AN INTRODUCTION TO
Educational Psychology

E. STONES

Lecturer in Education (Psychology)
in the University of Birmingham

GW00693571

Methuen & Co Ltd
11 NEW FETTER LANE, LONDON EC4

First published 1966, by
Methuen & Co Ltd,
11 New Fetter Lane, London EC4
Reprinted twice 1967
Reprinted twice 1968
Reprinted 1969 (twice)
Reprinted 1970 (twice)
Reprinted 1971

© E. Stones 1966
Printed in Great Britain by
Richard Clay (The Chaucer Press), Ltd
Bungay, Suffolk
SBN (Casebound)   416 28750 6
SBN (Paperback)   416 69420 9

DISTRIBUTED IN THE USA BY
BARNES AND NOBLE INC

Contents

CONTENTS

Acknowledgements

The author is grateful for permission to use the following figures:

Fig. 2 from *EEG and Behaviour*, edited by Gilbert H. Glaser, Basic Books, Inc., New York, 1963.

Fig. 3 from *The First Two Years of Life*, M. M. Shirley, University of Minnesota Press, 1933.

Figs. 5 and 6 from 'Teaching Machines', B. F. Skinner, *Scientific American*, Nov. 1961, © 1961 *Scientific American*, Inc. All rights reserved.

Fig. 20 from *Figure Reasoning Test*, J. C. Daniels, Crosby Lockwood 1962.

Fig. 21, the A. S. Otis Group Intelligence Scale B, reproduced by courtesy of George G. Harrap & Co. Ltd., and Harcourt, Brace & World Inc., New York.

What This Book is About

This book attempts to introduce students of education to the elements of educational psychology. It also relates as closely as possible the findings of research to classroom practice. It does not attempt, however, to provide teachers with ready-made classroom techniques. Each teacher develops his own classroom techniques. On the other hand the general principles for good teaching are discussed and concrete examples given where appropriate.

In order to make clear the fundamental processes involved in psychological development, the book starts with a study of the way in which the young child adapts its behaviour to its environment. This study involves a brief consideration of some of the key aspects of physical development, mainly the central nervous system. At the same time we consider the way physical growth and psychological development are influenced by the experience of the individual.

The discussion of development is followed by an examination of the processes of learning. Lower animals are considered, as well as man, since their much simpler behaviour helps to show more clearly the basic aspects of learning which man has in common with other animals.

In the discussion of learning the general aim has been to present an integrated view of the main features of conditioning theory without attempting to go into detailed discussion of the distinctions between the various views on the subject. This has meant a certain amount of oversimplification but the reader who wishes to explore the matter further will find more precise and detailed exposition of the subject in the references given and in other standard works on the subject.

Learning characteristic of man is considered next. The view is taken that the great difference between learning in man and the other animals, stems from man's life as a social being. In particular, it is argued, language is of fundamental importance in human learning since the use of language is crucial in the development of thought.

The way in which children form ideas about the world is discussed next and particular attention is paid here to the work of Piaget. A study is also made of the categories of thinking which are likely to be of most use to children.

We then examine the processes whereby the child acquires complex habits of thought through his use of language and we see how language deficiency holds back the development of the child's thinking.

The processes of learning so far considered are now related to specific classroom subjects, and suggestions are made to help the student to apply his knowledge of these processes to the classroom. Here we also discuss the application of programmed learning to the classroom and consider the psychological principles of programming and the use of teaching machines.

A section is devoted to the tests which a teacher might use in the classroom. The weaknesses of some traditional methods of testing and marking are discussed, and suggestions made to help the teacher avoid these weaknesses. Intelligence testing is given special attention and the changing views on the nature of intelligence are explained. Suggestions are made to the teacher about ways in which he can profitably use the various types of tests including intelligence tests.

Since the majority of teachers will at some time have children in their classes who, for various reasons, are less able than the other children, we discuss the causes of backwardness and its diagnosis. We also consider the way in which the teacher can help children to overcome their disability, and what he can do to get expert help for the more difficult problems.

Children are greatly affected by the social groups to which they belong and we therefore examine the effect of group influences on the child. Particular attention is given to the influence of the class and the school on the child's learning and emotional stability.

The final chapter deals with the teacher's work. It attempts to bring together the key aspects of educational psychology that the teacher needs to consider in his work in the classroom.

A note on the organization of the book

The salient points of each chapter are brought together in a summary which may be used by the reader to obtain a preliminary overview of the content of the chapter, and as an aid to revision.

References are given in brackets in the body of the text and are restricted to those which students may be reasonably expected to be able to follow up. The references are collected at the end of the book in numerical order as they appear in the text.

Acknowledgements

I should like to thank those friends and colleagues who helped with advice and suggestions at various stages in the preparation of this book, and in particular, Mr M. Smith, Dr J. C. Daniels, and Mrs Margaret Louise Stones, all of whom read the complete manuscript.

CHAPTER 1

The Foundations of Learning

Viki was a chimpanzee reared in the household of two American psychologists, C. and K. Hayes. They adopted her a few days after birth and reared her as far as was possible as they would have reared a human child. If Viki's development seemed to be deficient in any way as compared with human development, she was given special training. As a result of this unusual environment the chimpanzee developed more affinity with human babies than with other chimpanzees. She became capable of activity quite beyond the capacity of similar animals reared in more orthodox environments. She learned to dust, to wash dishes, to sharpen pencils, to paint furniture, and she could cope with psychological tests intended for children of her age so long as language was not involved. In many respects Viki made the same progress as a child of the same age; the most important difference was in language development where Viki made very little progress. The reason for this is probably that the brain of the chimpanzee is deficient in those areas which in humans we call the speech centres.

Viki was reared in an environment which for a chimp was extremely stimulating. She was continually being faced with problems to solve and she was given assistance where she had difficulty. In contrast chimpanzees in zoos have comparatively unstimulating environments and consequently develop much more limited abilities. The reverse is the usual case with children. The home itself generally provides a rich environment and the exceptional case is the child who is reared in an environment comparable to that of the chimpanzee reared in the zoo. The few existing reports which deal with such cases indicate that when the environment is grossly deficient in stimulation, the development of the child is correspondingly retarded.

One such report was made by R. A. Spitz in 1945 on the physical and psychological development of a number of children reared in a foundling home [1]. Their ages ranged from two to four years. Of twenty-one children five were totally unable to walk and only five could walk unassisted. Twelve could not feed themselves with a spoon, and only one could dress himself; none of the children was toilet trained. Six were unable to talk and only one could use sentences. Most of the children had the physical appearance of children about half their age. It should be stressed here that the children in the home were in no way maltreated. They had had excellent medical care, adequate diet, and had not been exposed to any injury or infection. The only abnormal thing in their life histories was the lack of social stimulation in the first years of life.

An extreme case of lack of social stimulation gave rise to one of the earliest attempts to apply scientific principles to the analysis, prediction, and modification of behaviour in man. Late in the eighteenth century a 'wild boy' of twelve was captured in a French forest. He was naked, walked on all fours, made unintelligible sounds, ate like an animal, and bit those who attempted to handle him. He was given to a French physician, J. M. G. Itard, to attempt to educate him. Itard thought that the child's gross deficiency was probably caused by his prolonged isolation from society. He analysed the boy's learning disabilities by a series of experiments and attempted to remedy them by a systematic programme of teaching. He was only moderately successful, one of the difficulties being that the boy probably suffered from some form of brain damage. But he did make some important progress, and his work foreshadows much modern work in education and psychology.

These investigations and experiments raise questions of fundamental importance for the teacher and the student of education. The key question is probably *to what extent can children be trained, and to what extent are physical factors which we are unable to control likely to frustrate our efforts?* The Hayeses produced behaviour in a chimpanzee quite out of proportion to the normal development of such animals. They failed to train Viki to use

16

language probably because her brain was inadequate. On the one hand a richer environment produced much more complex behaviour, on the other hand physical deficiencies prevented the development of language despite the best efforts of the psychologists.

With children similar problems arise. We might ask if young babies a few months old can be toilet trained, or if it is possible to teach the average child of four to read. The answer to the first question is clear. The child of three to six months lacks the physiological equipment to control his bladder movements, and no amount of sitting on his pot will train him to use it at the appropriate time. At best, his mother might find out the most likely moment and time her potting with the baby's evacuation. The answer to the question of teaching reading is less clear. Until quite recently many authorities would have stated that learning to read was dependent upon the child's reaching a certain stage of development, normally at about the age of six. They would say that to try to teach reading before the child was *ready* would be harmful. While it is clear that it would be impossible to teach a young baby without speech to read, it is by no means so clear that children much younger than six cannot be taught to read. It is more than likely that the waiting for the children to reach the stage of *readiness* for reading is the main factor in ensuring that they do not learn to read before six. In this case it is not so much inadequate physiological equipment as lack of stimulation and training.

What is it, we might ask, that underlies this difference between the two examples of child training we have just mentioned? To help us to find the answer to this question let us consider those aspects of our bodily make-up that affect profoundly the way in which we learn or don't learn.

Man in his environment

When an organism learns it adapts its behaviour to cope with changes in its environment. Man is an organism; more specifically he is an animal. He is undoubtedly a remarkable, and in many ways a unique, animal. Nevertheless he resembles other animals in bodily structure and functions. Because of this resemblance we can, by studying the ways in which other animals learn, gain insight into the way man himself learns. Although it is not possible to apply automatically the lessons we learn from the study of animal behaviour to human beings, there is no mysterious qualitative difference between man and the other animals which makes his behaviour inaccessible to our understanding. Many phenomena of human behaviour are still not understood, but this is probably because of inadequate knowledge rather than because the phenomena are forever inexplicable.

From the beginning of life until death, organisms are in a continuous state of interaction with their environments. In fact the term *environment* is used by some psychologists to designate the aspects of the organism's surroundings to which it is responding at a given time. This means that in the case of man he will be responding to such aspects of his surroundings as the things he can hear, see, touch, smell, taste, and feel. Such sensations may impinge upon him from his surroundings or from his internal environment, that is, from within his body.

The complexity of an organism's adaptation to its environment depends largely on the complexity of its nervous system. Thus a simple organism such as a worm with a very simple nervous system has a very low level of adaptation to its environment: that is, it is capable of only a very limited range of activities to cope with changes in its environment. Man, on the other hand, has a very complex nervous system and is therefore capable of a much greater range of activity.

The most complex nervous system would be of little use, however, if it were isolated from its environment. The nervous system of the worm receives information about the state of the soil through the worm's skin. When the soil dries, the worm burrows deeper to where the soil is damper. Man receives information about the environment through the various senses and because the channels through which he receives this information – the eyes, the ears, the nose and mouth, the skin, and the muscles – are so much more delicate and complex than the channels through which the worm receives its information, man is able to make much more delicate and complicated differentiation of the incoming information than the lower animal can do. Man has a further advantage over the worm. Not only can he take in more information and more complex information than the worm, he has the ability to deal with his environment in a more complicated way through the organs which act on the environment. The worm can act on its environment only in a limited way. It can take food and soil in through the mouth. It can excrete. It can wriggle around. Man, on the other hand, is capable of extremely delicate and versatile acts of manipulation because of the highly developed muscles and bone structure of his hands and fingers.

Ultimately, the adaptation of both man and worm will depend on the integrated activity of the organs which receive information from the environment, called the receptors. The nervous system that receives this information through nerve fibres, analyses it and passes it on to the effectors, i.e. the organs which act on the environment. In man all these organs are infinitely more complex than those of the worm hence the greater complexity of his adaptation to the environment.

If we compare man, not with a worm, but with a chimpanzee, we see that the differences are much less marked and yet man's activities are still infinitely more complex than those of the chimpanzee. What is the reason for this? Is it because one or more of man's organs are more highly developed than those of the chimpanzee? We shall discuss this at much greater length later when we shall see that physiological development is not the only thing that makes this enormous difference between the two species; however, on the physiological level there is a difference. This difference is in the level of development of the nervous system. In particular, it is the development of man's brain that provides the physiological basis for the development of the highly complex patterns of activity of which he is capable.

In very simple animals the nervous system consists of just a few nerve fibres. With a little increase in complexity the fibres increase in number and interconnect in a *neural net*. The higher up the evolutionary ladder we go the more complex this neural net until in man we find a complexity of interconnections beyond the scope of our imaginations. Judson Herrick, the neurologist, at Chicago University, has calculated that if a million of the nerve cells in the human brain were joined two by two in every possible way the number of combinations would total $10^{2,783,000}$. If this figure were written out it would take up the whole of this book. Even that would be only a fraction of the possible combinations, since every nerve cell can be linked with many more than one other, and also there are in the region of 10,000 million nerve cells in the human brain. It is this unimaginable complexity that makes for the complexity of man's behaviour.

The cortex

The cortex is the name we give to the part of the brain that accounts most for the tremendous complexity of the organ in man. Other parts of the brain are much more similar in man and the other animals. In man the cortex completely overshadows the rest of the brain and is the key factor in determining that man's behaviour is of a completely different order from that of other animals. The cortex is so important, not because of any difference in the kind of nerve cells which constitute it, but because of their enormous number and the richness of their interconnections.

Although most of the cortical cells are similar, various areas of the cortex have developed specialized functions. Some areas of the cortex are concerned with vision, with motor activity, with auditory stimulation, with speech, and so on. The detailed *maps* of the cortex sometimes given, which link with precision, areas of the brain with different bodily functions, probably give a misleading air of accuracy. It is not possible to define these areas with such precision. However, it has been discovered that when different areas of the cortex are stimulated electrically, experiences and activity specific to different bodily functions are evoked. The control by the brain of our behaviour is demonstrated vividly in these experiments as is also its role as the seat of memory.

W. Penfield, the distinguished neurosurgeon, stimulated different parts of the cortex of patients undergoing brain operations. The patients in these operations are quite conscious since the brain has no sensation and there is therefore no pain. He found that when areas of the cortex concerned with motor activity were stimulated by slight electrical discharges, movement of the limbs was caused. The patient could do nothing to stop the movement although he realized that he had not *willed* to do it. Stimulation of the area concerned with hearing cause the patient to experience sounds, and stimulation of the visual area evoke sensations of *brightness*, *colour*, and so on.*

Stimulation in other cortical areas produces vivid recollections of past events. Patients have heard music as it was originally played or sung. They will say to the surgeon that there is a man at the piano, or that the people are singing in church. In one case a patient who had been stimulated repeatedly in the same place heard the same song on each occasion and refused to believe, even in discussion later, that there was no radio in the room. All these experiments illustrate graphically how our knowledge of the world, the control of our behaviour, and the mechanisms of memory are seated in the nervous activity of the brain. One other experiment which Penfield carried out leads us to another important aspect of brain function which holds great promise for future investigations of the nature of brain mechanisms.

In one experiment Penfield placed electrodes on the exposed cortex of a man undergoing an operation. The man was asked to 'make a fist'. As he did so the pattern of electrical discharges from the brain, which was being picked up by the electrodes, changed. From the rhythm of the brain at rest the rhythm changed to that of the active brain. This illustrated the fact that motor activity is associated with changes in the pattern of electrical discharges of the cortex; this is one aspect of the discipline of electroencephalography; the study of the patterns of electrical discharges of the brain.

The electrical activity of the brain

The electroencephalograph is an apparatus which uses electrodes fixed to the scalp to pick up electrical discharges from the brain.

* PENFIELD, W.: in MAGOUN, H. W. (Ed.): *Brain Mechanisms and Consciousness*, Blackwell, 1954.

The brain does not need to be exposed as in the case of Penfield's experiments, and there is no pain in the attaching of the electrodes to the scalp. The discharges are picked up by the electrodes and are recorded by pens on moving paper, the frequency and amplitude of the discharges being conventionally recorded as a series of wavy lines on the paper; this is the electroencephalogram or EEG. Over twenty pens record the impulses from different parts of the brain in the typical EEG. The interesting thing about EEG patterns for the psychologist is that there is evidence that they are connected with patterns of behaviour. Eventually EEG patterns may be one of the factors which link psychological phenomena with the actual activity of the brain.

EEG records show that the electrical activity of the brain conforms to certain patterns or rhythms. When the subject is at rest with the eyes closed the brain produces a slow pulsing rhythm of about ten cycles a second. This is the *alpha rhythm* which represents a synchronization of the activity of many cortical nerve cells or neurones. When the eyes are open the alpha rhythm disappears and is replaced by quicker, less regular discharges. In sleep the alpha rhythms are replaced by the *delta rhythm* which is a slower rhythm (0·5–3·5 cycles per sec.). The British scientist, W. Grey Walter, has suggested that the alpha rhythm is a form of *scanning*. The brain at rest, with few sensory inputs from the environment, seems to be searching for a pattern by scanning as you might search for a particular word by scanning the page of a book. When the pattern is found, the scanning ceases, as your eye movements would cease when you saw the word. The cessation of the alpha rhythm indicates the desynchronization of the electrical activity of the cortical neurones. These will now be receiving stimulation from the various receptors. They will have 'found their pattern' and the nerve impulses will now be engaged in dealing with the information from the environment and not with searching for it [2].

In the young baby the brain rhythms are predominantly the delta rhythms. This suggests that the child is essentially in a passive relationship with its environment. The delta rhythms are those of the sleeping adult, and although the baby is being subjected to a great number of stimuli from his environment, he lacks the cortical development to perceive or to respond to them. If we now consider the baby at the breast, we see a profound difference between his activity and that of the man who was asked to 'make a fist', in Penfield's experiment. On the one hand the alpha rhythm of the man disappeared when he made a fist: scanning activity was replaced by neural excitation connected with the physical act. On the other, the baby takes the nipple and yet still exhibits the delta rhythm of the resting brain. The sucking response is automatic; the baby does not *know* what it is doing.

Grey Walter has suggested that the lack of alpha rhythms in the young child may act as a defence mechanism for the immature brain. If the very young baby were suddenly exposed to the flood of stimulation from the environment to which adults are accustomed, the results would probably be disastrous. The cortical discharge evoked by such a barrage of stimuli would most likely overwhelm the brain and bring about a seizure or convulsions. The delta rhythm indicating indifference to outside stimulation, insulates the immature brain and shields it from the complexity of the environment.

An experiment carried out with dogs by J. Fuller of Maine seems to offer behavioural corroboration of this hypothesis.* He found that when dogs reared in isolation and deprived of stimulation through contact with different aspects of the environment were released, they exhibited behaviour very reminiscent of human psychotic behaviour. Fuller suggests the hypothesis that since the puppies were reared in conditions of stimulus deprivation while their receptors were maturing, they were, on the moment of release from their confinement, subjected to an intense flood of stimuli to which they had no developed means of adequately responding. Under normal circumstances, as with the human baby, these organs and the cerebral cortex are insufficiently developed to take in the stimuli when they are first presented. The normal processes of development, which involve the gradual adaptations of the organs to increasingly complex patterns of

* FULLER, J. L.: *Discovery*, February 1964.

stimulation, enable the young animal to come to terms with his environment gradually and without disturbance.

'Knowing' and doing

The physiological processes we have been considering are the basis of our psychological activity. We have seen how the mother cannot modify the toilet habits of her young baby before the appropriate nerve cells have developed. Other factors of a physiological nature ensure that the psychology of babies and young children is very much different from that of the adult. Mothers often find it difficult to accept that their babies could hardly be said to *know* or *understand* something of what they are doing. They consider that the baby *knows* how to suck the nipple from the very beginning. In fact, the new born baby sucks *automatically* rather as most people respond to being tickled. It will respond to stimulation inside its mouth by a sucking activity; this stimulation is usually provided by the nipple, but it can be evoked by other stimulating objects. Lacking the development of the cortex and the elaboration of the complex neural circuits, the baby cannot control its activity and it would be incorrect to say that it *understands* what it is doing. This may be seen more clearly when we consider that babies born with no cortex have exhibited sucking responses, and the cortex is the seat of our conscious activity.

The infant's smile is another factor which causes misunderstanding of the psychology of the young child. The mother often considers that the child's first smile is a smile of recognition; perhaps even of recognition of *mother*. In fact the visual apparatus is so undeveloped that the child is incapable of distinguishing the mother from other adults and will smile at a hideous mask, or even at a row of dots or a group of dots.

The brain and learning

As we have seen, the brain is of supreme importance in the regulation of the activity of organisms. Parts of the brain other than the cortex have certain functions which greatly influence the

ability of the organism to learn but in man it is the great development of the cortex that has enabled him to learn the complex
skills that we shall be discussing in the pages which follow.
The other parts of the brain, sometimes referred to as the
subcortical parts, regulate such things as our level of alertness,
our awareness of basic 'needs' such as the need for food or water,
and our emotions. Clearly our level of alertness has a great deal
to do with learning. Unless we are alert we cannot attend effectively to our environment and the cortex will not receive the
stimulation it needs to form the links necessary for us to adapt
effectively to changes in the environment. The part of the brain
which maintains the level of arousal of the organism is called the
reticular formation and malfunction of this can have serious effects.
Monkeys with the reticular formation removed surgically, become comatose and show little or no reaction to the environment.
Some children who are mentally subnormal show irregularities
in function of the reticular formation.

The part of the brain which deals with emotions can also have
a great effect on learning. Malfunctioning of this, the so-called
limbic system, could cause disproportionate reactions to environmental stimulation which would prevent learning. For example, if
instead of maintaining a relatively stable level of emotionality, we
exhibit uncontrolled rage or excessive fear, the corresponding
activity of the limbic system would swamp that of the cortex and
prevent the connections necessary for satisfactory adaptation
being made. We should note in passing, however, that unsatisfactory emotionality can be learned, and need not necessarily
indicate malfunction of the limbic system.

The other important functional part of the subcortical areas of
the brain is called the *hypothalamus*. This makes us aware of our
basic needs. We learn to adapt to our environment to satisfy our
basic needs: if the hypothalamus does not function properly we
may not be aware of our needs and may take no steps to satisfy
them. Or, possibly, the effect is in the other direction and we find
it impossible to satisfy our basic needs. On the one hand the
organism would, for example, feel no need to eat and would die
of starvation, on the other hand it would eat but not feel satisfied

and so would continue to eat until it was incapacitated through overeating.

Under normal circumstances the subcortical regions of the brain and the cortex itself work as an integrated unit to maintain an organic equilibrium: all work together to ensure the optimum adaptation of the organism to the environment. The cortex is the essential organ in ensuring the best adaptation. It does this through the connections formed in the cortical nerve cells to which we have already referred, and these connections are the physical basis for our behaviour.

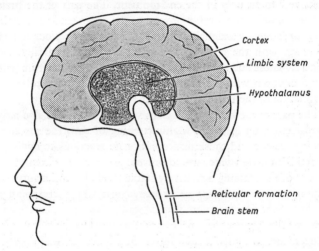

Fig. 1. Diagram of the main functional systems of the brain. Only those structures referred to in the text are shown. The diagram is not intended to be anatomical. As stressed in the text, these systems are richly interconnected and should not be considered as isolated structures.

These connections do not develop in predetermined patterns fixed at birth, but in systems of functional links depending on the stimulation they receive from the environment through the receptors. If stimulation is lacking, the links will not be formed and the patterns of behaviour will not develop. When we learn, we set up different patterns of connections in the cortex; these are real physical changes although they are not necessarily fixed once they are set up. We shall see in a later chapter how the connections are made and unmade in the process of learning.

If we consider our earlier question about the teaching of reading to young children, in the light of this discussion, it seems that the arguments about *reading readiness* have rather shaky foundations. At the age of six (average age of 'readiness') the brain is 90% of its adult size. Most of the connections with receptors and effectors are functioning and the physical apparatus to cope with reading is there. What is not there, are the cortical links which can only be formed in intercourse with the environ-

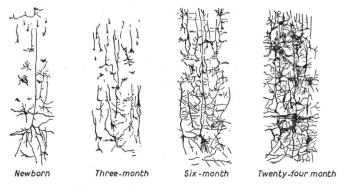

Newborn   Three-month   Six-month   Twenty-four month

Fig. 2. Stages in the developing human brain. The increasing complexity of the baby's behaviour is very largely dependent upon the growth of the number of cortical nerve cells and the intricacy of their interconnections.

ment; in this case, with the teacher teaching reading. It seems likely, therefore, that this is an opposite example to that of the baby and the pot. The latter could not learn because the nerve cells were not fully grown; the former has all the functional nerve cells but lacks the cortical links which can only be formed through experience. No amount of experience would teach the baby to oblige; no amount of waiting without experience would bring the latter to the stage of reading. The whole question of learning to read is discussed more fully in later chapters.

The evolution of the brain

We conclude our discussion of the function of the brain in man with a brief consideration of the factors which went towards making man so much different from the other animals.

It has been said that men were walking the earth 50,000 years ago who could have conducted a symphony orchestra, or read a paper to a scientific society. This refers to the fact that the brains of such men were much the same as those of contemporary men. There seems to have been very little evolutionary development of the human brain since those times. Prior to this, man's forbears, the pre-men or hominids, had much smaller brains. In fact the brain of modern man is some three times the size of that of the hominids.

Recent fossil discoveries have provided evidence of great interest and importance in this field. What has been called 'an explosion of brains', it is suggested, is not the cause of man becoming man as we know him, but that his taking to the social existence characteristic of man was the cause of the tremendous development of the brain which set man apart from pre-man. On the occasion of the one hundreth anniversary of Darwin's *The Origin of Species* Washburn and Howell at the Chicago Centennial celebration read a paper in which they said:

> The tool using, ground living, hunting way of life created the large human brain rather than the large brained man discovering certain new ways of life. [We] believe this conclusion is the most important result of recent fossil discoveries and is one which carries far-reaching implications for the interpretation of human behaviour and its origins. The important point is that size of brain, insofar as it can be measured by cranial capacity, has increased some threefold subsequent to the use and manufacture of implements. . . . The uniqueness of modern man is seen as the result of a technical-social life which tripled the size of the brain, reduced the face and modified many other structures of the body.*

We might well ask in concluding this chapter: 'Why, in fact, were there no men conducting symphony orchestras 50,000 years

* Quoted BRUNER, J. S.: in *American Psychologist*, January 1964.

ago?' The answer to this points to one of the most important aspects of human psychology and illustrates in a striking way the interdependence of man and his environment. The brain, we have seen, depends for the development of its most character- istically human feature, the cortex, on stimulation from the environment. The evolution of man has led to a progressively more complex social environment. This increasingly complex environment has provided the cortex with ever richer patterns of stimulation, which lead to more and more elaborate cortical connections. Man thus increases the complexity of his environ- ment and this new complexity makes possible the further develop- ment of the cortex and the complicated behaviour patterns which depend on it. In other words, there were no symphony orchestras 50,000 years ago because man had only just started to create the environmental conditions which were eventually to make sym- phony orchestras technologically and psychologically feasible. If we could whisk a child from those times to our present day, he would probably develop in much the same way as our own children. In the absence of a time machine he must stay at his primitive level, and instead of growing up to conduct an orchestra, he grows up to hunt and gather food; no doubt adding a little in the process to the complication of the environment we have been discussing. The whole process has been admirably summed up by V. Gordon Childe in the title of his book, *Man Makes Himself*.

Summary

In this chapter we have considered the factors which determine the extent to which children can be trained. We saw that chim- panzees in a stimulating environment develop more intelligent behaviour than chimps in zoos or in the wild. Conversely, children reared in environments lacking in stimulation grow up less intelligent than other children and are backward in many other respects. We saw that the chimp did not develop speech because it lacked the necessary development of the cortex. The child was unable to control its bladder activity because the necessary neural links had not yet been set up.

Man is considered as an organism in constant interaction with the environment. The patterns of interaction are determined by the activity of the central nervous system. Information about the environment is collected by the *receptors* and transmitted via the central nervous system to the *effectors* which control bodily movement.

The brain has four basic structures. The *reticular formation* maintains the state of alertness of the organism. The *hypothalamus* registers states of organic need, the *limbic system* is concerned with states of emotion. The *cortex* is the seat of intellectual activity. These four structures work together and influence each other.

The cortex is the most complex part of the brain. It is the part of the brain most concerned with regulation of man's interaction with the environment. The cortex of the young baby lacks the network of functional neural connections of the adult. EEG patterns in young babies suggest that they are mostly unaware of their surroundings. They only gradually become aware as an increasing number of neural connections are made. That is, consciousness is built up gradually in the child. It is likely that this is advantageous to the child, since if a new-born baby were fully conscious of its surroundings, the sudden influx of stimulation to the brain would probably cause organic breakdown.

Since the nerves of the very young baby are not yet sufficiently grown to make the necessary connections, it is impossible to build up habits which depend on these connections. It is, therefore, not possible to toilet train a very young child. On the other hand, behaviour such as reading which depends on the establishing of *functional* systems of links in the brain caused by changes in the nerve cells can be built up in children once the nerves are sufficiently mature. Children in general reach this stage by four or five, and whether, in fact, they learn to read will depend largely upon whether the teacher gives them the experience to build up the necessary cortical links.

The brain of modern man is very similar to that of man living over 50,000 years ago. The fact that modern man is capable of much more complex activity is not because of any evolutionary change in brain structure, but because men's brains today develop in a much more complex environment. Cultural change has replaced evolutionary change. One of the most important aspects of the changed environment involved in ensuring that man today is not as man was 50,000 years ago is his educational *milieu.*

CHAPTER 2

The Nature of Development

From the moment of conception, when the male sperm cell fertilizes the female ovum in the uterus, to the moment of death, the organism is in a constant state of change. Early in life the changes are dramatic and obvious and this is the field which mostly concerns the student of child behaviour. The process of change starts in the uterus where, for the first part of its life, the child is shielded from the vagaries of the world outside and rocked securely in an environment of great stability. It is an environment most congenial to the foetus but it is a relatively unstimulating one, and, despite the very great changes which take place in the embryo before delivery, the new-born child is completely unequipped to cope with the enormous complexity of the world outside.

Normal foetal change consists essentially of the gradual differentiation of the specialized organs from the original fertilized ovum. This development in the womb takes the child from the stage of the single fertilized cell to something recognizably human. Its development is essentially morphological, that is, it consists mainly of the development of the structure of the organs. Post natal development continues this structural growth but, in addition, functional development now becomes significant. From now on the baby adapts to its environment mainly by refining the functions of various organs. At birth the baby's movements are gross and undifferentiated; it tends to move the whole of its body rather than individual limbs; or the whole arm rather than the hand. It is capable only of the crudest reflex actions. These reflex actions are mainly elicited by touching the skin but there is also a good deal of uncoordinated spontaneous bodily movement [3]. This activity has been observed in malformed infants without a cortex which indicates that it is truly involuntary.

Growth of the brain and other parts of the body, together with the elaboration of neural links, make for the finer discrimination of activity. One of the first results of this development is that the child acquires the ability to control the former indiscriminate activity of his limbs. Instead of making gross movements of the arms, he gradually acquires the ability to move the hands to grip, then to manipulate. Bodily movement progresses from the gross activity of the recumbent baby, through the stage of crawling, to the complex coordination and balancing of the walking child. Later development brings the increasingly complex coordination of motor activity associated with the acquisition of various physical skills. After the differentiation of control over the various organs comes the complicated synthesis of their activities into coordinated movements. The baby eventually grows into the child who is capable of riding a bicycle or manipulating a pen with accuracy. Such advances depend on the growth and development of the various organs, and also on the satisfactory growth and development of the brain, including the elaboration of the necessary cortical connections.

When the new-born baby leaves the womb it leaves an environment which supplies everything it needs to keep it alive and in comfort: the foetus needs to do nothing to maintain a stable state of equilibrium. We might say that it lacks nothing. On being delivered, its state of equilibrium is shattered. No longer is it automatically fed, warmed, and kept free of impurities and damage; these functions, from the moment of birth, start to become the baby's own responsibility. It must come to terms with its new environment.

The fact that most babies do, in fact, learn to come to terms with their environment, and do, in fact, manage to take over responsibility for their own survival, is due to a great extent to the tendency of living organisms to maintain a state of equilibrium with the environment. What it once did in the womb with no effort, the baby must now do outside, often by the setting up of extremely complex patterns of behaviour. When the current state of equilibrium is upset, the organism adapts its behaviour in some way so as to restore equilibrium again. The new state of

33

equilibrium will not be the same as the original one since the organism will be changed in some way by the very act of restoring the state of equilibrium.

We may illustrate this by reference to one of the most fundamental states of disequilibrium. An organism needs food for growth and energy. When food is lacking the state of equilibrium of the organism is upset; it cannot replace the energy it is consuming or continue any processes of bodily growth. All organisms whose equilibrium is upset in this way will do what they can to obtain food so as to restore equilibrium. The term *needs* is sometimes used to designate the state of organic disequilibrium. The organism engages in behaviour to reduce its needs. A need is some deficit within the individual. In the case of lack of food the need may be referred to as hunger, although it must be said that some psychologists dislike the use of the term since it does not really explain anything although it may name it.

Neural connections between the hypothalamus and the limbic system link needs with *affect* (which is the general term used to refer to emotion). Thus the restoration of the equilibrium of the organism, through the ending of a state of need, results in a state of positive affect; for example, a mild pleasure after a meal, or the feeling of satisfaction after solving a problem. In addition, the cortex is linked with the hypothalamus and with the limbic system. Thus we are aware of needs and of our affective state. At the same time the cortex can influence the other centres. We eventually learn, with varying degrees of success, to 'control our emotions'. We learn also to satisfy our needs in conventional socially acceptable ways. Both these would be impossible without the integrated activity of the whole brain.

The affective states of the organism have their correlates in the autonomic nervous system. This is the system concerned with the control of our basic bodily functions such as heartbeat and the digestive system. Thus negative affect, such as is associated with what we term the emotion of fear, involves such physiological changes as increased heartbeat, dilation of the pupils of the eyes, the secretion of adrenalin into the bloodstream, and the inhibition of digestive processes. These physiological changes have survival value. They all help to enhance the physical capabilities of the organism to deal with an emergency. In adults, we can identify many emotions; fear, anger, hate, joy, and so on, but the young baby lacks these differentiated affective states. Instead he exhibits only positive and negative affect. Like much of the baby's development and activity, his affective life is gross and undifferentiated. Movement towards maturity brings the finer differentiation of affective states, so that we are eventually able to distinguish between behaviour associated with anger and fear, whereas in the young baby these would have been identifiable only as negative affect. The same applies, of course, to other emotional states.

From the first moments the behaviour of the new-born baby is *motivated* by the tendency towards the restoration of equilibrium. Behaviour which restores this state of equilibrium will be found satisfying or 'pleasant' so that the baby will be likely to repeat the behaviour on a future occasion. When the baby takes the nipple on the first occasion through reflex activity on having his mouth stimulated, the state of disequilibrium existing because of the need for food will be ended, and the sucking will be accompanied by positive affect. This behaviour is the prototype of the behaviour of the adult who goes to a restaurant and carefully consults the menu and then makes his choice of meal.

Thirst is another basic need. The organism deprived of water cannot survive and therefore is impelled to behaviour aimed at ending the state of deprivation.

Most animals are motivated at times by the need for sexual activity. This is another of the basic needs. The mature organism is stimulated by secretions from the sexual glands. Satisfaction of the need is provided by copulation. In primitive animals the activity which ends the state of need caused by the stimulation from sexual glands is largely automatic, but in more highly developed animals, as we have seen, while the need develops with the development of the organism, the manner of its satisfaction has to be learned.

For the organism to survive it must avoid damage to its tissues. Hostile environmental conditions such as intense heat, or

35

intense cold, or direct physical damage, are all inimicable to survival and produce a state of organic disequilibrium which the organism will seek to end. As with other needs there is a link between this and the affective side of behaviour. Tissue damage stimulates the connections to the limbic system producing negative affect, that is, sensations which we refer to as pain. The ending of the noxious situation ends the threat to the organism and thus removes the factors which disturb its equilibrium. The organism then returns to its normal state; the strong negative affect also ceasing. Were there no connection between the affective centres and the receptors signalling tissue damage, we should feel no pain on being cut or burned. This would mean that we should be in considerable danger of serious organic injury of which we would be unaware.

The needs so far discussed are those clearly connected with the survival of the organism, or in the case of the need for sexual activity, with the survival of the species. These needs may be regarded as the outcome of a long evolutionary process. Two other needs, which are basic to the survival of some organisms and which provide the motivation for much of their behaviour, are also of evolutionary significance, although less obviously apparent than the ones so far mentioned. One of these needs has been identified in recent years by H. F. Harlow who has conducted extensive experiments on the behaviour of monkeys. This is the need of the young mammal for contact with the mother or a substitute for the mother. Newly born monkeys will react by clinging to any surface which is placed in contact with the surface of the body. This reaction is similar to the automatic action of the baby's mouth when the nipple is presented. Its strength is strikingly demonstrated by one experiment in which very young monkeys who had shown no signs of being able to move around, followed a piece of cloth which was placed against the face and then gradually withdrawn. The animals automatically followed the cloth, sometimes even quite rapidly. In nature the evolutionary value of this behaviour is apparent; the monkey that did not cling to its mother would fall and die.

The baby kangaroo is born in a very immature state; it is little more than a foetus. On delivery it clings to the mother's skin and climbs upwards to her pouch. Eventually it reaches the pouch and attaches itself firmly to the nipple within and there it stays until mature enough to fend for itself. Any other pattern of activity would be disastrous for the young animal. It would, however, be wrong to say that the animal *knows* that it is climbing to safety. Kangaroos are not particularly intelligent when adult; the immature animal is a very much simpler organism and the activity can only be described as reflex.

The experiments which Harlow carried out demonstrated that the need for what has been called *contact comfort* was not dependent upon the need for food as might have been surmised. He devised substitute mothers from wire frameworks, one of which he covered with towelling. The other frame carried the feeding bottle. To obtain food the monkey had to climb up the wire *mother*. Despite this arrangement, the young monkeys developed an attachment to the towelling mother very similar to that normally formed to the real mother. They even clung to it in anxiety-producing situations, for example, when a strange object was put in the cage. Monkeys reared only on the wire frame did not cling to that in the presence of danger, but clutched themselves or rubbed themselves on the side of the cage until the danger was over [4].

One other basic motivator of behaviour is the need to know the environment. This is generally referred to as the *orienting reflex*. The orienting reflex is evoked when new stimuli enter the environment. An unknown stimulus in natural conditions may represent danger until it is thoroughly explored and seen to be harmless. When the new stimulus first appears, the equilibrium of the organism is upset by the change in the environment. Equilibrium is restored when the stimulus is thoroughly explored. The organism is then said to be *habituated*. Orienting activity is linked with the activity of the reticular formation. Work with the EEG suggests that the effect of the reticular formation is to increase the significance of stimuli for the organism so that the organism orients to these stimuli. Habituation is accompanied by a dying away of the discharge from the reticular formation.

37

There is evidence to suggest that organisms seek to maintain the input of stimulation through the senses at a relatively high level. Reduction of the input results in activity which continues until the sensory input is returned to the optimum level. The reduction of input of stimulation to a very low level can have deleterious effects for the organism.

In one investigation designed to examine the effects of stimulus deprivation, the experimenters paid college students to lie on beds in lighted cubicles for twenty-four hours a day. Sounds were kept at a minimum. Vision was controlled by goggles. The arms were placed in cardboard tubes which restricted the input through touch. Under these conditions mental skills deteriorated and emotional disturbances appeared. The students seemed dependent for their mental health on a continuing stream of stimulation from the environment.

In another experiment rhesus monkeys were given a discrimination problem to learn, the only reward being the opportunity to look out through a window for thirty seconds. The fact that the monkeys learned to solve the problem with this reward suggests that the need for stimulation is basic to the organism.

The suggestion is, therefore, that the need to know the environment is basic. It may be regarded as one of the important motivators of behaviour and one which is very important for the teacher. Applied to the classroom this suggests that we should maintain orienting activity related to current learning by ensuring that new elements are introduced before habituation takes place and the child loses interest. The point to bear in mind is that when the child is investigating new stimuli (new material or novel activity initiated by the teacher) he is in a greater state of arousal than when he is in a monotonous situation in the classroom. This means that the child's receptivity to the learning situation as a whole is heightened when controlled orienting activity is maintained.

The needs we have been considering have been related to simple, or even primitive patterns of behaviour. It is obvious, however, that the patterns of human behaviour are far from simple or primitive. But human behaviour patterns are, to a large extent, founded on these basic needs through the processes of learning that we shall take up in the next chapter. Before leaving the subject, however, we should note a potential difficulty. It is possible, and only too easy, to postulate a need appropriate to any observed behaviour. We could, for example, 'explain' the habits of the dipsomaniac or the chain smoker, in the one case by referring to a 'need' for alcohol and in the other to a 'need' for tobacco. This explanation is obviously spurious if we are using the expression *need* in the way we have previously used it. We do not really explain, we merely describe. Needs such as that for food or for drink can be founded on the physiological facts of tissue requirements and brain activity. Thirst and hunger have both been evoked in rats by electrical stimulation to the brain. Sexual activity has also been found to have its appropriate centres. A number of experiments in electroencephalography suggests that behaviour resulting from the orienting reflex has a physiological correlate which can be recorded by the electroencephalograph. Needs that can be demonstrated to be innate and based upon physiological foundations may be accepted as being real, others must await further evidence before they can be accepted with the same certainty as such things as hunger.

The needs that we have identified, either in their basic or highly developed forms, underly the processes of development which we are considering, and in the constant seeking for a state of equilibrium the organism will be motivated by these factors and the associated affect. Thus, as organic development proceeds, the patterns of behaviour which are related to the satisfaction of the basic needs evolve in intimate conjunction with that development.

Maturation and experience

The process of organic growth towards maturity is generally referred to as *maturation*. Maturation has figured large in our discussion of the child's adaptation to his environment, for we have talked about such things as the elaboration of neural links and the growth of the various organs. But this is only one side of the coin. The child's increasingly elaborate adaptation to its environment is dependent on the processes of growth and the pressures of the outside world. We have already mentioned the fact that at birth the child exchanges a congenial and extremely stable but relatively unstimulating environment, for an environment which is in comparison, unstable and extremely stimulating, and which, but for the intervention of adults, would be hostile. The new environment is stimulating *because* it is unstable, and it offers great possibilities to the baby *because* it is so potentially hostile. If a mammalian foetus could be transferred from the womb to a replica of the womb, which could cope with any increase in size, it would be safe from the vicissitudes of the outside world but it would never become anything resembling the adult animal. The new-born baby demonstrates dramatically its dependence on new experience for adaptive development, when it takes its first breath, not because it *knows* it must breathe air, but in response to the drastic change in its environment caused by the transition from life in a warm liquid to life in the relatively colder air. Sometimes, of course, the stimulus that produces the first essential reaction, the baby's cry, which fills its lungs with air, is the midwife's smack. The key to the production of the first breath seems to be the sudden increase in sensory input from the environment, whether it be chemical or physical. From the first moment we owe our existence to environmental stimulation. From this moment on, the development of the child is the result of the two forces of maturation and experience and it is quite impossible to determine which is the most potent factor at any one time [5].

This point may be made clearer by considering some of the ways in which fundamental human abilities develop. Visual ability is one of the most important of these and is one which is extremely limited in the young baby. The new-born baby is unable to focus his eyes for any length of time, and, as we have seen, he is unable to distinguish between different faces for the first few months. The eventual emergence of the ability to distinguish among various visual patterns may be ascribed to the maturation of the nervous connections with the cortex in conjunction with experience of using the visual apparatus. It is difficult to get a meaningful picture of the extent of the contribution of experience to the development of visual ability from the young baby, but investigations into the reactions of congenitally blind adults given their sight by operation has given us some idea of the importance of experience. Such adults have had great difficulty in progressing from the most simple visual discrimination. They have been able to distinguish a figure from its background and have been able to name colours after a little practice, but only rarely have they learned to identify simple geometric figures and read separate letters and numbers. One woman, who was attended for six months after her operation by two surgeons, was unable to tell one from the other at the end of the period [1]. Another patient who had learned to tell the time using a braille watch could not tell the time from the hospital clock but had to feel it on his watch.

Experiments with animals have given us further indications of the importance of protracted experience for normal visual abilities. Young chimpanzees reared in the dark until sixteen months of age were unable to fixate objects with their eyes, although normal animals are well able to at this age. They did not respond visually to their feeding bottles, although they were readily responded to by touch. They did not blink when a blow to the face was threatened. Other chimpanzees reared in the dark for seven months were unable to pick out a large yellow and black striped disc which gave them a mild electric shock, and took over two weeks to show any sign that they were connecting the disc with the shock, whereas other animals which had been allowed ninety minutes of light a day learned to avoid the disc after receiving one or two shocks.

Other experiments have shown that non-visual behaviour is also dependent upon experience. Chimpanzees, reared under conditions which precluded their being able to use their hands or feet, grew up incapable of many of the normal abilities of these animals. Experiments investigating the maternal and sexual behaviour of rats have shown their dependence upon adequate experience. Female rats deprived of the experience connected with nest building, do not construct such nests when they have litters and are very lax in the general care of the young. Rats reared in isolation and brought together at the height of sexual development exhibit a high degree of sexual excitement but a very low level of sexual competence. Such animals are so deficient in the skills of mating that males rarely reached the sexual climax. Chimpanzees reared in similar conditions are incapable of engaging in complete sexual relations.

Evidence about the effect of limited experience in children comparable to that we have observed in animals is lacking for obvious reasons. The investigation carried out by Spitz referred to in Chapter 1 is one of the few studies on the subject. The essential thing about the environment of the children in the foundling home was that they suffered from most severe social deprivation. As babies, all they saw was the ceiling above their cots except when the nurse's head appeared at feeding time. As toddlers the children had no toys and got no stimulation from adults. It was an environment unlikely to be paralleled in many homes, and the extreme retardation in physical and psychological development was ascribed by Spitz to unfavourable environmental conditions. Corroboration of this point of view was found by Spitz in a parallel investigation with children of similar physical and intellectual endowment early in life, who were reared in a nursery attached to a women's prison. Here the children were with their mothers for many hours a day and received a good deal of affectionate care and attention. In addition, there were toys to play with. The development of these children progressed normally while that of the children in the foundling home fell away, until as we have seen they were retarded in many ways. They even suffered from seriously decreased resistance to disease and the mortality rate of the group was extremely high.

As we have seen, the chimpanzee Viki reared in an extremely stimulating environment developed skills quite foreign to the normal development of these animals. This phenomenon can also be seen when these animals in the wild are compared with those in experimental laboratories. Chimpanzees in a beneficent habitat, where food is plentiful and the climate mild, have few problems to solve in order to survive. Few demands are made on them to learn new skills. In the laboratory, the reverse is usually the case and here the chimp has to solve different problems before he can eat. The result is that the laboratory animal is generally a far more intelligent animal than his opposite number in the wild.

The development of the school child

What is the significance of the findings from these experiments and investigations for the teacher and student of child behaviour? One of the most important is the fact that children do not just *unfold* inevitably as it were. Charts of child development and indices of child attainment such as are given in texts concerned with child development should be regarded in this light. They do not represent absolute levels of development, rather they refer to the *average* child of a given age, and also to the environmental *norm* of such children. Both these conceptions, in our case, are drawn from West European or American cultures. They cannot be carried over automatically into other cultures and they are unlikely to remain the same even in our culture. This can be seen clearly on the physical side where higher standards of living are radically changing the patterns of growth and development. Thus a child of five today is as big and as physically mature as a child of six thirty years ago. At school, children are capable of arithmetical calculations beyond the majority of adults of a hundred years ago; or of handling ideas in certain areas of science which would be out of the grasp of the teachers who taught their grandparents.

If children do not just *unfold* what are we to make of the statement that: 'Just as a child learns to walk and talk when he reaches the proper development for these activities, so he arrives at readiness for reading in his own time' [6]. This is a point of view commonly held until very recently. It was generally held that the average age at which a child *could* learn to read was about six and a half. At this age, it was said, the average child had developed the necessary physical and mental skills to cope with the complex behaviour involved in reading. The emphasis was almost entirely on maturation and the term *reading readiness* was used to indicate that state at which the child was capable of

Fig. 3. This is a well-known chart showing a sequence of stages of child development. This sequence cannot, however, be considered to be the *natural* or *inevitable* sequence; it will be the sequence appropriate to a specific environment. Children deprived of stimulation, such as those described by Spitz, not only do not pass through the same stages at the same time, but do not pass through some of the stages at all.

being taught to read. Attempts to *force* children to read before this age, it was held, would probably be abortive and have a bad effect on the child.

This point of view conflicts quite pronouncedly with the evidence we have been considering about the relationship between maturation and experience. If, as is almost certainly the case, young children need experience to enable them to make satisfactory visual and aural discriminations and to acquire suitable motor abilities then until they get that experience there is little possibility of them acquiring the skills. As was aptly put by the Scottish Council on Education: 'It is important to realize that reading readiness does not come by nature. The child brought up in a savage tribe that has no written records can have no reading readiness . . . reading readiness is not the product of maturation alone. Some degree of mental development and of other abilities and qualities must be attained before the reading task can be successfully performed, but the teacher's work cannot be accomplished by waiting on Nature.' Then later: 'Reading readiness is largely reading achievement in its early stages' [7].

For the teacher, then, it is important not to 'wait on Nature' but to arrange for the children to have the necessary experience involving visual discrimination and motor coordination, linguistic experience, and the desire and interest in learning to read.

What we have said about reading can be applied equally to other fields. If abilities are to be developed, experience and maturation must go hand in hand. From our observations of the children in the foundling home we have seen that the severe limitation of early experience can stultify the development of children enormously. The extreme deprivation of the children in this particular home was most unusual and is unlikely to be encountered in children brought up in a family. However, current investigations into the relationship of the abilities of children and their social and educational experience, all tend towards the conclusion that the quality of that experience is one of the most important things making for the satisfactory educational development of children. Children in stimulating homes will have much the same advantage over other children as the chimpanzee reared in the psychologist's home had the advantage over other chimpanzees.

When children go to school the same processes still operate. Children in a stimulating school environment will develop in order to come to terms adequately with that environment. Children in a school environment which makes few demands on them are likely to change little and make much less progress.

A recent report of research carried out by the School of Education at Manchester University, which is discussed at greater length later, lends support to this view. It was found that children in schools with progressive educational methods, good social backgrounds, and good teaching conditions achieve more than children in less favoured environments.

The Russian psychologist, L. S. Vigotsky, suggested an interesting view of the relationship between maturation and learning which bears upon our discussion. He suggests that learning goes before maturation creating a *zone of potential development*. He points out that the learning activity of the school child is something quite new for him, even though he has been learning in one way or another since birth. The child is capable of certain things which the teacher may determine by tests. If then the teacher interprets the results of those tests as determining the child's mental ability and proceeds to teach at that level, she will, according to Vigotsky, be teaching to the *yesterday* of the child's development. If, on the other hand, we test the child's ability to achieve tasks with help from the teacher, we find his zone of potential development. Should we now use the knowledge obtained from this type of assessment we shall be teaching for the child's future development: that which he will be able to accomplish *tomorrow* on his own. In Vigotsky's words: '. . . . the only good teaching is that which outpaces development' [8].

Individual differences

From what we have seen of the great effect of development on the abilities of the child at any given time, it is clear that individual children will differ according to their developmental state at any one time. The term *developmental state*, as used here, does not refer merely to the level of maturation, but to the resultant of the processes of growth and the effects of experience, including learning. Some psychology texts devote a good deal of attention to the question of individual differences, especially on the intellectual side, and in this country probably the major effort of educational psychologists in recent years has gone into devising increasingly accurate methods of assessing the extent of such differences. This phenomenon is considered in a later chapter, but while accepting that all children are different in some respects, it is the argument of this section that they are much more alike than they are different. All the facts and arguments so far advanced take as their necessary point of departure that, assuming a normal physiological state, then the psychological development of children will be fundamentally similar given similar environmental conditions.

The environment of every child, however, is unique; so is his experience. This applies even to twins. It is impossible for them to have exactly the same environment. Apart from the fact that the major aspect of the environment of each twin is the other twin; since they cannot occupy the same space at the same time, they will always be in a different relationship with their surroundings. One twin will be born first; in general they will be fed and attended to, one after the other, so that right from the start their patterns of experience will be different. Naturally, as soon as they become mobile and independent their environments will be even more different. We may see, then, that even with children whose genetic endowment is very similar, it is inevitable that differences will appear.

In the case of children other than twins, the hereditary material passed on to them by their parents is different in many respects. The results of some of these differences are readily observable. Eye colour, height, hair colour are some of the most obvious. There may be some inheritance of glandular or neurological organization which in turn could affect growth or behaviour. We should thus find differences in the way in which children react to their environment. For example, inefficient functioning of the reticular formation would depress orienting activity and

47

would have a deleterious effect on the child's learning ability. This has been found to obtain with some subnormal children whose EEG records show a lower level of activity of the reticular formation than normal people. Certain glandular differences may determine that this child is lively and quick, while the other is slow and lethargic. However, while gross deficiency in function of glands or nervous system may lead to learning difficulty, it is likely that the enormous number and complexity of neural connections in the brain provide an entirely adequate basis for satisfactory learning by most children according to our current standards. It is more than likely that no one who has ever lived has made use of the maximum potential of his brain in a lifetime of learning. There will, however, be undoubted differences in children in their current level of attainment in various school activities and in their interests. We shall consider these more fully when we have seen how they may be influenced by learning in school and home.

Summary

At birth the child moves from a stable, beneficent, but unstimulating environment, the womb, to an unstable, potentially hostile, but extremely stimulating environment, the world outside the womb. Change of bodily structure, which was the main characteristic of the foetus, is augmented in the newly born baby by the development of the functions of the different organs. Whereas the foetus maintained its state of equilibrium with the minimum of activity, the baby adapts to its environment by increasingly finely differentiated bodily activity. Disturbance of the state of equilibrium of the organism is accompanied by the discharge of negative affect; the restoration of equilibrium is accompanied by positive affect.

Functional development becomes more complex as the environment becomes more complex. Studies in animals and children have shown that the rate of development and complexity of patterns of behaviour in man depend to a great extent on the cultural environment. Children from different cultures will have different norms of development both physical and psychological.

Within a given culture different educational experience will play an important role in the production of different patterns of educational development. The fact that the environment and experience of every child is unique, together with the fact that the physiological organization is also unique, means that there will be individual differences among children. All children will be different. But systematic education would be impossible if children were not more alike than they are different.

Because of the very great effect of environmental stimulation on development, children's abilities cannot be expected to *unfold* automatically at a given time: relevant experience will assist the development of these abilities.

CHAPTER 3

An Introduction to Learning

As we have seen, the nature of children's development is greatly influenced by the environmental conditions in which they are brought up. The amount of social stimulation which they receive is of particular importance here, and even if physical conditions are adequate, an unstimulating environment which provides children with little opportunity or need to experiment or to solve problems, will result in a low level of achievement.

Perhaps the most important aspect of the child's social environment is beyond the reach of the teacher. For the first, very important few years of life, the arbiters of the child's development lie in the home. Genetical endowment and the cultural level of the family, coupled with the actual physical conditions of the home, will have decisive effects on the child's development and will continue to influence him throughout his school life. These factors are inaccessible to influence by the teacher but it is as well for him to have them in mind in his dealings with his pupils. In addition he will need to know how he may most effectively change his pupils along the lines he considers to be most appropriate. That is, he will seek out the most efficient ways of getting his pupils to learn.

We have already seen that learning has been going on from birth; possibly even before this; and probably the fundamental processes at work in this pre-school learning are applicable to learning in school. What the teacher needs is some systematic framework within which he can work with his children to ensure their most effective learning. This is one of the central problems in educational psychology. It is a problem to which there is no easy solution and the way in which learning takes place is by no means clearly understood. However, investigations in various fields are yielding findings which are helping us to understand the *conditions* under which learning takes place. The informed manipulation of these conditions by the teacher will enable him to improve the learning situation for his pupils.

It would be useful at this stage to establish what we have in mind when we talk about *learning*. The naïve idea that it is what happens to the pupil when the teacher *tells* him, is not only inadequate but misleading. It is misleading in two ways; it assumes a restriction on the use of the term which is unjustified and it assumes that the dispensing of information by the teacher necessarily involves its assimilation by the taught. The view of learning that many psychologists would accept, would be one that stressed its all-pervasive nature penetrating into spheres of human activity which the layman would not normally consider as being influenced by learning. For example, a person who is rehabilitated after some serious injury, *learns* to overcome his handicap. Neurotics *learn* the abnormal patterns of behaviour associated with mental illness. They also *learn* to overcome them. The addict's craving for tobacco or alcohol is *learned*. Knowledge of the learning process is helping therapists to teach patients to overcome their abnormal patterns of behaviour, and it may well be that this approach may be made to the rehabilitation of criminals in future.

As may be gathered from these examples, learning is to be considered as an active process. We are not likely to accept that the alcoholic has learned to do without drink unless we actually observe a change in his behaviour; or that the neurotic is cured without some manifestation of the disappearance of his neurosis. In other words, we cannot say that learning has taken place until we can observe in some way the changes in the behaviour of the animal or person, brought about by learning. This, of course, applies to school. The teacher is unlikely to assume that his pupils have learned, without checking in some way or other that their behaviour has changed. Perhaps we should note here that we are using the term *behaviour* in the sense in which it is used throughout this book, not in the sense of the children being well, or badly behaved; but in reference to the total activity of man or animal in response to a given situation. In the examples given, the essential part of the learning which takes place is the experience which builds up the changed behaviour. We might say, therefore. that *learning occurs whenever the activity of an organism brings about a relatively permanent change in its behaviour*.

This is a very broad definition and some psychologists prefer to take the view that there are different categories of learning ranging from the very simple learning of lower organisms to the complex learning of man. In all these cases, however, the general definition would apply. They all involve relatively permanent changes in behaviour even though the processes which bring about the changes are profoundly different.

The changes in behaviour referred to are the overt manifestations of learning; we might call them the evidence of learning. We may distinguish between these changes in behaviour and the processes within the organism which form the bases for these changes. On the one hand we have the actual changes within the organism, which we believe to consist mainly in changes in the central nervous system, this we may call learning; on the other hand we have the outward signs of learning, commonly referred to as *performance*. From what we have seen in earlier chapters, the complexity of the changes within the organism brought about by learning will depend partly upon the complexity of the central nervous system, and partly upon the life experience of the organism; the final outcome will be evidenced by the complexity of performance.

The definition of learning taken here clearly depends on the appearance of certain regularities in the environment. If the environment were completely chaotic, and if the laws of causality no longer obtained, organisms would be unable to build up the relatively permanent patterns of responses to which we have alluded. In such an environment it would be virtually impossible for an organism to adapt. Thus the relatively permanent changes which an organism makes in learning are changes which enable it to cope effectively with the regularities of the environment. If those regularities change then the patterns of behaviour will change as well.

With such a view of learning it will be clear that a very large field of investigation is open for students of the subject, and the work that has been done has included work with animals as well as human beings.

Experimental investigation into the nature of learning has developed only in this century. The study of its application to problems of learning and teaching of school subjects has hardly begun. In twenty-one years (1940–1961) only five papers on the application of learning theory were published in the three main journals in the field of educational psychology.*

Thus the experiments which we now consider were establishing new traditions: for the first time attempts were being made to introduce scientific rigour into the study of learning. This involved the abandoning of previous techniques such as *introspection* where the thoughts of the subject, reported to the experimenter, provided the data from which the experimenter drew his conclusions. An experimenter, using introspective techniques, would carry out an experiment, say in methods of learning, and then ask his subject how his thought processes worked during the experiment. As may readily be seen, such techniques cannot be checked objectively and must be affected by factors completely outside the experimenter's control. While the subject's thoughts might be interesting to the experimenter, he cannot legitimately take them down and use them as experimental evidence. Instead, emphasis is placed on experiments that are objective and amenable to corroboration and checking. Similarly, when we study learning in animals, care is taken to avoid *anthropomorphism.* That is, we do not invest animals with human attributes. We cannot say, for example, that the cat, curled up in front of the fire, is *content* or that a rabbit is *afraid.* These are human traits describing subjective human experiences. That animals feel as we do is highly unlikely and is certainly inaccessible to verification. To use anthropomorphic terms in describing animal behaviour is therefore a source of error. In the study of the application of learning theory to school, much remains to be done since the bulk of experimental work has been done with animals, and this necessarily means that we must pay a good deal of attention

* SKEMP, R.: *British Journal of Educational Psychology*, June 1962.

to animal learning. However, this is useful since we can see in the simpler behaviour of animals, some of the essential features of human learning. We must be careful, however, to avoid carrying over uncritically the findings of experiments with rats and monkeys to human learning.

The conditional reflex

The first and most important experiments to give us insight into learning processes were those started by I. P. Pavlov (1849–1936) a Russian physiologist [9]. As early as 1880, while carrying out investigations into the digestive systems of dogs, he noticed that the animal salivated not only when food was placed in its mouth, but when it saw the food. The function of saliva is to facilitate the digestion of food and the natural stimulus to produce salivation is the presence of food in the mouth. Salivation at the sight of food involves the responding by the animal to a stimulus other than the one which should naturally evoke the response. It seemed likely that this was an acquired response, since, presumably, the animal would have to learn in the course of its life which substances were food and which not food, otherwise it would salivate continuously. The point about this experiment is that the process of learning had come under experimental investigation. The animal had *learned* that the sight of food would soon lead to it being given something to eat. This might seem ridiculously elementary learning but it is the starting point for much of modern learning psychology. It is a basic pattern of learning which is far more complex.

Pavlov investigated this phenomenon and refined his experimental techniques until he was able to measure accurately the strength of the acquired response. In these experiments the dog would be placed in a harness in a specially designed room which cut out extraneous stimuli. A *neutral* stimulus such as the ringing of a bell would then be presented followed by food which would induce salivation in the dog. After repeated presentations the dog would salivate when the bell was rung. Pavlov measured the strength of the responses by the number of drops of saliva secreted.

It was soon discovered that although the natural response of

54

salivation to food in the mouth was stable and unchanging, the acquired response of salivating to a previously neutral stimulus was unstable and liable to die away if not followed by presentation of the natural stimulus.

It is useful to consider the value of this new response to the organism. Although salivating to the sound of a bell is an *un-natural* response it is of definite advantage to the organism so long as the natural stimulus follows. The organism responding to the new stimulus is ready to cope with the natural stimulus when it arrives. The dog salivating when it hears the bell already has a copious flow of digestive juices when food reaches its mouth: its digestive processes will thus be enhanced. Salivating before the food is therefore of definite advantage to the efficient functioning of the organism. Conversely, if food never follows the bell, salivation is of no advantage to the organism and, as we have observed, in these circumstances the response dies away.

Because of the instability of the acquired response, Pavlov called it a *conditional response** to illustrate its dependence on other factors. He called the response we have previously called a *natural* response, an *unconditional response*. The natural stimulus was called the *unconditional stimulus*. The whole pattern of stimulus followed by response is called a reflex. Thus, salivating to the presence of food in the mouth is called an *unconditional reflex*, since it occurs irrespective of other factors, whereas salivating to the sound of a bell is a *conditional reflex* dependent for its stability on other factors; notably, of course, the following of the conditional response by the unconditional stimulus.

It should be noted here that the term *conditioning* deriving from *conditional reflex*, is a scientific term which means simply the establishment of conditional reflexes. It has no sinister connotations in the context of educational psychology. That it has in common parlance is because of its being linked with such newspaper terms as *brainwashing*, and probably because of the

* In translating the Russian, the term *conditioned* reflex is commonly used instead of *conditional* reflex. I shall use the term *conditional* since it gives a more accurate meaning. The two terms, however, may be regarded as interchangeable.

writings of authors who have resisted the idea that the behaviour of human beings can be explained, predicted, or worse still, controlled. In fact teachers are constantly trying to do all three. The reason that they have escaped attack in the past is probably because the practice of teaching is largely based on rule of thumb and intuition. This is not surprising in view of the complexity of the processes of learning in man, but if we wish to use the knowledge gained from the study of conditioning to help improve our teaching, we should not be deterred by the emotive overtones which the term has acquired in popular currency.

Pavlov continued his experiments over a lifetime and elaborated laws of conditioning which dealt with the acquisition and lapsing of conditional reflexes and he considered that learning took place through the elaboration of intricate systems of conditional reflexes based on a foundation of unconditional reflexes. The simple conditional reflex has relatively little application in the classroom but the study of the laws which determine the waxing and waning of complicated patterns of conditional reflexes will help us to understand some of the ways in which learning can be facilitated. We shall consider these questions in a later chapter.

Trial and error

At much the same time as Pavlov was carrying out his experiments, E. L. Thorndike in America was investigating learning in cats. A hungry cat would be placed in a cage with food visible on the outside. On the inside was a release mechanism which could be operated by the animal.

When first placed in the cage the cat exhibits an apparently random activity, scratching and trying to escape to get the food. Eventually, it fortuitously operates the release mechanism which allows it to escape and obtain the food. Subsequent trials find the activity becoming less random and focussed on the part of the cage near the release mechanism. The time taken to escape decreases until the animal eventually operates the release as soon as it finds itself in the cage.

Thorndike's experiment was said to be an example of trial and error learning. However, it was later recognized to be of the type of learning called *instrumental conditioning*. Readers will see the affinity with Skinner's work outlined below.

Similar experiments, using white rats, have produced similar results. A hungry rat is placed in a maze and food is placed at the other end of the maze. The hungry animal, like the hungry cat in Thorndike's experiment, at first explores the maze in an apparently random manner, gradually working away from the point of entry until eventually it reaches the food. On subsequent

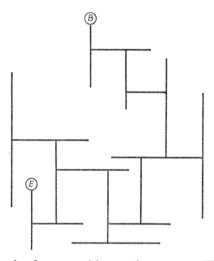

Fig. 4. Example of a maze with a random pattern. When investigating human learning the experimenter covers the maze with a piece of stiff paper or card with a small hole in the centre which he places over B. The subject has to find his way to E by sighting the maze through the hole in the card and steering the card until the hole covers E. The card must be large enough to cover the whole maze whatever position it is in during the experiment.

trials the preliminary investigatory behaviour is reduced and wrong pathways are avoided until eventually the animal will run through the maze without error and often at high speed.

Students presented with a similar problem tend to exhibit similar behaviour. This can be investigated as follows. A line maze is drawn on a piece of plain quarto paper. A larger piece of card or thick paper is pierced in the centre and placed over the quarto sheet so that the whole of the maze is covered except the small section immediately below the hole. The student must now manipulate or *steer* the card from the beginning of the maze to the end. A check is kept of the number of errors made and the time taken to get through the maze on each trial. An experimenter observing animal and student maze running will see a close similarity in attack and performance, the student exhibiting the same exploratory behaviour at the beginning and gradually dropping the incorrect manœuvres until he runs the maze without error.

On the basis of his experiments Thorndike suggested certain laws which he considered governed the learning of organisms, human and non-human. Some of these he modified during the course of his work, but the most important one is still of great importance: this is the Law of Effect. Thorndike states in this law that behaviour which is followed by reward or success will tend to be repeated, whereas, behaviour which is not rewarded will tend to die away. On the basis of subsequent work he was led to the conclusion that punishment was less effective in producing learning.

In general the control of learning in school has relied more on punishment than on reward. It is common enough to punish for failure to accomplish the set task, but rarer to reward success. Punishment may be meted out to the larger part of a class, reward is usually given to the most successful one or two children. The pun *seats of learning* was pregnant with meaning for many generations of schoolboys. Any other approach even now may be regarded with faint contempt as *psychological*, meaning *soft*, and the ineffective methods of teaching continue.

Need reduction

C. L. Hull, another American psychologist, built upon the work of Thorndike and Pavlov. He argued that learning takes place through a process of *need reduction*. A hungry animal reduces its need for food by pulling the release in the cage or by following the correct path through a maze: the animal's need is reduced when its activity produces food. Activity which results in the reduction of a need is said to be *reinforced*. In the case of the animal in the puzzle box the food which it reaches by successfully operating the catch is a reinforcer of the activity of operating the catch. Reinforced activity will tend to be repeated and thus the animal learns how to escape from the box. If, on the other hand, the animal receives a mild electric shock when it operates the catch it will learn to avoid the release mechanism. Noxious stimuli, such as electric shocks, which follow a given activity are referred to as *punishers*. Since such stimuli are deleterious to the wellbeing of the organism they may be looked upon as need producers rather than need reducers and if the organism is motivated to reduce its needs it will naturally avoid such stimuli.

Hull's hypothesis links the activity of the brain with the behaviour of the organism. The organism's needs which are based on its organic requirements and registered in the hypothalamus, are satisfied, or in Hull's terms, *reduced*, because new connections are established in the cortex, which lead to the new patterns of behaviour, thus ending the state of need.

Instrumental conditioning

B. F. Skinner in America has taken up the study of reinforcement and in a series of most interesting experiments has investigated the effect of the manipulation of reinforcement on various organisms [10]. Thorndike, Hull, and Skinner all approach learning in a similar way. Their work may be fitted into the broad category of what is called instrumental conditioning.* Skinner himself makes the distinction between instrumental conditioning and the conditioning studied by Pavlov; conventionally termed classical conditioning. The distinction between the two types of reflexes may be illustrated diagrammatically, following Skinner.

(S = stimulus, R = response, (S—R) = reflex,
→ = 'is followed by')

* The term 'instrumental conditioning' used here may be considered to be synonymous with the term 'operant conditioning' used elsewhere. There is a distinction but it is outside the scope of this book.

Classical conditioning

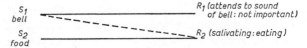

S_1 naturally evokes R_1 which is not important.

S_2 naturally evokes R_2 but since S_1 is presented almost at the same time as S_2, S_1 becomes linked with R_2 so that S_1 eventually elicits R_2. We may then write:

Instrumental conditioning

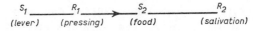

In instrumental conditioning the hungry animal is placed in a Skinner box, which is a highly sophisticated adaptation of the Thorndike puzzle cage. The pressing of a lever will bring, not escape as in the case of Thorndike's cage, but the presentation of a pellet of food. Thus our diagram may be explained as follows. The lever acts as a stimulus, completely neutral in the first instance. The animal responds to the stimulus by pressing the lever initially in the course of its investigatory behaviour. The pressing response is *instrumental* in producing a reinforcer (food) which then acts as a stimulus (S_2) for response R_2 (salivation). Since the pellet of food is insufficient to satisfy the animal, it continues its investigatory behaviour until it once again operates the lever and produces food. Eventually it will continue to press the lever until it is satiated.

At this juncture Skinner intervenes and arranges for the reinforcers (food) to be presented according to a variety of *schedules*. One schedule might be to reinforce every response; another might be to reinforce every tenth response; or perhaps the experimenter might reinforce at ten-minute intervals, and so on. Some very interesting patterns of behaviour have been built up, by varying the schedules of reinforcement, many of which have important bearing on human learning; these we consider in a later chapter.

Instrumental conditioning, then, differs from classical conditioning in that the required response is *instrumental* in producing the reinforcement. In the case of classical conditioning the reinforcement follows willy-nilly, i.e. it does not depend on the response made; the response may be regarded as anticipatory rather than instrumental. It is sometimes suggested that an important difference between classical conditioning and instrumental conditioning is that classical conditioning is a passive form of learning while instrumental conditioning is active. In this view classical conditioning relates to learning which involves involuntary responses, whereas instrumental conditioning relates to learning that requires voluntary responses. It is, however, difficult to draw a clear line of demarcation between the two and in fact, some psychologists argue that these two types of conditioning are different aspects of the same thing, but this is a refinement outside the scope of this book. In the experiments we have quoted we find that the rat in the Skinner box obtains food *because he presses the lever*. The dog in Pavlov's experiment is given food *whether or not he responds* after each presentation of the conditional stimulus. In both cases, however, the reinforcement of the responses (in both cases by food) leads to their being repeated. Both types of conditioning illustrate the importance of reinforcement in the setting up of patterns of behaviour.

Despite the fact that the experiments quoted have been carried out with animals much simpler than man, there is little doubt that the findings with regard to the effect of reinforcement have great application to the classroom. We consider this in more detail later, but the point could be made here that the teacher would be well advised to reinforce that behaviour in his children which he wished to be repeated. Skinner suggests that the adult can reinforce desired behaviour in a child by showing approval when the behaviour appears. He also holds that successful accomplishment of a given task often acts as a reinforcer of the activity which brought about success. Probably, because of the normal teaching situation, the teacher has far too many children to make possible the consistent reinforcing of desired behaviour. However, he should do his best to ensure adequate reinforcement within the limits imposed by the existing classroom situation.

'Learning is connecting'

Thorndike said: 'Learning is connecting.' Pavlov talked about *temporary connections* meaning conditional reflexes. Both were referring to the processes of conditioning. The investigations we have so far studied have suggested that learning depends essentially on making connections. The sucking of the new-born baby, at first a reflex activity, is soon connected with the reduction of its need for food and with positive affect. If the mother feeds the baby when it cries, she will reinforce the crying so that it will eventually repeat this activity whenever it feels the need for food. Its crying will be an example of instrumental conditioning. Newly born babies suck only when their mouths are stimulated. Within a week or two they are sucking when held in the feeding position in their mothers' arms. This is an example of classical conditioning. In the two examples the key to the babies' new activity is the setting up of new connections between two activities. The crying for food, and the sucking when nursed are both examples of learned behaviour.

The establishment of these connections depends on their being contiguous in time. A long delay by the mother before attending the crying child would work against the connecting of the cries with the appearance of the mother and food. Similarly if the mother held the child in the feeding position for a very long time before feeding it, the sucking behaviour would cease to appear when she picked it up to feed it.

There is little doubt that the principle of contiguity is of crucial importance in all forms of learning. Learning can take place without reinforcement but stimuli and responses which are not contiguous in space and time will not be linked. This discovery, made by observing simple organisms, can be observed in much more complex learning in man. Thus the complex mental activity associated with concept formation and problem solving depends on connections being made between the different aspects of phenomena and the necessary responses which constitute adaptive behavioural changes, resulting in the one case in the satisfactory formation of a concept and in the other case in the satisfactory solution of a problem. (See pp. 121-2 and 374.)

Stimulus–Organism–Response

Before leaving this introductory discussion it is important to consider the function of the organism itself in the establishment of patterns of behaviour. The diagrams taken from Skinner (p. 60) show a direct link between stimulus and response; we write S–R to indicate a reflex. From what has been said earlier about the role of the central nervous system in behaviour it is clear that this is an oversimplification. In any consideration of learning, the state and complexity of the organism must be borne in mind. By the state of the organism is meant its actual physical condition such as health or ill health, alertness or lethargy. By complexity we mean the level of development of the organism in the evolutionary scale; the main feature in this case being the complexity of the central nervous system. Thus when we consider conditioning we can never reduce it to simple 'muscle twitch' psychology as is sometimes suggested. Between the stimulus and the response comes the organism with all the complexity of (in the case of mammals) a highly developed central nervous system. Thus the practice has developed of representing the reflex in the form S–O–R where the central O symbolizes the organism.

Skinner has little interest in the stimulus–organism–response view of learning. He considers it quite legitimate to study, describe, and control behaviour by manipulating the stimulus–response situation. Other psychologists such as D. O. Hebb accorded it great importance as also did Pavlov, although this aspect of Pavlov's work is sometimes overlooked.

Current thought in psychology in many countries is taking an increasing interest in the S–O–R pattern. Instead of cutting off the study of behaviour from its roots in the organism, the organism and its behaviour are viewed as a single system. As was mentioned earlier the stimulus inputs from the external and internal environment are analysed and collated before a response is made. It is this analysing and collating activity which is the object of study at the moment by an increasing number of psychologists and scientists in other disciplines, such as those concerned with the activities of the brain, referred to in Chapter 1.

The Gestalt view

A different view of learning was put forward by the Gestalt psychologists who could not accept that learning was connecting. As W. Kohler, one of the leading Gestalt psychologists said:

'Explanation of our intellectual life in terms of conditioning would simply mean its reduction to the operations of an often most practical, but intrinsically blind, connection of mere facts. Promises that such an explanation will nevertheless be achieved cause in the present speaker a mild, incredulous horror.'*

The reasons for the Gestalt antipathy to conditioning theory are rooted in their view of human psychology. Their work in the first place lay in the field of perception, i.e. the way in which we perceive things. On the basis of their work they postulated certain laws of perception the details of which do not concern us here but which promulgate a basic axiom that the whole is more than the sum of its parts. The word *Gestalt* means *configuration* or *pattern*. The argument is that the significance of a situation or pattern of stimuli is in the total pattern, not in its separate elements. The significance of a piece of music is not in the individual notes but in the whole composition. This argument is opposed to the views of conditioning on the grounds that conditioning theory disregards the importance of the total pattern and stresses instead the separate elements. Pavlov rejected the assertion that it had ever been suggested that all the elements in a situation did not act upon one another, but the Gestalt psychologists made this a central point in their arguments when they ventured into learning theory. They said that conditioning theory was *bricks and mortar psychology* which added piece upon

* KOHLER, W.I in HENLE, M. (Ed.): *Documents of Gestalt Psychology*, University of California Press, 1961.

piece in the process of learning without ever seeing the whole structure [11].

The most well known experiments which underly the views of Gestalt psychologists are those carried out by Kohler between 1913 and 1917. During this period Kohler, a German scientist, was marooned on the island of Tennerife during the 1914–1918 war. He passed the time conducting experiments on chimpanzees. Many of these experiments were investigations into how the animals learned to solve problems. In many cases the problems bore certain similarities to those used by Thorndike in his experiments with cats.

In one of Kohler's crucial experiments the ape was placed in a cage on the outside of which was a banana out of reach. At the other end of the cage, within reach of the ape, was a stick. The problem would be considered solved when the ape picked up the stick and used it to rake in the fruit. Kohler claimed that the chimpanzee solved the problem, not like the cat in Thorndike's experiment, through random and undirected activity, but after failing to reach the fruit with its hands or feet, it reached the solution suddenly after surveying the total situation [12].

In another experiment food is placed in the cage out of the reach of the animal. A box in the cage can be used to climb on to obtain the fruit. Again Kohler claimed that his ape solved the problem through an intelligent restructuring of the total situation which he termed *insight*. The main characteristics of insight are that the solution to a problem is perceived *in a flash*, and that this solution results from the situation becoming organized in the brain.

The argument here is that the ape suddenly saw the total pattern or configuration of the situation and without any preliminary trial and error, solved the problem. This kind of learning was proposed as being a higher form of learning than trial and error learning.

The difficulty with the concept of insight is that it really explains nothing. To say that an animal learns through insight evokes the question as to what insight is. The Gestalt answer that it is the restructuring of the situation giving organization or pattern to what is perceived, merely removes the problem a stage, it does not explain it. Nor is the *suddenness* very useful. Other workers have discovered that chimpanzees sometimes come suddenly to quite erroneous solutions to problems and keep on repeating them.

Another difficulty involved in the concept of insight, is the part played by previous experience. The idea of insight is that new problems can be solved in this way without previous experience. The solution is reached when the total situation is apprehended. Yerkes, Pavlov and Birch carried out similar experiments to Kohler and came to the conclusion that apes exhibited *insightful* learning only after considerable preliminary training in simpler tasks. The work of Harlow which we discuss later provides evidence of a very similar nature.

Some Gestalt psychologists agree that previous experience is important in achieving insight. This position then raises the question as to what kind of previous experience this is likely to be. When the task is quite new trial and error is likely to occupy a very large part of this preliminary experience: only later when some learning has taken place is the learner's attack on a problem likely to show that understanding of the total situation which the Gestalt psychologists call 'insightful learning'. The fact that under experimental conditions animals or humans start new learning at the trial and error level does not mean that children must all go through this stage whenever they learn something new. The skilful teacher will try to short-cut the random nature of the early stage of learning.

Summary

Learning starts at birth or possibly before. We recognize learning when we observe a relatively permanent change in the behaviour of an organism brought about by previous activity. We cannot, therefore, assume that children have learned unless we observe some change in their behaviour.

While we may accept verbal responses as proof of a change in behaviour (learning), we cannot admit a person's own account of *how* he learned: in a scientific study of learning our evidence must be objective and subject to experimental investigation. For similar reasons we must avoid attributing human characteristics to animals.

Earlier views of learning which tended to be descriptive rather than explanatory, have been replaced in recent years by very widespread acceptance of *conditioning* as a basic factor in the processes of learning, and the scientific study of these processes has centred around the mechanisms of conditioning. A central theme in the study of conditioning, is the way organisms react to their environment. They normally react in two modes.

The first mode of responding is the *natural* or *inborn* mode. The basic unit in this mode is the *unconditional reflex*. The second mode of responding is an acquired mode. The basic unit here is the *conditional reflex*.

The unconditional reflex consists of the *unconditional stimulus* and the *unconditional response*. Under normal circumstances the unconditional stimulus will always produce the unconditional response. For example: the new-born baby will always suck when its mouth is stimulated.

The conditional reflex consists of *conditional stimulus* and *conditional response*. The term *conditional* is used because the response will normally be made only *on condition that* it is of value to the normal functioning of the organism. A conditional reflex is set up when a neutral stimulus is repeatedly followed by an unconditional stimulus. The unconditional stimulus acts as a reinforcer of the conditional response. Eventually the neutral stimulus elicits the response before the presentation of the unconditional stimulus. The neutral stimulus is now a conditional stimulus. For example: a person will blink if a puff of air is directed to his eye (unconditional reflex). If a bell is rung just before each puff, the blink is eventually elicited by the bell alone. This is the conditional reflex.

Conditional reflexes are extinguished or die away if they are not *reinforced*. When a response is reinforced it is confirmed as being of use to the organism. Thus the conditional eye blink will disappear if repeated ringings of the bell are not followed by puffs of air.

Instrumental conditioning differs from *classical* conditioning in that the behaviour is instrumental (i.e. it is the causative factor) in producing reinforcement. Thus, in the Skinner box, the animal obtains reinforcement by exhibiting a given pattern of behaviour. Typically this would be pressing a lever or pecking a button, which activity would produce food. Behaviour which produces reinforcement tends to be repeated; that which is not reinforced dies away.

Currently the S–O–R view of learning is receiving increasing attention. This view lays emphasis on the way in which the complex internal activity of the organism affects the way in which it adapts to the external environment. The organism and its behaviour are considered as a unity and not separately.

The Gestalt view of learning stresses the importance of considering the total situation and reacts against the atomistic view attributed to the stimulus-response psychologists. This view of learning also stresses the importance of *insight* which may be considered as a sudden seeing of the solution to a problem. The role of previous learning which may have been by trial and error is given little attention. Subsequent experiments have shown that insightful learning does not take place without considerable preliminary training. The investigations into the effects of limited experience in children show that the ability to engage in complex behaviour depends greatly on the quality of previous experience. The teacher can, however, help children to short-cut the random trial-and-error learning to achieve insightful learning.

CHAPTER 4

Mechanisms of Learning

The ubiquity of conditioning

Investigations into the processes of conditioning have mainly concentrated on mammals, notably the dog, the laboratory rat, monkeys, apes, and man himself. However, experiments have been done with other animals and the result has been that conditional behaviour has been found in all groups of animals which have been investigated. The picture which emerges from studies of different levels of animal life is one in which the capacity of conditioning seems to reflect levels of organization of the central nervous system. The more complex the nervous system, the more complex the processes of conditioning, i.e. the more can be learned. Such a view of conditioning stresses the essential similarity with regard to the mechanisms of learning throughout the animal kingdom. In this view there is no fundamental difference at the physiological level between man and the other animals in so far as conditioning phenomena are concerned. This is a view which coincides closely with the picture which is emerging from other sciences: the essential difference between man and the other animals is social, not physiological. This we consider later; now let us consider briefly how the level of complexity of the central nervous system is reflected in the complexity of the conditional behaviour which may be set up.

Learned behaviour has been observed in the protozoa, the simplest animals, which have only one cell. Conditioning in these animals is gross, i.e. not finely differentiated. One such animal, paramecium, learned to collect at a platinum wire where food was supplied. Multicellular animals such as flatworms and earthworms have been conditioned to make more complex responses. Earthworms have been trained to take the correct path through a T-maze; flatworms have been trained to avoid a light after it had been repeatedly paired with electric shock.

More complex animals have learned to make finer adjustments. Octopuses have been conditioned to discriminate between different geometrical shapes. Bees have been trained to come to specific shapes, colours, and odours. Fishes have been trained to colour, shape, and sound as conditional stimuli and have retained the learned habits for weeks. In one experiment a pike was conditioned not to attack fish which would normally be its prey. This was done by having a glass plate between the pike and sticklebacks. The pike attacked the sticklebacks but bumped into the glass plate. After a number of experiences of this nature the pike ceased to attack the sticklebacks. When the pike was then put into the same tank as the sticklebacks, it no longer attacked them, even though the barrier had been removed.

Mammals are capable of the most complex patterns of conditional reflexes. In a comparison of learning in animals of different order of complexity, the following pattern was found. When a choice between a triangle and a circle is presented and approach to the triangle is rewarded, fish, mice, pigeons, cats, dogs, and primates solve the problem. When circles and triangles are presented in sets of three and the odd one rewarded, the solution is not readily learned by any animals other than the primates.

We see, then, that the phenomena of conditioning are pervasive throughout nature. In general, conditioning works to the benefit of the organism. (That it sometimes does not, is discussed in a later chapter.) To help us get a clear understanding of the processes involved, we consider briefly another ubiquitous natural phenomenon; that of *feedback*.

Systems and stability

In recent years work in the science of *cybernetics* has contributed to our ideas about many natural phenomena, among them, learning. Cybernetics is the science which deals with automatic control. The word comes from the Greek, meaning helmsman or controller, and any system, living or non-living (we may regard animals as living systems), which produces automatic control, or self-regulation, may be considered a cybernetic mechanism [13].

Machines which are self-regulating incorporate a device called a *servomechanism*. This servomechanism exercises a control over the machine by using past performance to determine present operation. The machine is set up to operate in a given way: so long as the machine does this the servomechanism does not interfere. Any operation of the machine which deviates from the preset *norm*, is detected by the servomechanism which then reacts on the machine to return it to its original state.

A simple example of such an arrangement is provided by the thermostat in an electrical heating system. The thermostat is a device sensitive to heat, which is fitted into the circuit of the heater. The optimum temperature of the heating system is predetermined and the heater is switched on. When the temperature rises to the preset level, the thermostat operates a switch and cuts out the heater. The temperature will now begin to fall. This is registered by the thermostat, which then switches the heater on again. What, in fact, happens, is that the temperature will tend to fluctuate from slightly above to slightly below the operating temperature, the amplitude of the fluctuations depending upon the sensitivity of the thermostat.

This process whereby the results of the present operation of a machine determines its future operation is termed *feedback*. In our example, information about the results of the operation of the machine, i.e. the heater, are registered by the thermostat, which feeds back instructions to modify the operation of the heater, i.e. to switch on or off. Since an increase in heat above the optimum results in the switching off of the heater, and a decrease in heat results in a switching on of the heater, the process is called *negative feedback*. Were an increase in heat to lead to an increase in output of the heater, through the mediation of the thermostat, this would be *positive feedback*. Systems incorporating negative feedback tend to be stable systems, whereas positive feedback tends to be unstable and can cause the breakdown of the mechanism. In our example negative feedback could maintain water in a domestic hot-water system at a convenient temperature for use in the bathroom, positive feedback would result in ever increasing temperatures and finally to breakdown. But positive feedback can lead to growth. Thus technological advances react upon society engendering new techniques which permit further advances (p. 29). However, the term *feedback*, in general, implies negative feedback.

In man similar mechanisms are at work, for example, body temperature is controlled by a thermostatic mechanism. An increase in body heat results in dilation of the peripheral blood vessels which causes blushing and facilitates cooling: at the same time sweat glands operate causing perspiration which again cools the body through evaporation. On the other hand, cold produces the opposite result with contraction of the peripheral blood vessels, shivering, and the raising of body hairs (gooseflesh). Shivering is a bodily activity which generates heat; the raising of body hair is a vestigial primitive response to cold, which increases body insulation.

Many other bodily functions are of such a nature and this control of the body's organic equilibrium is known as *homeostasis*. While the bodily mechanisms may be regarded as examples of feedback, they may also be regarded as reflexes. Thus the homeostatic mechanism which ejects foreign bodies from the throat by coughing was regarded by Pavlov as an unconditional reflex. It is interesting and significant to note that many of these mechanisms which are not normally amenable to conscious control can be conditioned. The salivary reflex is an example of such a reflex, and such things as rate of heart beat, breathing, and the pupillary reflex have been conditioned. The yogi takes the process a stage further and brings the reflexes under his own control [2.]

While few of us learn to emulate the yogi, we all make use of feedback to control our bodily activity. Feedback is used in learning to ride a bicycle. If you lean over too far in one direction, you correct your balance by leaning in the opposite direction. When you aim at a target and miss the bull's-eye, you adjust your aim on the basis of feedback from the results of your first shot. If your first attempt is too high you aim lower; if too low you aim higher. When you pick up a pencil you are making a series of similar fine adjustments so that you grip the pencil correctly. The chances are that you will grip the pencil correctly first time, but a small child will have difficulty. In the case of the adult the feedback mechanisms are well established, in the infant they are not. If we adapt one of Thorndike's experiments we shall see another example of the ubiquity of feedback in human learning.

In this experiment the experimenter asks the subject to draw a line, say three inches long, freehand and without looking at the paper. After about ten attempts he is then asked to try again and this time he is told the length of the line he has drawn before he makes another attempt. In most cases the subject soon approaches the correct length; the lines he draws will generally fluctuate slightly above or slightly below the correct length in a manner similar to the slight fluctuations from the preset level of the temperature of a thermostatically controlled hot-water system.

Some cases of malfunctioning of limb movements may involve disturbance of the feedback mechanisms of the central nervous system. Such malfunctioning is occasionally manifested in tremor and uncontrolled oscillations of the limbs. What seems to happen is that the normal feedback mechanism is disturbed or even turns partly positive, so that when an attempt is made to regulate the movement of a limb, say in picking up a pencil, oscillations occur which are beyond control and the pencil cannot be gripped.

The feedback mechanisms maintaining a state of internal bodily equilibrium, or homeostasis, maintain a state similar to that of a thermostat: it is static equilibrium. Thus body temperature is controlled at 98·4° F. However, the human system maintains two states of equilibrium. In the case of such processes as the maintenance of a constant body temperature the equilibrium is fixed; the temperature always returns to the same level and the bodily processes which regulate the temperature are automatic: there is, in fact, a *thermostat* in the hypothalamus. Deviations from normal bodily states brought about by lack of food or water cannot be regulated in this way. These deviations are registered in the hypothalamus as we have seen, and manifested in what we have termed *needs*; but in order to restore equilibrium the organism has to engage in some sort of behaviour; it has to do something. In the examples we are considering, it looks for food or water. Since the accessibility of food and water varies enormously the behaviour of the organism must be correspondingly variable. The way in which the organism obtains food or water to restore its equilibrium will be different on every occasion but the experience of one successful or unsuccessful attempt to restore equilibrium will affect the method adopted on the next occasion. Equilibrium maintained in this way is *dynamic equilibrium* and in animals it is maintained by an intricate interplay of conditional and unconditional behaviour.

Animals maintaining a state of normal health and activity may be regarded as systems maintaining a state of internal fixed equilibrium through the mechanisms of homeostasis, and a state of dynamic equilibrium with the outside environment through the processes of conditioning.

The fixed equilibrium of homeostasis does not normally concern the educator, but its importance should not be underestimated. The French physiologist Claude Bernard said: 'The stability of the internal environment is the necessary condition of the free life.' Homeostasis leaves the higher centres of the brain free to develop functions of adaptation which result in the achievement of consciousness and the complex behaviour which we see built up in the intricacies of learning. The superstructure of dynamic equilibrium which we are now to consider, stands firm only because of the solidity of its foundation; the static equilibrium of homeostasis.

The conditions of stability

When any animal learns, it modifies its behaviour so that in general it moves from one level of stability to a higher level. I am referring now to behaviour which is adaptive, that is, is of benefit to the proper functioning of the organism. Since every new situation demands a new and different form of behaviour for adaptation, the mechanisms of adaptation must be fluid. As was suggested earlier, these mechanisms are found in the flux of conditional reflexes. So far we have considered only the simple essentials of these mechanisms; we must now consider in more detail the way in which we build up those patterns of behaviour which, because of their complexity, were referred to above (perhaps somewhat unscientifically) as the 'free life'.

It will be useful to take as our point of departure an example of learning in an animal before moving on to man. This should help us to see the basic principles clearly before we add the complicating factors involved in human learning. To do this let us consider a simple experiment of a type originated by B. F. Skinner [10].

In this experiment a classical conditional reflex is established in a laboratory rat by presenting food immediately after a suitable sound (in this case the side of the cage was tapped with a piece of metal). The rat eventually looks in the food box as soon as the sound is made. We then move on to the second part of the experiment. The experimenter now decides on some response to elaborate in the animal. A simple but graphic one starts by his putting a small object such as a button in the cage. The experimenter then watches the animal and when it touches the button the action is reinforced by the sound, followed by the food. After a few trials the animal will concentrate on the button and now the experimenter reinforces only when the animal picks up the object. By selectively refining the activity to be reinforced, the experimenter can produce quite complex patterns of behaviour in the animal. In the experiment outlined, a response of holding up the button in the front paws can generally be set up quite quickly. Thus the experimenter builds up the required behaviour by reinforcing activity which approximates more and more closely to that which he desires: he uses the technique of *successive approximation*.

This experiment provides examples of both classical and instrumental conditioning. It differs from Pavlov's first experiments in that a motor response (seeking the food) is elicited by the sound, whereas Pavlov concentrated on a digestive response (salivation). The picking up of the button is an example of instrumental conditioning. The animal picks up the object since this action has in the past been reinforced. It is a response of the same type as the pressing of the lever in a Skinner box or the operating of the escape trigger in the Thorndike cage.

Note in this experiment that *the sound* acts as a reinforcer of the activity of picking up the button. Now the sound itself is not normally reinforcing, but since it has been the conditional stimulus which has previously been followed by the unconditional stimulus of food, it now functions as a reinforcer. However, since it depends for its stability on an unconditional stimulus, it is referred to as a *secondary reinforcer*. One of the most potent secondary reinforcers in man is money. Quite elaborate patterns of behaviour have been set up because they have been reinforced by money. However, these patterns would not be set up were it not clear that money is the key to the satisfaction of many needs, both primary and derived. Young children who have not yet connected money with the reduction of primary needs will generally prefer sweets to money.

The shaping of behaviour

Skinner calls the technique of building up patterns of behaviour by manipulation of reinforcement, *shaping* behaviour. He illustrates how this can be done in man by giving an example of the way in which a pattern of activity can be set up in a baby. The experimenter decides on some activity for the child to exhibit; say raising his arm. For reinforcement Skinner suggests the switching on of a reading lamp. This is adequate reinforcement for the baby. The experimenter first switches on the lamp when the child raises his arm slightly and switches it off when the arm is dropped. Gradually a higher raising of the arm is required by the experimenter before reinforcement until the child is raising his arm appreciably.

Two important things should be noted here. One is that the switching on of the light acts as a reinforcement. It seems that the successful manipulation of the environment by itself acts as a reinforcer. It may well be that this phenomenon is connected with the orienting reflex and orienting activity towards new aspects of the environment. We meet this again when we consider Skinner's views on the role of reinforcement in programmed learning (Chapter 9). The important thing for the teacher is that the child finds the successful accomplishment of a given task reinforcing in itself. The other point to note in the experiment with the baby is that the whole operation is accompanied by positive affect. Far from being 'cruel' the baby enjoys the game. In fact the baby's rattle fulfills very much the same function as the switching on of the lamp, the great difference being, of course, that the baby himself manipulates the rattle most of the time. On the other hand the adult who shakes the rattle to get the child to smile or make some particular movement is shaping the baby's behaviour in just the same way as in the experiment. In the classroom the same effects are to be noted. Successful coping with a problem is reinforcing and is accompanied by positive affect. The teacher who arranges the work he gives to his children so that they achieve success will not only stimulate them to further activity, he will also probably find that they like the work as well.

Extinction

To return to our experiment. If we now cease to reinforce the behaviour we have built up, the animal will soon cease to respond. Thus repetitions of the sound not followed by food will eventually lead to the disappearance of the response. This phenomenon is termed *extinction*. We may state it generally in these terms. Responses which are not reinforced will tend to drop out of the behavioural pattern. A well known story may illustrate this. When the shepherd boy first cried 'Wolf!' the men responded to the stimulus by turning out to deal with the threat. There was of course no wolf to reinforce their activity. On the repeated occurrence of this procedure the response eventually died away to the chagrin of the shepherd boy. In a similar way the efforts of certain municipal authorities to get rid of the immense flocks of starlings which roost on public buildings have come to nothing. The startle cry of a starling, greatly amplified, was broadcast through a loudspeaker. This was effective at first and the birds flew off. However, since the cry was not reinforced by real danger, the startle response died away and the starlings sat through the

77

playing of the record with equanimity. It should be noted, however, that reflexes which have been extinguished do not die away entirely but will be established with greater facility if the conditioning procedure is repeated, and the conditional stimulus reinforced.

Parents and teachers can make use of extinction to check undesirable behaviour in a child. If such behaviour is ignored it will gradually be given up. Approved behaviour should be rewarded with affection and approbation and will be strengthened. It is desirable, of course, to adopt this approach early in the child's life since it is much more difficult if several unsatisfactory patterns are established and the child is 'spoiled'. The main difficulty here, however, is more likely to be the parents' lack of fortitude to ignore the undesirable behaviour in the first place, than to the lack of efficacy of the training procedure. It is perhaps worth stressing the point, however, that affection and attention must be given to approved behaviour otherwise the child will be confused and there will be little chance of a happy solution to the problem.

External inhibition

External inhibition is another phenomenon of conditioning which leads to the disappearance of a conditional response. In this case the response does not appear when an extraneous stimulus accompanies the conditional stimulus. In other words the intruding stimulus inhibits the response to the conditional stimulus. Pavlov found that in his early work extraneous sights and sounds interfered with the establishment of conditional reflexes and to eliminate this effect he had to introduce sound-proof laboratories.

This phenomenon is fairly obvious: it is what we might commonly refer to as a distraction. Pavlov's difficulty was in getting rid of the distractions, hence the soundproof laboratories. The teacher in the classroom will know a good deal about distractors: the P.E. lesson in the playground outside the classroom window, or the first snowfall of the winter are powerful external inhibitors of the responses the teacher is aiming to establish. Other factors in the classroom situation may not be so obviously distracting but may well be providing stimuli which interfere considerably with the children's learning. We shall consider some of these potential distractors later in the book.

Reciprocal inhibition

Another aspect of the processes of inhibition which has had particular application in psychotherapy, is that of *reciprocal inhibition*. Behavioural psychotherapy regards neurotic behaviour as 'persistent unadaptive learned behaviour in which anxiety is almost always prominent and which is acquired in anxiety-generating situations'. Pavlov investigated neurotic behaviour and produced experimental neuroses in dogs. The American psychologist, J. B. Watson, created a maladaptive response to furry objects in a child by pairing an innocuous stimulus, a tame rat, with a sudden loud noise. A fear response to a sudden loud noise may be regarded as adaptive since such a sound often signifies danger. The learned fear response evoked by furry objects however, is maladaptive, since such things do not normally signify danger.

Phobias may be cured by reciprocal inhibition. This is done by pairing the anxiety-producing stimulus with another stimulus or stimulus situation which produces the opposite effect. Fears, we may remember, are accompanied by negative affect; on the other hand the reduction of a state of need is accompanied by positive affect. Positive affect cannot coexist with negative affect. If, therefore, we couple the noxious stimulus with one that acts as a need reducer, we shall be presenting two stimuli which produce opposing affective states. If we arrange for the stimulus which produces positive affect to predominate, it will be possible to present the noxious stimulus without evoking the phobia. By gradually increasing the strength of the phobic stimulus the phobia can be eliminated by a process of controlled reciprocal inhibition.

One of the earliest examples of the use of this technique was reported in 1924. The therapist, Mary C. Jones, cured a three-year-old child's phobia for white rats, fur, cotton wool, and other similar objects. Therapy involved the gradual introduction of the child to contacts with a rabbit during his daily play period. Playing along with him were three children who were not afraid of the rabbit. The rabbit was first introduced in a cage and was kept at a distance. The cage was gradually brought nearer and nearer on successive days and eventually the rabbit was let free in the room. In this case the phobic stimulus was being paired with a pleasurable situation, the child's playing with his friends. In addition the therapist also paired the appearance of the rabbit with a pleasant stimulus by giving the child sweets when the rabbit was brought into the room. Eventually the child overcame his fear of the rabbit and also his fear of the other similar objects.

The present author eliminated a conditioned fear of aircraft by a similar technique. A child of about two acquired a fear of aircraft when one produced a rather frightening sonic boom. She would run indoors crying and screaming whenever she saw or heard an aeroplane. She was then given a sweet every time an aircraft came near; she improved very rapidly and was soon looking for aircraft to earn a sweet. Her phobia was completely removed and never returned.

J. Wolpe, of the University of Virginia School of Medicine, has made a significant contribution to this work and has evolved a variety of techniques for the conditioned inhibition of mal-adaptive behaviour. Many of these techniques involve the use of reciprocal inhibition, the pleasant stimulus acting on the anxiety-arousing stimulus or stimuli to produce its extinction. These techniques show great promise in the treatment of neuroses and will undoubtedly be of great value in the treatment of children's problems when they are more widely known.

The practising teacher can learn much from the study of the formation of children's neuroses. The school itself can produce such problems and Wolpe refers specifically among some of the anxiety-producing stimuli found in neurotic patients to 'hostile school teacher'. The hostile teacher, the unsympathetic teacher, or the teacher who makes unrealistic demands on a child, could be building up neuroses which would stay with the child for years. Incorrect treatment in school may sometimes lead to school phobia, a condition in which the child is so afraid of school that physical sickness at the idea of going to school eventually makes it impossible for him to go. A less intense but far more common reaction may be truancy.

Stimulus discrimination

If we were unable to distinguish between one stimulus or stimulus situation and another we should find it impossible to make the correct response to the appropriate stimulus. We should be unable to build up any stable patterns of adaptive behaviour to the regularities of the environment. The ability to discriminate is, therefore, of crucial importance to our survival. To take a simple example of discrimination at work let us consider once again the experiment with the rat referred to above. Remember that, for the rat, behaviour which produced food was adaptive behaviour, behaviour which did not produce food was not adaptive behaviour. The rat has therefore to discriminate between behaviour which produces food and behaviour which does not.

In order to obtain food the animal in the experiment has, in the beginning, to discriminate among the stimuli comprising the test situation. Activity which concentrates on any aspect of the situation other than the button receives no reinforcement. If, in our experiment, we were to set out to elaborate a pattern of behaviour, involving picking up an object, without using the method of successive approximation described, it would have taken a considerable time, since the animal is unlikely to pick up the button in its normal activity.

A graphic illustration of the educational use of the method of successive approximation of discriminatory responses is seen in Skinner's work with so-called *tone-deaf* children. The child is seated at an apparatus which presents him with a range of musical notes: there is in addition a panel for his responses.

He is asked to listen to the sounds and to indicate whether they are the same or not by pressing the appropriate button on the panel. A light indicates whether or not he is correct. Notes are then presented which are an octave apart. These are followed by notes which gradually grow closer together until eventually the child is discriminating between notes with a precision of half a tone. In this technique, discrimination is achieved by the reinforcement of the correct responses by the light signal on the panel.

Stimulus discrimination has been the subject of considerable investigation. Pavlov's experiments showed that animals learned to discriminate quite precisely among different stimuli such as musical tones, geometrical shapes, and taste. His method was to present the stimuli at random to dogs. One would be reinforced, the other not. Discrimination between visual stimuli of some complexity was built up while aural stimuli were also sharply differentiated.

The great importance of the phenomenon of stimulus discrimination is very clear. Animals in the wild must of necessity distinguish with accuracy among the many different stimuli; visual, aural, olfactory, and tactile if they are to survive. The zebra that mistakes the roar of the lion for the call of its mate is unlikely to have to face many further problems in discrimination. Much the same applies to the motorist who persistently fails to discriminate between red and green. The fact that our digestive juices might flow when we hear the dinner bell and be inhibited when we hear the fire bell, is also evidence of stimulus discrimination. An interesting application of this phenomenon in animals, is the experimental training of pigeons to work as inspectors on a production line. The bird is trained to discriminate between perfect and imperfect samples of such things as pharmaceutical pills or transistors. A conveyor belt carries the products past the pigeon's cage and the pigeon is taught to peck one button if the samples are perfect, and another if they are imperfect. The operation of the buttons accepts or rejects the products. Checks can be made by sending through imperfect samples to test the pigeon's discrimination.

Stimulus generalization

Stimulus generalization is complementary to the process of discrimination. This may be illustrated by further consideration of our original experiment with the rat. If into the cage we now introduce another small object of similar size to the original button, the animal will react much as it did previously and pick up the object. We may say generally, that, when an organism has been conditioned to respond to a particular stimulus, other similar stimuli will elicit the response even when these stimuli have not been used in training.

Under normal circumstances such generalization is adaptive; that is it is of benefit to the organism in maintaining itself in a viable relationship with its environment. Outside the psychological laboratory and in nature, stimuli are never identical. If the zebra responded with flight only to one specific sound from a predator in one specific circumstance, it would be most unlikely to survive. In a similar way, if our response to a danger sign were conditioned only to one particular shade of red it would be of limited practical value.

It has been found that generalization spreads according to the similarity of the stimuli to the original one; the strength of the response to the stimuli most like the original one being greater than the response to the least similar. Thus a child, in the early stages of learning to read, may say the word *cat* when presented with the stimulus *cat* on a card and make the same response to such stimuli as *hat*, *cap*, *fat*, and so on. It is likely to read *sat* as *cat* with more assurance than it would *pot*, while it is most unlikely to read *elephant* as *cat*. In this case stimulus generalization would be undesirable and here the teacher would need to train the children to discriminate between stimuli, in this case, between the letters in words. This will be considered at greater length in Chapter 8.

In school the teacher will be concerned to establish a delicate balance between stimulus generalization and stimulus discrimination. This will involve his careful scrutinizing of the material he intends to use with his children to look for the common elements which will aid generalization and for the differences which will help discrimination. If he finds few or no common elements in different parts of the material he hopes to use he must expect little or no generalization of learning. On the other hand if there is little difference between the different elements the children are likely to be faced with problems of discrimination that are too difficult.

As a general rule an effective procedure to help children to discriminate will be gradually to increase the difficulty of discrimination as in Skinner's experiment with tone-deaf children. In reading, for example, one might start children off by asking them to discriminate between *car* and *banana* and gradually ask them to discriminate between words which are more and more alike until they are able to discriminate between, for example, *car* and *can*. In work involving measuring or assessment, start with easy discriminations; for example, measuring to the nearest yard and then progress gradually until the children are measuring to the nearest inch or whatever is relevant to the task in hand. The teacher should, of course, take an active role by pointing out things which will help the children in the task, directing their attention to the important factors in discriminating, and ensuring feedback of results.

It should be noted that the processes of discrimination and generalization are based on relationships between stimuli and not on stimuli in isolation. This is sometimes overlooked by some psychologists who conceive of the ability to perceive relationships and differences as one of the higher processes of learning only to be explained by *insight*. A well-known experiment quoted to illustrate this argument is that of the Gestalt psychologist, Kohler, who, after training a hen to go to the lighter of two grey containers for food, removed this container and replaced it by a dark one. The hen then went to the medium bowl for the food, it now being the lighter of the two. This has been taken by Gestalt psychologists as a refutation of stimulus response theory since the hen responds to a different stimulus. As Grey Walter says: 'A pathetic fallacy. What the nervous system receives from the sense organs is information about differences – about ratios between stimuli.'

Pavlov proved this rather neatly. He elaborated a reflex in a dog to two tones with an interval of a fifth of a tone. He then began to set up responses to other pairs of tones, some of them separated by a fifth and some by a third. The response was set up

84

to the pair of tones separated by a fifth more rapidly: the tones were different but they were related to each other in the same way as the first pair. The animal had thus learned a relationship and not a response to a specific stimulus.

Some interesting current work along these lines is being carried out by Skinner. He is teaching discrimination and relationships to children using similar techniques to those used by Pavlov. The design of his stimulus displays resemble remarkably the type of patterns used for obtaining an estimate of non-verbal intelligence (see p. 278) [10].

Transfer of learning

From what we have seen of stimulus generalization we can see that learning a response to one stimulus will produce similar responses to similar stimuli. This is a case of transfer of learning. If both stimulus and response are kept constant there will be maximum transfer: in fact, of course, this will be merely a practice of the original response. Should the stimulus be changed slightly but the response kept the same, then learning of the first stimulus-response association will transfer positively to the new situation where the stimulus is slightly different. This is called *positive transfer* of learning. In the classroom positive transfer takes place when a child who has learned to add two digit numbers moves on to deal with three digit numbers. The work he has done with the two digit numbers helps him to cope with the three digit ones.

A different situation obtains when the stimulus situation is held constant and the required activity is changed. For example a person who learns to drive a car with one type of gear change will have difficulty when he tries to drive a car with a similar gear lever but with the gear positions differently arranged. This would be a case of *negative transfer*. In this case the learning of the first skill interferes with the learning of the second skill. It should be noted, however, that the two skills involved in this case, changing gear in two different ways, were incompatible activities. In cases where the two activities are not incompatible there may not be negative transfer, there may, in fact, be positive transfer.

An example of this kind of transfer is provided by an experiment in which a dog was trained first to lift its right hind leg to the conditional stimulus of a buzzer in conjunction with an unconditional stimulus, an electric shock. The dog was then trained to lift its left hind leg in response to the buzzer. In both cases the dog was supported by a sling so that it could lift both feet at once. In this experiment positive transfer was found, the dog taking less time to learn the second response than it would have taken had it not had any other previous training.

When a previously existing skill affects new learning either positively or negatively the transfer is called *proactive transfer*. (*Proactive* from the prefix *pro* meaning before; hence transfer effects arising from previous activity.) When new learning affects already exisiting skills either positively or negatively the transfer is called *retroactive transfer*. (*Retroactive* using the prefix *retro* meaning acting back upon.) When experiments are carried out to test the transfer effects of different types of activity we get the following experimental designs.

Proactive design

| Experimental Group: | Learn A | Test B |
| Control Group: | Rest | Test B |

In this experiment the transfer of learning from the prior learning of skill A to skill B is tested. Should the experimental group cope better on test B than the control group it will be evidence of positive transfer, should they fare worse it would be evidence of negative transfer from A to B.

Retroactive design

| Experimental Group: | Learn A | Learn B | Test on A |
| Control Group: | Learn A | Rest | Test on A |

In this experiment the effect of learning skill B on learning which has occurred in A is studied. The effect could be either to improve or worsen performance on a test of skill A.

A widely used laboratory experiment to test both types of transfer is the mirror drawing test. In the proactive design for this experiment the subject is asked to trace the outline of a star with only a mirror image to guide him. He is thus in a situation where his already existing skills of drawing and tracing come into conflict with the new task since the motor activity needed is the reverse of what would be normally required as responses to the visual stimuli of the outline of the star. Not surprisingly there is a good deal of proactive negative transfer from the already existing skills of drawing and tracing to the new situation and the subject has great difficulty in moving his pencil in the right direction.

When the mirror drawing test is used to study retroactive transfer the experimental and control groups are both given practice in tracing the star with their non-preferred hand. The experimental group is then allowed to practise tracing with the preferred hand while the control group rests. Both groups then have more trials using the non-preferred hand. In many experiments positive retroactive transfer has been found and the experimental group has performed better on the subsequent test than the control.

What is the significance of the phenomena of transfer for the teacher? First, it should be stressed that only where there is fairly close similarity between stimulus situations can transfer be expected. Thus it is futile for a teacher to expect that training in one subject will improve performance in other subjects which are dissimilar. Thus training in mathematics cannot be expected to improve children's ability to deal with other subjects because, as is sometimes suggested, it 'trains you to think logically'. Second, the teacher needs to bear in mind that teaching children one method of tackling a problem and then later introducing another method of solving the same problem which involves different and antagonistic activities from those previously learned, will make their learning of the second method much harder than if the first method had never been employed.

Learning sets and transfer

One of the most interesting series of experiments related to the process of transfer has been carried out by H. F. Harlow who investigated the ability of rhesus monkeys to solve problems [14]. In his experiments monkeys were confronted with a small board on which lay two objects different in colour, size, and shape. If the monkey chose the correct object (as determined by the experimenter) he was rewarded by finding a nut or a raisin underneath. The objects were moved around from trial to trial until the monkeys learned to choose the correct object. The test was repeated many times with several hundred pairs of objects. The interesting feature of this experiment was that the animals were given a large number of problems, all different, but all of the same general type.

When the monkeys were first introduced to the problems, they attacked them in a slow process of trial and error. As they tackled more and more problems, they gradually became more adept at reaching a solution, until after about 300 experiences of the test situation they were able to solve the problems at once. Thus these monkeys learned the method of solving a particular *type* of problem, not just one specific problem. When presented with a new problem of this type they would solve it at once. To an observer not aware of the previous experience of these animals, it would have seemed that they solved the problem by *insight*. In fact, the insight was learned through a long process of trial and error.

Harlow repeated his experiments on young children aged between two and five and found very similar results. The children took less time to learn than the monkeys as a group, but the brightest monkeys learned more quickly than the slowest children. Harlow called the learning of a method of attack on problems, a *learning set*. He suggests that we learn organized sets of habits that enable us to meet new problems of the same general nature, more effectively. While the acquisition of one learning set would be of little use in a complex and constantly changing environment, a large number of different learning sets would be of very great use indeed. Harlow, in fact, considers that the acquisition of learning sets may be closely related with human thinking. We will return to a consideration of this in later chapters when we discuss the work of Piaget and the role of language in human learning.

Harlow repeated the experiments with more difficult tasks of a discriminatory nature. He found that monkeys were able to learn to choose the odd object from three (two alike and one different) in a similar way to the way they learned to choose between the two objects in the earlier experiment. In the oddity experiment the animals had to choose the odd object. If they were given two cylindrical blocks and one cube, they were to choose the cube. If two cubes and one cylinder they were to choose the cylinder. The pattern of learning was the same as in the first experiment, a slow process of trial and error at first, followed by the gradual acquisition of 'insight'.

Once a learning set is acquired it seems to persist for a long time. Harlow found that after the lapse of a year, monkeys soon regained their former skill when presented with problems of a type for which they had previously acquired a learning set.

The kind of learning that we are discussing here is one of the most potent for producing maximum transfer. It is more an example of the learning of concepts than of the learning of specific methods of solving specific problems. It is a subject that we shall return to later when we discuss classroom learning more closely.

Reinforcement

Reinforcement is most important for all forms of learning. We have mentioned Hull's 'need reduction,' and we have mentioned the principles of homeostasis. Either could be regarded as a model for the processes of reinforcement. (Note that no claim is made that these models *explain* reinforcement.) Food is no reinforcer to a satiated animal. Or, to put it differently, there must be some need (in this case for food) to be satisfied if learning is to take place. Homeostatically we might say that the internal equilibrium has been disturbed (by lack of food) and therefore the organism seeks to restore equilibrium by ingestion.

Until recent years the study of reinforcement has concentrated on such phenomena as the effect of strength of reinforcement and the spread of reinforcement. It has been discovered that it is important that an action be reinforced as soon as possible to ensure its rapid learning. The optimum time between the onset of the conditional stimulus and the onset of the unconditional stimulus has been found to be about 0·5 sec.

Skinner at Harvard has made a special study of the use of reinforcement in the shaping of behaviour patterns [10]. One of the main techniques in this process has already been mentioned; that of successive approximation. In the case of our original experiment with the rat, behaviour was *shaped* by the reinforcing of activity which gradually grew nearer and nearer to the pattern we wished to establish.

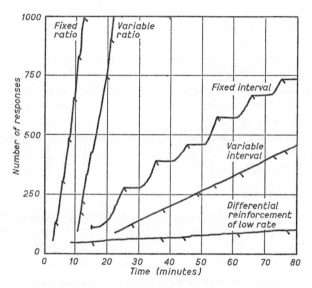

Fig. 5. Pigeon response curves differ markedly according to the schedule, or rate, of reinforcement. The curves are drawn by pen on moving paper. Each time the pigeon responds the pen jogs upward, creating a cumulative record. Reinforcement is shown by an oblique mark. The highest response rate is elicited when the animal is reinforced each time it completes a fixed number of responses. Similar rates are achieved by reinforcing for some average number of responses (variable ratio). If rewarded for the first response after a fixed interval the animal soon learns not to respond early in the interval. When the interval is varied it works steadily. The lowest response rate results when it is reinforced only after an interval (in this case three minutes) has elapsed since its last response.

Schedules of reinforcement

Once a pattern of behaviour has been set up by reinforcing every desired response made, different patterns of responding can be maintained by arranging for the activity to be reinforced intermittently according to different schedules of reinforcement; thus, for example, we might reinforce every fifth response. This we would term a *fixed ratio schedule*. Or we might reinforce the first response which occurs ten minutes after the previous one; this would be a *fixed interval schedule*. We may have *variable interval schedules* or *variable ratio schedules*.

Typical patterns of behaviour set up by different schedules may be seen in the diagrams. Fixed interval schedules generally show a pause after reinforcement followed by an increasingly rapid rate of response just before reinforcement. Variable interval schedules produce a constant rate of responding over long periods of time. This pattern has great stability. Fixed ratio schedules produce a very high rate of responding with a pause after each reinforcement. Variable ratio schedules produce a similar pattern of behaviour but pauses occur at times other than after reinforcement.

Different schedules have different characteristic patterns of behaviour and different patterns of behaviour have been set up in the same animal by different stimuli.

In one experiment using these schedules Skinner built up nine different patterns of behaviour in a single pigeon by projecting different coloured lights as stimuli on to a translucent key (which the pigeon pecked as its response) and reinforcing them on different schedules. Thus when the key was red the animal was reinforced on a six-minute fixed interval schedule, when the key was green the pigeon was reinforced upon completing sixty responses. When the light was green the pigeon produced the curve of responding appropriate to a fixed ratio schedule, when it was red its responses were characteristic of a fixed interval schedule. All that one had to do to get the pigeon to shift into another schedule of responding was to change the colour of the light on the key.

A most interesting aspect of these reinforcement schedules is that they produce very similar patterns of behaviour in quite different organisms: pigeons, monkeys, rats, and human beings produce the curve of responding characteristic of the schedule of reinforcement rather than of the species. A striking example of this phenomenon is the experiment by D. S. Blough, who, by

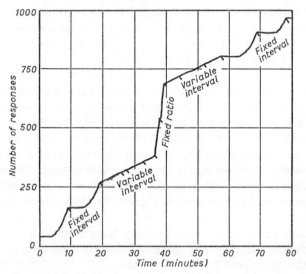

Fig. 6. Mixed performance curve results when a pigeon has been conditioned on different schedules to different stimuli. As the stimuli change, the performance changes appropriately. The stimuli were changed by changing the colour of the key which the pigeon had to peck.

arranging suitable control over schedules of reinforcement, has obtained curves showing the sensitivity of the pigeon's eye to light, which are almost identical to the curves obtained from humans, which were obtained through the use of complex verbal instruction.

As Skinner points out the extremely persistent and high rate of response characteristic of the fixed ratio schedule of reinforcement, is the equivalent of piece work in industry. Here, the size of the pay packet is dependent not upon the lapse of time (fixed interval schedule), but on the amount produced. As is well known, this method of payment sustains high levels of production. Similarly, the pattern of behaviour, produced by variable ratio reinforcement, is exemplified in man by the high rate of activity, produced by relatively slight reinforcement, exhibited by the habitual gambler. The hall full of *bingo* enthusiasts, or the arcade full of fruit machine operators, is remarkably evocative of the battery of reinforcing apparatuses with pigeons pecking keys, or rats pressing levers.

Piece work plays a large part in the lives of many people, so does gambling. However, most of our day-to-day existence is probably dependent upon similar kinds of variable ratio schedules of reinforcement. It is plausible that these *life schedules* approximate to those of the experiments involving the shifting of the subject, human or subhuman, from one schedule to another, as in the case of the pigeon which was reinforced to different schedules according to the colour of the operating key. As Skinner says: 'We are all constantly shifting from schedule to schedule as our immediate environment changes, but the dynamics of the control exercised by reinforcement remain essentially unchanged.'

Negative reinforcement and punishment

So far in our consideration of reinforcement we have dealt with positive reinforcement, in popular terms, reward. Negative reinforcers have similar effects to positive reinforcers but they work in an inverse way. In the case of negative reinforcement, the organism is subjected to a noxious stimulus which can be terminated when the response to be learned is produced. In a typical experiment with humans the subject is seated before an apparatus with one hand on a metal plate. A high voltage low amperage shock is passed through the plate immediately after the flashing of a light or the presentation of some other neutral stimulus. The avoidance activity of withdrawing the hand is the learned response in this experiment and this learning of avoidance behaviour is the central feature in negative reinforcement. In school a negative reinforcer could be the teacher's displeasure which could only be terminated by the pupil's doing what the teacher wants him to do.

Punishment is similar to negative reinforcement in some respects, but differs from it in that the noxious stimulus follows the activity. In the case of school it could be the teacher's displeasure which follows a misdemeanour and which is calculated to prevent the recurrence of the misdemeanour. In everyday life avoidance activity constitutes an important part of our behaviour and much of the apparatus of government and law is based on punishment and negative reinforcement.

Punishment and negative reinforcement may be used to remove undesirable or maladaptive patterns of behaviour. In one case a boy aged ten used to wake up between 1 a.m. and 2 a.m. and go to his mother's bed where he would then be able to go to sleep. The parents had tried to cure the habit by not allowing the child in the bed, but this was most unsatisfactory and the child spent hours crying to get to his mother's bed. When he was questioned he said that although he was most keen to go to his own bed and stay there, he woke up every night and felt anxious immediately. Unless he could get to his mother's bed he would become panic-stricken.

Treatment involved asking him to imagine himself in his mother's bed. When he had a clear picture of the situation he was instructed to say *mother's bed*. He was then given a mild electric shock. When he could tolerate the shock no longer (average 3·2 secs) he had to say *my bed*. The current was then switched off. This was done fourteen times over a period of ten minutes. In this case the shock which followed the child's saying *mother's bed* was a punisher, whereas the cessation of the shock when he said *my bed* was a negative reinforcer.

For the five nights following the treatment the child awoke but went back to sleep again. On the sixth night he slept through and from then on had no relapse up to the time the report was written (six months).*

The obvious drawback to techniques using negative reinforce-

* LAZARUS, A. A.: in EYSENCK, H. J. (Ed.): *Behaviour Therapy and the Neuroses*, Oxford, 1960.

ment and punishment is that they depend for their efficacy on anxiety-evoking stimuli. This may be well worth while in extinguishing an incapacitating neurosis under close clinical control, but it can rarely be justified in normal school conditions where the anxiety generated may spread indiscriminately. Another consideration is that while negative reinforcement and punishment may be used to inhibit a pattern of behaviour, it is much more difficult to use them in the production of behaviour. It may be possible to stop a child throwing ink pellets by punishing him, but it is very difficult to teach him to read using the same techniques. Briefly, punishment can be used to get rid of undesirable activity but it is of doubtful value in getting children to learn anything. Even in the case of classroom misdemeanours, ignoring the activity, so long as it is not upsetting other children, may be more effective than giving the child attention. At the root of much undesirable classroom activity is the need for attention, and this activity is reinforced if the teacher makes a fuss or punishes the miscreant. The effect of reinforcement of this attention, and possibly the approval of some of the other children, may well be greater than the effect of punishment the teacher might use. The point should perhaps be made, however, that ignoring behaviour is by no means the same as being unaware of it. On the contrary, the teacher would do well to develop a keen sense of awareness in the classroom so that he has a fair idea of what *all* the children are doing. One of the most common mistakes of the student teacher is that he tends to concentrate his attention on one part of the class and becomes unaware of the rest of the children. A similar mistake is losing contact with the class through excessive concentration on the material. Apart from any question of class control it is most undesirable to lose contact with the class since it becomes impossible to assess how they are reacting to the lesson. But the fact of being alive to the current activity of the class has other advantages. Often the mere realization that the teacher is aware of what is going on will be sufficient to prevent some forms of undesirable behaviour; but whether he decides to take action or not to prevent a given piece of behaviour, it is important that the children realize that he is fully aware of the situation and that if he ignores the activity, he does so deliberately.

The effects of punishment on behaviour have by no means been as clear cut as those of reward. In certain circumstances punishment has even increased undesired behaviour. This phenomenon is not unknown in schools where repressive corporal punishment often leads, not to the elimination of disciplinary problems, but to their increase. This often brings an increase in repression which exacerbates the problem, so setting up a vicious circle which is broken only by a change in the situation.

Skinner found that rats which were well conditioned to bar pressing and then shocked when they pressed the bar, stopped pressing very rapidly. However, as soon as the bar became harmless, pressing developed rapidly once again. In other words, all that the punishment had achieved was a temporary suppression of a particular pattern of behaviour. This was an experiment on animals and one cannot carry over the findings to human beings. However, as many of Skinner's experiments have shown, there is often close resemblance between the records of responses made by humans and those made by other animals when subjected to the same schedules of reinforcement so the evidence may be taken as suggestive of human behaviour. There is some evidence from schools that this does apply to children and we shall consider this at greater length later (p. 354).

Experiments have been set up in classroom situations to check the relative merits of punishment or reward. Punishment has generally been blame, and reward, praise. The findings of such experiments showed clearly that reward was substantially more efficacious than punishment in classroom teaching. In one experiment an ignored group given the same instruction as a praised group showed no improvement. This fits in closely with what one would have expected on theoretical grounds. Unreinforced behaviour is extinguished and the children remain almost as before.

The main conclusion that can be drawn from the investigations into punishment is that it is of very limited value in education. Apart from its dubious efficacy, the problem of precise control is extremely difficult. Furthermore the undesirable emotions aroused by punishment, that is anxiety, or fear, do not remain confined to the one stimulus but spread like the ripples on a pond to every aspect of a class's activity.

The educational tradition which comes down to us from schools of the past, is one where the hallmark of a competent pedagogue was the strength of his arm. It was to escape the ingeniously contrived *schedules of negative reinforcement* that led children to learn their numbers and their letters. Unfortunately, such techniques are still with us and punishment is still used in a vain attempt to teach. Skinner considers that in many ways the control of learning in most classrooms is still aversive today: the teacher's reproof, the low marks on an exercise, the imposition for an incorrect piece of work are all of this nature and much of the learning that takes place is avoidance learning and very inefficient (p. 379).

Motivation

The obverse of reinforcement is *motivation*. This term has been used to designate the phenomena involved in the operation of incentives or drives. Reference has been made to Hull's views on need reduction and the idea of homeostasis; motivation may be regarded as the tendency of the organism to reduce its needs or to return to its state of equilibrium (but see below).

The great danger in discussions of motivation is the tendency to suggest mechanisms which act as prime movers of behaviour similar to the mainspring in a clock. The psychologist, McDougall, for example, suggested that instincts were the great motivators. Man fought because of his aggressive instinct, gathered in communities because of his gregarious instinct, and so on. This clearly is mere verbalizing: there is no limit to the explanations accessible to this technique. As an American psychologist put it: 'If man gathers in crowds it is the gregarious instinct, if he goes alone it is the solitary instinct: if he twiddles his thumbs it is the thumb-twiddling instinct: if he does not twiddle his thumbs it is the thumb-not-twiddling instinct.' At the same time research into animal behaviour has revealed mechanisms which resemble instincts but might be more accurately regarded as chains of unconditional reflexes. Such reflexes are fewer than is commonly supposed and much of the behaviour of the lower animals which was previously described as *instinctive* has been discovered to be learned. A striking example of this is in the happy family cage to be found in some zoos where such *natural* enemies as cats, dogs, mice, rats, and birds, live together in harmony. The relationship of a predator to its prey is largely a learned pattern of behaviour, not instinctive.

Objections similar to those made against instincts can be made against *drives, urges, forces, needs,* and other suggested agents of motivation. They can be hypothesized but not demonstrated. R. S. Peters, in a critique of causal models of motivation, argues that human behaviour is not motivated in the same way as animal behaviour. Human behaviour, he considers, cannot be explained as being determined by previously occurring events. Instead, he considers that man behaves according to rules, and works towards ends.*

Although this view describes rather than explains, it is a view which we can accept in part; our main reservation being to argue that the rules by which man lives, and the ends to which he works, are derived from his actual experience of living: they are, in fact, learned. The fact that man is not at the mercy of his immediate physical environment, springs from the fact that man, alone among the animals, lives in a world of symbols. Because man has language, which represents the world symbolically, he is able to respond to patterns of stimuli from the past, and project himself into the future. We shall consider this in greater detail later.

Although we may accept the concept of man as a rule following purposive animal, the problem of the basic motivators still remains. The view espoused in this book is that referred to in earlier chapters. The basic needs of the organism (which can be expressed in physical terms) such as lack of food, or air, or water, stimulate the organism to activity of a homeostatic nature. When equilibrium is achieved, the activity, in the normal organism, ceases. Behaviour in the lower animals will almost entirely be

* PETERS, R. S.: *The Concept of Motivation*, Routledge, 1958.

related to the direct reduction of these basic needs. In man, biological motivators are also important, but in addition much of human activity is controlled by acquired motives. These are generally regarded as having been built up on a biological foundation. Hull argues that during the upbringing of children derived needs such as the need for affection, or for approval, gradually take the place of the more primary biological needs with which they are very often associated. The reinforcing effect of the successful solution of a mathematical problem may well be based on the orienting reflex; the reinforcement provided by parental approbation may ultimately be based on a complex amalgam of the reinforcement provided by the contact comfort, warmth, food, and drink which have almost invariably accompanied it.

Objections to views of motivation based on concepts of the reduction of organic needs have sometimes hinged on experiments in which animals which are not hungry have learned mazes. The answer to such objections may well be in the functioning of the orienting reflex mentioned earlier. This reflex causes the organism to pay attention to any novel stimulus in the environment and to investigate. Should the stimulus persist without any further change in the environment, habituation takes place and the organism no longer reacts to it. The orienting reflex is extinguished. We notice this phenomenon, for example, if we go to live near a waterfall. At first the unusual stimuli secure attention, but eventually we become accustomed to the noise and cease to notice it actively. Exploration of a new environment is a similar orienting followed by habituation. This phenomenon has obvious survival value: an animal that did not react to disturbances in the environment would have an extremely brief existence. At the same time continuous active responding to all stimuli would be an impossible task which would be equally disastrous for the animal.

Work done by E. N. Sokolov the Russian psychologist, shows that changes in the EEG pattern are correlated with the arousal and suppression of the orienting reflex.* The characteristically

* SOKOLOV, E. N.: in BRAZIER, M. A. B. (Ed.): *The Central Nervous System and Behaviour*, Josiah Macey Jr. Foundation, 1960.

regular rhythms of the brain at rest are suppressed when new stimuli impinge on the organism. After repeated presentation of the stimuli, habituation takes place and the rhythms return. Sokolov found that if, after habituation to a light stimulus of a certain duration, the time of presentation was increased, the rhythm was again suppressed, the extension of the signal apparently changing its significance. On the basis of the research done in this field Sokolov suggests that under repeated presentations nerve cells in the brain preserve information about the intensity, the quality, the duration, and the order of presentation of stimuli. This he describes as a neural model. He considers that when the pattern of stimuli from the environment no longer synchronizes with the pattern of nervous activity in the cortex, the orienting reflex is produced. Thus the nervous system apparently forms a programme of stimulation. This programme is compared with the real stimulation. If they do not coincide, an orienting reflex is evoked at each point of disagreement. This effect serves to increase discriminatory power for the obtaining of new information about the unusual properties of the stimulus.

Sokolov's neural model is a hypothesis only but it is allied to others put forward by learning theorists such as Bugelski in America, by cyberneticians such as Wiener, and electroencephalographers such as Grey Walter. The work of neurologists, electrophysiologists, neurocytologists and other disciplines tends in this direction. It is a field which has been hitherto unexplored mainly because of its enormous complexity. It does, however, seem a most promising area of research which will add considerably to our knowledge of the processes of learning as it becomes more thoroughly explored.

A synthesis

We have now considered in a simplified way some of the most important principles of learning. These principles not only regulate our cognitive development, but also our day to day conduct and our emotional behaviour. We may now attempt a synthesis of these ideas and their embodiment in man.

The behaviour of organisms is regulated by two main agencies, the unconditional and the conditional reflexes. The lower in the evolutionary scale the animal the more likely it is that unconditional reflexes will play the major role. Thus, for example, the solitary wasp shows the typically stereotyped behaviour of an animal largely controlled by innate responses.

This animal selects a small hole in which to conceal its prey, usually some small insect. Before it puts its catch in the hole it leaves it at the mouth of the hole, investigates the hiding place and, if it is satisfactory, returns to pick up its prey and take it into the hole. Should one remove the prey a short distance from the mouth of the hole while the insect is inside, it will emerge, collect the prey, take it to the mouth of the hole, enter, and reconnoitre again. Should one repeat the procedure, the wasp will go through the same routine. This could go on indefinitely; it is a mechanical chain of reflexes.

This chaining of unconditional behaviour in primitive animals has its counterpart in the chaining of conditional reflexes in higher animals and in man. In the case of man chains of learned responses are the habits we build up in the course of our lives which eventually resemble the unlearned chains of reflexes, called *taxes*, of the wasp. They are of great use because we can run off such a chain of responses without conscious attention and can, in fact, attend to other things at the same time. Children learn to cope with such things as dressing and undressing sequences where the response to one stimulus becomes the stimulus to the next response. Thus the completed action of putting on a sock provides the stimulus for the next response of putting on a shoe, which is in turn followed by the tying of the shoe lace.

The difference between the chain of conditional reflexes and the taxis is well illustrated by the action of the professor who, because of the excessive heat in his laboratory one summer day, took off his jacket and his tie. Because these two actions were part of a chain of conditional reflexes built up and practised for many years, he automatically continued the chain by starting to take off his trousers. However, because the chain was learned and not innate, he soon perceived the inappropriateness of the stimulus situation and broke the sequence.

In man the basic reflexes are few, the acquired activity, i.e. the learning, is complex. It is very difficult to say with any certainty which reflexes are innate in man especially since experiments have shown that the human foetus is susceptible to conditioning. In our view human learning must therefore include learning in the embryo. Once started, learning becomes increasingly complex. As the child grows older his environment expands phenomenally and he is constantly having to make new adjustments to it. He is also learning that the environment itself is manipulable. The child's early learning involves the activation or inhibition of responses, the generalization or discrimination of responses, and the chaining of responses. This early learning forms the basis for learning set formation.

These kinds of learning are common to man and to the lower animals, and it is not unreasonable to consider that the more complex forms of learning, which we are to discuss, are built upon these foundations. However, when we consider the kinds of learning which are characteristically human we find an additional complication which, Pavlov suggested, makes human learning very different from that of the other animals. This complicating factor is what Pavlov called the second signalling system; that is, language.

In lower animals information about the environment is provided by such organs as the eyes, ears, etc. These are the vital links in the formation of conditional reflexes. They transmit to the animal signals (stimuli) concerning the nature of the world around it. They make up the first signalling system.

In man the same process operates. In addition, however, man receives signals of signals: these second order signals are words. Possession of language is probably the most important distinguishing feature between man and other animals, for, as can be readily seen, the ability to reproduce the world symbolically, emancipates man from his immediate temporal and spatial environment and introduces stimuli not only from the here and now, but from a distance and from past and future. This in itself is enough to extend the human stimulus field unimaginably.

If we also consider the abstractive and synthesizing properties of language another dimension is added. We will consider these questions more fully in the next chapter.

The nature of reinforcement is also of great importance. The type of schedule, as we have seen, largely determines the pattern of response in both man and other animals. This is a further complicating factor in explaining learning and behaviour.

Finally, it should be added, it is impossible that any individual response is identical with the ones that precede or follow it. After one response both organism and environment are changed, even if only slightly. Furthermore the state of the organism itself must be considered. Work with EEG patterns has shown how the sleeping brain reacts differently to stimuli from the way the waking brain does. This confirms our common-sense observations but also adds point to it. The health of the organism also affects the elaboration of conditional reflexes, as it affects the physiological reactions of the body.

Taking all these factors into account we arrive at a picture of man maintaining a state of dynamic equilibrium in a highly complex patterning of reactions, which are not only determined by the facts of the physical world, but by the impact of abstractions of and generalizations about that world through the medium of language.

In the next chapter we look more closely at the nature and function of language in an attempt to build up an outline picture of the child learning. This is a tall order and any picture can only be tentative. Without an analysis of the influence of language, however, it would be impossible.

Summary

The processes of conditioning have been observed in all animals which have been investigated. The higher in the evolutionary scale the animal, the more complex and finely discriminating the behaviour which can be conditioned.

Feedback is also found throughout nature. In animals it is fundamental in the preservation of the fixed bodily equilibrium called *homeostasis*. Homeostasis is the fixed equilibrium upon which the more adaptive *dynamic equilibrium*, which the organism maintains in face of changes in the environment, is based. Learning involves the adoption of patterns of behaviour which bring about more adaptive states of dynamic equilibrium.

Learned behaviour, especially in human beings, is often reinforced by *secondary reinforcers*. These are reinforcers which fill the role of the basic or organic reinforcers such as food and drink. Secondary reinforcers in man are such things as the approbation of the teacher, the admiration of others, and money.

When behaviour is not reinforced it tends to die away. This phenomenon is called *extinction*. Teachers and parents can make use of extinction by ignoring undesired behaviour so that the child gets no attention which might otherwise reinforce the behaviour and lead to its repetition.

Stimulus discrimination involves distinguishing between different stimuli. The more similar the stimuli, the more difficult will be discrimination. Young children are generally less able to discriminate between stimuli than adults. In nature, animals depend on accurate discrimination for survival.

A response learned to one stimulus will be evoked by other similar stimuli. The greater the similarity, the greater the strength of the response. This phenomenon is called *stimulus generalization*. Much learning in school involves the cultivation of fineness of discrimination of some things and the fostering of generalization in other spheres. The two processes are complementary. Both generalization and discrimination are based on the relationships between stimuli and not to stimuli in isolation.

Experiments have shown that monkeys build up learning sets. That is, they learn the method of attack on problems if faced with the same type of problem a large number of times, rather than just learning the individual correct response.

When a response is being conditioned to a stimulus, the occurrence of an extraneous stimulus of sufficient strength at the same time may lead to the response being suppressed. This is termed *external inhibition. Reciprocal inhibition* occurs when a response causes emotional states which interfere with learning. The emotional states could be negative or positive. Thus reciprocal inhibition could be used to eliminate undesirable responses such as phobias; however, it may also have a deleterious effect on learning if the desired responses are inhibited by inappropriate stimulus situations. Negative reinforcement and punishment may produce inappropriate stimulus situations in school which could interfere with children's learning.

Reinforcement is essential for effective learning. Different schedules of reinforcement produce different patterns of behaviour. To establish a pattern of behaviour, reinforcement should follow each correct response. Once the required behaviour is well established reinforcement can take place intermittently.

The term *motivation* refers to whatever it is that causes behaviour. In general terms this refers to the tendency of the organism to achieve a state of equilibrium. An organism deprived of food will be motivated by its state of deprivation to seek food. Human motivation is similar to the acquired drives described by Hull. These are social motivators founded on the basic or organic needs.

Conditioning processes in man are basically similar to those of other animals. However, on top of these processes man builds a complicated superstructure based on the symbolic properties of language. This superstructure is the most important aspect of human learning.

CHAPTER 5

Learning and Language

Previous chapters have dealt with problems of learning of a general nature and we have considered the fundamental mechanisms underlying the modifications in behaviour which enable organisms to adapt most effectively to changes in their environment. While we have stressed that the basic mechanisms of adaptation, conditional reflexes, are fundamentally the same in all organisms, there are great differences in the complexity of the adaptive behaviour. As we have seen, the behaviour of the most elementary organisms is largely governed by the inherited reflexes and is therefore rigid and stereotyped, whereas the behaviour of the mammals is highly adaptive and complex (perhaps most complex when working for man in such conditions as looking after sheep or performing in a circus).

Behaviour in man is infinitely more complex than that of the other animals including the mammals. Indeed, it is possible to say that, despite the fact that the underlying mechanisms are the same, learning in man is different *in kind* from that of all other animals. To see why this is so we must consider the way in which the life history of the animal differs from that of man.

The individual and the species

The behaviour of an animal is the resultant of two influences, its genetic endowment and its life experiences. The genetic endowment consists of bodily forms and dispositions to particular reactions in particular circumstances. This is called the *genotype*.

The genotype is the product of biological evolution. The bodily form (morphology) and the inborn reactions are both of fundamentally adaptive significance for the organism and for the species. The genotype is, in fact, primarily the morphological and behavioural adaptations which the individual animal inherits. For example, the long neck of the giraffe is one such morphological adaptation; the cowering behaviour of small birds at the sight of a predator is an example of behavioural adaptation.

The life experiences of the animal, operating through the mechanisms of conditioning, facilitate the organism's adaptation to rapid changes in the environment. The total behaviour of the animal may then be regarded as the complex working out of hereditary tendencies through the agencies of conditional reflexes. On the rigid base of the adaptations of the whole species, the individual makes its own life story through the mechanisms of fluid temporary reflexes that come and go according to the flux of the environment. The life style of the individual animal is called the *phenotype*.

While all this applies to man there is one other influence which makes his adaptation to the environment fundamentally different from that of any other animal. It is the fact that he acquires, in the course of his life, experience of a social nature. This experience has an historical aspect and, in fact, could be described as the collective adaptation of the whole species over the whole of recorded history. The behaviour and development of the child of today is determined not only by the biological adaptations made by the species in the normal course of evolution, but also by the accumulated collective experience of the whole of mankind. This is in part manifested in technological developments, which make the concrete physical environment of man in technologically advanced societies fundamentally different from the natural environment, and also in the forms of social organization and social customs which have evolved through the centuries of man's history. The enormous changes brought about by this social evolution could not have been produced by the slow mechanisms of biological adaptation, nor would evolutionary change have produced the same effect. Mammoths grew woolly coats to accommodate to the slow change in their environment brought about by the Ice Age. They took thousands of years to do this and when the ice retreated producing an environment which was incompatible with his adaptations to life in the cold, the mammoth became extinct. Man, on the other hand, adapted to life in the Ice Age by using fire and protective clothing. Man, that is, did not change himself to cope with environmental change, but changed the environment to fit him. Consequently when the ice retreated all he had to do was to wear less and to rely less on fire to keep him warm.

In animals other than man, then, adaptations to major environmental changes are generally accomplished through changes in the bodily structure, such changes being of an evolutionary character transmitted through the hereditary mechanisms from generation to generation. Such bodily changes have no effect on the environment and occur very slowly. Man, on the other hand, adapts to environmental changes by altering part of his environment to facilitate his survival; he builds huts, lights fires, wears clothes, constructs boats and so on. These adaptations are transmitted not in the hereditary genetic mechanisms but in the form of the material and social products of society and, of course, become then, part of the environment of man, to act in turn as further agents of change. You may care to consider how much of your present environment is *natural*, and how much is produced by society.

What is the significance of the facts of social inheritance for our study of the development of the child? Clearly, since the inherited accumulated wisdom of mankind is manifested not through hereditary biological mechanisms, but instead is embodied in the material of the social environment and in the laws and customs of organized society, each baby is faced with problems of learning or, in other words, of developing adequate behavioural patterns, to ensure satisfactory adjustment to the complexity of social living. He is not born with the ability to make boats, to control fire, or even to use a spoon; all these patterns of behaviour have to be acquired by the child in the process of living. The acquisition of these behaviour patterns constitutes the greatest part of the child's adaptation to the environment, in other words, its education.

The American J. S. Bruner suggests that man's technological advance has produced three implement systems which act as amplifiers of human capacities. These are amplifiers of human *motor* capacities from the cutting tool to the lever, the wheel, the pneumatic drill, and other modern devices; amplifiers of human *sensory* capacities, for example smoke signals, talking drums, the electron microscope, radar, etc.; and amplifiers of human *thought* processes from language systems to myth and theory and explanation. The important point about all this for man's psychology, is that each of these extensions of man's capabilities demands for its effective use, a counterpart in the form of skill which he must develop in order to use these devices. These skills are selected in the course of evolution. That is, those skills needed for optimum employment of the technological implements will be at a premium for survival and will therefore be influential in the morphological development of the species so that the tools man used had an influence on the way his bodily structure developed.*

But morphological change is very slow and as we have seen man has been much the same morphologically for many thousands of years. The crucial factor in human psychological development is therefore the acquisition by the individual of the skills related to the use of the technological extensions of man's capacities. For the young human being the most important factor in the acquisition of these skills is the influence of adults.

Many of the higher animals learn the behaviour patterns of the species through the example of the parents. The kitten learns through imitation to stalk the mouse or bird. But in the case of man the process of education is transformed. The human parent teaches not only by example but also by telling. This means, of course, that patterns of behaviour can be set up in the absence of the situation to which they are relevant. The mother or the teacher can instruct a child in the elements of kerb drill without actually being on the road, but a mouse cannot instruct its young to avoid the cat unless the cat is actually there.

Since so much of the experience of mankind is embodied in his culture and not his bodily forms, the child is dependent upon adults to a very great extent in his attempts to master the social environment. As we have seen earlier, left to himself it is unlikely that a child will learn any of the common skills involved in feeding or dressing and so on. He will certainly be very unlikely to learn,

* BRUNER, J. S.: in *American Psychologist*, January 1964.

unaided, the use of any of the many common tools: the spade, the knife; and in our society, such things as pencils, brushes, and other relatively sophisticated instruments. But this is only one aspect of the child's dependence on adults. Without the influence of parents and society at large, all the processes which we regard as characteristic of civilized man: reading, writing, number, are inaccessible to the child. Speech itself would be non-existent. In other words, the social heritage transmitted to the child by adults is what differentiates man from the other animals. Without these man is dependent on biological inheritance and the vagaries of a *raw* environment.

In primitive societies it is possible for the transmission of knowledge to be done on a non-specialist basis. Skills were handed on from parents to children adequately because they were relatively simple skills. But with scientific and technological advance skills and techniques became increasingly complex and their transmission became more and more a specialist job. Today, in a society of extremely rapid technological and scientific change, teachers need to be educated to a much higher level than ever in the past. The school life of the child is also extended to make it possible for the school to make some approach towards preparing him to cope with the new aspects of the social environment which are coming into being with ever increasing rapidity.

We thus have a picture of learning in animals which consists of the development of the individual through the mechanisms of conditioning, interacting with inherited behaviour patterns to produce an individual pattern of behaviour. This pattern will differ from that of other members of the same species mainly to the extent to which the individual experiences differ. By and large these differences will not be very great since most of the adjustment to major environmental change is accomplished through the mechanisms of biological inheritance and the organism will *by nature* be maximally adapted to its environment.

In man a similar picture may be observed; up to a point. He has his biological inheritance, his bodily structure, and his innate behaviour patterns, upon which he constructs his life story, in small part as the other animals through simple conditioning;

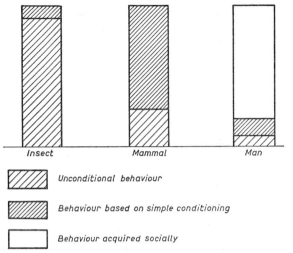

Fig. 7. Diagram to suggest the various elements in the total behaviour of different animals. Note the large part played by
inborn or unconditional behaviour (coarse shading) in the
insect; the large part played by simple conditioning (fine
shading) in the mammal; and the predominant role of behaviour acquired socially (unshaded) in the case of man.
N.B. No attempt is made to convey the differing complexities
of behaviour, nor should the shaded parts be taken to represent
definite measurable quantities; they are illustrative only.

but mainly, as we have seen, his individual biography is
written through the assimilation of the cultural achievements of
generations of mankind. And the main agent for this assimilation
is language.

Signals and symbols

When Gulliver visited Laputa he encountered an interesting
group of scholars in the School of Language. One piece of research
which they were carrying out involved the abolishing of all words.
The aim of this was to cut down strain on the lungs and thereby
to increase the lifespan. The argument was that this was expedient
since words were '. . . only names for things, [and] it would be
more convenient for all men to carry about them such things as
were necessary to express the particular business they are to

discourse on. . . . I have often beheld two of those sages almost sinking under the weight of their packs, like pedlars among us, who when they meet in the streets, would lay down their loads, open their saddles, and hold conversation for an hour together, then put up their implements, help each other to resume their burdens, and take their leave.'

Swift was not unaware of the complex nature of language. His satirical thrust reminds us vividly how language cuts us loose from the ties of the here and now. Even at its most primitive level (. . . words are only names for things) it emancipates us from our specific concrete environment and opens to us dimensions of experience otherwise inaccessible. At its more complex levels it enables us to enter into relationships with others which remove human social intercourse to a completely different plane from that of other animals.

The most elementary aspect of the word is its property as a signal. Signals are the stimuli we perceive and they are used by the lower animals and man. Animals, however, attend only to the physical stimulus properties of the word and not to its *semantic* properties, i.e. its meaning. In other words a dog obeys when its owner says *sit*, not because it understands the *meaning* of the word, but because the word acts as the stimulus in a conditional reflex which has been set up during the training of the animal. Similarly, the talking of a parrot is the mechanical imitation of speech signals and is completely without semantic significance. Words are not the only signals, however; the shepherd uses whistles to control the behaviour of his dog and animal trainers use hand and other signals. These fulfil the same function as the word in these circumstances. Skinner has described how pigeons can be trained to respond to verbal stimuli so that they will obey the printed command *peck* or *don't peck*. The pigeon in this case, however, is not reading: the visual signal stands in the same relationship to the pigeon as the spoken signal *sit* to the dog. Both are conditional stimuli of the first order.

On the other hand man is a symbol-producing organism. He gives signals meaning. To the animal the signal has significance only in relation to the activity with which it is linked; to man it has wider significance bestowed on it by society. It then almost ceases to be a signal and instead of merely directing our attention towards things it serves to remind us about things, that is, it represents things. It is a secondary signal, a symbol.

Probably the crucial thing which follows from the use of language as a symbol system is that it enables us to bring into contiguity stimuli which could not otherwise be brought together. In our earlier discussion of the processes of learning, it was pointed out that unless things were contiguous in space and time, connections would not be set up between them. Without some system of symbolization which allows stimuli to be represented by other stimuli, responses can only be set up to things which are physically present here and now. However, in fact, through the use of language the teacher is able to present to children at the same time and in the same place stimuli which could not possibly be brought together otherwise. Thus, for example, he can juxtapose stimuli which signify such things as the sea, mountains, clouds, rivers, lakes, ice, snow, sun, rain and mist. He is also able to present stimuli which cannot exist without a symbol system, for example, such stimuli as x + y, or 12 × 12.

Language, as a symbol system, therefore, complicates man's environment by crowding it with complex systems of stimuli which call forth the correspondingly complex patterns of behaviour which makes human learning so extraordinarily more complicated than that of any other animal.

Psychologically speaking, the property of the word as a symbol, as a stimulus of extraordinarily wide generalization, constitutes its meaning. In the words of E. Sapir, the eminent linguist:

The world of our experiences must be enormously simplified and generalized before it is possible to make a symbolic inventory of all our experiences of things and relations and this inventory is imperative before we can convey ideas. The elements of language, the symbols that ticket off experience, must therefore be associated with whole groups, delimited classes, of experience rather than with single experiences themselves. Only so is communication possible, for the single experience lodges in an individual consciousness and is, strictly speaking, incommunicable. To be communicated it needs to be referred to a class which is tacitly accepted by the community as an identity. Thus, the single impression which I have had of a particular house must be identified with all my other impressions of it. Further, my generalized memory or my 'notion' of this house must be merged with the notions that all other individuals who have seen the house have formed of it. The particular experience that we started with has now been widened so as to embrace all possible impressions or images that sentient beings have formed or may form of the house in question. This first simplification of experience is at the bottom of a large number of elements of speech, the so-called proper nouns or names of single individuals or objects. It is essentially, the type of simplification which underlies or forms the crude subject of history and art. But we cannot be content with this measure of reduction of the infinity of experience. We must cut to the bone of things, we must more or less arbitrarily throw whole masses of experience together as similar enough to warrant their being looked upon – mistakenly, but conveniently – as identical. This house and that house and thousands of other phenomena of like character are thought of as having enough in common, in spite of great and obvious differences of detail, to be classed under the same heading. In other words, of a convenient capsule of thought that embraces thousands of distinct experiences and that is ready to take in thousands more. If the single significant elements of speech are the symbols of concepts, the actual flow of speech may be interpreted as a record of the setting of these concepts into mutual relations [15].

The 'convenient capsule of thought' constitutes the meaning of the word: the sound now symbolizes a concept.

A concept is an abstraction from objects, situations, or events of the attributes these phenomena have in common. The words we use symbolize or stand for these concepts. The idea of *tree* is a concept. *Tree* refers not to one thing but to a class of things. From the multitude of different types of tree: the oak, the ash, the eucalyptus, the palm, the fir, the pine, we abstract the essential similarities and ignore the inessential differences. We call them all *tree*. *Tree* is a generic term. That is, it does not refer to one thing in particular, it refers to all such things in general. In fact *tree* cannot legitimately be used of one thing and when we say: 'That is a tree,' we are really classifying the thing, not making a specific reference to *that* object. Some primitive societies lack the sophisticated concepts which we possess. Certain Australian tribes have no concept for *tree*. They have to refer to particular things as we might have to refer to oak, ash, etc., if we had no concept for *tree*. (In actual fact, of course, even the less abstract concept of *oak* is nonetheless a concept, since from all the oaks one sees, one must abstract the essential quality of the oak.) Another primitive people, the Eskimoes, have no generalized concept of *snow* and no word for it. Instead they have a different name for it depending on the kind of situation in which the snow is found. Thus they have a word for snow falling, a different one for frozen snow, and still another for melting snow. In our culture we have one word for all three; we abstract the essence of *snowness* and give it one word. The child in our culture acquires the word for and the concept of *snow* by experiencing snow in different circumstances while at the same time hearing only one sound so that *snow* to him acquires all the connotations for which the Eskimoes have separate words.

Bruner makes some very similar points in his book *A Study of Thinking* (see pp. 165 ff.). He points out, like Sapir, that the categorizing of phenomena which takes place when we form concepts reduces the complexity of the environment enormously. He says that there are seven million colour differences to which human beings could respond but in fact we normally make use of only a dozen or so commonly used colour names: that is, we categorize a very large number of different colours under the one name of *brown* or *green*, etc. Another important result of classification is that we can identify things when we see them if we put them into a previously existing concept class. Thus we are spared the problem of relating every particular aspect of our environment to every other specific item. If we had to treat each new phenomenon as a thing in itself and were unable to fit it into a previously existing class it would be quite impossible for us to cope with any more than our immediate environment. A most important further aspect of concept formation is that once we establish a category we reduce the need for constant learning. Once we have abstracted the properties that constitute a concept we can recognize newly encountered phenomena as being examples of the concept if they possess the necessary attributes; we don't then have to learn anew the features or attributes of the new phenomena. As Bruner says: 'We do not have to be taught *de novo* at each encounter that the object before us is or is not a tree. If it exhibits the appropriate defining properties it "is" a tree. It is in this crucial aspect . . . that categorizing differs from the learning of fiat classes. Learning by rote that a miscellany of objects all go by the nonsense name BLIX has no extrapolative value to new members of the class.' This last point is an important one for the teacher and we shall return to this later. The point is that learning to classify verbally without at the same time seeing the defining attributes of the class is arbitrary learning to the child and will have no relevance outside the specific situation in which it was learned.

Bruner refers to other aspects of conceptual thought which we deal with in general terms elsewhere. However, he stresses one point which is often overlooked and yet which is of great importance for learning and thinking. He points out that the categories which we make use of when we classify things in the course of forming concepts, are not in the environment *by nature*. That is, they are not *there* to be discovered by man. They are, in fact, *invented* by man. Man imposes his own system of regularity on nature and the classifications and concepts he uses will depend to a very large extent on the level of technological development and the culture of the society in which he lives. However, since concepts can only be referred to by the use of language the level of children's linguistic ability will have a great bearing on their ability to categorize the world and impose a system upon it.

In the pages which follow we shall make repeated reference to concepts and concept formation. We should, however, avoid thinking of concepts as *things* which have a clearly defined structure and which are finite entities. A more accurate way of looking at them would be to regard them as complex psychological phenomena built up over the years which enable us to react to our present environment not only through our present perception but through a synthesis of present experience and experience of the past. In this synthesis concepts will be likely to act as a complex dynamic integrated system, rather than a collection of autonomous entities. In our discussions, however, we may well refer to such things as the concept of weight, or the concept of number. This will be a matter of convenience and should not be taken to imply that concepts can be isolated, ticketted off, and categorized like collections of concrete objects.

Conceptual learning

Man's use of language has a profound influence on the processes of conditioning. Because of the symbolizing and conceptual nature of language the processes of conditioning are greatly modified in man. Instead of responding only to the physical nature of stimuli, most of his behaviour is influenced by the symbolic aspects of stimuli. The effect of this is to introduce an extraordinary flexibility into learning in man. Because, during his childhood, he builds up complicated systems of classification through the use of language, he is able to assess and categorize stimuli, and make the appropriate response on the basis of previous responses to stimuli in the same category, even when those stimuli are very different in their physical properties. As an example we may take the experiment in which a conditional response elaborated in children to the *sound* of a bell was elicited by the spoken word *bell* and by the written word *bell*. In the one case a completely different sound signal – the spoken word, *bell* – evoked the response previously linked with the *ringing* of the bell. In the other case a visual signal replaces the sound of the bell in the evocation of the response. In both cases there is *immediate substitution* of the new stimulus for the one which originally produced the response [16]. Such flexibility of behaviour is completely beyond the scope of the most highly developed non-human animals; it is the foundation of human learning.

Other experiments have investigated the way in which the conceptual aspect of words affects the processes of conditioning. Children were conditioned to respond in a certain way to a number of different birds' names. They were trained to make the response for such words as *hawk*, *owl*, *hen*. They were not trained to respond to other birds' names, so that, for example, they would not respond to words such as *thrush*, *sparrow*, etc. However, when the word *bird* was presented, the children responded with the reaction which had been linked with the specific birds' names. It was also noted that the reaction was produced at once by the word *bird*. Thus the generalized symbol *bird* included the specific symbols *hawk*, *owl*, *hen*. The learned response was transferred perfectly to the new word, a feat completely beyond the abilities of the most intelligent of other animals.

This quality of language is that which transforms completely the way in which human beings adapt to their environment; that is, the way they learn. It should be noted, however, that the very great extension of the power of the learning processes brought about by the symbolic nature of language, is only the first in a number of stages of increasingly complex abstractions. From the initial symbolizing of the thing, we move to the manipulation of classes of things. We deal with abstract attributes of things. For example, we abstract from a variety of objects the idea of colour. We conceive of the form of things. We construct complex relationships such as *before* and *after*, *today* and *tomorrow*. In nature there is no today or tomorrow; such concepts can only exist through man's use of language in a social setting. Since all these abstractions and many more besides, abstractions of abstractions, the common currency of everyday life for the child in our schools, are contingent upon language and accessible only through language, the absolute primacy of adequate linguistic ability as an educational goal is clear. The deleterious effects of linguistic inadequacy being exposed by current research emphasize this point. We shall consider this research later. For the present let us note that man's use of the symbolizing and conceptualizing qualities of language invests his learning with *meaning* in the fullest sense.

Learning and meaning

Emphasis has been placed on the role of language in human learning because it is the key to meaning. The question of meaningful learning is one which concerns the teacher every day of his working life. But care must be exercised here. Merely verbalizing the learning operations is no guarantee that meaningful learning is taking place. The work of Piaget which we consider later shows that correct verbal responses often cover over quite inadequate concepts. At worst, the word could have merely the property of a signal of the first order for the child, in much the same way as the word *peck* was merely a visual stimulus for Skinner's pigeons. Between the response to a stimulus at this level and at the level of full comprehension lies a multitude of shades of understanding. On the other hand, to suggest as some have done, that it is necessary to build concepts on experience with the concrete, involving the physical manipulation of the environment with minimal attention paid to language, is to cut off the child from the most potent source of conceptual experience. The importance of this is discussed below; the point, essentially, however, is that only through language can many of the concepts involved even in dealing with the concrete, have any existence.

The symbolizing and conceptualizing function of language has another very important implication for human learning. Whereas the lower animals transfer learned behaviour to new situations only by the mechanism of primary stimulus generalization, man, through language, has infinite potentiality for transfer. As Piaget and the followers of Pavlov have pointed out, language enables the child to bring the past into juxtaposition with the present. He does this because he is able to express verbally the relations between things and the operations he performs so that he can carry these forward to the new situation. For example, once the child has established the idea of *left* he will be able to apply the idea in many different circumstances other than the ones in which the concept was established. Now, however, transfer takes place between stimuli (words) which are semantically similar and not between stimuli which are similar physically. That is, we carry over the habits and learned behaviour, set up in certain situations, to situations related in *meaning*. A simple example of this would be the child who learns a response to a word and generalizes the response to words of similar semantic significance and not to words which are phonically similar. A response set up to the word *doctor* generalizes to the word *physician* but not to *dicktor*. However, work with imbeciles has shown that they generalize to the phonic similarity and respond to *dicktor*.* Similar work with young children has shown that they generalize to homonyms; as they grow older they start generalizing to synonyms and antonyms. Only gradually do they start responding to, or using, the conceptual qualities of the word. This is the kind of result that we might expect from our study of language development since the generalization to the phonic similarity is at a more primitive level than generalization to the semantic similarity.

The words of Sapir remind us of another very important factor in generalization and transfer; the fact that each word in itself is already a generalization. Thus the word *doctor* has far-reaching connotations for most of us which will differ according to our experience of doctors. Similarly a child will carry over into new situations, through the medium of words, the convenient *capsules of thought* whose richness and relevance will depend on the extent to which they crystallize real experience of the things and operations to which they refer. If the child lacks the experience which endows the word with this generalized significance, there will be little chance of transfer since the word has little *meaning* for the child. The job of the teacher is, then, to ensure that the child has adequate experience to load the word with the significance at least appropriate to the next stage of learning.

Language and concepts

We have so far talked of concepts in close conjunction with the symbol system which embodies them, that is, language. The question might be asked if language is essential for concept formation.

From the experiments which Harlow and others have carried out with various animals it does seem that concepts can be learned without language. Harlow, for example, showed that monkeys were able to solve tasks involving the use of the concept of oddity. The Frenchman, P. Oléron, investigated the concept formation of deaf children and found that they were able to form

* O'CONNOR, N. and HERMELIN, B.. *Speech and Thought in Severe Subnormality*, Pergamon, 1963.

concepts of shape, size and colour, but had great difficulty in forming class concepts which depend on the mental manipulation of several attributes of phenomena at once. (See Chapter 7.) It seems, therefore, that concepts can be formed without the use of language but, generally speaking, a child without language of any kind, and this includes sign languages, will have very much more difficulty in forming concepts than normal children.

The American psychologist, R. Gagné [17], in an interesting book on learning, suggests a model of concept learning showing its connection with language. His model is similar to those put forward by Luria (p. 131) and Bruner (p. 181) although they are stressing different aspects of the process. Gagné argues that the first step in learning a concept is probably for the child to learn the word which symbolizes it through an instrumental conditional reflex so that the child can repeat the word at will when asked. Gagné takes the concept of 'edge'.

The next step is for the child 'to identify two or three specific edges by saying *edge* whenever an actual edge is pointed to'. From this he goes on to give practice in discriminating between different examples of edges and stimuli which are not edges. Words are probably not essential at this stage but they are no doubt very useful. The teacher should present the child with a sufficient range of situations to ensure that an adequate coverage of the concept is made. How can the teacher decide this? This is probably impossible to answer. The best he can do probably is to provide representative examples of the various stimulus situations in which the concept is likely to be met. Dienes (p. 217) suggests a principle in the formation of mathematical concepts which he calls 'the more the merrier' principle. This is an argument for providing as large a number of different exemplars of a given concept as possible. There is a possible difficulty here, however, in that if the presentation of exemplars is not carefully controlled the combination of different stimulus situations may cause confusion such as we have discussed when we talked about external inhibition.

When the child is able to discriminate, among different exemplars of the concept (in Gagné's illustration the child can now say 'edge' to three different stimulus situations, a three dimensional object, a flat piece of paper, and a drawing, when they are presented all at the same time), he is ready for the last step in forming the concept. The teacher now shows the child a new object or drawing 'with which he has not previously associated the word *edge* and says *Where is the edge?*'. If the child picks out the correct part of the object or drawing, the concept has been acquired.

The reader might care to consider how much more difficult the teacher's task would have been to teach this concept without the use of language. It is also instructive to compare Gagné's model with the work of Vigotsky and Bruner reported in Chapter 7.

Language has other properties which we now consider. One of these properties is the syntactical aspect of language. Language is more than a random collection of words, it has a logic and form imposed upon it by society. This logic is the logic of grammatical usage. The manipulation of symbols according to grammatical conventions makes possible the elaboration of complex relationships between things, actions, and attributes otherwise impossible. It would probably be true to say that this represents a higher level of abstraction, and of the analysis and synthesis of these abstractions, than the initial mastery of the semantic properties of words. In the words of A. R. Luria, the Russian psychologist, this enables the child '. . . to form concepts . . . to draw conclusions from accepted assumptions, to master logical connections, to cognize laws, far surpassing the boundaries of direct, personal, experience' [18]. The complexities of thought made possible by the syntactical elaboration of language may be seen in the abstract relationships which it produces. Such expressions as, *if this then that: because of this that occurred: unless this that will not*, are highly abstract concepts utterly dependent upon language and incapable of being generated without language. Sapir illustrates the same point graphically when he demonstrates that in the sentence: *The farmer kills the duckling,* there are expressed thirteen distinct concepts. Some are concrete: *farmer, kills, duckling,* but there are also ten relational concepts working to produce the exact sense of the sentence. These concepts express such things as subjectivity and objectivity (acting as subject or object), singularity, and time (expressed by the form of the verb). In the normal course of events we are not consciously analysing each sentence in this manner, but unless we have acquired the necessary concepts in the course of our lives we cannot fully understand the meaning of the sentence. Piaget has pointed out that children use such forms long before they grasp the structures of meaning corresponding to these syntactical forms. The work of Vigostsky (Chapter 7) indicates that this is because the child forms *pseudo-concepts* through intercourse with adults which have the outer form of adult concepts but the content of much more primitive mental processes.

Language and emotion

The word, however, is more than the capsule of thought to which we have referred. It bears the mark of our animal origins. Communication in the lower animals consists essentially of the spread of affect. As Vigotsky says, the frightened goose contaminates the flock with fear but does not tell what he has seen. The child's early sounds are of this nature. But when the child begins to acquire language he acquires each new word in an affective context. That is, the word will carry with it the emotional overtones of the situations in which it was acquired. This does not imply that the affective content of the word will reflect only the conditions obtaining when it is first used by the child. As the significance of the word as a concept changes with the flux of experience which gives it its generalized nature, so the variety of affective tones obtaining in the circumstances in which the word is used become generalized. Thus words of prohibition or admonition used by the mother to the young baby will carry with them the generalized emotional content of the different situations in which they are used, as will the words of comfort and approval used in other situations. The word will also have the power of evoking not only the objective generalized notion of the class of things to which it refers, it will carry with it the affective associations of those phenomena. Few, if any, words are entirely free of affective overtones. R. H. Thouless has pointed out that words have three functions of which the two main ones are the conveying of information, asking questions, making statements, and so on; and the affective use as a means of arousing feelings.* Such words as *coward, hero, patriot, filthy,* convey both information and affect. Newly coined words or the specialized jargon of branches of science often have the very minimum of affective overtones, while the politician and demagogue often use words which convey little information but much affect. Vigotsky expressed succinctly the relationship between the informative and affective aspects of language when he said: '. . . every idea contains a transmuted affective attitude towards the bit of reality to which it refers.' We see this particularly well illustrated in poetry which derives much of its power from the subtle blending of the intellectual and the affective.

Language and thought

The question which naturally arises from a discussion of the role of language in learning is the relationship between thought and language. Some behaviourist psychologists have argued that thought is internalized speech accompanied by vestigial movements of the speech apparatus. Plato suggested that in thinking the soul was talking to itself. The question is a very difficult one to resolve since it is hard to investigate language without using language itself as part of the experimental technique. The view that would probably gain most acceptance at the moment would regard thought and language as being probably independent in early life, growing together as speech appears. The relationship then becomes a dialectical process; in the words of Sapir: 'We must . . . imagine that thought processes set in, as a kind of psychic overflow, almost at the beginning of linguistic expression; further that the concept, once defined, necessarily reacted on the life of its linguistic symbol, encouraging further linguistic

* THOULESS, R. H.: in REYMERT, M. L. (Ed.): *The Mooseheart Symposium on Feelings and Emotion,* McGraw-Hill, 1950.

growth. . . . The instrument makes possible the birth of the product, the product refines the instrument.'

The work of Oléron with deaf children suggests that a kind of 'thought' can exist without language. However, much more evidence is needed in this field since one of the great difficulties in investigations of this nature is ensuring that the children have no system of symbolization at all. Most deaf children brought up in normal circumstances will have some form of symbol system (possibly sign language) even if it is not spoken language and such symbol systems fulfil the requirements of a language system such as normal speech even if they are less effective. It does seem quite certain, however, that the acquisition of a language transforms the nature of thought.

Thus, in addition to the aspects of language we have considered previously, its role in cultural accretion, in releasing us from the here and now, and in extending our horizons through the generalizing property of words; it is the tool which shapes the most characteristic human faculty, that of thought. The teacher concerned with the intellectual development of his children cannot afford to ignore the development of their linguistic ability.

Learning to speak

The language of the child, with its profound influence on his behaviour, has a complex history of development. The mere acquisition of the correct speech forms is in itself an immense task. The baby probably makes thousands of attempts to echo the sounds made by adults before it achieves complete control and is able to utter the words correctly at will. (This is not to suggest that adults dictate to babies the sounds they shall use. It is highly likely that the sounds made naturally by the young baby have been taken as a basis for many words used in early life.) It is probable that the acquisition of correct speech forms follows the patterns of other learned behaviour. That is, the sounds made by the child which approximate to adult forms are reinforced by the approval of the adult, or in the early months, by the fact that they produce tangible results such as food or attention. Such sounds, by virtue of the fact that they are reinforced, will be repeated, sounds which are not reinforced will be dropped and fall out of the child's repertoire. This process is similar to Skinner's technique of shaping the behaviour of animals by the method of successive approximations.

The acquisition of the correct speech forms, although only one aspect of language, is undoubtedly very important, for without the ability to discriminate finely among the speech sounds of others and among his own imitations of these sounds, the child could never build up a recognizable set of speech sounds. The chimpanzee lacks this imitative ability and consequently, although one of the most advanced of all mammals and nearest man in brain development, the chimpanzee does not have a language. Chimpanzees in a human environment such as those brought up in the Yerkes family in America learn to perform quite complicated tasks. The animal referred to in Chapter 1 was able to perform such actions as turning on the switch of an electric fan. When it failed to work, she would check the wall socket and plug in the wire. She would replace a faulty bulb when operating the switch failed to light it up. She used a carpet sweeper and dialled the telephone, besides coping with many other problems involving such things as form boards, peg boards, picture puzzles, piling blocks, and buttoning. Despite this very obvious ability, the animal showed no signs of developing speech spontaneously. When the experimenter decided to intervene to teach her to speak she found it extremely difficult. She first tried to teach her to vocalize on command. In five months she had only managed to teach Viki to produce a hoarse staccato grunt. To make any advance it was necessary to manipulate the ape's lips so that they formed the required sound: she could not produce the appropriate sound by imitation. This is not due to any deficiency in the ape's vocal apparatus which is quite well developed; it may well be due to a difference in brain structure as compared with human beings. The Hayes's suggested that this may bear some resemblance to the state of aphasia, a human brain abnormality which manifests itself in speech deficiencies. On the other hand parrots with a very primitive brain are adept at imitation and can produce the speech sounds of human beings with great accuracy. The sounds they produce, however, are devoid of meaning. The American psychologist, Yerkes, suggests:

If the imitative tendency of the parrot were combined with the calibre of intellect of the chimpanzee, the latter would undoubtedly possess speech, since he has a voice mechanism comparable to man's as well as an intellect of the type and level to enable him to use sounds for purposes of real speech.

Man combines the imitativeness, the voice mechanisms, and the brain development necessary for the production of language. It is thus possible for the human baby to learn to reproduce the speech sounds of adults with accuracy. This is only the first stage in language development, however, the speech sounds in themselves are empty. After the early mastering of speech skills comes a long process of linguistic and psychological development before the forms of the words are filled with the meaning which transforms them from simple signals to symbols with all the richness of adult concepts. The word charged with meaning is the hallmark of human learning.

Summary

The behaviour of animals is formed by the genetic inheritance typical of the species which we call the *genotype*, and the patterns of behaviour developed by the individual in its life experiences. The inherited bodily form and reflexes, together with the acquired patterns of behaviour of the individual, constitute the *phenotype*.

In animals other than man the main influences forming the phenotype are the conditional reflexes acquired during the life experiences of the individual. Each individual has to learn the appropriate patterns of behaviour himself. Man, on the other hand, learns from the experience of others. Man transmits changes beneficial to the species through his culture and the species is thereby able to adapt rapidly to changed circumstances. In the process of adapting, man changes his environment. The changes he makes in the environment prepare the way for more adaptation so that man's adaptive behaviour becomes increasingly more complex.

The patterns of behaviour which man transmits through his culture are passed on from generation to generation by the use of language. Language and society go hand in hand; neither can exist without the other. Language releases us from the here and now and, through its symbolizing properties, enlarges our environment to an unimaginable extent. This is because language enables us to create categories of things which have no existence in the real world. Language facilitates the formation of concepts. Concepts abstract the essence of things in the real world and enable us to classify and index reality. Through language we create concepts which would not otherwise exist. Such abstract relationships as *before*, *after*, *because*, depend on language. Words, for human beings, have a much greater significance than the sounds which clothe them. *Sit* to a dog is merely a noise to which it has been conditioned: *stand* would do equally well. To man it has meaning. The dog responds to the signal significance of the word; man responds to its semantic properties.

Language not only conveys information; it carries affective overtones. The affective content of words develops while the words are being learned. Words learned in situations strongly charged with affect will become associated with the affective tone of the situation and will arouse a similar tone when they are used in other situations.

Language and thought are very closely linked. After the first few years of life they develop together. The development of complex linguistic skills is essential in the education of children.

Children are able to learn to speak because they possess a central nervous system of sufficient complexity and the necessary receptors to enable them to discriminate finely between different sounds and because they are able to imitate the speech sounds of others. In learning to speak the baby imitates the adult sounds, the sounds which are reinforced by adult attention are repeated, those ignored gradually die away. Eventually the child is able to speak using adult sounds and inflexions.

CHAPTER 6

Learning and Concept Formation

Human learning differs fundamentally from the learning of other animals in its extensive use of concepts. Concepts are formed through the experience one has of reality, and one of the most important elements in concept formation is the process of perception. Until one perceives an object as a thing in itself it is impossible to develop a concept of a class of such things. Similarly, unless we single out the important features of an object or action it is difficult to generalize from our experience. In order to illustrate this process let us first examine what happens when we perceive the world around us.

When the intricate pattern of visual stimuli from our environment passes through the lens of our eye, it forms an image on the retina. However, this image is not conveyed in that form to the brain any more than the image picked up by a television camera is delivered intact to your set. In fact the visual pattern is transformed into a pattern in a different medium. In the case of television the medium is electromagnetic waves which pass through space to the receiving set; in the case of vision it is electrochemical nerve impulses bearing some affinity to electric currents. Similarly the disturbances in the air which give rise to what we term sound, impinge upon the mechanisms of the ear and are transferred into the mechanical vibrations of a diaphragm which in turn are converted into similar nerve impulses as in the case of vision. As M. D. Vernon points out: '. . . between the projection of this visual pattern on the brain, and our full consciousness of the world of objects, a series of elaborate mental processes takes place which converts the visual pattern into the perception of the world as we know it.'* Part of these mental processes, which are at present somewhat obscure, is concerned to give stability

* VERNON, M. D.: *The Psychology of Perception*, Pelican, 1962.

and constancy to an ever changing pattern of stimuli. We have to learn to distinguish movement of the image, signifying movement of the environment, from that signifying movement of the body. Also involved is the development of the ability to impose constancy on the shape of objects even though we see a different shape according to the angle from which we view it.

It seems likely that during the early stages of life the child has no notion of separate identity. He is immersed in and part of his environment. In the first year he gradually begins to apprehend that objects in his environment have a discrete existence independent of him. His orienting activity will lead him to pay attention to changes in his perceptual field. These will mainly involve changes in the position or state of concrete objects and this will help him to the realization that they have an independent existence. Some psychologists argue that the ability to distinguish figure from ground is inborn. As the Gestalt psychologist, D. Katz, puts it: '. . . the tendency to form objects would become operative in the consciousness of a child from the start, even without experience of any sort. This would be equally true in the visual field of an individual who was born blind but had undergone a successful ophthalmological operation.' Katz continues by outlining the Gestalt laws which are considered to operate in the perception of objects '. . . even in a consciousness that has had no opportunity to have experience with objects' [11]. The laws to which Katz refers, concern the qualities of objects which make for their organization as independent units in the visual field. Thus such factors as proximity, similarity, continuity, completeness, enable us to single out visual forms by nature: individual experience, according to Katz, merely amounts to 'consolidation of a natural response of the visual system'.

As was mentioned earlier the experience of congenitally blind people given their sight when adults sheds some doubt on this. In fact such persons have had difficulty in perceiving and identifying objects, even those which they had previously handled. This is not really surprising from a developmental point of view. If we build up an impression of the world based on senses other than sight the optic nerve cells and the appropriate areas of the brain will have been virtually unstimulated and there will have been no opportunity for the elaboration of the pattern of nervous processes associated with sight.

Although babies may possibly be able to distinguish objects from early in life, there seems little doubt that most babies get a lot of help from their mothers. One of the most potent of the mother's aids in this field is undoubtedly her speech. Luria has carried out many experiments with children which illustrate the influence of speech in determining the nature of the child's perception. He argues:

> When a mother shows a child something and says *cup*, first her pointing and then the name of the object cause an essential modification in the child's perception. By the laws of temporary links [conditional reflexes], the mother's gesture and the word designating the object become secondary signals *causing marked changes in the range of stimuli acting upon the child*. In isolating the object from its environment, the action of pointing strengthens the stimulus, making it a figure set in a ground. The word designating the object delineates its essential functional properties and sets it within the category of other objects with similar properties; it serves a complex task of analysis and synthesis for the child, and later settles into a complex system of links acting on him and conditioning his behaviour [18].

In the experiments which led to the formulation of this argument, Luria commonly used language to change the relative significance of stimuli. Children aged three to five are given the task of reacting to certain visual stimuli. These consist of a red circle on a grey ground and a green circle on a yellow ground. The child is asked to squeeze a bulb with his right or left hand according to whichever pattern appears. This is soon learned and the stimulus which dominates the response can be seen to be the circle by presenting red and green circles on different grounds. The child responds to the stimuli as he did previously indicating that the circles are the important elements in the stimuli.

The child is now asked to squeeze according to whether he sees the grey ground or the yellow; that is, speech is used to alter the relative strengths of the stimuli. Children up to the age of three or four do not generally adapt; they continue to press in response to the appropriate circle. Children from four to five seem to be in an intermediate stage, while children of five to seven adapt their responses in accordance with the verbal stimuli with some stability and press in response to the background. In an extension of the experiment, circles are replaced by the shapes of aeroplanes of the same colours on the same grounds. The child is told that aeroplanes can fly only when the sun is shining (yellow background) and must stay on the ground when it is rainy (grey background). The child is once again asked to respond to the background. Under these conditions the great majority of all children, including those three to four years old, began reacting to the backgrounds. In this manner we see the beginning of the process whereby we often disregard the *physically most potent* stimulus in a situation and attend to another stimulus which is more *meaningful*. In the case of the children the meaning was introduced by the adult, in our case we orient ourselves on the basis of meaning which we have ourselves built up through experience in countless similar situations. In the case of the adult, language frequently transforms the stimulus situation. Out of the confused mass of stimuli in an urban street scene, one will single out an obscure stimulus such as the sign above a shop because one's attention is directed to it by another person's use of language. Here language isolates an unobtrusive aspect of the perceptual field and brings it to the forefront of attention with a force out of all proportion to its physical stimulus strength. The word is still more powerful. It can quickly transform the situation by dismissing the first stimulus and calling out another immediately and with the same force as the first.

Concept formation in children

Although perception is a very important feature in the development of concepts it is not the only feature. To perceive is not necessarily to conceive. Just as the child has to learn to see the world in the way that the adult does, so he has to learn to conceive of the world in an adult fashion. It is not always clear to the adult that the child's view of the world is not the same as his. The child may use the same words as the adult but his understanding of the things and actions the words refer to may be quite different. It is not just a case of the child thinking in the same way but with fewer ideas; the child thinks in a qualitatively different way from the adult. Rousseau said many years ago that the child is not a miniature adult and his mind was not the mind of an adult on a small scale, but many adults have not really grasped this, and many teachers are only now finding the truth of this and astonishing themselves when they repeat some of the experiments of Piaget into the way children's thinking develops. Piaget's influence in this field has been seminal, and although I cannot, in a short space, attempt to indicate the scope of his contribution to our understanding of the thought of the child, I will attempt to outline the salient points and show how they relate to our study [19].

Professor Jean Piaget at the universities of Paris and Geneva has made a fundamental contribution to our knowledge of the way in which children build up a picture of the world. He has not been mainly interested in learning and teaching but rather in the origin and development of thought in children. He has, therefore, deliberately arranged many of his experiments so that they are outside the normal experience of the children. He seeks, as it were, to uncover the basic processes which underly concept formation and to promulgate the laws which govern these processes. It is sometimes suggested that here he is chasing a Will-o'-the-wisp; learning experience and development of thought cannot be separated. Certainly most of the evidence we have so far taken from other sources would confirm this view.

However, over a period of about forty years through a multitude of clinical investigations into the way children tackle problems, he has produced a number of theories concerning the nature of the child's thought which have sparked off much replication of his experiments, and new thinking about classroom practices, especially in mathematics.

Piaget has a genetic approach. That is, he starts from the relatively simple behaviour of the infant and traces the progression to ever more complex levels of activity. This development he conceives of as being phased, with the child passing from phase to phase in a given sequence. Let us now consider the main stages of intellectual development in the child as Piaget sees them.

Stage 1. Sensory-motor period (birth to 18 months–2 years)

Piaget's model of the child's early life is similar to the Pavlovian one. The new-born child has a basic equipment of unconditional reflexes. On this basis he elaborates conditional responses which maintain his dynamic equilibrium with his environment. Piaget would express this by saying that the child achieves this balance or *adaptation* through a process of *assimilation* and *accommodation*. The child has to accept his environment in part and to organize his behaviour making allowances for its occasional intractability. He comes to realize that he cannot pass through a closed door: he *accommodates* to this feature of the environment. Later, by *assimilation*, he learns to open the door: he then changes the environment to suit his behaviour. Clearly the two processes are never independent; child and environment are in a continuous state of interaction which maintains the state of *adaptation* (Piaget), or *dynamic equilibrium* (Pavlov).

Closely linked with the process of adaptation is the construction of the *permanent object*. This is very similar to what we saw when we considered the early processes of perception. The child gradually differentiates out from the shifting mosaic of his environment, patterns of stimuli which he eventually recognizes as the attributes of separate objects. At first the child also behaves as though objects disappear or cease to exist if they cannot be seen. With further experience he shows through his behaviour that he realizes that the object still exists although it may be hidden. He will, for example, look for a toy which he has seen hidden whereas a child at an earlier stage will not.

Stage 2. Pre-conceptual intelligence (2–4 years)

This is the phase where the child is beginning to develop concepts and before he is capable of distinguishing between the specific concepts relating to an individual object and the generic concept relating to a class of objects. A common example of this is the tendency of children of this age to call men generally *daddy*.

As we have already seen, language plays a most important part at this age in the formation of concepts. In addition, the actual physical activity of the child is accompanied by a kind of 'running commentary' of speech. Piaget originally considered that speech which accompanied activity at this stage was mere babbling. In other words it was a by-product of the activity and of no relevance. He now agrees with the views of Vigotsky (see below) that such *egocentric speech* in fact plays a role in the regulation of the child's activities. Far from being a by-product of the child's activity, it may well be its prime mover. This is considered in more detail in the next chapter.

Stage 3. Intuitive thinking (4–7 years)

This is the stage when children first start school where they begin to acquire the basic skills and effective communication. Piaget's work has suggested to us that these basic skills may be more complex than we used to think. At this age we introduce children to such concepts as number, weight, length, height; we sometimes take for granted their grasp of spatial

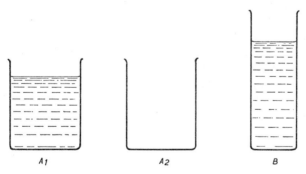

Fig. 8. Investigation of conservation. A child lacking conservation of substance agrees that the containers A_1 and A_2 contain the same amount of liquid. When the contents of A_2 are poured into B, as in the illustration, the child says there is more liquid in B despite the fact that the child saw the liquid being poured.

relationships; and the idea of causality is so much part of our nature that we rarely imagine that children may not have the same view of the world. And yet this is what seems to be the case at this stage. Children assess quantities on their most obvious perceptual appearances, not on the more complex qualities that we, as adults, use. For example, two sticks of equal length will be accepted as equal so long as they are parallel and in line. If we move one forward of the other the child will now say that one is the longer. Similarly a child will agree that two identical glasses filled to the same level contain the same amount of liquid. If the liquid from one glass is now poured into a tall narrower glass, he will aver that there is more liquid in the taller glass. This implies lack of what Piaget calls *conservation*. The child does not see that although the outward form may have changed, the quantities involved are the same (i.e. they are conserved). This latter experiment relates to conservation of quantity; the former referred to conservation of length. We meet similar phenomena in experiments dealing with substance, weight, volume, and number. Children in the stage of intuitive thinking are likely to lack conservation in all these fields.

Stage 4. Concrete operations (8–11 years)

By *operations* Piaget means actions which are internalized and reversible. That is, the child is able to *think about* actions which previously he had only been able to carry out at the sensory-motor level and he is also now beginning to achieve conservation in certain fields, notably substance (at approximately 7–8 years), of weight (approximately 9–11 years), and volume (approximately 11–12 years). We can see this by carrying out the following experiment with children. Two balls of modelling clay which are accepted by children as equal are taken. One is rolled into the shape of a sausage. The children are then asked questions couched in appropriate language to find out if they think there is still the same quantity in each lump, if they think the lumps are the same weight, and if they think the lumps have the same volume. Children at stage 3 will say that the sausage contains more clay than the ball. At stage 4 children with conservation of substance say they

Fig. 9. Investigation of conservation. The ball is rolled out into a sausage and the children asked questions to determine whether or not they have achieved conservation. Children who have not achieved conservation will say that there is more clay in the sausage than in the ball.

are both the same but will deny conservation of weight. They maintain that the ball contains as much clay as the sausage but weighs less. Such children, however, would not accept that the volume is the same until a year or two later. We see, therefore, a gradual progress from acceptance of conservation in one aspect to conservation in three aspects at once. However, the child is still tied to the concrete; he is not yet able to formulate his operations into a generalized system independent of objective reality.

Stage 5. Formal operations (11–14 or 15 years)

At this stage the child starts to become independent of concrete reality. He is now able to reason by hypothesis. Instead of reasoning about actions or reality he now reasons with propositions: he manipulates relations between things besides *establishing* these relationships. Piaget gives as an example of a problem demanding this type of thought, an item from one of Burt's tests: 'Edith is fairer than Susan: Edith is darker than Lily, who is the darkest of the three?' Piaget declares that few children below age 12 solve this problem. Before that age he suggests the reasoning goes as follows: 'Edith and Susan are fair, Edith and Lily are dark, therefore Lily is darkest, Susan is the fairest, and Edith in between.' In other words the child reasons as younger children do when serializing sticks according to size. This is because the problem is posed and is to be solved verbally without recourse to concrete operations.* However, although children eventually develop the ability for formal thinking and reasoning by hypothesis, it by no means follows that from then on they use only this method of thinking. Adolescents and adults will often revert to simpler modes of reasoning when faced with an entirely new situation.

Piaget thus suggests a pattern of development moving from relatively simple thought processes greatly dependent upon the objective environment, to ever more complex systems of mental organization becoming more and more independent of concrete reality. This view agrees closely with much of what has been discussed earlier. The main difference, of course, is that while the other workers have attached great prominence to the role of the adult in the formation of concepts, Piaget has tried to deduce the *natural* sequence of development divorced from such influences. Some research has been done in England, and generally Piaget's stages have been confirmed although the ages at which they occur have tended to be somewhat earlier. Much more work still has to be done in the repeating of Piaget's work, not the least in the schools where the extent of the validity of his theories can have an important influence on our classroom practice.

Readers will probably be interested in some of Piaget's additional findings concerning the development of concepts which have relevance to school.

Children of infant age seem not to be able clearly to differentiate number and space. A child of four or five asked to place on a table as many red counters as there are in a row of green counters, will make a row of the same length. If the counters in one row are now spaced out a little he will say that there are more counters in that row. The ability to establish a one-to-one correspondence eventually develops and then the child is able to collect one of the rows into a bunch and still grasp that the number is unchanged. Piaget observed the way in which the ability to see a one-to-one correspondence develops. Other investigators have experimented to see if the development can be speeded up by the teacher. E. M. Churchill gave a group of five-year-old

* PIAGET, J.: *The Psychology of Intelligence*, translated by PIERCY, M. and BERLYNE, D. E., Routledge and Kegan Paul, 1947.

children special encouragement in a play situation to discover for themselves constancy of numerical relations. For example, a child is helped to match a row of egg cups with a corresponding row of eggs. She found that this group made a highly significant improvement as compared with a control group, in a battery of tests derived from Piaget. Similar results have been obtained by other research workers. This suggests that teaching can influence very considerably a child's attainment in these stages. (See also pp. 180–81 and pp. 218–20 for experiments which produce quite different results from those of Piaget.)

Other concepts which have been investigated are time, movement, and speed. Piaget's experiments in these fields show that the child does not have *a priori* understanding of those concepts. Our idea of time, for example, undergoes a process of development. Piaget's experiments indicate that at first a child confuses the idea of age with its outward manifestations. Thus when one of two children born at the same time outgrows the other, the child considers the taller one to be older. Similarly, if two trees are represented pictorially the child will accept that the one planted first is older than the other until the latter grows taller than the former. Older children achieve the concept of objective time, they become able to manipulate conceptions of time in thought. Time is abstracted from the physical changes in the environment which give rise to the concept.

When we investigate the notions of movement and speed we find some further interesting facts. Speed at first is not seen as a time–space relationship. The child fixes on one aspect of the situation. For example, if a toy car is sent along one side of a triangle while another car is sent along the other two sides at the same time, both reaching the same point simultaneously, the child will say that both cars travel at the same speed. A car in the act of overtaking another will be said to be going slower until it is actually forging ahead.

Investigations into the child's conception of space and spatial relations have yielded some interesting results. At first the child cannot discriminate between such forms as the circle, triangle, and square sufficiently to copy them. Instead he will draw an irregular figure for all of them. This phenomenon was used by Binet in his first intelligence test, the child's ability to copy a circle or later a square being marks of a child's relative level of attainment.

The concept of independent vertical and horizontal planes is another phenomenon which follows a similar process of development to other concepts. At first the child does not have this concept. If he draws trees on a hill they will be at right angles to

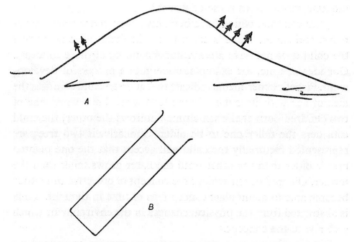

Fig. 10. Children who have not attained the concept of a horizontal plane independent of actual objects draw trees as in A and draw the level of a liquid in a tilted container as in B.

the side of the hill. If he draws the water-level in a tilted container it will be at right angles to the side as it was when the container was upright.

Thus, as before, we see in Piaget's work the gradual progression from the partial understanding of concepts with the child fixating on one and later on more aspects of the phenomenon, to a full grasp of the concept and its many attributes.

He has given us a great insight into children's thinking but has been criticized on some grounds. One criticism has been the lack of statistics. This is a feature of the clinical genetic approach to research. It goes counter to much of English and American research but it knits closely with Luria's and Skinner's. Skinner defends his position, however, and tells of another psychologist who contemplated dedicating a book to the mathematicians and statisticians '. . . with whose help this book could not have been written'! However, both Piaget and the Russians are beginning to pay more attention to statistical methods and there is a complementary move by some Americans into genetic studies.

A more important weakness in Piaget's work may well be in the fact that the phenomena that we see in the Piagetian experiments are culture-bound. By this is meant that the culture in which a child is born determines the age at which concepts are formed, and whether in fact they are ever formed. For example, as Lewis Mumford has pointed out, the concept of abstract time is a social product, it is not native to mankind. Some societies have flourished on a loose basis in time and have been so indifferent to it that they lack authentic chronology of the years. And yet only when we conceive of the day as an abstract span of time which we divide up into set periods, can we study the development of the concept of time in the child. Similarly with space. One child in an English industrial city, who was retarded intellectually in many respects, was found to have a precocious understanding of three-dimensional topography. It was found on investigation that she lived high up in a block of flats from where she could see a large part of the city almost as in a three-dimensional model. Margaret Mead has also pointed out that young children in a primitive society, such as the Manus, who live in houses on piles in salt lagoons near the fishing grounds, demonstrate in their daily activity knowledge of conservation of weight long before comparable Swiss children. If a child loading and handling canoes thought things changed in weight when they changed shape the results could be fatal.*

Piaget's present view on the influence of culture on the development of the various stages is that while they cannot be tied down

* MEAD, M.: in TANNER, J. M. and INHELDER, B. (Eds.): *Discussions on Child Development*, No. 4, Inter. University Press, 1955.

to given age ranges, they will follow the same sequence of development when they do appear. The Russian psychologist, P. Y. Galperin, takes a different view and argues that the development of the various concepts will follow different patterns according to the kind of training the child gets. He has carried out experiments into the formation of mathematical concepts in young children which seem to substantiate his argument. (See pp. 218–20.) Piaget, himself, suggests that investigations of cultural differences in concept formation would be a most fruitful area of research.

In an investigation which replicated many of Piaget's experiments with English children, R. M. Beard found that although in general Piaget's ideas of stages of development obtained, there were variations. Some children were advanced in some fields and retarded in others. She found the largest divergences from Piaget's findings 'occur in children's conceptions of the world and in their understanding of physical causality and spatial conceptions. These are fields most affected by the general advance in scientific and technological knowledge which increase both information and the tendency to question beliefs and theories'* (see also p. 195).

This is very much in line with the views of Galperin and the comments of Mead. J. S. Bruner has also suggested that the stages of development can be affected by cultural pressures; in this case by the deliberate use of language in the problem situation. We shall consider this aspect of Bruner's work later. At this stage, the most important thing for the reader is to remember that Piaget's findings on concept formation should not be interpreted too rigidly.

A schematic view of learning

Piaget's views on the schematic nature of mental and motor operations are of particular interest to the educator. He considers that the child gradually develops an increasingly complex adaptation to his environment through a series of increasingly

* BEARD, R. M.: 'Nature and Development of Concepts', in *Educational Review*, Vol. 12, No. 3 and Vol. 13, No. 1, June and November 1960.

complex *schemas*. The idea of the schema was first put forward by the neurologist, H. Head. Similar views on the subject have been proposed by the Canadian psychologist D. O. Hebb and by F. C. Bartlett who regarded a schema as '. . . an active organization of past reactions, or of past experiences, which must always be supposed to be operating in any well-adapted organic response. That is, whenever there is any order or regularity of behaviour, a particular response is possible only because it is related to other similar responses which have been serially organized, yet which operate not simply as individual members coming one after another, but as a unitary mass.'*

Pavlov had similar views. Of the way in which we organize our experience of the world he said: 'Countless stimuli, different in nature and intensity, reach the cerebral hemispheres both from the external world and the internal medium of the organism itself. Whereas some of them are merely investigated others evoke highly diverse conditional and unconditional effects. They all meet, come together, interact, and they must, finally, become systematized, equilibrated, and form, so to speak, a *dynamic stereotype*' [9].

There is no universally agreed definition of the term *schema*. Applied to motor activity, it is analogous to an habitual skill. Applied to cognitive processes, it is analogous to the term *concept*. However, schemas are not *things*. The word is used merely to refer to behaviour which operates in a unitary nature rather than in isolated bits. Let us now consider some of the views held about the place of the schema in learning.

The schema has its neurological aspect in the activity of the cortex. The work of Sokolov mentioned earlier suggests a possible model for this activity. A schema, on this view, would be not a random firing of neurones, but an integrated pattern of cellular activity built up in the course of repeated experience in similar situations. This pattern would be linked with the situations in which it was set up and would be evoked by the pattern of stimulation characteristic of those situations. Hebb has also put forward suggestions of this nature. He calls the integrated

* BARTLETT, F. C.: *Remembering*, O.U.P., 1932.

activity of cortical cells the activity of 'cell assemblies', but as with the suggestions of Sokolov the suggested model should not be taken as a demonstrated phenomenon, it is a hypothesis only.

The suggested neural model has its behavioural component which can be more readily observed and when the appropriate stimulus situation arises the appropriate behaviour is evoked. Thus the information received by the cortex from the receptors will elicit a *pattern* of cortical activity and not disconnected impulses. The neural pattern might then initiate a pattern of activity which could involve moving from place to place but could equally well take the form of speech or writing or 'just thinking'.

The schema can be contrasted with the chains of reflexes exhibited by the lower animals such as the wasp we considered in Chapter 4. In the case of insects, the *taxis*, which is the name given to this reflex activity, is stereotyped and fixed. It is unconditional. The schema, however, while being stereotyped to a degree, is dynamic and can change since it is essentially conditional behaviour. Schemas also differ from the chains of conditional reflexes mentioned in Chapter 4 in that they act as units. The individual aspects of the schema coalesce and act as a complex whole whereas the different links in reflex chains remain separate and strung out in time. Schemas of motor activity are the skills which we build up in our everyday activity. When we first start to build up the skills we have to think about what we are doing. Later we are able to carry out the activity which took all our concentration when we were learning it while doing something else at the same time. When we use a skill such as typewriting, or serving at tennis, we deploy complex acts of perception, discrimination, and motor activity in an integrated pattern.

Schematic behaviour involves integration of specific responses into more complex, virtually automatic activity. This more complex activity will be applicable to a greater variety of situations than single responses. The extent of the versatility of the activity and its application to different situations depend on the variety of experience on which it is built. Thus the tennis player who built up a schema of serving in one set of circumstances only, say, with no wind, with the sun behind him, and with the same type of ball would have a very limited schema and would be at a disadvantage compared with a player who had trained in a variety of circumstances.

Piaget gives an example of the way his children built up motor schemas of sucking, progressing gradually from the setting up of simple responses to the more versatile (for a baby) activity. He suggests that in the course of repeating routines, various positional, tactile, acoustic, and visual stimuli become associated to build up a schema. The assimilation of stimuli to the schema, he considers, correspond to the phenomena of conditioning and generalization. His child Laurent, nine days old, who was sleeping in his crib, opened his mouth and began sucking the moment he was placed on his mother's bed. Later, being picked up by the nurse, he started both sucking and groping behaviour. At three months of age, both Laurent and Lucienne stopped crying and made sucking motions at the sight of their mother unfastening her dress for nursing. At approximately five months, Jacqueline opened her mouth as soon as she saw the bottle. By seven months she opened her mouth in one fashion at the sight of a bottle and in another fashion at the sight of a spoon. As Piaget remarks: 'An accommodative differentiation was clearly evident.'

We see here, at a very primitive level, the emergence of a motor schema. The gradual assimilation of different responses to a common schema built up a pattern of activity more complex than a simple reflex and more adaptive because it was applicable in different situations (feeding from a spoon or from a bottle).

A schema, therefore, unifies past adaptations to the environment into complex and virtually automatic systems of responses. Such a system of responses will follow whenever we encounter a given stimulus situation which is relevant to one aspect of the schema. Thus once a tennis player has built up in a number of different circumstances, a schema of serving, he will use the common core of the schema every time he serves but will also select from it special aspects to cope with variations in wind, weight of balls, skill of opponent and so on. If, on the other hand, the tennis player had to learn a different set of responses to cope with every different serving situation, he would have to learn an infinite number of quite distinct responses. Apart from the enormous time which would be taken in such learning, there would be the serious drawback that since the responses are quite self contained, no matter how many he learned he would be unable to cope with a new situation.

So far we have discussed motor schemas. However, the term *schema* is often applied to ways of thinking. Such cognitive schemas operate, like motor schemas, as integrated patterns of activity which tend to become habitual. However, whereas in motor schemas individual responses are fused into an integrated pattern, cognitive schemas are probably more like integrated patterns of concepts. We discuss the evidence for and the implications of this view, below.

Learning a new schema will be slow but once a schema has been learned it will facilitate the learning of new material. Because it embraces many aspects of cognitive activity, the schema will have greater potential of transfer than the isolated reflex.

Although we have used the term stereotyped when referring to schemas, we must not forget the dynamic aspect. Schemas change in the course of learning to take in new elements, sometimes to drop out others, but in general to become more comprehensive. Piaget suggests that when faced with a new problem of learning the child brings to bear his past experience in the form of a previously elaborated schema. This schema is potentially adequate to the solution of the problem. Piaget calls this schema an *anticipatory schema*. If this coincides closely with the demands of the present problem, the solution will be easily reached. If there is less common ground the schema will need to be altered, in Piaget's terms, *restructured*. The restructuring will be complete when the new learning is mastered. The changed schema will now be more comprehensive and more relevant to the solution of the new problem as well as to the earlier ones. Thus learning advances by a series of schemas which increase in complexity as they assimilate new elements.

The use of cognitive schemas may be regarded as an important aspect of meaningful learning. Learning which does not make use of such schemas will have less wide application. Behaviour which does not involve schemas will tend to consist of arbitrary linkages of stimuli and responses. This we shall refer to as *rote learning*. A child learning by rote in this sense would be able to go through the motions of, say, an arithmetical computation and get the correct answer without comprehending the process by which he reaches it. For example, to divide by a fraction he 'turns it upside down and multiplies' because he has been told to do it that way. The child here builds up a response to a stimulus situation, which is virtually devoid of any experience relating to the properties of fractional quantities. Instead of learning in a situation impregnated with meaning, he learns isolated facts which he cannot carry over into other situations. The difficulty arrives, of course, when the problem is placed in a real-life context (as opposed to the artificial arbitrary world of the arithmetical textbook); the automatic response no longer occurs; the teacher has not helped the child to build up a schema relevant to the situation.

Piaget regards the process of development as a series of stages of *equilibration*. By this is meant that behaviour moves from one level of equilibrium to another. Learning and development involve the acquiring of a series of schemas of increasing complexity.

Before concluding this present discussion of the schema, it will be instructive to consider some of the points made by M. L. J. Abercrombie in an interesting discussion of the role played by schematic ways of thinking and perceiving in the way we react to our environment.* While recognizing the value of the schema in ways similar to those mentioned above, she points out the dangers which may follow from too rigid schemas. If the schema becomes too stereotyped and too resistant to change it may become unadaptive. In Piaget's terms, the schema would not be restructured to take in new phenomena. For Abercrombie the term *schemas* seems to refer to organized systems of concepts which operate habitually and in an integrated fashion. We might think of such cognitive schemas as our total outlook in a given field. She instances many cases of medical students who had built up schemas

* ABERCROMBIE, M. L. J.: *The Anatomy of Judgement*, Hutchinson, 1960.

in different fields which, because they were inflexible and stereotyped, were leading them to unscientific attitudes. For instance, students' judgements were greatly affected by their generalized concepts of human nature. Their cognitive schemas relating to these concepts tended to be resistant to change. 'Some thought that people can be, and should be, trusted to do good work and to tell the truth; that one should always put the best possible interpretation on statements even if they were vague and confused and should assume that certain necessary precautions had been taken even if they were not described. Others thought that one must always be on one's guard against being taken in. Some did not like to be harsh, others thought that scientists must be sceptical.' Students in discussion on the topic of human nature found that their judgement on straightforward scientific matters had been influenced, among other things, by whether in general they trusted people. Students with different schemas made different judgements. In other circumstances students diagnosed the same case differently because they approached the problem of diagnosis with different schemas which were stereotyped in different ways and relatively inflexible.

We might draw a parallel in school by considering the teacher who is experienced in teaching young children beginning reading trying to teach backward secondary children the same skill. Although the processes are similar in many ways, unless the teacher adapted the schema he had built up in his dealings with the younger children, he would be misled if he tried to draw the same conclusions from his observations of the older children. Similarly, his approach to teaching the older children will have to be modified to be successful. If his schema is inflexible his success will be limited.

D. P. Ausubel has recently put forward a view which resembles in some respects the schematic view of learning.* He suggests that meaningful learning is learning which can be related to and assimilated into what he terms *existing cognitive structure*. Ausubel suggests a hierarchical view of cognitive structure. His model helps us to relate schemas and concepts a little more clearly.

* AUSUBEL, D. P.: *The Psychology of Meaningful Verbal Learning*, Grune and Stratton, 1963.

According to this view, meaningful new learning is not just tagged on to previously learned concepts but is fitted into a hierarchical structure. At the bottom of this hierarchy are the most specific concepts, but these specific concepts are subsumed under fewer concepts of greater generality. These more general concepts are themselves included in still more general concepts, and so on to the few extremely general concepts which cover a person's full knowledge in a given field. Ausubel suggests that (cognitive) schemas are the equivalent of concepts of a high degree of generality (i.e. concepts very high in the hierarchy).

This model applies to meaningful learning. However, when new learning takes place which is not related to existing cognitive structure it cannot be fitted into the hierarchy of concepts. Consequently, it remains an isolated response. Because of this the new learning lacks meaning. It also tends to be specific and does not transfer to new situations. This is rote learning. Rote learning, it is argued, tends to be more difficult, since it cannot be anchored to any existing knowledge. It is also likely to be forgotten more easily.

Ausubel reports an experiment to investigate this hypothesis. A group of Illinois students were given an exposition of the ideological background to the American civil war before a lesson in which they learned the Southern point of view. The idea was that the students, being from the North, would not have sufficiently adequate general concepts to which they could relate the new learning and the new ideas would tend to conflict with rather than to fit in with their existing ideas about the civil war. A control group was given a purely descriptive passage about the Southern point of view. In the test on the Southern point of view which followed, the experimental group performed better. The instruction about the ideological background may be considered to have established a schema which could subsume both the Northern and Southern points of view. A similar experiment by A. Z. Redko [8] showed that concepts such as *slave* and *slave owner* were learned more effectively when the higher-level concept (or schema) of slave-owning system had been formed. In another experiment, R. R. Skemp gave first-year grammar school boys (11–12 years) two learning tasks. One involved schematic learning, the other rote learning. Schematic learning was considerably more effective both immediately and also in terms of amount remembered later (p. 53 n.).

The question of transfer

The argument for a hierarchical view of cognitive structure has implications for the question of transfer of learning. As has been suggested earlier, conceptual learning transforms the basis of the transfer of learning. In simple response learning, transfer depends on actual physical similarities among stimuli. In conceptual learning transfer transcends the limits of physical similarity.

The American psychologist, R. Gagné, holds a view which bears on this point [17]. He suggests a hierarchy of types of learning ranging from simple response learning to problem solving. The higher in hierarchy the form of learning the greater the potentiality for transfer. At the level of concept learning he holds that concepts may be linked into chains which then make up principles which taken together make up what we term 'knowledge' in a given field. For example, the principle *water flows downhill* is a chain of three concepts. Once this is learned a child has a principle which he will be able to apply in a variety of situations which may be widely different from the situation in which he learned the principle.

Gagné suggests that response learning is at the bottom of a hierarchy of types of learning. Next comes the chaining of responses, then multiple discrimination learning, concept learning, principle learning, and finally problem solving. Gagné is primarily concerned with the *methods* of learning. The content of this learning, however, is very similar to Ausubel's model, although the terminology is not quite the same. In both cases learning at the higher levels of the hierarchy is more general than at the lower levels. That is, it covers a much greater range of phenomena and thus has greater potentiality of transfer.

A classical experiment on transfer which bears strongly on the question of the learning of principles was carried out by C. H. Judd in 1908. He had two groups of children; one group was taught the principle of refraction. Both groups were then given practice in throwing darts at a target placed twelve inches under water. The darts had to be thrown obliquely which made it a fairly difficult task to learn. The target was then raised to four inches and the children were asked to continue throwing at the target. The group that had been taught the principle of refraction adjusted to the new conditions much more readily than did the control group. The control group showed little transfer from the learning of the original task.

Piaget's work has made clear to many teachers how easily children can learn the appropriate verbalizing without grasping the underlying concepts. In such cases not only is there no transfer but the child gives the appearance of understanding while in reality remaining in ignorance. Teachers might wonder if they can do anything to help children to learn the concepts as well as the words. To this Piaget offers no answer. He attempts to study children's thinking in isolation from its development and the children's learning. Other writers, as we have seen, have attempted to answer this question, and we shall see later how Piaget's formulation about children's cognitive development are by no means universally applicable. One particular difficulty in Piaget's work, however, is the fact, pointed out by M. M. Lewis, that Piaget investigates the child's thought through the child's language and the child's language is a very important factor in the way in which the child constructs his picture of the world [20]. On the other hand some psychologists have made the study of the role of language in the development of the child's thought pre-eminent. We now turn to a consideration of some of their work.

Summary

Human learning differs fundamentally from learning in other animals because it involves the extensive use of concepts. Perception, or the impressions we get of the world through our senses, is a very important aspect of concept formation. Through experience of the world we learn to perceive objects in our environment as having their own separate existence: if we did not we should not be able to form concepts. Language used by others can have an important effect on our perception by helping to isolate from the environment those features which are of most significance.

Piaget has studied the formation of concepts in children over a long period. He suggests that concept formation follows a series of stages. Stage one is the *sensory-motor* stage (birth–2 years) when the child is entirely dependent for his knowledge of the world on his sense impressions of the concrete. At this stage he eventually recognizes the *permanent object*. Stage two is *pre-conceptual intelligence*. The child is now beginning to form concepts but so far he has no idea of classes of things. He will accompany his activity at this stage with a running commentary of speech which relates to his actual motor activity. Stage three is *intuitive thinking*. Children at this stage assess reality on the basis of its dominant perceptual appearances. Because of this they will confuse superficial changes in phenomena with fundamental changes. Piaget says that such children lack *conservation*. Stage four is *concrete operations*. The child has now achieved conservation in many fields, but he still depends on concrete reality for the working out of the mental operations. Stage five is *formal operations* and now the child can reason without being dependent on the concrete. He can now reason using relationships. However, he will not always reason in this way.

Piaget's investigations have shown that concepts are not born with us but that they develop during childhood. Although he attempts to study the development of concepts in isolation from learning it seems clear that experience and teaching affect the processes of concept formation and that the ages and stages he suggests may vary according to the cultural background and education of the individual child.

Piaget's concept of the schema is of particular interest in learning. Fully adaptive behaviour does not consist of isolated reflexes but of organized patterns of cognitive and motor activity built up in various situations and which can be applied to similar situations in the future. Ausubel and Gagné have suggested hier-archical views of learning which bear strongly on this question and on the problem of meaningful learning.

CHAPTER 7

Language and Thought

A study of concept formation

One of the most interesting views of the growth of conceptual thinking has been put forward by the Russian psychologist Vigotsky. In a series of ingenious experiments he investigated the formation of concepts using a method which dealt successfully with the problem that concept formation and language are closely correlated. [21] Instead of using words that already carry with them elements of thought and possibly even fully developed concepts, Vigotsky used words which had no symbolic significance at all at the outset, but which gradually acquired such significance in the course of the investigations. He presented two sets of stimuli to the subject of the experiment, one set as the objects of his activity, the other as signs which can serve to organize that activity. The translators of Vigotsky's book give this description of the use of his apparatus.

The material used consists of 22 wooden blocks varying in color, shape, height, and size. There are 5 different colors, 6 different shapes, 2 heights (the tall blocks and the flat blocks), and 2 sizes of the horizontal surface (large and small). On the underside of each figure, which is not seen by the subject, is written one of the four nonsense words: LAG, BIK, MUR, CEV. Regardless of color or shape, LAG is written on all tall large figures, BIK on all flat large figures, MUR on the tall small ones, and CEV on the flat small ones. At the beginning of the experiment all blocks, well mixed as to color, size, and shape, are scattered on a table in front of the subject. . . . The examiner turns up one of the blocks (the *sample*), shows and reads its name to the subject, and asks him to pick out all the blocks which he thinks might belong to the same kind. After the subject has done so . . . the examiner turns up one of the *wrongly* selected blocks, shows that this is a block of a different kind, and encourages the subject to continue trying. After each new attempt another of the wrongly placed blocks is turned up.

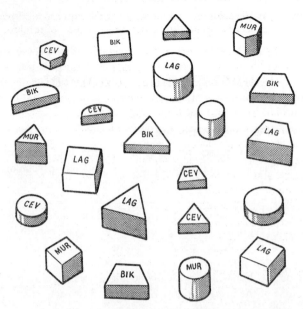

Fig. 11. The blocks used by Vigotsky in his investigation of concept formation. Note that the blocks are also in five different colours, but that the colour is not a criterion in the required conceptual response.

As the number of the turned blocks increases, the subject by degrees obtains a basis for discovering to which characteristics of the blocks the nonsense words refer. As soon as he makes this discovery the ... words ... come to stand for definite kinds of objects (e.g. LAG for large tall blocks, BIK for large flat ones), and new concepts for which the language provides no names are thus built up. The subject is then able to complete the task of separating the four kinds of blocks indicated by the *nonsense* words. Thus the use of concepts has a definite functional value for the performance required by this test. Whether the subject actually uses conceptual thinking in trying to solve the problem ... can be inferred from the nature of the groups he builds and from his procedure in building them. Nearly every step in his reasoning is reflected in his manipulations of the blocks. The first attack on the problem; the handling of the samples; the response to correction;

the finding of the solution – all the stages of the experiment provide data that can serve as indicators of the subject's level of thinking.

Vigotsky and his associates studied several hundred people using these techniques. From these investigations a number of general findings emerged. It was established, in agreement with Piaget, that although the processes of concept formation begin in childhood, they do not in general reach the adult stage until adolescence.

Three stages on the road to concept formation were isolated. In the first instance the child groups the experimental objects in unorganized heaps of three main types. The first type is based on pure trial and error and when the child is shown that his grouping is wrong he merely adds to the collection he has made, replacing the *wrong* one by another chosen at random. A somewhat more complex organization follows the child's immediate perceptual field. He groups things according to whether they are contiguous in space or time. The things he attends to first, or the things fortuitously juxtaposed by the experimenter become the groups. From the heaps built up randomly and through contiguity, the child may construct a third type of group from elements taken from these groups. Such an arrangement is still unorganized. In Vigotsky's words it is a 'Vague syncretic* conglomeration of individual objects that have somehow or other coalesced into an image in his mind. Because of its syncretic origin, that image is highly unstable.' The child substitutes for real connections between things, what he considers to be the associative factors. Sometimes they overlap with adult concepts; when they do the adult and the child are able to understand each other. As can be seen, when the child groups the test objects in these vague conglomerations which do not coincide with the adult organization, there is a real lack of contact between the child's understanding and adult views.

The next stage in the child's thinking involves the use of *complexes*. Whereas a concept groups objects according to one abstract attribute, the complex consists of elements grouped according to any number of concrete factual connections.

* 'Syncretic' when the objects are grouped accidentally with no logical connection.

Groupings of this nature will be formed when the child adds to the first block another block because it is of the same colour, another because it is the same as the first block in shape or size or in any other attribute that strikes him. He may add blocks to the nucleus on the strength of differences and similarities or possibly because the blocks are contiguous. Vigotsky suggests that at this level the child groups things in a way similar to the grouping made under a family name. The name of the block in the experiment is now something more than a proper name but it does not involve *conceptual* identity any more than Mr Jones and Mrs Jones are identical because they have the same name. This complex, the *associative complex*, makes use of bonds such as contiguity, colour, similar shape, etc. Another form of complex groups the objects according to the extent to which they resemble collections. As knife, fork, and spoon, form a set because of their differences, so the objects now selected by the child compose groups which resemble such sets in that they are placed together on the basis of some one trait in which they differ and consequently complement one another; so, for example, a group would include blocks each of a different colour, or form, or size.

The *chain complex*, another form of grouping, strikingly illustrates the difference between thinking in complexes and thinking in concepts. The child now selects objects for his grouping on one criterion or other and adds to the group until some other attribute of the latest addition attracts his attention. His focus then shifts and he begins to select on the basis of this new attribute. For example, if the original block were triangular, he might select the next few blocks because they are the same shape until his attention is taken by the colour of the latest addition to the group; say yellow. His attention now focuses on yellow blocks of any shape until some other shift takes place and he choses circular or rectangular blocks for example. The child is now paying attention to one attribute of the object at a time; that attribute, be it colour, shape, or size is not *abstracted* from the object but is regarded as one of its distinguishing features. Because of this, each of the different characteristics of the experimental apparatus are of equal importance; the child does not attempt to subordinate the attributes of the objects to any one main aspect. The only thing that matters when the child chooses the next block, is, 'has it any features in common with the last one?' There is thus no nucleus to a chain complex and it is quite possible for the final addition to the collection to have no features at all in common with the original chosen by the experimenter.

The links in the chain complex often become vague and diffuse. The common factor between two objects may become fluid so that the child might follow a yellow object with a green, a green with a blue, a blue with a black. Or a square will be followed by a hexagon, a hexagon by a circle and so on. This type of grouping was called a *diffuse complex* by Vigotsky and he points out that its boundaries are limitless in the child's dealings with the real world. The child still does not abstract from the various phenomena any of the common or quasi-common attributes. Phenomena are linked by their concrete physical characteristics but the child's apprehension of the nature of the connecting attributes is unclear and liable to fluctuate.

One final type of complex can be discerned in the development of the child's thinking before he begins to manipulate true concepts. This Vigotsky called the *pseudo-concept*. The pseudo-concept resembles the adult concept; for example the child might select all the triangles to form a group. He does not, however, make his selection on the basis of *triangularity* but upon the concrete visible likeness rather like the associative complex.

To illustrate the difference between the pseudo-concept and the real concept let us consider first the subject who groups according to true classification. After completing a grouping and being shown by the experimenter's turning over one of the wrong choices that his grouping is incorrect, he will make some remark to the effect that the criterion of classification is not colour or shape, etc., and will brush up the blocks and start looking for another criterion. On the other hand a subject may approach the task with all the signs of an attempt at true classification; for example, he may select all the blue blocks. When being shown that they are not all LAG by the experimenter's turning over one of the wrong blocks, the child will allow the block to be removed but will not remove the rest of the blocks from the specimen LAG. If the examiner now asks if the remaining blocks still belong together and are LAG, he answers quite definitely that they do because they are all blue. This reply shows that his first attempt was not a true attempt at classification and that the original group he formed was not based on the *concept of blueness* but on the *concrete physical attributes* of the blocks. In other words, the grouping was based on a complex which gave the impression of a concept; it was in fact a pseudo-concept.

As may be imagined the transition from the use of the pseudo-concept to the true concept passes unnoticed, but the use of true concepts is the culmination of the child's progress through the processes of manipulation of complexes. The use of pseudo-concepts predominates over all other complexes in the young child. This is because complexes are formed not spontaneously in real life but under the influence of adult language. The adult supplies the word ready made and the child uses it; but the adult does not and cannot pass on the meaning of the word. The child thus forms a complex around the word supplied by the adult, he does not reach it through his own experience.

Vigotsky identifies one other stage on the road to concept formation in the construction of the *potential concept*. At this stage the subject in the experiment groups things on the basis of one common attribute rather than on the basis of maximum similarity. The difference between this and complex thinking is that although the child may attend to the same attribute, in complex thinking his associations are vague and floating, whereas in the potential concept there is stability so that the child is able to carry over the identifying attribute from one situation to another. The potential concept is not a true concept because the child has not yet abstracted the quality which the objects possess in common and is unable to view this common attribute *as an abstraction* apart from the objects which embody it. The child may group the triangular shaped objects consistently and yet not grasp the idea of triangularity.

There is a close link here with the results of Piaget's investigations. We have seen how children before the level of formal operations in his experiments, although to all intents and purposes fully conversant with a variety of concepts, show that in fact they are familiar with the verbal trappings only. They are fully able to juggle with the verbal forms but have no real grasp of the conceptual content. Children in the junior school are able to talk about such things as weight and speed and age, and to do sums involving these concepts, and yet on closer investigation they are seen to be attending to the physical aspects of the situation which are obviously and concretely comparable. (The size of the tree is the physical manifestation of its age; and long before Piaget, children were being caught out by the question: 'Which is heavier, a ton of lead or a ton of feathers?')

Preliminary investigations with English junior school children have produced very similar results to those obtained by Vigotsky. As with other investigations into concept formation, the stages do not coincide with clearly defined age levels but seem to reflect the child's background of experience. However, children in the top classes of the primary school (10–11 years) complete the classification with more consistent success than younger children, a large proportion of whom never satisfactorily solve the problem. An interesting feature of the test situation is the way in which children who successfully classified the material conceptually now attach meaning to what were formerly nonsense words. This was demonstrated by asking the children at the end of the test whether they thought the tester and his assistant were LAG, BIK, MUR, or CEV, and how many of the children in their class were LAG.

Vigotsky carried over his experimental findings to real life situations. He found evidence of complex thinking in young children and in primitive tribes. He quotes as an example of the chain complex, the case of the child who used *quah* '. . . to designate first a duck swimming in a pond, then any liquid, including the milk in his bottle; when he happened to see a coin with an eagle on it, the coin also is called *quah*, and then any round, coinlike object. This is a typical chain complex. Each new object included has some attribute in common with another element, but the attributes undergo endless changes.'

In the thought of primitive peoples he refers to the phenomenon called *participation*. He discusses the case of the Bororo people of Brazil who had the same word for red parrots as they had for the tribe. One anthropologist concluded but there was no mistake about it, and the Bororo really considered themselves to be red parrots. Vigotsky suggested that the real explanation of this seemingly fantastic idea ties in with the fact that words to the Bororo people designate groups of objects and not concepts. The word for parrot is the word for a complex that includes parrots and the Bororo people. 'It does not imply identity any more than a family name shared by two related individuals implies that they are one and the same person.' Vigotsky points out that although this bizarre example is likely to attract attention, it is merely a spectacular instance of a common phenomenon. Thus much of children's thinking is of this nature although often their complexes are such that they do not apparently transgress the laws of adult logic. The fact that the thought processes underlying the outward manifestations are not identical to those of the adult, is only revealed when the child operates in a novel situation, where he is unable to make use of behavioural patterns already established under the influence of the language of the adult, and partaking of many of its characteristics.

In his study Vigotsky is using the term *concept* to apply to what would generally be called *class concepts*. Class concepts are more complex mental phenomena than such concepts as, for example, the concepts of *yellow* or *square* which are attributes of some of the blocks used in the experiments. The concepts symbolized by the words LAG or BIK embody the attributes of perceptually different things. Thus a yellow block of circular cross section is classified with a red block of square cross section. These objects are perceptually very different but on the criterion of classification adopted by the experimenter they are conceptually the same. They belong, that is, in the same conceptual class. On the other hand such concepts as yellow or square do not demand this classifying of perceptually different things except insofar as there are different shades of yellow and different sizes of squares.

After an extensive research programme into the problems of classification Piaget came to very similar conclusions as Vigotsky. He found that the development of classificatory ability had a long period of growth in the child. Piaget considers that the ability to classify underlies the child's ability to think logically. Only when a child can classify unambiguously and recognize the criteria for his own classification will he have reached the stage of logical thinking. Thus while a child of nine or ten may be able to recognize that objects can be large and light in weight, or large and heavy, or small and heavy, he cannot arrive at a true understanding of specific gravity. This is because specific gravity involves the comparison of the weight of an object with the weight of the same volume of water. As E. A. Lunzer points out in the introduction to the report of the work on classification,* it is one thing to be unambiguous about the properties of a thing when it exists or can be imagined to exist (a familiar object used in an experiment) but it is another thing to be unambiguous about the properties of a thing which can only be imagined or constructed from the given properties (in this case the weight of an equal volume of displaced water). To construct an object from its given properties involves the complete *abstraction* of the properties of the object from its physical reality.

Piaget uses the expressions *intension* and *extension* to refer to the processes involved in classification. Intension refers to the properties common to a set of elements: Piaget suggests that a grasp of intension harks back to the sensory-motor level since the actual observable physical similarities among the elements are the important aspects of intension. The child, at a relatively early age, is able to cope with the intensive aspect of classification as in the example of specific gravity because the properties of weight and size are observable physical attributes of actual things. Extension, on the other hand, refers to the process of abstraction of the essential defining properties of a given class. Although little children may be able to cope with the intensive aspect of classification

* INHELDER, B. and PIAGET, J.: *The Early Growth of Logic in the Child.* Trans. LUNZER, E. A. and PAPERT, D., Routledge and Kegan Paul, 1964.

they will be less successful with the extensive aspect. This is because they are still very much dependent upon the concrete and if they try to extend the defining attributes of an exemplar of a class concept to embrace other exemplars they can only do this through the actual concrete appearance of the exemplars. This means that they can only pay attention to such things as contiguity or pattern (what Piaget calls graphic collections which they can actually perceive). Thus children at this stage produce collections and complexes as Vigotsky discovered. Only later when they can deliberately and consistently abstract from the concrete exemplar its defining properties and use them in categorizing other material can true classification take place. In order to abstract the defining attributes of an exemplar of a class concept and carry them over to other possible exemplars language seems to be essential. Thus while the intensive aspect of class concepts may be possible without the use of language, the extensive aspect seems to depend on symbolic representation. Piaget considers the coordination of intension and extension to be the key feature in classificatory behaviour. Vigotsky did not approach the problem in the same way as Piaget but there is a great deal of similarity in their findings.

Other research workers studying classificatory behaviours have, in general, found that classification can be carried out without the use of language, but with increasing complexity (and therefore increasing abstraction) language becomes essential. In most cases it is considered that the ability to classify is the basis for complex logical thinking.

The importance of investigations into concept formation is to demonstrate convincingly that the child acquires a view of the world recognizably similar to that of the adult only gradually. He is not born with a ready-made set of concepts, the characteristic feature of adult thought. Conceptual thought is a higher form of thought than the non-conceptual thought of the young child. Adult thought, because of its conceptual character, is far more versatile and of much wider application. Because the word is the carrier of the concept it assumes great importance. It is important because it enables the concept to be crystallized. If one tries to form any concept even by contemplating abstract geometrical designs, one often finds that the best way to pin the concept down is to fix it with a word.

Language is also important because in real life the adult imposes on the child the patterns of speech appropriate to conceptual thought. The child acquires true conceptualization only gradually, but as we have seen, without the influence of language used conceptually, it is conceivable that the child in our society would stay at the level of the Bororo and not progress further than thinking in complexes. The adaptation to the environment flowing from thinking in complexes cannot but be at a lower level than when conceptualizing begins to take place. As an illustration of this we may take the example from Vigotsky of the child who says *before* for both before and after, or *tomorrow* for both tomorrow and yesterday. The child is here thinking in complexes. He has not grasped the concept as an adult and he associates the two situations because there is an associative link between them. A related example is the common confusion of *borrow* and *lend* by young children.

In the face of evidence of the relatively primitive nature of the child's thought, teachers have asked whether or not they can do anything to help children to acquire concepts. In essence, the whole of education works towards this end. However, the direct teaching of concepts does not work. Merely *telling* the child will, in Vigotsky's words: '. . . accomplish nothing but empty verbalism, a parrot-like repetition of words by the child, simulating a knowledge of the corresponding concepts but actually covering up a conceptual vacuum.' In the next chapter we consider experiments on the teaching of concepts to school children. The general conclusion that emerges from this research supports Vigotsky's contention: it is impossible to relay concepts from teacher to pupil. This, of course, is precisely what it attempted in rote learning. To foster real conceptual learning the teacher must give the child controlled experience involving the use of new concepts in familiar contexts so that he gradually builds up accurate notions of the concepts. We discuss this procedure at some length in the next chapter; we might, however, at this juncture, consider that although the child might build up concepts through his own unguided experience, they would be few and probably less complex than those formed under the teacher's guidance. For example, the whole range of mathematical and scientific concepts would be beyond his grasp. The teacher, therefore, plays a vital role in the development of children's concepts by providing suitably selected and arranged experiences which form the raw material of the concepts and without which they will be empty and valueless for future learning.

A key feature of conceptual learning is that it has significance wider than that of any specific situation. Language is the main instrument whereby the significance of learned behaviour is generalized and extended in scope and complexity. And yet, paradoxically, it can be a real obstacle to meaningful learning if used consciously or unconsciously by the teacher to cover up a conceptual vacuum. The difficulty is that ostensibly the child has adapted his behaviour to accord with adult procedures, but in fact has made only a partial, or even an incorrect, adaptation. Piaget's work is, of course, particularly illuminating here, but some of the work on the formation of scientific concepts mentioned in the next chapter is of interest. We see, through these investigations, time and again concrete evidence that the child's 'correct' reactions in a given situation are in fact wrong and undetected only because they have the verbal trappings appropriate to the situation. To adapt Margaret Mead's example of the Manus child who would drown if he had not acquired conservation of weight, we might say that the child who had acquired the verbalizings appropriate to conservation of weight (see Chapter 6) including the ability to get sums right, would nevertheless come to grief in the real life situation of the Manus child, where what is needed is not the appropriate automatic verbal response but a true knowledge of the concept.

On the other hand, once a child has had the basic experience of reality to make a body of concepts really meaningful he will be able to use these concepts as a basis for future learning. He will be able to absorb these concepts into an organized body of previously acquired concepts so that verbal learning in the classroom will be meaningful for him. It will thus be possible for the teacher in the secondary school to use teaching techniques which are highly verbal and do not depend to any great extent on the concrete. However, should the teacher introduce a new subject to the children, which cannot make use of existing concepts, he will have to do his best to give them the necessary experience of reality upon which to build the concepts relevant to the new field of learning. The secondary school is able to make greater use of verbal learning than the primary school since secondary children have in general had greater experience than those in the primary school and they will have therefore acquired a more comprehensive body of concepts upon which to base their learning. They will, also, of course, have reached the stage of formal operations and be able to reason by hypothesis without being dependent on the presence of the concrete object.

Concept attainment

Once a child has reached the stage where he is capable of reasoning by hypothesis his thinking makes ever increasing use of concepts. By the time he is adult he will have formed a complex repertory of concepts. He will not always think conceptually but when faced with new situations or with new phenomena he will seek to impose some order on them drawing on his stock of concepts. When a situation arises where his existing stock of concepts is inadequate to cope with the new phenomena he will have to form new concepts to enable him to cope with the new situation. The problem of an adult faced with the need to enlarge his stock of concepts is different from that of a child who is learning to conceptualize. The adult is already sophisticated in this way of thinking and will approach the problem with a certain expertise: he will adopt certain strategies to help him to acquire the concepts. The process of acquiring additional concepts is called *concept attainment* in distinction to *concept formation* which is our chief concern when we are considering the way children learn to think conceptually.

J. S. Bruner and his associates have made an authoritative

study of the attainment of class concepts.* They presented adult subjects with the task of discovering the defining attributes of a concept when presented with a succession of objects some of which exemplified the concept and some of which did not. The examples used were eighty-one cards with different geometrical figures and borders printed on them. There were, for example, a card with one green circle, a card with two green circles, cards with one, two, or three black circles or crosses or squares. All cards had one, two, or three borders. In all there were 255 possible ways of arranging the cards in such groups as 'all cards with three circles', or all cards with one border, or all cards with black crosses and three borders. The experimenter selects one concept such as we have suggested and then shows the subject a card which exemplifies the concept. The subject is told that some of the cards in the total display of eighty-one cards exemplify the concept, others do not. His task is to choose cards from the array one at a time to test whether or not they are exemplars of the concept and eventually decide what the concept is. He is told after each choice of card whether or not it exemplifies the concept. He may offer a hypothesis as to what the concept is after any card although he is not asked to do so but is told to reach the concept as efficiently as possible and may select the cards in any order he chooses.

There are two main important strategies for arriving at the correct concept. In the first case there is *scanning strategy*. Using this method the subject frames one or more hypotheses about part of the concept exemplified by the first card. He selects, that is, one or more aspects of the card as being crucial features of the concept. So long as other cards which are examples of the concept show the same features he maintains his hypothesis or hypotheses. When he meets a card which contradicts a hypothesis he discards it and seeks another which is consistent with the cards he has so far seen.

When the subject tries to scan with all the possibilities in mind it is called *simultaneous scanning*. As may be well imagined this is a

* BRUNER, J. S., GOODNOW, J. J., and AUSTIN, G. A.: *A Study of Thinking*, Wiley (N.Y.), 1956.

very difficult procedure for the subject needs to deal with many independent hypotheses and carry them in his memory. If on the other hand he scans with one hypothesis in mind at a time, that is, using *successive scanning*, he reduces very much the difficulty of the task. However, at the same time, the procedure approaches more nearly trial and error with the subject trying out a hypothesis directly rather than trying to arrive at the defining principles of the concept by a systematic logical approach.

The other main strategy is the *focusing* strategy. Here the subject chooses a card which exemplifies the concept and uses it as a focus or example. He then makes a sequence of choices which alters either one or more of the attributes of the first card to test whether the change leads to another example of the concept or not. The *safest* strategy is to change one attribute of the concept at a time and this method is what Bruner called *conservative focusing*. This method ensures that each choice will produce some information which is of direct value to the subject but it does mean that he may have to go through a very large number of cards before he reaches his goal. The other approach to focusing whereby more than one attribute of the focusing card is changed is called *focus gambling* and this does carry the risk that although one might, by taking a chance on varying more than one attribute at a time, reach the solution much more quickly than by use of conservative focusing, there is also the chance that one might take longer. This follows because by varying the attributes to be changed more than one at a time the subject is placed in a quandary when he chooses a card which is not in the concept category he is looking for. When he chooses such a card he can get no information to help him see wherein the original correct card exemplifies the concept. In such a case he has to discard the card as evidence or revert to a scanning procedure.

Bruner found in his experiments that the majority of his subjects chose focusing to arrive at the defining principles of the concept. Focusing avoids the strain of simultaneous scanning and the trial and error nature of successive scanning; it is particularly useful when time is limited and in fact 63% of subjects who used focusing techniques under timed conditions were successful as compared with 37% who used scanning techniques.

What is the relevance of this work for the teacher? In the first place it should be borne in mind that the experimental conditions were highly artificial. Under normal conditions we are not subjected to such a heavy bombardment of instances and non-instances of concepts among which to discriminate. In addition we normally experience instances and non-instances of new concepts in a familiar environment which gives us a great deal of help in the attainment of new concepts. However, bearing in mind these facts we can derive some pointers which should be of use in understanding the way in which children in the secondary school are likely to attack the problem of concept attainment.

We might, for example, take note of the difficulty posed when a very large number of examples and non-examples of a concept are presented. The sheer enormity of the task of carrying a large number of hypotheses in the memory from one discrimination to another will deter most people from attempting the most abstract approach of simultaneous scanning. The teacher will therefore be well advised if he wishes the children to use this method, to ensure that the number of examples and non-examples of the concept to be attained is kept fairly low. If, on the other hand, he has not the same control over the presentation of stimuli so that the most likely strategy to be used is a focusing strategy, he should give some thought as to whether he prefers the children to take the long, safe route of conservative focusing or whether it would be more useful for them to adopt a focus gambling approach. If the latter is likely to be used the teacher should attempt to keep to a minimum the non-examples of the concept because these are the possible sources of difficulty. As we shall see when we discuss programmed learning, if we keep error low in the early stages of learning the children will build up the concept and then will be able to discriminate non-examples more readily later. It would be difficult, if not impossible, to suggest a *recommended* best approach. Much will depend on the circumstances in which the problem is presented. But this is a field where the teacher has some influence and it will often be up to him as to which strategies for concept attainment the children adopt. Even though the work described very briefly here is from circumstances different from the classroom, and even though the findings apply only to one aspect of conceptual thinking, a teacher who takes note of Bruner's work will be better able to help his pupils in attaining class concepts than one who does not (see page 225).

Thought and action

The acquisition by man of conceptual thought invests his apprehension of his environment with a depth and complexity completely beyond the range of any other animal. As we have seen, however, this understanding of the world is built up through man's interaction with reality; it does not grow spontaneously. Similarly, conceptual thought, once developed, does not become cut off from the real world without becoming sterile. That is, the whole function of the complexities of thought is to render man's adaptation to his environment more effective. As systems of conditional reflexes regulate the activity of the higher animals, such as the mammals, at a much higher level of complexity than the primitive organisms, which are largely controlled by unconditional reflexes; so man's thinking makes possible a still higher level of self regulation. Pavlov suggested that the main factor in this process of self regulation is one's own speech. Language, in this view, not only acts as the main agent of conceptual thought, it is the medium which links conceptual thought to practical activity. It would, of course, be wrong to suggest that there is a one-way process from thought to activity or from activity to thought; the two interact. As children acquire more complex patterns of thought they acquire more complex patterns of self-regulatory activity. Since Pavlov, investigations have been made into the way in which speech acts to regulate our behaviour; much remains to be done but we now consider the findings of research in this field.

Speech and self regulation

If we consider the beginnings of language in the child we can see how speech begins to control behaviour at a very early age.

The speech which controls behaviour at this stage is not the child's own, however, but that of the adult. M. M. Lewis illustrates this, citing the case of a child aged 1 year, 1 month, 5 days [20].

'The child was playing on the floor. His ball was in a corner of the room, where it had lain unheeded by him all day. His mother said, *Baby, where's ballie?* The child turned and crawled towards the ball. On the way there he halted at the coal-box, a favourite plaything. His mother repeated the question, whereupon he resumed his journey, seized the ball and looked up at her.'

As Lewis points out, this is a remarkable event. The mother has directed the behaviour of the child towards part of his environment which was outside his immediate centre of attention. But it is not a spontaneous reaction; the adult has paved the way for the emergence of this reaction by many months of speech activity involving the child. From now on, the child is more and more directed by the speech of the adult. Control by physical means gives place to control through the medium of speech.

This is only the first stage in the development of speech as a regulator of activity. From being the instrument with which the adult regulates the activity of the child, it becomes the instrument whereby the child regulates his own behaviour. In order to see how speech assumes the role of regulator of behaviour we need to consider the main stages in the progress of speech development.

Speech, as is suggested in the example from Lewis's observations, originates and evolves in social interaction with the mother. Early speech is communication at a primitive level, linked to the comfort and discomfort sounds made by the child in the first months of life. From the very early days these sounds have a social function. Before the child is able to use words he finds that sound has the effect of changing his environment. His cries will produce food, or perhaps comfort. These early sounds fulfil many functions and the adult is not always sure what the cries of the child indicate. Is the crying indicative of hunger, or is it a carelessly fastened safety pin? As speech develops, its functions become more differentiated; the child uses words which refer unequivocally to things within the shared experience of the child and the mother. Language is still, however, fulfilling a social function.

The next stage in speech development sees speech increasingly used for the directing of the child's own activity. Words originally used in social contexts are now used in a similar way to plan the child's own activity. Another example from M. M. Lewis will illustrate this phenomenon in the child of almost two and a half years.

'Playing the game of hiding a pencil in a book: *Ever can you be, little pencil?*'

'Looking for his toy, "Billy-boy": *Billy-boy, where Garkie put it? Where is it?*'

The term applied to speech of this type is egocentric speech. Piaget originally considered it to be a mere accompaniment to the child's activity; a sort of babbling which served no obviously useful purpose. Vigotsky's researches revealed that in fact the child uses language in this way to direct his own activity. In the example given, the child's activity is impelled along by the language he uses. Vigotsky demonstrated this function of speech in a number of experiments. Children were observed in various situations and their speech was noted. In one experiment children were drawing. Just as a child would be preparing to draw, it would find the pencil missing. At such a moment the amount of egocentric speech almost doubled. The child '. . . would try to grasp and to remedy the situation in talking to himself: "Where's the pencil? I need a blue pencil. Never mind, I'll draw with the red one and wet it with water; it will become dark and look like blue." ' Although egocentric speech is speech for the child himself, it is still of a social nature. Vigotsky also showed that when children were in a situation where they thought no one could hear them, their egocentric speech disappeared.

Egocentric speech gradually becomes more abbreviated and elliptical. In ordinary speech the speaker has to make explicit the subject of his statement; when one is thinking or talking to oneself there is no need for this. One's speech or thought can be completely predicative (i.e. the subject need not be stated). Abbreviated, predicative speech is speech on the way to becoming internalized. Later, egocentric speech disappears to be replaced by inner speech and eventually by thought. Inner speech, according to this view, is by no means the equivalent of social speech. The movement towards the elliptical, seen in late egocentric speech, continues, so that inner speech loses its phonetic aspect and becomes entirely semantic. As speech becomes internalized, its functions as a director of activity are internalized, so that the process of regulation started by the mother's speech and continued by the child's egocentric speech, is replaced by control through the internal flow of meanings and concepts. These, it is suggested, are the mechanisms of self-regulation characteristic of man.

The work of Vigotsky has been repeated and checked by other scientists who have confirmed his findings. Luria, who was a colleague of Vigotsky, has continued his work and has examined the way in which man's use of speech changes the way he adapts to his environment and becomes the prime factor in the regulation of his activity. His research suggests that the principles of generalization and discrimination, of growth and inhibition of conditional reflexes, assume a different form when speech is involved. This does not mean that the ordinary processes of conditioning no longer apply, but that when language is involved it changes the nature of the learning process. As we have seen in Chapter 5, the principles of stimulus generalization are modified by language. The children who had been trained to make a response to the word *doctor* would, without language, have probably generalized their responses to *dicktor* as would an animal. Certainly there would have been no tendency for the response to be generalized to *physician*. When generalization to *physician* occurs, the semantic significance of the words takes precedence over their phonic properties. Thus when new connections are being built up man does not react automatically to the physical properties of stimuli, but to their conceptual significance.

Luria demonstrates this by establishing a reflex by presenting a child or an adult with a neutral stimulus such as a red light followed by the order *press* (the bulb on a recording apparatus). The subject is then shown a light of another colour unaccompanied by reinforcement (the order *press*). An animal in a similar situation would either respond or not respond; man's reaction is not so immediate. A young child asks the question when he sees the different-coloured light: 'Shall I press for this too?' The adult makes a verbal generalization, either: 'I press for red and not for yellow,' or: 'I press for a light of any colour.' Once a verbal rule is made it modifies all subsequent reactions. The stimulus is now '. . . not a mere signal but *an item of generalized information*'. We might phrase this in everyday terms by saying that we now attend to the meaning of the stimulus.

One of the effects of this process is that once a pattern of responses has been established to a class of stimuli, any new stimulus belonging to the same class will evoke a similar response, even when the stimulus is presented for the first time. Conversely, whereas an unreinforced response in an animal dies away, in man this need not happen. The acceptance of a particular stimulus as a member of a class to which a pattern of behaviour is established, will itself act as a reinforcement. As Skinner has said: 'An obvious fact about behaviour is that it is almost never invariably reinforced.' In Luria's terms we should say 'directly reinforced', but it may well be that because of the symbolic function of speech, the reinforcement of one activity in a class of actions will reinforce the activity connected with the whole class.

Once a conditional reflex is set up in an animal it is generally very difficult to reshape and it is extremely persistent. Skinner gives examples of pigeons which, after a period of three years, responded to a stimulus in exactly the same way as they did when the responses were established. However, experiments with children and adults have demonstrated that in man this process is quite different. If the reinforcement is changed, say, from *press* to *don't press* the reversal is made at once. This, of course, renders the behaviour of man far more adaptive and versatile than that of other animals. It is interesting to note, however, that this does not apply to very young children (see below).

The important thing to note here, is that the elementary properties of stimuli as simple signals is transformed by language.

Thus, although the processes of conditioning still operate, when the symbolic processes of language are involved, the significance of stimuli can be changed at once, even though the physical properties are the same. In Luria's experiments, children would change from pressing when they saw a light, to not pressing, even though the same light was shown: the only change in the situation being that the experimenter said to the children *don't press*. Children at this stage are already greatly ahead of all other animals in the versatility of their behaviour and capacity for learning.

Luria's investigations into the way in which speech assumes the role of regulator of behaviour, suggest that it falls into a number of stages. In the first stage the speech of the child is insufficiently developed for it to regulate the child's motor reactions.

A child of about eighteen months told to take its stockings *off* when it is putting them *on* is unable to do so. Similarly, although it is possible to start a child of eighteen months pressing the bulb on a recording apparatus by telling him, verbal instructions cannot stop him. However, when the experiment is modified to include a feedback signal the situation changes. Now when the child, following instructions, presses when the light appears, his action puts out the light. He is then aware that his action is at an end and he ceases to press. If the feedback system is now disconnected, the earlier lack of clear-cut responses recurs and he presses when he should not. Thus, although a child of this age is capable of a voluntary self-regulatory act, this act is not entirely under verbal control.

In the second stage the regulatory efficiency of speech is still weak. If a child between about three and three and a half years is asked to press for a red light and not for a green, he is incapable of doing so. Although he understands the instructions, he can't help responding to any light.

If the child is now asked merely to say *press* or *don't press* in response to the signal, he has little difficulty in doing this. He can also cope with the experiment which demands that he responds to one light with the word *press* accompanied by the action, and to the other with the response (not pressing) unaccompanied by the phrase. If he is then asked to respond to the green light (by not pressing) and at the same time to say *don't press*, the child presses without realizing it. Speech impels him to action, functioning as a signal devoid of semantic significance. Only later, at about age five, does this *impulsive* reaction to speech weaken to be replaced by behaviour accurately regulated by a more developed speech ability. This may be considered to be the third stage.

Finally the stage is reached when the child ceases to use external speech and regulates his behaviour by internal speech. Now: 'The verbal analysis of the situation begins to play an important role in the establishment of new connections: the child orients himself to the given signals with the help of the rules he has verbally formulated for himself, this abstracting and generalizing function of speech mediates the stimuli acting upon the child and turns the process of elaboration of temporary connections into the complex, "highest self-regulating system" [human behaviour].'

Briefly, the regulation of the child's behaviour follows a series of steps. In the first place the child is regulated physically by the adult. Later the adult is able to control the child's activity by speech. At first, however, the speech has only an impelling function; acting almost as a signal and nothing else. Speech will initiate activity but this activity once initiated takes precedence over further instructions. This is because the motor activity (in the example above, taking off his stockings) evoked by speech is more powerful than the semantic aspect of speech. In the example, the semantic significance of 'take *off* your stockings' is less powerful than the motor activity of the child. In the next stage the semantic aspect of speech begins to play a decisive role. The child now attends to the *meaning* of the words and regulates his activity on the basis of their semantic significance. By now speech is becoming internalized and the child does not need the reinforcement of his own externally heard speech. This is the prototype of adult self regulation.

It is interesting to note that, when recordings are made of

muscular activity of the speech organs in sub-vocal speech, activity is noted only in the first stages of internalization. Later no muscular activity is noted. However, should a difficult problem be presented, the muscular tensions characteristic of earlier stages reappear. In ordinary children this is registered in the mechanisms of speech, but in deaf-mute children it is registered in the muscle tension of the hand, because gesture is connected with this and gesture in such children often takes the place of speech.

Luria discovered that in all the experiments he and his associates carried out, a crucial stage was reached between the ages of four and five years. At this age speech is internalized, voluntary movements are developed and performed and Luria considered that there must be some intimate relation to maturation. At this time the child begins to organize his behaviour without external reinforcement, which, Luria suggests, may mean that an internal system of feedback has been developed.

Self regulation and the elaboration of complex modes of thought are thus both profoundly affected by language. Together they present a picture of the human organism achieving a delicate and highly elaborate state of dynamic equilibrium with the environment. Whereas other animals are dependent almost entirely upon the external world for the regulation of their behaviour, that is, their behaviour is controlled by the mechanisms of conditioning which we considered earlier, man assumes the regulation of his own activity. He obeys generalized rules of behaviour. He responds to his own commands. He becomes capable of *voluntary activity*.

Thus through the medium of language and conceptual thought man is able to regulate his behaviour according to pre-formulated strategies. The child develops from the stage where his activity is almost entirely regulated by the immediate environmental forces, to a stage where he is able to plan his activity taking into consideration generalized laws about the nature of the world.

Language and cognitive development

Bruner has made an interesting contribution to our ideas on the course of intellectual development which links many of the ideas of Piaget, Luria, and Vigotsky. He suggests that man has developed skills which enable him to 'represent' the environment to himself in three main ways. The importance of representation is that it enables us to deal effectively with recurrent regularities in the environment. The names Bruner gives to these modes of representation are *enactive representation, iconic representation,* and *symbolic representation.* Bruner suggests that these three modes of representation appear in the child in the order given.*

By enactive representation Bruner means the mode of representing past events through appropriate motor responses. He points out that we cannot give adequate descriptions of familiar pavements or floors over which we habitually walk, nor do we have much of an image of what they are like. 'Such segments of our environment – bicycle riding, tying knots, aspects of driving – get represented in our muscles so to speak.' Such enactive representations are much the same as the motor schemas to which we have referred earlier. Through repeated encounters with the regularities of the environment we build up these virtually automatic abbreviated patterns of motor activity which we run off as units when in the appropriate situation.

Bruner illustrates enactive representation by drawing on the work of Emerson and similar work by Werner. In a series of experiments children were asked to place a ring on a board with seven rows and six columns. They had to place the ring in the same position as a ring on the experimenter's board. The child's board could be placed in various positions relative to the experimenter's: right next to it, 90° rotated away from it, placed face to face with it so that the child had to turn full around to make his placement. Children from three to twelve were tested. The older the child the better his performance but when the board was alongside the experimenter's the young children did nearly as well as the older ones. The more they had to turn the greater the

* BRUNER, J. S.: in *American Psychologist,* January 1964.

difficulty the young ones had in coping with the problem. They were clearly depending on their bodily orientation to solve the problem. Older children succeeded even when they had to turn fully around, either by imagery (discussed below) or by carrying symbolic self-instruction back to their own board, by saying which row and which column the ring was on.

Iconic representation takes place when we build up a 'mental image' of things experienced. Generally such images are composite, being formed from a number of experiences of similar situations. Only rarely are these images 'photographic' as in the *eidetic imagery* of young children who are sometimes able to reconstruct with great accuracy the scene depicted in a picture after it has been exposed and then removed. Little is known of the way in which mental images are formed but Bruner points out that it seems essential for a certain amount of motor skill and practice to take place before one can form an image to represent a sequence of acts. The reader might care to try this by learning a maze in the way outlined in Chapter 3 and at different stages of learning trying to imagine the path of the maze. In learning situations such as this adults are generally unable to form an image which can be used to solve the problem until they have mastered and practised the task by successive manipulation.

A great difficulty in discussing iconic representation is that it shades gradually into symbolic representation. As might be seen in the experiment cited above dealing with children's ability to copy the experimenter's placement of the ring on the board, a child could use either an image of the experimenter's board or just remember the number of the row and column. It would be very difficult, however, to say categorically that the child used one technique or the other; it is possible that a combination of the two was used. It is the transition from iconic to symbolic representation to which Bruner devotes most of his attention.

Symbolic representation, in Bruner's terms, has the characteristics which we have discussed at some length earlier in our consideration of the nature of language and its importance for human learning. Bruner considers that '. . . the translation of experience into symbolic form, with its attendant means of achieving remote reference, transformation, and combination, opens up realms of intellectual possibility that are orders of magnitude beyond the most powerful image forming system'. He gives accounts of experiments with young children which illustrate the way in which symbolic representation brings about this transformation.

One experiment carried out by J. Huttenlocher was performed with children between six and twelve. Two light switches were placed before the child; each one could be in one of two positions. There was also an electric light bulb. The child was asked to tell on the basis of turning one switch only, what turns the light on. There are four ways in which the problem can be presented. In the first the light is off and when the child turns the switch it comes on. In the second it is on and when the child turns the switch it goes off. In the third case the light is on and when the switch is turned nothing happens. In the fourth case the light is off and when the switch is turned nothing happens. In this experiment the nature of the steps needed to reach the solution is the same whichever way the problem is presented. The difference between the four cases is that in the first case the child has only to realize that the position to which the switch is moved is responsible for switching the light on. The remaining cases demand more than one connected inference. For example in the last case the child has to take four steps. First, he has to reject the present position of the switch he has just turned. Then he has to reject the original position of the switch. Third, he has to reject the present position of the switch he has not turned (because the light is off). Fourth, he accepts the alternative position of the switch he has not turned as being the one which puts the light on. Only when the child can integrate these four steps can he solve this problem. The results of the experiment show that six-year-old children do very nearly as well as twelve-year-olds on the first case (the on–off display). In general the more inferential steps needed the poorer the results of the six-year-old children. The twelve-year-olds, however, coped in very similar ways with the tasks no matter how many inferences were involved.

Another experiment by F. A. Mosher, the 'Twenty Questions'

experiment, quoted by Bruner makes the same point. He asked children from eight to eleven to find out by 'yes–no' questions what caused a car to go off the road and hit a tree. Two kinds of questions are broadly possible. On the one hand there are the constraint-seeking questions such as: 'Was it night time?' followed up by other appropriate questions. Or, on the other hand, there are the questions which test hypotheses directly, such as: 'Did a bee fly in the window and sting the man on the eye and make him go off the road and hit a tree?' The younger children, in the main, made direct tests of hypotheses; the older made great use of constraint-seeking questions. When the younger children on one of the rare occasions asked a constraint-seeking question, they followed up immediately by trying a hypothesis. Thus younger children try to solve the problem by a series of guesses, whereas the older children try to adopt a systematic approach that gradually builds up and integrates information in a structure that will eventually produce the solution. The younger child cannot do this. As Bruner points out, the younger children are seeking one-step substitutes for direct sense experience, the older ones are cumulating information in a very different and more complex way.

One other type of experiment reported by Bruner which illustrates in a most interesting way the powerful influence of speech on cognitive processes uses Piaget-type experiments with certain variations. In one of these experiments children aged from four to seven years were presented with the classical problem of the pouring of water from one container to a container of different cross section and it was determined which children had achieved conservation. Next, two standard beakers were shown and the children agreed that they both had the same amount of water. A third, wider beaker was then introduced and the three beakers were screened, except for their tops. The experimenter then poured the water from the standard glass to the wider one without the children being able to see the level of the water. When asked now which container had most water there was a striking increase in the number of children showing conservation. When the screen was removed all the four-year-old children reverted to their original judgement and said there was more in the tall glass. However, virtually all the five-year-olds stuck to their judgements and although they said 'it looks as though there is more in that [the standard] one', they argued that it must be the same 'because it was only poured from there to there'. A few minutes later another test was given this time using a tall, narrow container and the two standard ones. The four-year-olds were unaffected by their previous experience and showed no conservation. Conservation in the five-year-olds rose from 20% in the pre-test to 70% while conservation in the six- and seven-year olds rose from 50% to 90%.

How can we interpret these results? Bruner suggests that by activating the children's speech (symbolic representation), that is, having them 'say' their description in the absence of the things to be described, there would be less chance of the visual display producing an iconic representation which would then become dominant and interfere with the operation of symbolic processes. This accords with much of what we have said earlier with regard to children's speech. For the teacher it suggests that when there is a likelihood of the visual display misleading the children, getting them to 'say' what is going on will help them to develop the more effective form of thinking, that is symbolic representation.

What can we learn from these experiments? Bruner suggests two main conclusions. The first is that as children mature: '. . . they are able to use indirect information based on forms of information processing other than the act of pointing to what is immediately present. Second . . . they seem able to cumulate information into a structure that can be operated upon by rules that transcend simple association by similarity and contiguity. In the case of "Twenty Questions", the rule is best described as implication – that knowing one thing implies certain other things and eliminates still others. In the experiments with the light switches, it is that if the present state does not produce the effect, then there is a system for tracing back to the other states that cause the light to go on.' Bruner considers that in effect, by these processes the child constructs a manipulable model of the environment governed by the rules of implication which enables him to go beyond the here and now and to integrate longer series of events.

This point of view is much the same as we have already when we have discussed the way in which language transforms human behaviour and it is not surprising to find that Bruner urges that the fundamental feature in the development of the ability to construct the models of the environment to which he refers, is the development of the language ability of the child. Without language, i.e. symbolic representation, man is at the mercy of the immediate environment; with it, in Bruner's words, is linked 'a unique set of powers to man's capacity'.

What is the significance of all this to the teacher? It seems clear that the use of language can transform the way children adapt to their environment. The use of language probably forms the basis of reasoning, and therefore children should be encouraged in its use. Children are not born with the ability for reasoning or for using language. It will develop, in Bruner's words, only through 'exposure to the specialized environment of a culture'. In view of the prime importance of language in the development of complicated techniques of coping with the environment the cultivation by the teacher of modes of symbolic expression of increasing complexity is the crucial factor in the cognitive development of children.

Language deficiency

Language, we may see, is of great significance in the formation of our mental processes and also in the development of our patterns of behaviour. It might well be inferred, therefore, that any deficiency in the development of language would cause difficulty in the mastery of complex systems of thought. A clear illustration of this may be seen in the case of deaf children, who, if their disability is not detected become retarded intellectually.

Cases are known where children with severe deafness have been diagnosed mentally defective and sent to mental deficiency hospitals. Apart from any pathological conditions in the child, environmental influences will clearly affect the quality of the child's speech and thereby the quality of his thought and the versatility of his behaviour.

Luria has made a classical study of the way in which unfavourable environmental conditions operate to produce speech retardation, which, in turn, produces a low level of mental life [22]. He was able to study identical twins five years of age who, through a combination of unstimulating home circumstances, and the fact that they played almost entirely alone, had stayed at a very primitive level of speech development. Since they had little contact with adults, they had had no encouragement to talk and there had been little progress towards the symbolic use of words. Instead there had developed what Luria calls *synpraxic* speech. This is a primitive form of speech in which the child cannot detach the word from the object or the action. In the case of the twins their communication with each other consisted of words and actions inextricably mixed. Words on their own had no permanent meaning and could only be understood in a concrete situation. They had different meanings according to the situation in which they were used and the tone in which they were spoken. Luria gives an example of the use of one of their names. ' "Lioshia" could mean: "I [Lioshia] am playing nicely" – or – "Let him [Liosha] go for a walk" – or – "Look [Liosha] what I have done".' Luria found that synpraxic speech accounted for over 90% of the children's speech. There was almost no speech of a narrative or planning nature. The speech of the twins was also autonomous; that is, because it did not possess the developed system of normal language, their understanding of other people's speech was rudimentary. They had, in effect, a private system of communication but little removed from rudimentary signalling.

According to Luria the twins were perfectly normal in many ways nor did they seem to be mentally retarded. However, it was interesting to see that they never played with other children and when they played together the content of their play was always very primitive and monotonous. In general it consisted entirely of the manipulation of the toys, there was never any attempt at construction. Luria considered that language deficiency was the cause of their backwardness. Lacking the power of abstraction and of generalization they lacked the abilities which are crucial in the organization of planned complex activity.

The twins were separated and placed in different nursery schools. One twin was given special remedial treatment for his speech deficiency. Both twins made progress and the synpraxic speech died away. The important thing from the teacher's point of view, was that the twin given remedial treatment made more rapid progress than the other and, when the report of the investigation was made (after ten months), was still significantly in advance of his brother.

Luria comments: 'Even more significant was the fact that the whole structure of the mental life of both twins was simultaneously and sharply changed. Once they acquired an objective language system, the children were able to formulate the aims of their activity verbally and after only three months we observed the beginnings of meaningful play: there arose the possibility of productive, constructive activity in the light of formulated aims, and to an important degree there were separated out a series of intellectual operations which shortly before this were only in an embryonic state.'

Luria claims that the results of the experiment demonstrate the role which speech plays in elaborating new forms of communication, but also in the calling forth of '. . . significant changes in the structure of their conscious activity, built upon the basis of verbal speech'.

Restricted and elaborated codes

Investigations carried out by B. Bernstein with English children have complemented the work of Luria and his associates. Much of what we have studied so far has naturally dealt with the younger child since it is in the early years that patterns of speech and behaviour are built up. Bernstein examines similar processes at work in older children. His work has certain affinities with Luria's work with the twins, but in the case of Bernstein the factors limiting the development of elaborate forms of speech are of a widespread social nature. He found that language deficiency was correlated with inefficient modes of thought in adolescents, which seemed to reflect social background [23].

Bernstein made a study of the effect of class differences in language upon the ability of the child. He compared the performance of boys from lower working-class homes and boys attending a famous public school on tests of verbal and non-verbal intelligence. He found that working-class boys who scored high on the non-verbal test made lower scores on the verbal test, in some cases amounting to over twenty points of I.Q. On the other hand, the scores of the boys from the public school did not show this pattern. Bernstein ascribes the discrepancy in the scores of the working class boys to their poor linguistic background.

Although by no means so serious as the deficiency described by Luria in his report on the twins, there are certain common features. We find a language closely linked with the concrete and rigid in its application. The child who lacks experience of language which is mobile and versatile, encouraging abstraction and classification, will lack the opportunity to develop the higher symbolic processes we have already considered.

In addition to restrictions imposed by the content of the language, the mode of communication also has its effect. In a way somewhat akin to the way *autonomous speech* developed in the twins in Luria's investigation, a language which depends to a great extent upon the actual social context in which it is used, develops in groups such as the family, or as Bernstein suggests, in combat units in the armed services. Following Vigotsky, Bernstein suggests that the more the subject of a dialogue is common the more will speech be condensed. Married couples of long standing, or old friends, communicate within a matrix of shared experience where the wealth of significance in a change in inflexion or an elliptical comment makes elaborate verbal expression redundant.

This form of language is likely to arise in any such intimate groupings: problems arise when this elliptical language, coupled with the lack of syntactical sophistication of much working-class speech, is the only language available to the child. As in the case of the twins, the restricted nature of the language confines children from such backgrounds to the relatively simple forms of expression. The elaboration of sophisticated concepts and the mastery of the intricate processes of generalization and classification present very great problems to such children.

Children from middle-class homes are in a very different position. Whereas in the working-class home, generally speaking, speech is constantly related to the concrete situation within the family and therefore containing a persisting, substantial common element; in the middle-class home speech is constantly seeking to shake itself free from the common ground of unverbalized experience, to express itself in individual idiosyncratic speech. The reason for this is to be seen in the parent–child relationship. As we have seen when we discussed the verbal regulation of behaviour, the child's behaviour is at first regulated by the parent. In time the child gradually takes over these regulatory functions himself. However, the functions which are assumed by the child inevitably bear the stamp of the parent. As we saw above, it is initially the parent who gives meaning to the signals from the environment and the meaning given to these signals by the middle-class parent will differ from that given by the working-class parent.

Bernstein considers the language of the lower working-class family a linguistically *restricted code*. He considers that of the middle class an *elaborated code*. He suggests the main attributes of the restricted code are its syntactical crudity, its repetitiveness, its rigid and limited use of adjectives and adverbs, short, grammatically simple, often unfinished sentences, and above all, much of the meaning is implicit and dependent upon a commonly held system of speech habits.

The elaborated code is a much more flexible instrument. It has an accurate grammar and syntax. It employs a range of subordinate clauses unknown to the restricted code. It makes much more widespread and flexible use of conjunctions, prepositions, adjectives, and adverbs. It is much more discriminating and it has a much greater potentiality of abstraction. It also differs from the restricted code in that the pronoun *I* is used frequently reinforcing the personal and individual nature of the language.

Bernstein illustrates the nature of the restricted code for the learning child. He gives an imaginary example of two conversations on a bus. A mother has a child sitting on her lap.

First conversation:

Mother: Hold on tight.
Child: Why?
Mother: Hold on tight.
Child: Why?
Mother: You'll fall.
Child: Why?
Mother: I told you to hold on tight, didn't I?

Second conversation:

Mother: Hold on tightly, darling.
Child: Why?
Mother: If you don't you will be thrown forward and you'll fall.
Child: Why?
Mother: Because if the bus suddenly stops you'll jerk forward on to the seat in front.
Child: Why?
Mother: Now darling, hold on tightly and don't make such a fuss.

As can be seen in the restricted code the symbolic function is slight; the words have little more than signal significance. With the elaborated code, a wide range of concepts is deployed, the words have elaborate semantic significance. Furthermore, as Bernstein points out, in school the language of a working-class child acts as a filter to restrict what gets through from the teacher (an elaborated code user), to the elements of the restricted code.

Following from this Bernstein concludes that the problems facing a lower working-class child in a school situation aimed at improving his language skills will be very different from that of a middle-class child. The latter has merely to *develop* his linguistic skills, the former has to *change* them. This makes it extremely difficult for the user of a restricted code to schematize the learning he is asked to make, since it is presented in the unfamiliar forms of the elaborated code. It is not dissimilar to the difficulty the twins experienced in Luria's experiment when a third person tried to communicate with them. As a result, the learning of these children will tend to be mechanical. They may be able to produce the correct answers, but, as we saw when we discussed Piaget's work, these answers do not spring from an understanding of the basic concepts involved, but are surface responses mechanically acquired, rootless and short-lived. The trouble is that the older the child gets the more difficult the problem becomes since the educational process becomes more abstract.

Bernstein's analysis suggests a reason for the discrepancies between the verbal and non-verbal intelligence scores of lower working-class children. It also bears on the fact that a high proportion of such children are in the lower classes of streamed schools, and that relatively few are selected for grammar schools. However, the fact that the two different languages are socially generated and not innate presents the teacher with the possibility of extending the language of the working-class child.

The existence of this possibility of improvement, however, does not produce a solution to the problem. The teacher has to make contact with the child and this will initially have to be through the restricted code. He will need to make this contact in similar conditions to those of the child's home. This demands small classes. Elaborated code users are better equipped to cope with large classes and formal methods; users of the restricted code need the small informal groupings. Bernstein actually suggests smaller classes for these children. This may or may not be achieved. But a small step forward may be made if teachers become aware of the enormous importance of language in the education of their pupils and of the specific difficulties of the child who uses only the restricted code.

It is likely, however, that the deleterious effects of cultural deprivation can only really be ended by changing the conditions producing them; when they are changed they can have a dramatic effect as Luria's work shows.

Summary

One of the difficulties in investigating the role of language in learning is that any investigation must rely heavily on language itself. Vigotsky sought to overcome this problem by placing the learner in a situation in which he was able to build up concepts and at the same time acquire verbal symbols for the concepts. Vigotsky was thus able to study the way in which words gradually come to stand for concepts and how they are then used in solving problems more economically than formerly.

Vigotsky found that true class concepts did not, in general, develop before adolescence: before then children use mental actions which often resemble concepts but lack their abstracting and generalizing nature. Some primitive people also use such mental actions. Piaget also studied the formation of class concepts and found, in general agreement with Vigotsky, that true classifying ability involving the genuine abstraction of a number of exemplifying attributes was very dependent upon language. Concepts cannot be transferred from the teacher to the child by simply telling. To build up adequate concepts the teacher has to arrange for learning situations which will give the child the relevant guided experience for him to acquire the concept. Lack of guidance by the teacher could result in the concept not being acquired at all, or being inadequate. Should the teacher try to transfer the concept 'ready made' to the child by 'telling' him, the child is likely to learn the word without having a grasp of the concept it symbolizes. This is rote learning, mere verbalizing which covers a conceptual vacuum.

In a study of concept attainment in adults, Bruner and his associates found that presented with exemplars and non-exemplars of class concepts, subjects employed four main methods of attaining concepts. These were simultaneous scanning, successive scanning, conservative focusing, and focus gambling. Most subjects chose focusing strategies.

Luria suggests that language is of key importance in the control of our behaviour. The child's activity is at first controlled physically by its mother. Later the mother is able to use speech to control the child's activity. The child then begins to regulate his own behaviour by talking to himself; telling himself what to do. Later his speech becomes internalized and abbreviated until eventually the child regulates his activity through his thinking. In moments of stress, however, or when faced with a difficult problem, speech activity, either internal or overt, is likely to appear.

In the early stages of speech development, the signal properties of language predominate in regulating the behaviour of the child. Later the semantic properties usually predominate. Until the semantic properties of language predominate, the regulation of the child's activity lacks flexibility and tends to have an impulsive character.

The symbolizing and conceptual nature of language modify drastically the processes of conditioning and introduce a new flexibility into the child's activities. Language makes possible the setting up of generalized classes of responses based, not only on the physical properties of stimuli, but mainly on their meaning. Thus, once a stimulus is seen to belong to a given class of stimuli it will immediately evoke the response appropriate to that class. Language also makes possible planned behaviour in which the child formulates the aims of its activity according to generalized rules about the world.

Children's ability to solve problems has been seen to improve greatly when they are able to express them symbolically using language. The more steps there are in reaching a solution to a problem the greater the need for linguistic ability. Children who have not yet developed the habit of using symbolic means of tackling problems tend to guess at solutions to problems, whereas children who use the symbolic properties of language with greater facility employ constraint seeking strategies in a systematic approach to the problem.

When language development is retarded it usually results in some form of intellectual deficiency. Luria found that a pair of twins brought up with little contact with adults, developed a form of speech in which words had virtually no symbolic content but acted merely as signals. This very primitive speech resulted in a low level of mental development, which changed drastically, when the children's speech became normal through their being separated and placed in nursery schools where they had to communicate using accepted speech forms.

Bernstein found that the non-verbal intelligence scores of working-class boys were higher than their verbal intelligence scores, whereas public school boys scored similarly on both tests. He suggests that this discrepancy may be due to the poor linguistic skills of the working-class boys.

CHAPTER 8

Learning in School

Learning and meaning

Experimental psychologists often use nonsense syllables to study aspects of learning. Such syllables are intended to be devoid of meaning so that the subject of the experiment will be learning material with which he has had no previous acquaintance. Examples of these syllables could be *lib*, *jal*, *paj*, and so on. The subject of the experiment may have to respond to the experimenter's demands by saying or writing the syllables he has previously learned. When comparisons are made between learning rates using nonsense words and meaningful material, subjects have most difficulty with nonsense words. Similar results are obtained if the experiments are concerned with the retention of learning.

Such experiments serve to stress a most important aspect of human learning that we have already discussed; the importance of the role of meaning: this applies to the classroom as well as the psychological laboratory. If we look again at the nonsense syllables, we can see that what the experimenter is investigating is not essentially the learning most characteristic of man, but rather that which is typical of the lower animals. The nonsense syllables are being used merely as aural or verbal stimuli and responses and the subject's learning is of the same character as that of the parrot learning to 'talk'. As Vigotsky says: 'A word without meaning is an empty sound, no longer part of human speech.' By seeking to remove all extraneous cues from the learning situation the experimenter removes that which is most important in human learning.

In the classroom this kind of learning is of little value. The aim of the teacher is diametrically opposed to the aim of the experimenter; he is concerned to provide as many cues as possible to facilitate learning and the main thing we gain from the experiments with nonsense learning is to ensure that as little as possible of it takes place in the classroom. This follows directly from the results of experiments which show the importance of meaning for efficient learning, and it also follows from what we have said previously about animal learning and human learning which uses the abstracting and symbolizing power of language. In the experiments using nonsense words, the learning is similar to simple conditioning. There is the least element of transfer through stimulus generalization and no chance of learning of a conceptual nature.

The learning of tables is one of the nearest approaches to the learning of nonsense syllables in school. It is not, perhaps, wholly a case of rote learning without any abstraction at all, since the idea of number is itself an abstraction. Once the child understands *one*, or *two*, or any number unconnected with any concrete object, he has begun to abstract. In the case of the recitation of the tables, however, all too often the stimulus *twice two are* . . . elicit the response *four* in a manner similar to the response of an animal in a conditioning experiment, or the parrot doing its tricks in its cage.

Other examples of rote learning, where the amount of generalizing and conceptualizing is very low or nil, may be seen in such cases as the learning of the names of capes and bays which passed for geography in nineteenth century state schools, or in the learning of dates in history. In neither case is the child likely to gain any concept of a geographical or historical nature. In history, it has been demonstrated that young children have very unclear concepts of time, as we have already seen, so that the linking of the names of kings and queens (stimuli) with the responses (dates) is again at the lowest level of learning with virtually no generalization or conceptualization. One of the most splendid examples of this type of learning is provided by Dickens in his novel *Hard Times*. In school, the teacher, Mr Gradgrind, has just asked pupil Bitzer to tell him what a horse is. Bitzer replies:

Horse – quadruped, gramnivorous, forty teeth – namely, twenty-four grinders, four eye-teeth, and twelve incisive. Sheds coat in spring, in marshy countries sheds hoofs too. Hoofs hard, but requiring to be shod with iron. Age known by marks in mouth.

Bitzer makes the required response to the teacher's stimulus but any concepts he may have about what a horse actually *is* will have been formed outside the classroom.

The teaching of concepts

It may be that there is a place in school for some learning of a rote nature; the case of the tables may be one example, but before any teacher uses rote learning he should consider whether the learning has any value *in itself* since the amount of transfer into other fields is likely to be limited.

In general, however, the teacher should aim to make the learning of the children as meaningful as possible. This involves arranging the educational environment so that the changes in behaviour, which he wishes to produce in the children, necessitate their acquiring concepts which will have the potentiality of transfer to related situations. Concepts do not arise spontaneously; they are formed out of the child's experience of grappling with different aspects of his environment. To enable children to form appropriate concepts the teacher must arrange for the experiences of the children to be relevant and in sufficient variety to ensure as full a grasp of the concept as possible.

It is likely, however, that it will not be enough for the teacher merely to arrange a variety of experiences for children to encounter, possibly fortuitously, in the course of classroom activity. Learning by discovery, in the sense that the children's experiences are not guided, is unlikely to guarantee adequate concept formation. There is, indeed, evidence to suggest that guided learning is more effective than pure discovery learning. Ausubel, in a review of research (p. 148 n.), quotes experimental evidence, none of which shows discovery learning to be particularly effective. He concludes that guided discovery, where the children are encouraged to learn by their own efforts but with guidance from the teacher, is more effective.

The way in which the intervention of the teacher affects the course of concept development is exemplified in an investigation carried out by Vigotsky. He compared the formation of concepts of a scientific nature with those of everyday life. He found that: '. . . as long as the curriculum supplied the necessary material the development of scientific concepts runs ahead of the development of spontaneous concepts [those from everyday life]'. He ascribes this phenomenon, which is probably the reverse of what one would expect at first blush, to the fact that, whereas everyday concepts are formed unsystematically, in the case of scientific concepts, the teacher working with the pupil '. . . has explained, supplied information, questioned, corrected, and made the pupil explain. The child's concepts have been formed in the process of instruction, in collaboration with an adult.' (See also pp. 121–2, and 142.)

We see here the great importance of the active intervention of the teacher into the child's learning. It is the systematic approach to the teaching of concepts and mental skills that speeds up mental development. But the teacher will have difficulty in developing adequate concepts in different fields if the speech of his children is insufficiently developed, and in fact children's linguistic inadequacy is almost invariably reflected in their low level of intellectual attainment. This may be observed by a comparison of the linguistic ability of the children in the bottom stream of a junior or secondary modern school, with that of children in the A stream. It could be argued (and often in the past it was argued) that the low intellectual level of the children was the cause of their linguistic difficulty. This point of view is no longer tenable in its extreme form, although it may be that linguistic and cultural deprivation interact with limited ability to the detriment of both. There is little doubt, however, that systematic concentration by the teacher on the speech of such children would have considerable beneficial effect. (The Newsom Report recommends that research be conducted into the effect of linguistic disability on school children.) It is important, then, in view of the effect of speech on intellectual development, that a good deal of attention be paid to the development of children's speech, and activities involving the children in the use of speech should form an important part of the curriculum. This does not mean, of course, teaching children to 'talk proper'. It may sometimes be thought that oral work is wasteful of time and there is often a feeling that since nothing concrete is produced comparable to a page of sums, or an essay, or some such exercise, then the time could have been more valuably spent. This is far from the truth and most research in the field suggests that work involving the children in linguistic experience is well worth while. It is probable, however, that most benefit will be derived from a systematic approach .to work in this field with a planned attack on the problems involved, and thàt much more limited results will flow from a desultory *ad hoc* approach. A danger to be avoided here, is the confusing of linguistic ability with the ability to memorize words and phrases with a view to reproducing them later in a rote fashion. Merely handing out dictionaries and stocks of words and phrases could result in the empty verbalizing which we mentioned earlier.

If we remember that all words are abstractions, that merely naming something is an act of abstraction, and that all words except proper nouns are abstractions which refer to classes of things or actions, we may get some insight into one important aspect of our approach to language work with children. If we are to avoid parrot-fashion learning we must ensure that any new words or phrases are apprehended in as full a manner as possible. Behind the symbol (the word) the child must see the reality (the thing). It is true that the significance of a concept changes throughout life: for example, the word *man* has different connotations for the author or the reader at different times of his life. So for children the content of a concept changes, becomes more complex as they grow older and enlarge their experience. The linguistic experience which the teacher attempts to arrange for the child will therefore build concepts much less complex than those of the teacher, since the child's experience is much more limited. If, however, the words used are stripped of any contact with reality, they will tend to remain at the level of simple aural signals similar to the names of capes and bays of the nineteenth century geography lesson. Once a word has been given a basis in reality, or perhaps in some graphical representation of reality through film, film strip, or pictures, it becomes possible to build on it; but until it has that basis any attempt to build on it will be similar to building a house on the shifting sand. This argues the need for a great deal of experience of a concrete nature in the junior and infant schools when new words and concepts are being introduced.

Once the child has formed adequate concepts he may use them in combination with other concepts, but it will be necessary to ensure that such combinations are accurate and consistent. To do this it will be necessary to build up other concepts of a more abstract nature. Adjectives, adverbs, conjunctions, prepositions, are all essential to the development of adequate systems of analysis and synthesis of the child's experience, and to facilitate the generalizing and discriminatory function of the language he uses. It should be noted here, however, that this is not an argument for the teaching of grammar in the junior school. The idea of *noun* is an abstraction of an abstraction and it is doubtful that children of junior school age gain much from grammar lessons.

Thus, in building up concepts, the teacher uses language to direct the child's attention to specific aspects of the real world to help him to make abstractions from it. The child will not build up concepts without this basis in reality, but the development of complex speech abilities is essential for him to make the necessary abstractions, and is, of course, the basis for the generalization of learning which is based on the *semantic* properties of words and not on their properties as simple signals.

Language and learning

The different aspects of language that we have just considered work together to make human learning more complex than learning in the other animals. Because man is able to form concepts, to learn abstractions, to manipulate relationships mentally and to formulate rules it becomes possible for his learning to be logical. The learning of a lower animal such as a pigeon or a rat in a learning experiment is essentially what Skinner calls *superstitious* learning. That is, there is not necessarily any causal link between the activity of the organism and the subsequent reinforcement. The animal learns the behaviour because reinforcement follows, not because it *knows* there is a chain of cause and effect between its activity and reinforcement. The reinforcement might be provided quite arbitrarily by the experimenter as in the shaping experiment described in Chapter 4. Human learning, on the other hand, to a very great extent takes into account the logical connections between things. We are able, not only to understand causal relationships between phenomena, but to manipulate symbolically logical systems such as may be found in mathematics or science.

Although human learning generally makes use of the logical connections between phenomena, it does not always. For example, situations arise in school where the teacher may adopt two different methods of teaching. He may, on the one hand, teach children to solve a given problem by helping them to see its logical structure, or he may get them to follow a set procedure which will produce a solution without their comprehending the underlying logic of their activity. Such activity is akin to the superstitious behaviour mentioned above. Superstitious learning in school may be found in most subjects. Mathematics is often quoted as an example, probably because the contradictions between the two approaches to learning are particularly clear in this field. In early work with number we often find children learning to subtract will 'borrow one' from the tens and 'pay it back' without having any idea of what they are about. One child who had a fair grasp of the logic of the task was able to work out the answers to a page of these sums in her head. However, after she had written down the answers she was observed to go through the sums putting in the small 'borrow' and 'pay back' digits. This activity meant nothing to her, it was, in fact, a piece of superstitious behaviour. Other subjects may be instanced, such as the experiments in science where the children follow mechanically a set of instructions given by the teacher, or the blind following of grammatical rules with no understanding of their underlying logic.

Learning such as we have described which has no basis of logic, is generally inefficient learning. Such learning is highly specific and the learner finds it difficult to transfer to a different situation. He will also have difficulty if he goes wrong since he will be unable to examine the logical structure of his activity or the material he is working with to see where the fault lies.

This logical structuring of the material is very closely related to the schematic learning to which I referred in Chapter 6. While schemas involving motor activity may be developed without a linguistic basis, cognitive schemas depend upon concepts and the understanding of laws and logical connections which are formed through language. A child with a low level of linguistic ability will have poor conceptual ability and will be unable to understand the system of logical relationships which constitutes a cognitive schema. This means that he will find it difficult, if not impossible, to see the way in which the various elements in a schema are related and will therefore be unable to learn that particular schema. For example, it will be difficult for a child who lacks understanding of the logical connections between verbal statements to develop a schematic approach to written language. Thus, instead of learning a skill which enables him eventually to construct sentences and paragraphs correctly as a habit requiring little deliberate detailed application, he will almost certainly use confused illogical paragraphs, or, at a lower level, he will write incomplete sentences which fail to convey what he intends. The latter child may well be able to define a sentence according to the textbook and yet still be unable to write good sentences.

The fostering of cognitive schemas based on an understanding of the logical connections between things is therefore a very important part of the work of the teacher. We consider some specific practical applications later in this chapter. In the meantime, we might say in general that the teacher in the classroom would do well to concentrate upon so arranging the children's activity that they see its underlying logic. Meaningful learning of this nature will be of more general application than the rote learning which we may take to be a rough equivalent of what we have referred to as superstitious learning. Meaningful learning will also give the children a deeper insight into what they are doing.

Teaching children to solve problems

Skilful use of language by the teacher can help children to build up skills in problem solving. P. Y. Galperin has made a detailed study of the way in which the teacher can help children in their problem-solving activity by judicious use of the verbal analysis and reinforcement of that activity [16]. Galperin considers that mental actions, or cognitive schemas, are formed in the following five stages:

(1) Creating a preliminary idea of the task.
(2) Mastering the action using objects.
(3) Mastering the action on the plane of audible speech.
(4) Transferring the action to the mental plane.
(5) Consolidating the mental action.

In stage one, two approaches are available. In the first approach the teacher explains the operation to the child and then allows the child to make himself familiar with the material under the teacher's directions. In the second method the teacher carries out the operation while the child watches and 'helps' by prompting. Galperin found that the second method was superior to the first, which was an unexpected occurrence since the first method seems more active. He suggests that the reason for this is that, freed of the concrete activity, the child is more easily able to concentrate on the material and organize his orienting activity towards it.

In stage two the child manipulates the material himself; the teacher guides, explains, and corrects. The speech of the teacher directs the child's activities to the manipulation of the material, singling out the objects, the goals of the activity, and the methods of achieving the goals. At this stage the child is working in the concrete and is not abstracting or working things out in his imagination.

At stage three the child has mastered the activity using objects. He now moves to the stage where he can *represent* the activity by audible speech. He can now explain, or give an account of the way the activity is carried out. What was formerly a practical activity is now a theoretical one. It is, however, still reinforced by the child's own speech.

At stage four the child is encouraged to whisper to himself instead of speaking out loud. He is still using language. However, as the activity becomes more habitual it becomes more and more compressed and abbreviated.

At stage five the action is completely internalized. It is now extremely compressed and elliptical. The flow of speech of stage two has now become a flow of concepts, and the child has transformed what was initially a concrete objective action into a mental phenomenon. Galperin stresses that if the pupil does go wrong and fails to learn, it is essential to return to an earlier stage and start again. Giving the child practice at the stage where he fails is merely reinforcing his error.

An experiment by Gagné and Smith confirms the work of Galperin insofar as the effect of verbalizing on problem solving is concerned.* In this experiment children 14–15 years old were set a problem in concept formation. Some of the children were asked to verbalize during practice, others were not to verbalize. Some children were also asked to look for a general principle to be stated verbally on completion. The results of the experiment showed that the children who verbalized took less time to solve the problem and made fewer mistakes. The children who verbalized also produced significantly more adequate statements of general principles than the children who did not verbalize.

We have now considered in general terms points to be noted in ensuring that children's learning will be efficient and meaningful. We shall take up the question of problem solving again in Chapter 15. Let us now turn to some specific teaching situations to see how some of these ideas might work out in practice.

The teaching of reading

I have said that language plays a key role in the extension of the child's intellectual activity. Let us now consider the part played by reading in this process.

* GAGNÉ, R. M. and SMITH, E. C.: *Journal of Experimental Psychology*, 1962, **63**, 12.

Reading is one of the most potent means of extending the child's experience of language. When a child becomes a fluent reader he is no longer directly dependent upon the teacher or other adults for language experience. Through reading he extends his knowledge of the physical world, of society, of human relationships, and of his cultural heritage. At the same time he comes to grips with increasing complex concepts. By grappling with the abstractions involved in reading, especially when he has advanced from the stage of reading narrative, he learns to master complicated relationships between ideas. All this activity enables him more easily to generalize his learning and at the same time to discriminate more finely. It is thus most important that the child learns to read as soon as possible; and when he learns to read it is also important that his first steps will allow him to generalize his experience as soon as possible to allow of the maximum of transfer from the material he masters to new material.

It is perhaps as well, before discussing the teaching of reading, to consider how complex an activity it is. We have seen that speech constitutes a second signalling system. That is, the spoken word symbolizes aspects of the external world in the first instance and later symbolizes abstractions from the real world; that is, things which have no concrete existence. The spoken word, then, is a symbol. We now take the spoken word and give it concrete form; we write it down. The arbitrary squiggles which we commit to paper are symbols of symbols. The written word is an abstraction twice removed from reality since it reconstitutes in graphic form spoken symbols which themselves are abstracted from reality. It may, perhaps, seem to the adult who has been reading for many years that undue emphasis is being placed on this aspect of reading; contact with a class of children just beginning to learn reading will probably give a different impression. Without an appreciation of the extremely complex nature of the written word it is difficult to apprehend the extent of the problem facing any young child when he first starts to learn to read.

Before a child can possibly learn to read he has to be able to distinguish among different written shapes. Learning to read, therefore, involves the learning of visual discrimination. If a child cannot discriminate between two words he clearly cannot 'read' them. It is thus important that before a child is expected to discriminate among the fairly complex stimuli that constitute words, he has plenty of practice in discriminating among other easier shapes. From what has been said earlier about *readiness* it should be clear that just to wait 'until the child is ready to read' is to leave to chance that which the teacher should be teaching. The ability to discriminate among shapes is one of the first steps in reading and children can be helped to acquire good visual discrimination as they can be helped with other things.

While children do start school unable to discriminate effectively between shapes, it is likely that more have difficulty with aural discrimination. This means that they will have trouble when it comes to distinguishing between spoken sounds. They will be unable to decide with which sound a word starts or finishes. Such children need training in phonic discrimination before they start reading. For such children the teacher can arrange games such as 'I Spy', or encourage children to make rhymes. It is worth while paying particular attention to this aspect of pre-reading experience since persisting difficulties of phonic discrimination have been observed at secondary school and higher education level, and these difficulties have caused the students difficulties in reading comprehension.

Once the child can discriminate among shapes and symbols and can also discriminate among different spoken sounds, the next problem is to teach him to link the spoken sound with the written symbol. In practice this will generally be done by presenting the printed word together with a picture of the object and the spoken word. It might be considered that this procedure links the spoken word with the object, but in fact, of course, it merely links a symbol with a representation of the object. The drawing of a dog is an image of a real dog, not the dog itself. It is an image which abstracts many of the essential features of *dog* but at the most this will only be a fraction of the total characteristics of *dog*. Furthermore, it is two dimensional and monochromatic, with no smell or sound. In other words it is a highly conventional representation of reality and not reality itself. This point has been stressed because children have to learn to see pictures and the teacher should not forget that while most children will have had a lot of practice in this field, especially through watching television, stylized textbook pictures might not be so easy to identify. The teacher will, of course, establish that the child understands the pictures in the book before attempting to start linking them with words.

There are two main points of view as to the most effective way of setting about teaching the early stages of reading. On the one hand we have the *Look and Say* method which consists of teaching the children to read either whole words or sentences right from the start. There will be no attempt to get the children to discriminate among the different letters in the words; instead they will be encouraged to read the words as *wholes*. On the other hand we have the *phonic* approach which emphasizes the fact that words are made up of letters and that letters in various identifiable combinations symbolize sounds, either words or parts of words. In the first place, naturally, the words would be monosyllabic to simplify the task for the child. Later on, combinations of syllables make up longer words and gradually the more complicated phonic rules which are essential for the composition of interesting material are introduced. It is, perhaps, worth noting that these more complicated spelling rules are not all, as is sometimes supposed, arbitrary irregularities, there is a consistency about many of them even though they are clearly fairly complex. The number of these complicated rules and phonic irregularities need not be very great in the early stages but as the child's vocabulary grows then he can be introduced to more and more of these words. Eventually, of course, when the child becomes really fluent, he will read words at a glance in the same way as an adult does, stopping only to analyse words that are unfamiliar.

Protagonists of the *Look and Say* method claim that children see words as *wholes*, or as patterns. They base this argument on the views of the Gestalt psychologists who consider that a fundamental aspect of perception is the tendency of the organism to see things as *wholes*. According to Gestalt psychology, the brain imposes patterns on the raw material of perception according to certain laws, the gist of which is that the patterns tend to make complete forms, that like things are linked in a pattern, and that incomplete forms will be completed by the organizing activity of the brain. The Gestalt psychologists also claim that the ability to perceive such patterns is innate and therefore young children have the ability to distinguish among shapes. The last point, as has been suggested earlier, seems not to be a tenable one and it seems that the ability to discriminate among shapes is a learned ability. Congenitally blind adults, when given their sight, have proved to have very great difficulty in learning the visual discrimination that the Gestalt psychologists claim is inborn. Thus, although there is little doubt that the fluent reader does not analyse every word that he reads, there is equally little doubt that this ability is a learned one and not an innate one.

The *Look and Say* method of teaching reading bases its approach on word patterns. It claims that by introducing children to words with clearly defined patterns they will be able to learn words much more readily than they would if the words conformed to similar or identical patterns. Simple phonic monosyllables such as run, man, sun, can, would be difficult to discriminate since they all conform to the same basic overall pattern, i.e. run, sun, etc., while possibly longer but less uniform word-shapes such as elephant or mother are easier to distinguish.

Linked with the attention paid to the shape of the word is the argument that because no attempt is made to restrict the vocabulary to phonic words, the writer of reading primers is emancipated from the worst horrors of stilted and uninteresting subject matter. F. J. Schonell makes this point, giving as an example of a phonic atrocity: 'The pig with a wig did a jig in the bog' [24]. This exemplifies two key criticisms, made by exponents of the whole word method, of the phonic approach: the fact that there is little difference in the patterns of the words, and the content of the sentence is meaningless. The need to find words which are phonically regular produces both the undifferentiated pattern of words and the uninteresting content.

Advocates of the phonic approach point out that whole word methods ignore the fact that the letters in words symbolize sounds and that the sequence of the letters in space (reading from left to right) represents the sequence of sounds in time when the word is spoken [25]. Teaching children to read English by concentrating on the whole word is to ignore the fact that the English language is an alphabetic language and to attempt to teach it by whole words is to treat it like a non-alphabetic language such as Chinese. It is interesting that the Chinese at the moment, recognizing that the nature of their language is an obstacle to the goal of universal literacy, are planning to go over to an alphabetic script as soon as possible.

If we consider the case of Chinese script in comparison with our own we see one of the main disadvantages of *Look and Say* methods in teaching reading. We have been concerned in recent pages with the problem of making learning *meaningful*; with attempting to ensure that what is learned is readily transferred to related situations. One of the difficulties that anyone learning Chinese is faced with is the fact that it is necessary to learn words as wholes; the words are in fact stylized pictures of the actual thing and as such one has to learn to identify thousands of different shapes in order to be able to read Chinese. A child learning to read English by the whole word method is in a similar position. He has to learn a different shape for each new word. Consequently if he is to build up a reasonably large vocabulary he will have to learn to recognize a large number of different shapes. This presents difficulties since many words have the same general outline but have absolutely no semantic similarity. Thus all words will have to be of different shapes, which restricts the words available, and the child taught by the whole word method learns to discriminate between words by criteria (their shapes) which are quite irrelevant to the meaning or sound of the words.

Learning to read by these methods closely resembles the mechanical rote learning which we have discussed earlier. The child learns *specific* responses to *specific* stimuli, there is virtually no transfer. I have seen this on many occasions when I have asked children who are 'fluent readers' of *Look and Say* primers, to read from different material which contains phonically less difficult words. There has been virtually no transfer, the learning is specific to that particular book and that particular reading scheme. Such children have no real key to reading; they are in a similar position to Skinner's pigeon which learned to peck the button marked *peck*. If on the other hand the children are taught from the beginning to discriminate among words according to the correct criterion, the letters which constitute the word, they are able to discriminate meaningfully among words, to generalize their learning and carry it over into new situations.

When a child has built up a set of phonic concepts relevant to one aspect of reading, he is able to use this when he approaches new material. On the other hand, a child coming to new material with experience of dealing with the shapes of words will be baffled since he focuses on aspects of the printed word which have nothing at all to do with sound or meaning. Some teachers seeing this disadvantage of *Look and Say* material, attempt to supplement their work using the whole word method by introducing phonic work at the same time. On the face of it this may appear to be a middle road which combines the virtues of both methods. This is illusory since the methods are mutually exclusive: the whole word method encourages children to ignore the letters in words, phonics teaches them to pay attention to them. At the same time the teacher who tries to base phonic training on whole word books will be using the most unsatisfactory material since the words will almost certainly be complex phonically even in the introductory books, whereas a systematic phonic scheme will start with phonically simple words and gradually introduce more complex material later. The child attempting phonic analysis with whole word material is getting the worst of both worlds.

The relative merits of *Look and Say* and phonic methods have been hotly debated for many years, and the opinions of educators and teachers are still divided on the issue. The various arguments are very clearly set out by the American, R. Brown, in his book *Words and Things*. Brown, himself, presents a point of view with which the present author would agree and which is probably gaining support at the moment. This approach would start with work in phonics, not drilling in the alphabet but with whole

* BROWN, R.: *Words and Things*, The Free Press, 1957.

words spelt consistently from which the child could extract meaningful generalizations. From this beginning the child would soon have to learn as total patterns such words as *the*, *but*, etc., because they are so common in English that it will greatly speed up reading if they can be read at a glance. In the early work with phonics it would be important to ensure that the children were given words to read which were already in their spoken vocabulary. After the earlier stages the child would gradually be introduced to the more complex phonic rules while any important irregularly spelt words would be learned as wholes. Eventually, of course, the child is able to recognize words at sight although not necessarily by their shapes, but possibly because he can identify certain phonic regularities at a glance and these regularities provide sufficient information for him to recognize the word without reading the whole of it. At the moment it is probably true to say that more schools teach reading using a *Look and Say* approach than use a phonic approach. It is probably also true, however, that the method suggested here is becoming more widely used and although more research evidence is needed, what is available indicates that teachers would do best to adopt a systematic approach to phonics as the key aspect of their teaching of reading.

In recent years a new approach to beginning reading has been introduced. In an attempt to simplify the complexities of traditional English orthography for children beginning to read, a new alphabet has been devised by Sir James Pitman which is intended to circumvent the irregularities of normal English spelling. This alphabet called the Initial Teaching Alphabet (i.t.a.) consists of forty-three characters which are intended to constitute a consistent phonetic system. Children are taught to read using this alphabet and when they have achieved fluency they transfer to orthodox reading. The idea is that the biggest stumbling block to beginning reading for young children is the irregular alphabet and by introducing this new alphabet their first steps on the road to reading will be made much less difficult.*

To investigate the efficacy of this method a number of experi-

* DOWNING, J. A.: *The i.t.a. Reading Experiment*, Evans, 1964.

ments have been set up in different parts of the country where groups of children using i.t.a. have been matched with groups of children using traditional orthography (t.o.). The proof of the effectiveness of i.t.a. will be revealed when a comparison of the reading attainment of the groups is compared.

At the time of writing it is difficult to assess the merits of this new method since full details of the experiment have not yet been released. In addition there has been a very great deal of publicity which is having the effect of making objective assessment of the method very difficult. One point could be made, however, and that is that the experiment is using a whole word reading scheme done into i.t.a. with the experimental group on the one hand, the whole word method used in orthodox form with the control group on the other hand. Thus what is being compared is not only i.t.a. and t.o., but a whole word or 'look and say' scheme with a phonic approach. What is really needed to give a meaningful appraisal of the merits of i.t.a. is a comparison with a systematic phonic scheme using t.o.

As has been suggested, learning to read, as all other learning in school, is based in its early stages on the concrete object or action. The child learns first to associate the spoken and written symbols with their referents in the real world. At this stage the teacher will arrange for activities which link the word with the thing. The child will say the words out aloud and will need a good deal of help from the teacher. At a later stage the child will be less dependent on the thing and will be able to read the word itself without reference to the concrete object. Books will still be lavishly illustrated at this stage to give him support with new material. He will be less dependent on the teacher but will still read the words out aloud. Later still, he will be less dependent on illustrations and the teacher, and his reading will be internalized with only the occasional regression to overt speech when he encounters a new or difficult word. The teacher will encourage this progression ensuring that the child masters each stage thoroughly before moving on to the next, and at the same time, ensuring that he does not stay at any of the stages longer than is necessary or his progress will be delayed.

The teaching of English

During the time when the child is moving towards fluency in reading he should, as has been suggested above, be having considerable practice in the use of the spoken language. The linguistic experience which he derives from these exercises will help him to develop his reading ability. At the same time as he masters the more complex aspects of language he will be mastering increasingly comprehensive concepts. When these concepts spring from sources unfamiliar to the child it will be important to see that they are rooted firmly in situations that are comprehensible to him. In general terms this will mean that the teacher will need to ensure that the children have adequate experience of practical activity to give a solid foundation to the concepts which they are acquiring [26].

Practical exercises to develop the children's ability to manipulate concepts should incorporate practice in explanation, in description, in giving accounts of events. Such exercises should link up with other aspects of the curriculum and indeed could be very closely integrated with many different subjects. Work in geography and science provide ample opportunity for such techniques and give point to the value of and need for techniques of classification. Classification, which deals with real things, insects, birds, geographical features, etc., can only be expressed through the medium of language; the practical experience of classifying activities and their designation through language interact to reinforce each other. Work in the traditional field of *English* is, of course, of great value in extending the child's grasp of concepts. The reading of good children's literature either by the teacher to the class, or by the children themselves, will help them to develop and refine their abilities to generalize and discriminate through the awareness of the finer shades of meaning of near synonyms and related groups of words. Poetry, especially, will encourage the gradual development of an appreciation of the way in which overtones of meaning can spread out from words like the ripples in a pool. The teacher needs to be aware in this field, however, of the children's books in which the language is limited, tending to consist of reach-me-down phrases with no richness of vocabulary and expression. Such writing is of limited value, since the thought clichés which it uses do not extend the experience of the child, and can therefore have little effect on his mental development. This does not mean to say that a good children's book will sacrifice enjoyment and appeal for the sake of 'improvement'. There are many books these days that combine appeal to children with a richness and variety of word and linguistic expression. Teachers of English have for many years used a technique with their classes which has involved the comparing with the children of two pieces of writing on related themes, one which deployed a rich vocabulary and an original syntax and the other which used a predictably stereotyped style and vocabulary [27]. By examining writing in this way children are made aware of the deficiencies of the mediocre and of the advantages of language used well.

One other aspect of language development might be mentioned under the heading of English. It is possible to use dramatic work to strengthen the associations of words and to elucidate the content of phrases and other units of meaning. It is relatively easy to provide some sort of concrete reference for nouns, and probably adjectives, but when verbs, adverbs, prepositions, are introduced it is somewhat more difficult to give them a basis in reality. Simple dramatic work can often give some clarity. Nuances of meaning between different verbs can be illustrated in this way. For example, with verbs indicating movement: 'He ran down the street; he walked, ambled, sauntered, proceeded, limped, wandered, prowled, marched, plodded, trudged, strode, toddled, stole.' Adverbs: 'He walked, swiftly, slowly, proudly, cautiously, impatiently, defiantly, boldly, furtively,' and so on. Prepositions: 'He walked, in, out, over, under, along, around, into, beneath,' etc. When children are first faced with new material, more adequate concepts will be built up if they are founded in the children's own experience through their actually performing the activities in the classroom.

In this consideration of the application of language to the classroom much stress has been placed on the role of the teacher in influencing the development of satisfactory forms of language. Ideally the teacher would be able to coach each child individually, correcting and giving examples, explaining and recapitulating in the course of instruction. In practice with large classes, especially in the junior school, where this is particularly important, this individual attention is impossible. In present circumstances the best that can be done is to use group techniques and give individual attention to the children when possible. Some of the techniques in language training do in fact lend themselves to group techniques; for example, the dramatic work to which we referred earlier; and there will always be great need for group discussions. In the field of individual instruction with the teacher monitoring the child's own linguistic efforts, the future probably lies in some form of auto-instructional device such as we are to consider in the next chapter. This may be in the form of a language laboratory, or in some form of computer-based system. This would provide for the child to be led through a systematic course of language provided automatically by a tape recorder and probably incorporating visual material. He would go at his own speed and the machine would present him with the material most necessary for his particular needs. It would, in effect, simulate the human teacher in an individual teaching situation, with the added advantages that the machine would not get bored and that its programme would have been devised by an expert in the field of linguistics. Systems of this type have been used so far mainly for the teaching of foreign languages but the potentialities for their use in ways such as have been suggested above are very great.

The teaching of mathematics

The learning and teaching of mathematics is a fruitful field when we discuss effective learning. As we have seen, rote learning in this field would include such activities as reciting the tables, learning that to divide one fraction by another 'you turn one upside down and multiply'. Even counting to five might be a rote activity for a child of two or three. In all these examples the rote element is essentially the unenlightened verbalizing of the child.

The young child who learns to count up to five may be unable to manipulate more than two or three objects in matching activities where some notion of number is needed. The mere fact that he is able to recite these (to him) meaningless sounds, is no guarantee that he has a comprehension of number commensurate with his verbalizing. This, of course, can apply throughout school. The secondary school child learning geometrical theorems off by heart may be able to cope with the stereotyped problems of some of the textbooks without having any true idea of the mathematical significance of his activity.

In this, as in other fields, the problem is to ensure that the child comprehends the reality behind the abstraction; unless he does this his facility with the language of mathematics becomes mere symbol manipulation. It is true that, once an abstraction has been made effectively, it becomes possible to build on it, but as the work of Piaget, Galperin, and Dienes (see below) suggests, concrete experience is almost always necessary to underpin the conceptual learning of new material. Thus it is necessary to give infants experience in the manipulating of concrete objects in order to build up their ability to count using matching operations (i.e. actually counting real things, not merely repeating the numbers). When the children have accomplished this, they may then be able to count with understanding, that is having some knowledge of the significance of their counting. Later, when counting is automatic and fully apprehended, the child will come across other arithmetical activity of a more complex nature which will demand that concrete material be again introduced. Such a situation would be reached when the child starts work with fractions. It is perfectly possible to teach children to work out sums involving the manipulation of fractions without reference to any concrete fractional quantities. To build up a satisfactory concept of the relation of the fraction to the whole, however, it is necessary to provide the children with experience of working with concrete material involving fractional quantities. For example, chocolate blocks are familiar to most children and they can be readily obtained sectioned in a variety of ways into three, four, five, six, eight, ten, and twelve. The children can also be given experience constructing their own fractions using paper and cardboard for cutting out. It should be noted here, however, that it is possible, and may be desirable, to approach the teaching of number in a different manner, introducing children to measuring first and then moving on to counting. This approach introduces ideas about fractional quantities together with simple counting (see pp. 218–20).

In ensuring that children have experience of the concrete as an essential precursor of the formation of arithmetical and mathematic concepts, there are broadly two approaches. On the one hand the child is given a great deal of largely *undirected* play with concrete material. This often takes the form in the primary school and in remedial classes in the secondary school, of practical activities involving weighing, measuring, and counting in *real life* situations. Children will weigh such things as packets of sugar or flour, potatoes, peas, etc. They will measure using rulers or yardsticks, and they will calculate through buying and selling activities in a classroom shop or post-office. The teacher will provide *tasks* for the children which they can solve only in the activity with the material. The great difficulty here, not always realized, is that mathematical concepts are not normally to be derived from real life situations since they are far too complex and 'artificial'. Thus the experience children get in the work we have mentioned so far will be insufficient to develop mathematical concepts. The teacher who wishes to develop such concepts in his children will need to arrange artificial situations which embody these complex mathematical structures. This can be done by using material from everyday life but the schemes chiefly in use which employ concrete material for concept formation make use of structural material specifically designed for the purpose. The use of this material does not, of course, preclude the use of other *activity methods*. Only brief mention can be made here of the nature of the structural material used in mathematics but there is extensive literature on the subject to which the interested reader can refer.

A well known approach to arithmetic using structural apparatus is the one devised by Catherine Stern.* This uses coloured blocks,

* STERN, C.: *Children Discover Arithmetic*, Harrap, 1953.

of unit width and height, and ranging in length from one to ten, each block ruled in units. The blocks are used to represent number relationships. For example each whole number between 1 and 10 is represented on a counting board by a block. It is thus possible to demonstrate in concrete form such facts as that 6 is the number value of a group of six units, that it contains one more unit than 5 and one less than 7. The blocks may also be arranged on a *number track*, which is a series of ten sections, each of ten units in length, which placed end to end can represent the number scale from 1 to 100. The child is also able to build up squares of four, nine, sixteen, and so on by the use of cubes which are arranged in square trays.

The idea behind the Stern apparatus is that the child is enabled to perceive the visual structures of number arrangements. These structures like the patterns of dots on dominoes, are apprehended, not as an agglomeration of single elements, but as organized wholes. The child does not count when he uses the apparatus, he measures: he *sees* the difference between 6 and 7, he does not count them out. From his experience with the apparatus, repeatedly seeing the patterns and relationships, it is considered that the child will evolve the corresponding mental structures. It might, however, be asked whether the theoretical bases of the Stern approach, which owe much to Gestalt views of perception, do not miss the mark. Children will not see the visual structures of numbers without training, and the ways in which numbers are arranged to form patterns are arbitrary anyway. The question at issue is whether learning to see numbers as patterns is an effective method of teaching children mathematical concepts which will be of general application. It may well be that children learning to distinguish between numbers by their shapes, will be focusing their attention on the unimportant aspects of the situation, the shapes, and thus missing an important aspect, the quantitative difference between the numbers.

The Cuisenaire apparatus is one of the most well known of the different structural approaches to mathematics teaching. This material consists of 241 coloured wooden rods 1 cm. in cross section and ranging from 1 cm. to 10 cm. in length. Rods of the same length are the same colour and the rods are also grouped in colour families. The unit rod is white; the rods 2, 4, and 8 are coloured in different shades of red; the rods 3, 6, and 9, are different shades of blue; 5 and 10 are the yellow family, and 7 is black. There are also cards and games used mainly for learning and memorizing number combinations. After a preliminary period where the children are allowed to play with the apparatus in an undirected way, they are encouraged to use the rods to build models which will help to make clear the differences of colour and size. They will also see the relationship between the rods of different colour. Later work involves their learning to discriminate first between rods which are obviously very different in length and then gradually getting them to make finer and finer discriminations until they can distinguish among all the rods. Later systematic work introduces them to the four rules and work on fractions and proportion can be introduced. The aim throughout is to provide a concrete basis for the abstractions which will eventually come to constitute the various concepts.*

Z. P. Dienes [28] has produced structural material which has been used in some schools for the past few years. He explicitly declares that the everyday environment of the child does not provide the situations from which many mathematical concepts can be derived. It is thus necessary to provide material which will enable the child '. . . to structure his own experiences in his own way and thus allow him to reach mathematical abstractions and their symbolic formulation . . . following a path natural to him'. He considers there to be three stages in the forming of a new concept:

    (a) a preliminary or 'play' stage;
    (b) a more structured 'becoming aware' stage;
    (c) formulation of the concept, followed by a 'practice' stage.

In the first stage the child plays with the material in relatively unstructured games so that he encounters experiences relevant to the concepts to be formed. During the second stage he will be given tasks which provide experiences similar to those connected

* GATTENGO, C.. *A Teacher's Introduction to the Cuisenaire–Gattengo Method of Teaching Arithmetic*, Reading, Gattengo–Pollock, 1960.

to the relevant concept. Here the child will be helped to direct his activity along the right lines to help him eventually to form the concept. The third stage involves the child becoming aware of the nature of the concept and becoming competent in applying it to relevant situations. Another very important aspect of Dienes's approach is what he terms 'The more the merrier principle'. The argument here is that in building up concepts it is important to give adequate experience of a varied nature from which the concept may be abstracted. The more varied the experience embodying the principle to be abstracted, the more complete will be the concept. 'If what the child *perceives* varies a great deal as long as there is a common core for him to discover, he will eventually *conceive* this common core.'

The apparatus which embodies these ideas consists of two sets: the Multibase Arithmetic Blocks (M.A.B.) and the Algebraic Experience Material (A.E.M.). The M.A.B. material consists of pieces of wood of four different sizes. The units are $\frac{3}{8}$-inch cubes, the other sizes are grooved so as to appear constructed of the unit cubes. The sizes are in geometrical progression with the common ratio of 4 : 4 units = 1 long; 4 longs = 1 flat; 4 flats = 1 block. There are other sets of similar material using different ratios, 3, 5, 6, 10. Tasks involving the use of this material give the children the concrete experience necessary to give them insight into the arithmetical concepts underlying the four rules. The different ratios in the various sets help the children to develop the general idea of *base* which perhaps rarely occurs normally, despite the fact that we have a coinage (at the moment) which works with base 12 (pence and shillings) and base 20 (pounds and shillings), and systems of weights and measures which use bases 3, 8, 16, etc. It is perhaps of particular importance that children acquire this concept today since electronic computers use base 2 for their calculations and it is probable that many millions more calculations are performed using base 2 than using the base 10 of the decimal system.

The A.E.M. apparatus is designed to complement the M.A.B. and, by use of a variety of material, Dienes claims that children are helped towards a fundamental grasp of quite abstract mathematic concepts. It should be noted here that with both the A.E.M. and the M.A.B. the role of the teacher is essentially that of supervisor arranging the experiences of the children so that they will discover the concepts in the way most suitable to them as individuals.

We have already discussed the experiments of Piaget and it is not proposed here to examine them in any further detail. Nor is it possible to outline a method of mathematics teaching based on 'Piagetian principles'. However, all teachers should note well what his experiments have demonstrated; that children do not form concepts spontaneously or suddenly but that there is a history of development from the partial to the full understanding of a process. It is also important to note the complementary aspect of this; the fact that children who have only a partial grasp of a mathematical concept can show all the signs of complete comprehension as assessed by the conventional rote learning procedures.

The work of Galperin into the teaching of mathematics suggests that the observations which Piaget made of the way in which children formed ideas of quantity, may be products of the mathematical training which they had had. He also suggests that the traditional way of introducing children to counting and measuring may not be the best approach and he has carried out research which throws an interesting light on this problem.

In the Piaget-type experiment when children are presented with a set of cups and saucers, each cup with a saucer, the children will say that there are as many cups as saucers. If the cups and saucers are now separated, children will say there are more saucers. Galperin argues that this shows that the children had not been taught mathematical thinking as a new way of approaching the physical world. The normal approach to elementary mathematical thinking builds on the primitive perceptual ability of the child to distinguish between objects. Galperin considers that a more effective approach to the subject would be to introduce the children to numbers as *arbitrary* measures.

Galperin argues that the normal way of teaching elementary mathematics, which introduces counting and then measuring, is the wrong approach. He suggests that the normal course of the child's development is the opposite, and he would teach measuring first and then numbers. He considers that if this method were adopted children would learn both measurement and number more easily and more thoroughly.

Galperin investigated this hypothesis experimentally. He took two groups of six-year-old children and gave them a set of tests similar to the ones Piaget used to investigate children's concepts of number and quantity. One group of children was introduced to elementary mathematics in the orthodox way: they learned to count to 10 and to add the quantity *one* to any number from 1 to 9. The experimental group was introduced to measurement rather than to numbers. The children in the experimental group first visited shops where they saw people measuring the lengths of different articles for sale. They were then taken back to the classrooms to do some measuring themselves. The children were given unmarked paper measures of different lengths and were shown how to use them for measuring different objects. To measure a table the child would take a number of the unmarked measures and lay them end to end to see how many were needed to cover the distance between two ends of the table. (Note, the children did not count these measures.) The next step followed when the experimenter took away some of the measures so that the children did not have enough to cover the distance of the things they wanted to measure. When they protested, they were shown how they could achieve the same end by using one measure, putting a small marker at the end of the measure and using the measure again. The training went on until the children had mastered the ideas of *more*, *less*, and *equal*.

The children were now introduced to numbers. *One* was defined as the fractional length of an object (e.g. table) covered by a measure of a particular length. The children were then taught to count and write from 0 to 5, each number being paired with an appropriate number of markers; then to add and subtract using these numbers; and then to count, add, and subtract the numbers from 6 to 10.

The two groups were retested at the end of the experiment with the following results. The experimental group did far better than the control group and 55 out of 60 in the experimental group made no errors at all on the test. (The test was the same one as used at the beginning.) The test was also given to fourth year junior children (10–11 years) and the experimental group did better than these children.

Much more information is needed about experiments such as this before any definite pronouncements can be made as to the efficacy of the method, but any teacher interested in building up simple concepts in young children might well care to try such an approach.

Many psychologists have stressed what Dienes mentions in the manual to his structural apparatus; as one concept is acquired it becomes the basis for an attack on the next. Piaget says that the newly acquired schema becomes the anticipatory schema for the next problem of a similar nature. And as we have seen (p. 200), Galperin suggests that the formation of mental actions proceeds in stages and that, if one stage is not adequately mastered, subsequent learning is impaired. It is thus most important to ensure that each step in the progress towards mathematical understanding is thoroughly consolidated.

The teaching of geography

Much of what has been said about the formation of mathematical concepts may be applied to many other areas of the curriculum. Throughout, the main danger is that the teacher may employ techniques which do not provide adequately for the grounding of the concepts to be formed in the child's experience with the material world. An allied danger, of course, is that the teacher may make unwarranted assumptions about the level of the child's understanding at any one stage and attempt to teach that which is beyond the child's current ability to conceptualize. In geography a good deal of map work is done in the junior school and sometimes in the infant school, and yet research has suggested that children in the primary school often have little real comprehension of what a map is. The research of Piaget on the conservation of area is relevant here. Children aged about seven will assess area according to its obvious perceptual appearance. In one experiment children at this age were shown two pieces of card which they were told were toy fields. On each were placed toy houses representing the farmers' houses and outbuildings. On one of the 'fields' the buildings were scattered, while on the other they were placed together. The children were then asked if the cow belonging to farmer Brown (buildings scattered) had more, less, or as much grass to eat as farmer Jones's cow (buildings together). Some children had acquired conservation of area and said that there was the same amount of grass no matter where the buildings were placed, but others, lacking the concept of conservation, averred that the field with the buildings scattered about had less grass than the one where the buildings were close together. These children had paid attention to the fact that there was a greater uninterrupted space in the one field than in the other and had based their answers on this partial view of the situation. This was a relatively simple situation; with more difficult map work it is likely that such incomplete understanding is more extensive. Adults sophisticated in the reading of maps may easily forget the complexity of the formal symbols used in map design, not to mention the formidable conceptual jump required to move from a three-dimensional view (that often few children have experienced) to a two-dimensional, scaled down, highly conventional representation. Children, it is true, may well be able to learn to differentiate among different maps and to learn that this shape is Britain, this America, and so on. This achievement need have nothing geographical about it, it is often merely the ability to discriminate among different geometrical shapes; the ability to put 'towns' in their correct position on these shapes is often an exercise in spatial perception. Learning of this nature is analogous to simple stimulus-response learning which we have previously referred to as rote learning. True understanding of maps needs considerable grounding in practical activity so that the abstractions of outlines and contours, and the conventional symbols, are genuinely related to those aspects of the real world which they symbolize.

One geographical concept which is difficult to investigate directly and to represent in a model, is the relationship between vertical scale and the horizontal scale on the Earth's surface. Geography textbooks and atlases tend to show sectional diagrams across contours with a highly exaggerated vertical scale, since, if vertical and horizontal planes were drawn to the same scale, it would be difficult to discern differences of height along the section since the vertical dimensions are so small compared with the horizontal. The result of this is that few people ever achieve a realistic concept of the relationship of the vertical to the horizontal on the Earth's surface. Thus student teachers when asked to draw what they would consider to be a section across a given geographical area, using the same horizontal and vertical scale, produce drawings in which molehills have literally become mountains and where mountains soar to orbital heights. It is fairly certain that if more attention were given to this concept in schools with diagrams, films, and models, children would acquire the concept. But merely presenting the scale as arithmetical quantities has no impact of a geographical nature.

Many other geographical concepts are based on direct perception. It is not always possible for children to be brought into contact with the geographical features underlying the concepts, but it is important that this is done wherever possible. The tremendous expansion of travel in recent years should have a positive effect in this direction. Films, slides, models, and diagrams all help to enrich the concepts which the child is being helped to build up, but the mere reading from a book is of limited value to the child. (It is different, of course, with the adult who may have had years of experience with the actual geographical features or graphic representations of them. In his case his understanding is already so rich that the mere verbal reference is sufficient to evoke complex patterns of relevant concepts.)

The teaching of history

The teaching of history presents a rather different problem to the teacher. Piaget's investigations into the child's understanding of time, as we have seen, demonstrate that children will have little real comprehension of the meaning of dates, or time scale. It is therefore quite pointless to insist on the accurate memorizing of lists of dates unless it is considered that this has an intrinsic value, which is highly unlikely. Such learning, as has been suggested, is a form of rote learning; it is the mechanical pairing of arithmetical symbols with the appropriate verbal stimuli. It is a different matter, of course, attempting to give the children a broad view of historical developments. To do this, however, will require imaginative reconstructions of past eras using a wide variety of aids: films, pictures, stories, description. The local environment is also often a potent source of historical associations which should not be neglected, and the use of original documents in photostat form as has been developed at the University of Sheffield in their 'Teaching Archives' (now available as 'Jackdaws'), is a good example of the use of visual material.

Activity which helps the children to experience imaginatively the life of times past should be encouraged. Some excellent programmes are produced by the B.B.C. which do this admirably, while an interesting technique used by one history teacher has involved the children 'publishing' simultaneously two news sheets entitled respectively: *The Barons' Chronicle* and *The Serfs' Gazette*. The aim of all this activity is to give the children as full a knowledge of the past as possible so that they may better know the present. The amount of historical understanding derived from formal exercises in manipulating dates and dynasties or taking down notes is virtually nil.

The teaching of science

As we have seen from the work of Piaget and Vigotsky, children acquire concepts only gradually and often give the impression of having formed them when in fact they have not. Work by R. G. Natadze of the University of Tbilsi [8] into the formation of scientific concepts in biology has confirmed their findings in the learning of school subjects. He found that children between seven and ten had difficulty in learning to classify animals despite careful explanation by the investigator. Although children were able to learn by heart the defining attributes of mammals, reptiles, fishes, birds, etc., when they were asked to classify different animals it became clear that their learning was conceptually inadequate. Younger children, when shown a picture of a dolphin, would say that it was a fish even when they had been told that it breathes air and suckles its young. Children of about nine would classify a whale as a fish and would justify their decision by saying that it has gills and spawns. Throughout, the perceptually dominant features overwhelmed the children's activity, and although they 'knew' the definitions of the various animals, they could never be depended upon to classify them accurately. A teacher who accepted the repetition of the definitions as evidence that the children had learned the various concepts would have been very much misled.

Until fairly recently much science teaching has depended upon the learning of formal definitions and principles to be used quite mechanically. Experiments were (and are) performed by the teacher 'to prove' this, that, or the other. Children have copied down notes on experiments which they have seen performed by the teacher and have acquired the most sketchy scientific concepts.

In recent years a major movement for the reform of science teaching has developed in many countries. In America the Physical Sciences Study Committee has been engaged in a fundamental reappraisal of science teaching since about 1950. In England the Nuffield Science Teaching Project has been in operation since 1962, and similar work is proceeding in other countries. In essence, the aim of the new approach is to present the sciences as systems of inquiry rather than simply as bodies of knowledge.* To this end the emphasis is laid on having children first come to grips with phenomena through laboratory and field experience, directly if possible, but if necessary through the use of aids such as film and television. Laboratory experiences are no longer to be used merely to verify previously stated principles. Ways are sought to encourage pupils to discover ideas for themselves and to learn the sciences by developing, so far as is possible, the viewpoints and modes of attack of scientists confronting problems. The Nuffield project has developed this kind of approach in the junior school, as well as at the secondary level, using apparatus improvised from everyday materials in addition to orthodox equipment.

While the new teaching will almost certainly foster concept

* See COMMONWEALTH EDUCATION LIAISON COMMITTEE: *School Science Teaching*, H.M.S.O., 1964.

development, it is perhaps worth stressing that there is little virtue in providing children with heterogeneous collections of phenomena for them to investigate at random. It would seem more economical of time and more conducive to the establishment of accurate concepts if the teacher guides the experience of the children so that they are neither overwhelmed by the complexity of the stimulus situation (as might happen in a Bruner type experiment, see pp. 165–9) nor do they miss the essential experiences for ensuring the adequacy of the concepts. The teacher who guides or 'programmes' the science experiences of his children will probably be making the best approach to the establishment of scientific concepts (see Chapter 9).

From abstract to concrete

The discussion in this chapter has largely centred around the way in which learning in various subjects is made most effective. The value of building up sets of coordinated concepts, related to the activity in question, has been stressed in order that learning may be of general application and imbued with meaning. These concepts have their roots in concrete reality but the more complex they become the more abstract they will tend to be. This poses certain problems in connection with conceptual learning. If care is not taken, the child who has mastered sets of concepts may have difficulty in applying them to the real world. It is perhaps easiest to see this in scientific and mathematical problems. E. A. Fleshner [8] found that older students set problems in physics, some of which had a concrete content and some of which had an abstract content, solved the ones with abstract content more effectively. The more the problem resembled the orthodox textbook question the more chance the children had of solving it. In mathematics a problem involving the knowledge of the properties of triangles was solved more easily when it was in the form of a textbook diagram than when it was presented as part of a real situation with the triangle depicted as two sides of a roof resting on the walls of a building.

Fleshner points out that in the textbook diagram the textbook writer has performed a major act of abstraction. He has simplified the problem by making it more abstract. This is not so paradoxical if we consider that the act of abstraction peels off the inessential and reveals the relevant core of the problem. The details in the real-life problem act as distractors which confuse the student. The moral of this is clear; while the teacher will help children to build up schemas with as wide an area of generalization as possible, he should also provide for adequate experience of the application of the knowledge to practical problems. There should be a two-way process; the abstract and the concrete interact to make the child's understanding of both richer and more profound.

Summary

The learning of nonsense syllables sometimes used in psychology experiments is learning without understanding. It has little use in the classroom since there is no generalization of learning and no transfer. The teacher's aim is to foster learning with understanding; that is, conceptual learning. Concepts are not inborn, they develop through experience. The teacher can help in the formation of concepts by controlling the experience of the children.

Through the use of speech, the teacher can explain to the children and direct their attention to the essential features of situations so that a systematic approach to the formation of concepts is possible. To improve the quality of the children's thought, the teacher should try to improve their speech. This does not mean teaching them to *elocute*, or to lose a regional accent. It involves inculcating speech habits which make use of increasingly complex and abstract ideas. The use of complex speech habits and modes of thought makes it possible for the child to understand the logical basis of learning. Wherever possible the teacher should encourage this type of learning.

Galperin found that children were helped in problem solving activities by guiding them through a series of stages. 1. The child watches the teacher working with concrete material and prompts him. 2. The child manipulates the material himself while the teacher guides and corrects. 3. The child gives a verbal account of the operation. 4. The child whispers to himself the verbal account. 5. The action is completely internalized. Gagné and

Smith found that verbalizing helped secondary school children to solve problems.

Reading is a potent method of developing language and teaching children to read is probably the most important function of the primary school. Reading is a complex activity involving the manipulation of symbols twice removed from reality. Learning to read should be based firmly on concrete material at the beginning but the *props* should be withdrawn when the children can cope without them. Of the two main approaches to the teaching of reading the phonic approach holds the greatest possibility of transfer from one set of material to another. In order to help children over the difficulties caused by traditional orthography, the initial teaching alphabet has been introduced in experiments in beginning reading.

In mathematics it is necessary to ensure that children see the concrete reality behind the symbols in the textbooks. Various types of structural apparatus are helping children to do this by involving them in practical activity.

In geography it is necessary to ensure that children have real experience on which to found geographical concepts. Field work and aids are essential here. Care should be taken in the use of maps, to ensure that children genuinely understand what a map is: research suggests that young children do not understand.

Young children have difficulty in apprehending a time scale. Dates have little significance for them. In history they will achieve more by attempting imaginatively to reconstruct the past through the use of appropriate aids and contemporary material.

Much of what has been said about the teaching of mathematics can be applied to the teaching of science. Science cannot be taught entirely verbally. Children need actual experience to form scientific concepts. They cannot be relayed from teacher to pupil merely by the teacher's telling.

It is important to remember that although conceptual learning is essential, it is useless if it cannot be referred back to the real world. Teachers should make sure that their children can apply their learning to the solution of real-life problems as opposed to the simplified textbook problems.

CHAPTER 9

Programmed Instruction

In recent years some of the ideas derived from the experimental study of the processes of learning have been transplanted from the psychological laboratory to the classroom. This new link between theory and practice has been made through the techniques of programming. Programmed instruction is a field in which the work of the psychologist and the teacher fuse. In the words of one American psychologist it is '. . . . the first application of laboratory techniques utilized in the study of the learning process to the practical problems of education'. The laboratory techniques referred to are those exemplified by Skinner in his control of behaviour [10]. As we have seen above, Skinner, through the judicious use of reinforcement, was able to shape the behaviour of an organism 'almost at will'. His laboratory animals learned most elaborate sequences of behaviour: his pigeons learned to play ping-pong while other pigeons have been trained to pick out faulty pills on a production line.

This effective control of the behaviour of organisms has not been accomplished without the most careful scrutiny of the factors involved and elaborate analyses of the part played by reinforcement. However, when the psychologist looked at the classroom situation he found none of this. He found instead traditional techniques evolved empirically, not subjected to scrutiny or analysis; and where controversy existed, it did not question these conventional methods but rather dealt with peripheral matters. To some extent this is the result of an attitude held by many educationists, past and present, who have adhered to the belief that teaching is intrinsically an art and not a science. Such an attitude would, presumably, refuse to admit the concept advanced by Skinner of education as a branch of technology. It is, however, developments in technology which are now making

228

possible for the first time the detailed scrutiny of the behavioural processes which lead to learning. As Skinner puts it:

In the experimental study of learning it has been found that the contingencies of reinforcement which are most efficient in controlling the organism cannot be arranged through the personal mediation of the experimenter. An organism is affected by subtle details of contingencies which are beyond the capacities of the human organism to arrange. Mechanical and electrical devices must be used. . . . Personal arrangements of the contingencies and personal observation of the results are quite unthinkable. Now, the human organism is, if anything, more sensitive to precise contingencies than the other organisms we have studied. We have every reason to expect, therefore, that the most effective control of human learning will require instrumental aid. The simple fact is that, as a mere reinforcing mechanism, the teacher is out of date [29].

Two points are involved here; the first refers to the need for mechanical aid in studying learning; the other concerns the need for a mechanism to improve the efficiency of certain aspects of teaching. It is the latter which chiefly interests us at the moment. What can replace the teacher *as a mere reinforcement mechanism*?

Reinforcement in the classroom

To answer the question we need to consider briefly the place of reinforcement in the classroom. As we have seen previously, when a given pattern of behaviour is to be induced in a laboratory animal, the designated behaviour is reinforced immediately. A reinforced response might well be a single unit in a more extensive pattern of behaviour; the important point is that reinforcement follows each small increment of learning. To present the organism with random, infrequent, and delayed reinforcement would be a very unlikely procedure to produce effective change of behaviour. However, a glance at the average classroom procedures reveals a situation where reinforcement assumes precisely this unsystematic nature. Typical classroom instruction would normally consist of an exposition of the material to be learned followed by class activity calculated to give the class a deeper insight into the subject. Often this activity involves the pupil in problems intended to give practice in the use of the new material.

In arithmetic this might consist traditionally of a number of exercises involving the use of new techniques. In English it might be the use of new grammatical concepts in a set of exercises. In geography, history, and other subjects it could be an exercise to test the degree of memorizing of the new material. In all these cases reinforcement of correct responses is almost entirely unsystematic. Even when the teacher goes from child to child while the exercises are being done, it is clearly impossible to ensure that no child has to wait for the reinforcement of a correct response, or that no child is forging ahead and building up an elaborate sequence of incorrect responses.

If we are to systematize reinforcement in the classroom we must somehow ensure that virtually no correct response goes unreinforced and no incorrect response is reinforced. Since this is clearly an impossible task for any teacher we must accept the point of Skinner's remarks and look elsewhere for our 'reinforcing mechanism'. Skinner and other American psychologists have looked elsewhere and have found what they consider at least a possible answer to the problem of efficient reinforcement in what has been termed *Programmed Instruction*.

Origins

The term may be new but the practice is not. It had its most immediate origins thirty or more years ago when S. L. Pressey of the Ohio State University presented two papers which described an 'automatic teacher' which '. . . tells the subject at once when he makes a mistake (there is no waiting several days, until a corrected paper is returned, before he knows where he is right and where wrong)'. Thus, Pressey pointed out, the device made use of the *Law of effect* mentioned above (Chapter 3). Pressey dropped work on his automatic teaching device in 1932. The next major development came with Skinner's presentation in 1954 of an immediate reinforcer teaching device. Whereas Pressey's machine demanded that the student chose one of a number of suggested answers to a given question, that is, it was a multiple choice device, the Skinner machine demanded a constructed reply. Another important development in technique incorporated in the Skinner machine was the organization of the material. Whereas other devices presented relatively unrelated questions, Skinner *programmed* his material in an organized sequence, the increment of learning in each step of the sequence being so small that the pupil, having solved one problem, finds little difficulty in solving subsequent ones. Thus he is reinforced frequently and is led step by step through the material to be studied with the minimum of error and the maximum reinforcement. (Skinner considers that the successful manipulation of the machine is generally a sufficient reinforcement.)

Since Skinner's paper, work has gone on apace in America and in the last few years a flood of literature on automated teaching has appeared, together with various types of machines. In Great Britain a similar phenomenon is occurring and recently there has been a progress from almost complete disregard or ignorance of the subject, to a very lively and expanding interest evinced by teachers, psychologists, publishers, and commercial firms interested in the 'hardware'. At the moment the whole subject is in a state of flux. Machines at present in use will probably appear very crude in a short space of time and it is likely that new developments will take place in programming. However, it is possible to single out certain factors which will provide exemplars of the present position and likely future developments.

Linear programming

Linear programming is based on the ideas advanced by B. F. Skinner. As we have seen these ideas spring from a particular view of the learning process. This involves the immediate reinforcement of the 'correct' response to a given stimulus. 'Correct', in this context, means that response which the experimenter wishes to evoke. 'Incorrect', or undesired responses, are not reinforced and gradually drop out of the behavioural repertoire until only the desired responses remain. The hungry pigeon in the experiment receives food when it performs an arbitrarily chosen manœuvre: the student making a response to a verbal stimulus is 'rewarded' when he makes that response to a question deemed to be the appropriate one by the teacher. The reinforcer in the case of the student will generally be the satisfaction of the successful manipulation of the environment rather than the obtaining of food, but experience so far has shown that this is generally adequate.

It would be a mistake, however, to regard student learning under these conditions as the mere accumulation of arbitrarily connected responses. A good programme will take into consideration the underlying logic of the subject and help the student to see its structure. Reinforcement should have this aim in view and not the production of an unthinking and mechanical behavioural

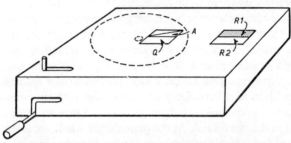

Fig. 12. The Skinner disc teaching machine. The frame appears at Q, the response is written at R2. When the programme advances the answer to the frame appears at A. The student can compare his response with the correct response, but cannot alter his response, since it has now moved to R1, where it is covered by a perspex shield.

pattern. The behaviour of the pigeon is sometimes called ritual or superstitious precisely because it has no logical foundation, whereas human learning generally has.

Skinner's first approach to the problem was the production of a simple machine, which, with some minor modifications, may be regarded as the prototype of the linear apparatus. This device consists of a disc operated by a lever. The lever rotates the disc through approximately 12° at each operation. The disc is enclosed in a slotted cover which exposes a small section of the disc and under the same cover is a roll of paper, part of which is exposed through another slot. The stimuli (written instructions and questions) are printed radially on the disc so that one item is exposed through the slots each time the lever is operated. The student is required to write his answer (the response) on the answer tape alongside. The next movement of the lever brings into view the correct answer and moves the student's answer behind a transparent panel. The student can now compare his answer with the correct answer. If he decides he was correct, he moves the lever which marks his answer correct and presents the next item. He also operates a lever which reduces the number of times that item will appear again. When he has completed one revolution of the disc he continues a second time, being presented only with those items he answered incorrectly the first time. Many subsequent machines have dispensed with the 'drop out' of correct responses and the student goes through the programme once only. The disc method of presentation has also been largely replaced by paper on rollers or by devices presenting items on standard-size paper or cards. A 'teaching board' devised by Reid, of the University of Aberdeen, simply presents the item on a piece of paper which is overlapped at one end by an answer roll. When the answer has been written the child pulls out the over-lapped end of the item paper and exposes the answer which he then compares with his own.

We can see from the above how Skinner achieves the immediate reinforcement both he and Pressey considered essential. We can also see how Skinnerian methods permit of constructed responses rather than multiple choice answers. But so far the apparatus need be nothing more than a 'quiz machine' presenting a number of test questions and differing only from the traditional test in that the student receives knowledge of results without delay. The degree to which it transcends this will be a measure both of the programmer's competence and of the value of the device as a genuine teaching machine.

As we have seen, Skinner's other main contribution in the design of his apparatus, was in the orderly presentation of the material. The subject matter to be taught is broken down into a series of simple sequential steps. These steps are designed to present information and at the same time to evoke a response which tests whether the student has understood. As an animal can be taught economically to run a maze by reinforcing a sequence of correct turns, so a pupil can be led economically through complex material by reinforcing correct responses. It is clearly essential, however, that in addition to sequential presentation of the material, each item must be so designed that the correct response is almost invariably evoked. If this is not so then the

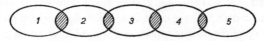

Fig. 13. Diagrammatic representation of a linear programme. Note the chaining. The items are linked by a certain amount of common content, shown shaded.

student is not reinforced by getting the correct answer and begins to lose interest. Material presented in this way is called a *programme*, a term which embodies the idea of progression, and clearly the programme will be a gradual progression from simple to complex behaviour.

The most well known of all linear programmes is the one produced by Skinner and Holland, *The Analysis of Behaviour*. The excerpt from this programme printed below will give the reader an idea of the linear mode of presentation. It should be noted that the frames are short because they had originally to fit in the Skinner machine which had a fairly small aperture. There is no theoretical reason why the frames should not be much longer. The extract is taken from the middle of the programme but readers may find that they are able to complete the frames on the basis of their reading of the chapters on learning. When the student is using the programme he should cover up all the frames except the first, read and complete (mentally or on paper) the first item, and then move on to item two for feedback and for reinforcement.

Extract from *The Analysis of Behaviour*

1. A stimulus which follows a response is called a .... if the rate at which similar responses are emitted is observed to increase. (Answer: reinforcer.)

234

2. A hungry pigeon pecks a key and is immediately given food. The .... of pecking will increase since presenting food .... a reinforcement. (Answer: rate, is.)

3. If, instead of presenting food after the pigeon pecks the key, a loud noise is turned *on*, the rate of pecking will *not* increase. Presenting a loud noise .... a reinforcement. (Answer: is not.)

4. When pecking a key *turns off* a very loud noise for a few moments, the frequency of pecking in the presence of the noise is observed to *increase*. Ending the loud noise .... a reinforcement. (Answer: is.)

5. Reinforcement which consists of *presenting* stimuli (e.g. food) is called positive reinforcement. In contrast, reinforcement which consists of terminating stimuli (e.g. painful stimuli) is called .... reinforcement. (Answer: negative.)

It is extremely important that the answer demanded must not be trivial but must involve the student's actively reacting to key material that will advance his understanding. To illustrate this point, the same material rewritten to demand minimal understanding of the subject is given below for comparison.*

1. A stimulus which follows a response is called a reinforcer if the rate at which similar .... are emitted is observed to increase. (Answer: responses.)

2. A hungry pigeon pecks a key and is immediately given food. The rate of pecking will increase since presenting .... is a reinforcement. (Answer: food.)

3. If, instead of presenting food after the .... pecks the ...., a loud noise is turned *on*, the rate of pecking will *not* increase. Presenting a loud noise is not a reinforcement. (Answer: pigeon, key.)

4. When pecking a key *turns off* a very loud noise for a few moments, frequency of pecking in the presence of the noise is observed to *increase*. Ending the loud .... is a reinforcement. (Answer: noise.)

5. Reinforcement which consists of *presenting* stimuli (e.g. food) is called positive reinforcement. In contrast, reinforcement which consists of terminating .... (e.g. painful stimuli) is called negative reinforcement. (Answer: stimuli.)

* MARKLE, S. M.: 'Faulty Frames', in *Programmed Instruction*, The Center for Programmed Instruction, New York, December 1961.

Another commonly used technique is 'fading' or 'vanishing'. Here the student is presented with material to be learned. A simple example might be a short poem. He would first be presented with the poem in full. A frame would then follow with blanks or dashes in the place of some of the words. (Definite and indefinite articles would be obvious choices here.) The pupil's response would be to supply the missing words. Subsequent frames would fade more words until eventually the pupil was writing out the whole of the poem. In a similar way spelling could be taught by fading out the different letters of the word until the student can reproduce the word without any prompts. This method is not only applicable to the learning of simple material; Holland and Skinner used the technique in parts of a programme on neuroanatomy.

Other methods are used in the construction of programmes but they all have similar features; they aim, by textual cues and prompts to build up a complex behavioural repertoire from simple elements with the aim gradually to render the pupil independent of such cues and prompts.

It is possible to group prompts into a number of classes, the main ones being *formal* prompts, *sequence* prompts and *thematic* prompts. Formal prompts are the kind of prompts which the tyro programmer is likely to make use of when he starts writing. Such prompts give cues such as the initial or terminal letters of the missing words. The sequence prompt depends on the preceding frames having built up a train of thought that will help the student to understand and complete the frame. The thematic prompt depends on the content of the frame to channel the student's thinking so that if he reads the material of the frame he will be directed by his thoughts about the content of the frame to arrive at the appropriate answer. Experienced programmers will tend to avoid formal prompts which tend to reduce programmes to extended cross-word puzzles and will concentrate on the other two mentioned so that the student is really thinking about the subject of the programme all the time he is trying to complete a frame and not working through his stock of words beginning with this or that letter.

Intrinsic or branching programming

The intrinsic approach to programmed learning has been developed largely by N. A. Crowder of the Educational Science Division of U.S. Industries, Santa Barbara. As we have seen, Skinner based his programming techniques on a specific theory of learning, Crowder's approach is different. He states his position thus:

> The person who creates a teaching machine might seem to be claiming that he understands human learning in sufficient detail and generality that he can set up, via the machine, those conditions under which efficient learning will inevitably occur. However, we who work with intrinsic programming devices do not have access to any such educational philosopher's stone. Rather, we suspect that human learning takes place in a variety of ways and that these ways vary with the abilities and present knowledge of different students, with the nature of the subject matter, and with a number of interconnections between the sources of variation, and with other sources of variability of which we are not even aware [29].

Since Crowder does not work from a theoretical standpoint, his programmes do not attempt to force the student into a Procrustean bed of Skinnerian frames; instead he proceeds pragmatically allowing each student to 'prove' his own programme. 'The student is given the material to be learned in small logical units and is tested on each unit immediately. The test result is used automatically to control the material the student sees next. If the student passes the test question he is automatically given the next unit of information and the next question. If he fails the test question the preceding unit of information is reviewed, the nature of his error is explained to him, and he is retested. The test questions are multiple-choice questions and there is a separate set of corresponding materials for each answer that is included in the multiple choice alternative. The technique of using a student's choice of answer to a multiple choice question to determine the next material to which he will be exposed has been called *intrinsic programming* . . .' [29].

We see, then, that in general, Crowder's techniques involve multiple choice or directed responses and a programme which involves, in addition to the main route through the material, branches, like the branch lines on a railway, which are used when the student has difficulty on the 'main line'. Diagrammatically the branching programme in its simplest form would be as illustrated in Fig. 14. A student who works his way through the programme without error would go from 1 to 2 to 3 to N making N correct choices. Another student who made all the errors possible would go through the programme making XN errors where X is

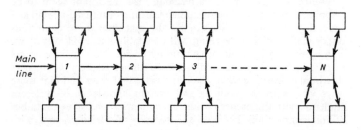

Fig. 14. Branching programme showing main line and branches. A mistake at any one step would lead to a sub-sequence via a branch, and then, after additional information, back to the main line for another try.

the number of alternative choices at each question assuming the same number of choices. Clearly there is a very large number of different paths through the programme and this is the key to Crowder's provision for individual student differences, which claims to convert the programmer's linear monologue to a student generated (intrinsic) dialogue between student and programmer.

Within this general framework more complex programmes can be constructed making allowances for students with different measures of difficulties. Branch lines can branch again, and sub-sequences to the main programme can themselves generate their own sub-sequences. Thus a student having difficulty in a sub-sequence would be routed to a further branch with additional remedial material and thence back to the main sequence (Fig. 15). Such a method produces a much more flexible programme than simple branching and increases the number of alternative routes

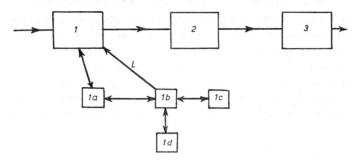

Fig. 15. Branching programme with sub sub-sequences. A mistake at 1 could lead to 1a; a mistake here could lead to 1b; a mistake here could lead to 1c. A correct response at 1a, 1b, or 1c, could lead back to the main sequence via the branch lines or via a special return line L.

enormously. Many complex systems of branching are possible but care must be taken not to lead the student so far off the main track that he has difficulty getting back.

The remedial material in such sub-sequences is generally designed to explain difficult points more thoroughly. Here is an example of one frame in a Crowder programme with the various sub-sequences: note the conversational approach in the presentation and correction. Note also the directing of the student back to the main sequence.

[Sequence from *The Arithmetic of Computers* by N. A. Crowder.] Electronic digital computers perform complicated logical and arithmetical operations in thousandths or even millionths of a second. Inside the computer, numbers are represented by sequences of electrical pulses. But the number system used usually differs considerably from that commonly employed in pen-and-paper arithmetic.

To understand how a computer uses its peculiar number system, we shall have to spend some time dissecting and examining closely the number system we already know.

Our familiar number system uses ten different numerals: 0, 1, 2, 3, 4, 5, 6, 7, 8, and 9. Each single numeral is called a digit. Because the system uses ten different numerals or digits it is called the *decimal* system (Latin *decem* = ten). The arithmetic we learned in school is decimal arithmetic.

239

We are so familiar with the decimal system and decimal arithmetic that the decimal system may seem to us the 'natural' system. Actually it is only one of many systems of writing numbers.

Now here is a question on the material you have just read. Select what you believe to be the correct answer and turn to the page number indicated to the right of the answer you choose.

Would you say that the two numbers 492 and 0·29 are both written in the decimal system?

ANSWER

Both 492 and 0·29 are written in decimal system. Page 4.
Only 0·29 is written in the decimal system. Page 8.

Turning to Page 4 we have:

YOUR ANSWER: Both 492 and 0·29 are written in the decimal system.

You are correct. The word 'decimal' refers simply to the fact that our common number system uses only ten different numerals, or digits. With these ten single digits (0, 1, 2, . . . 9), we can count up to 9. Beyond 9 we must use combinations of these numerals, such as 1 and 0 for ten (10), and 1 and 1 for eleven (11), etc.

Turning to Page 8 we have:

YOUR ANSWER: Only 0·29 is written in the decimal system.

Well, let's see.
You once learned that $0·29 = 29/100$
and $ 0·4 = 4/10$
and $ 0·333 = 333/1000$.

Fractional quantities such as 0·29, and 0·4, and 0·333, written with the aid of the decimal point, are called decimal fractions. You probably were thinking about this use of the word 'decimal' when you decided that the decimal fraction 0·29 is written in the decimal system and the whole number 492 is not.

The fact that no decimal point is shown does not exclude the number 492 from the decimal system. The word 'decimal' means 'ten'. The decimal system is a number system which uses ten different digits. Both whole and fractional numbers may be written with decimal system digits.

The number 492 and the number 0·29 are both written in the decimal system because they both use the decimal system digits – which are 0, 1, 2, 3, 4, 5, 6, 7, 8, and 9. Please return to Page 1 and choose another answer.

In this example there are only two alternative answers, but there could be more than this if necessary.

Since Crowder does not base his techniques on any consistent psychological theory it is not surprising that his views on reinforcement differ from those of Skinner. Whereas Skinner holds that knowledge of results is important in order to reinforce correct behaviour, Crowder allows the student knowledge of results in a merely incidental way. He uses the student's response to decide the choice of the next step through the programme: feedback is for information rather than for reinforcement.

Another very important factor arising from Crowder's lack of a specific theory of learning is his attitude to errors. Skinner seeks to minimize errors since he would view them as punishers which are uneconomical in the formation of routines of behaviour. Crowder covers this point by his insistence that reinforcement from the knowledge of results is incidental and that the main aspect of the wrong choice of path is that it gives additional information.

Perhaps one of the most vulnerable of Crowder's specific techniques is the multiple choice answer. As we shall see when we consider the use of objective tests, there are a number of disadvantages involved in this kind of answer. The most obvious one is that it is difficult to construct plausible alternatives to the correct response but there are other possibly more important ones.

One of them links with our last point. Should really plausible alternatives be presented side by side with the correct answer there is a possibility that the incorrect response might be learned. In addition it seems likely that the selection of one possible answer out of a presented group involves the student in less active consideration of the subject. It could, at its worst, become, in the words of the American educationist, Jacques Barzun, 'just pointing'. (See p. 268.) On the other hand Skinnerian techniques involve not the recognition of the correct answer but its construction, which demands a greater creative effort. Another very important point in favour of the constructed response is that it is likely to '. . . contain more feedback of information [to the programmer] than multiple choice answers: and it is axiomatic that programmers must feed on feedback'.* Multiple choice items automatically cut off much of the very important information that arises from the errors students make, since the content of the errors is preformed by the programmer. However, it should be remembered that the alternatives given in multiple choice items in well-written programmes are based on the actual answers given by students when the programme was being developed. The feedback to the programmer of information on the student's learning activities has been an unexpected 'bonus'. But here, for probably the first time, we are taking a close look at pupils in the process of learning in a way that the lecture or the textbook can never do.

The main advantage of the branching programme with the multiple choice question is that it adapts itself to the student. It is a cybernetic device whereas the simple linear machine is not. (This by no means precludes the possibility of a linear programme which is cybernetic, and in fact machines which present such programmes do exist.) The cybernetic qualities of the branching device make it an attractive proposition for computerized teaching machines. It is this feature which has led some writers to argue that because the branching programme adapts to the student, it is in fact more truly a teaching machine than the linear programme.

The fact that both linear programmes and intrinsic programmes work quite well suggests that too close a comparison between programming and the shaping of behaviour as in animal conditioning is ill advised. When Skinner shapes the behaviour of a pigeon he reinforces the exact response which he wishes the animal to make. In a linear programme the child may make a verbal response which is important only because it indicates that he has grasped the material in the particular frame; the actual word or words which constitute the response may well be quite unimportant. Thus it seems possible that a more fruitful way of looking at programmes, linear or branching, may be to consider the frames as sequential experiences of guided problem solving

* SIME, M.: 'The Sheffield Teaching Machine', in *Teaching Machines and Programmes*, Sheffield University Bulletin, January 1962, p. 21.

activity, small in themselves but whose cumulative effect is to enable the child to cope with more extensive and more difficult problems in the same and related fields.

The two main approaches to programming at the moment in general use are by no means incompatible. Programmes can combine linear and branching sequences and constructed or multiple responses; in fact, one of the growing points in programmed instruction is likely to be in the devising of different ways of presenting the programme and controlling the student's behaviour as he works his way through it. Most programmes, however, demand frequent responses from the student, give him immediate feedback, and allow him to progress at his own rate. Any student who works through a programme is of necessity active. A student listening to a lecture or a child listening to a teacher explaining new material, may or may not be actively grappling with the novel stimuli. Either child or student reading a textbook, could be attempting an active assimilation of the contents, or could be reading in an almost passive way with responses at the minimum required to comprehend the words at the lowest level. In the case of the programme the minimal response is at the level of active comprehension. This factor, coupled with the indispensable logical arrangement of material (not always a feature of textbooks or lectures!), ensures an active approach which is essential for effective learning.

It by no means follows, however, that programmed material will automatically be superior to orthodox methods of presentation. A programme is as good as the programmer and programmers will no doubt vary in competence as do teachers and textbook writers. One of the present dangers in the field of programmed learning is that while machines to present programmes are interesting and relatively easy to produce, the writing of programmes is a difficult and arduous task. Consequently, while machines proliferate, the supply of good tested programmes is very limited and the temptation of commercial interests to take advantage of the new and potentially expanding field, may very well result in the production of indifferent programmes, which could eventually, in the apocalyptic tones of Holland, bury

'. . . the whole movement in an avalanche of teaching machine tapes' [29]. In the light of this warning, let us consider the principles involved in the construction of the linear programme.

Programme construction

An important factor to be considered is the body of pupils for which the programme is intended; in the jargon: *the target population*. It is relevant to consider such things as age, sex, previous educational history, and probable level of competence in the basic skills relevant to the level of material to be dealt with. With this in mind we next consider the syllabus of the programme. This can be done most effectively by deciding what we consider should be in the repertoire of the pupil at the end of the programme. This may be determined by the composition of an *objective test* (see Chapter 10) which will consist of items intended to test the extent to which the student has achieved the objectives set in the programme. By comparing this *post-test* with a statement of the level of present pupil attainment, we can arrive at the general field of coverage of the programme.

Having clearly in mind the target population and the changes in behaviour which he wishes to bring about in the students, the programmer now makes a detailed scrutiny of the syllabus. He seeks to determine the key concepts which the programme is to present to the students. When he has isolated these he arranges them in what he considers to be the most logical sequence and ensures that they are linked with each other within the sequence. Most programme writers will continue the analysis, breaking down the concepts into sub-concepts until the skeleton of the programme is clear. They will then start to construct the individual *frames* which are presented to the student one at a time.

When writing frames it is important to avoid writing them so that they are merely test items, they must be guides to learning. They will present information and demand that the student think about it before making a reply to the question based on the information presented. It is also important that the individual items are linked with each other and are not isolated gobbetts.

The draft programme is now tried out on a few students drawn from the target population. Their responses are analysed and unsatisfactory frames exposed and rewritten. It may also be necessary to add frames. This process may be repeated a number of times before the programme is ready for a field trial. In the field trial the programme is given to a reasonable number of the target population (say at least thirty). The trial group is then tested on the post-test. The responses to the post-test will be scrutinized to see if the programme seems to be teaching any section of the syllabus inefficiently; if it is, that area of the programme will be rewritten and the programme tried again until a very large proportion of students using the programme score high marks on the post-test. The final criterion of efficacy of the programme may well be of the order of 90% of students using it obtaining 90% marks in the post-test. The procedure of revising the test and trying it out until it meets the programmer's criterion is termed *validation*.

The process of validation is an interesting new development in educational practice. For the first time the teacher is taking full responsibility for the children's learning. Instead of placing the onus on the pupil and blaming his lack of ability for his educational failure, the programmer recognizes that his technique is probably faulty and adapts it so as to improve its efficacy. The detailed study of the objectives of the syllabus, the attempt to organize the key concepts logically, and the close scrutiny of the programme in its development, are subjecting teaching to an operational analysis which is unprecedented and which cannot but lead to improvements in teaching techniques. Student teachers learn a great deal by attempting to write a short programme, but so also do teachers who have been teaching for many years.

It should be stressed that programmed instruction by no means reduces learning to rote learning of facts. A good programme will make use of all the techniques of the good teacher. It will direct the attention of the pupil to the necessary concrete material to help him to form real and relevant concepts and it will employ all the aids the teacher is likely to use in the classroom. Such programmes will be far from entirely verbal; they will look outwards and control the student's learning in active intercourse with his environment and not only through working through the programme. Furthermore, it should always be borne in mind that there is no suggestion at all that the teacher is to be superseded by the machine, or the programme. Rather, programmed instruction will help him to do his job more efficiently in certain fields: what those fields are likely to be is an open question at the moment which further experiment and classroom practice will help to answer.

The machines

The simplest method of programme presentation in general use is the programmed textbook. This can be either linear or branching. The linear type may incorporate a technique of having the answer placed separately from the question so that the pupil constructs his response and then consults the answer. We have already seen how a branching programme can be presented in book form by our example from Crowder's programmed book. It is likely that this method of programme presentation will become popular since it does not need machinery and is therefore less expensive than other techniques.

Machines currently available include simple linear ones which present the programme on rolls or sheets of paper and machines using film or continuous stationery which present intrinsic programmes. The simple linear machines function mainly as anti-cheat devices preventing the child from looking ahead to anticipate the anwer called for. They also, with younger children, help with motivation since the children get satisfaction from working the machines. The same can be said about some of the electrical devices, although some of these machines may be linked to ancillary equipment such as tape recorders or film projectors and are of particular use in technical subjects where techniques have to be demonstrated.

It may be asked, if material can be presented in textbook form, why machines are necessary. The main reason at one level is that 'cheating' can be prevented by a machine, since the programme once in the machine is inaccessible to the student, who can only run the programme forward, and is thus prevented from consulting the answer before making a response and cannot alter his answer once made. In the textbook the student can look ahead or go back. It is by no means certain, however, that it is essential to prevent cheating. Homme and Glaser claim that experience shows that a cheat-proof device is not essential for college students and I found that student teachers fared much the same whether they used a cheat-proof device or a non-cheat device when using a programme on educational psychology.* It may perhaps be more necessary with younger pupils, but even here it may well be that our fears about cheating are part of our heritage of aversive educational practices where the chief concern has been the punishing of undesired or incorrect responses, rather than the positive reinforcement of desired or correct responses. Should future experience show that the approach to learning, implicit in programmed instruction, renders old ideas of aversive control patently obsolete (as many teachers already maintain), then the programmed book will be of very great importance and much of the gadgetry now being produced will be unnecessary.

Another reason for using machines involves quite different issues. The programmes we have described have so far been of the non-cybernetic simple linear type, or the simple cybernetic ones of Crowder. Using modern computer technology it becomes possible to produce a machine that not only teaches but 'learns'. This involves the machine in the analysis of the student's past performance on the programme in order to present him with the appropriate material. The machine, that is, adapts to the behaviour of the individual student. To some extent, of course, this is merely an elaboration of the branching programme; its value lies in its ability to handle a much more complex range of behavioural contingencies. It is also possible for one computer to cope with a number of students each getting individual attention.

A further possibility in this field is the use of computers to

* STONES, E.: *An Experiment in the Use of Programming Techniques in the Training of Student Teachers*, University of Nottingham Institute of Education, 1966.

make a detailed study of the learning process in man. We have seen how the feedback from the student's working through a programme teaches the programmer a lot about the student's learning. However, this feedback is probably a very crude measure of the complexities involved in human learning. It is possible that as Skinner needed elaborate electrical equipment to investigate the learning process in lower animals, it will be essential to use the most advanced computer technology to investigate learning in man. Work is now proceeding in several universities where computers are being used to study the fundamental processes of human learning. This is probably the most significant aspect of the current interest in teaching machines for educational psychology. It is also of interest that the work which led from the laboratory to the classroom has now moved back into the laboratory at a much higher level.

Summary

Programmed instruction applies some of the ideas which have evolved from the laboratory study of learning, to the classroom. Skinner argues that in the normal classroom situation feedback of knowledge of results and reinforcement are very inefficient. Programmed learning was developed by Skinner to bring these aspects of learning under closer control.

Pressey developed an early testing device in the 1920s which, he discovered, not only tested but taught. In recent years Skinner provided the main impetus for the development of programmed learning using *linear* techniques. Crowder has been instrumental in fostering the development of *intrinsic* techniques.

Linear programmes take students step by step through the programme providing rapid and regular reinforcement by arranging that, after each short step, the student is informed of the result of his effort and that the student will almost invariably be correct. Intrinsic programmes usually present material in larger portions. The student makes a selection of an answer after reading the material and, according to the nature of his answer, will take one path or another to the next item of information. In the intrinsic programme students will in theory take different paths through the programme, whereas, in the linear programme, they will all take the same path. However, there is no clear dividing line between the linear and intrinsic approach and the programmer will draw on the techniques appropriate to the subject in hand.

The most important features in programme construction are the detailed scrutiny of the syllabus, its breaking down into key concepts, and the ordering of these concepts in a logical sequence. When the frames have been written, thorough validation is most important. A programme should not be used unless it has been tried and found effective.

Machines range from simple linear devices presenting the programme on rolls or sheets of paper, to sophisticated cybernetic appliances linked up to computers. Programmes, can, however, be presented without machines. Research is now going on using programming techniques and computers to investigate factors involved in human learning.

CHAPTER 10

Examinations and Tests

Our discussion so far has centred on the process of learning; we now turn to a consideration of the ways in which the teacher can measure the extent to which children have learned. If we consider some of the techniques involved in programming we shall have some idea of the approach to the assessment of learning. Programme writing starts from the position where the programmer defines what he hopes will be the terminal behaviour of his students. This he terms his behavioural objectives. These objectives will specify what he expects the students to be able to do at the end of his programme. He may expect them to have acquired certain skills or to be able to answer a number of questions which they were unable to answer before the programme. The programmer will attempt to assess to what extent he has achieved his objectives by using a test to assess the students' terminal behaviour. Such a test could be a practical one involving the knowledge of techniques, or it could be a verbal one. In the main, tests in education are of the verbal type. This is the situation in ordinary teaching. The teacher rarely specifies his objectives so precisely as the programmer, but when he administers a test he is doing essentially the same thing. That is, he is attempting to assess the degree to which the terminal behaviour of his students differs from their initial behaviour. Traditionally he uses a test to do this, although in some subjects this may be augmented by practical exercises.

The essay type test

The test most used in this country to assess the efficacy of learning is the essay type test. This is used commonly in the classroom and in public examinations such as the General Certificate of Education. These tests consist of a number of questions which demand a short essay as an answer. Here, for example, are a number of questions taken from tests given at different educational levels. Note that some of the questions are intended to test practical knowledge.

'What are the essential differences between the microstructures of whiteheart and blackheart malleable cast irons? Discuss the variations in metal composition and in heat treatment which give rise to these differences.'
(City and Guilds, Foundry Practice, 1959, Paper No. 62/4)

'What are the advantages and disadvantages of finishing the joints to face brickwork:

'(i) as the work proceeds;
'(ii) on completion?'
(City and Guilds, Brickwork, 1958, Paper No. 82/1)

'Discuss the economic and political geography of continental shelves.'
(General Certificate of Education, Geography, Advanced, Paper 1, June 1954; Northern Universities Joint Matriculation Board)

The candidate is expected to write a short essay in answer to these questions. The scripts are then marked by the examiner, who awards marks generally in one of two ways. He may prepare a detailed marking scheme awarding marks for specific aspects of the answer; this method is generally termed analytical marking. Or he may award what he considers to be the appropriate marks after reading through the question, without making any detailed analysis. This method is generally termed impression marking. Impression marking is quicker, and some examiners view it with suspicion. But in some subjects, such as English composition, it produces results which are almost as consistent as analytical marking, and in view of the time saved, it would seem to be more practical in these subjects than the analytical method.

One of the weaknesses of the essay-type test springs from the fact that the examination has a limited coverage. In a G.C.E. 'O' Level paper, for example, where the candidate may be asked only four or five questions, he may have studied for four or five years. The questions may demand insight and understanding but they do not cover the whole field and often they are to some extent predictable. We therefore get the widespread practice in almost all public examinations of 'question spotting' and 'cramming'. This involves the teacher's attempting to single out that area of the syllabus which he considers most likely to be the subject of questioning, and concentrating intensively on it, often with the aid of prepared model answers. In the worst cases in some examinations it has been known for candidates to have been given a supply of model answers to swallow for regurgitation later in the examination room when the appropriate questions were presented. If the examinations could be more inclusive the practice of cramming would be much more difficult, if not impossible.

Another disadvantage of the essay test may be exemplified by the case of the grammar school teacher who was interrupted in the marking of a batch of essays. The next day when she went to continue the marking she took up the first essay and after reading it through was preparing to give it a mark of four or five when, on turning the last page, she realized that she had marked the essay the previous day and had awarded it eight. Experiments have been conducted in the marking of essays by teams of markers and it has been demonstrated many times that the mark awarded by one marker very often varies considerably from that awarded by another marker for the same essay. In the same way, inconsistency in the same marker, as outlined in the case of the grammar school teacher, has been discovered on many occasions.

Public examination boards are not unaware of the problem of inconsistency and take steps to solve it. A typical procedure to increase marker consistency of such examinations is to have a closely coordinated team of examiners under a chief examiner. Such a team meets after the examination and discusses a mark scheme for the examination. Examples of answers made are considered and considerable discussion ensues to decide on a common standard of marking. Sometimes this may involve the marking by the whole panel of photostat copies of a sample of scripts with comparison of marks awarded and a final agreed standard of marking. The marking of the scripts by the team now goes on with continuous checking of the examiners' standard of marking by the chief examiner. With all this detailed coordination a very high degree of marker consistency can be attained. Another procedure, sometimes used in the secondary selection examination, is to have each English essay marked by several markers. The average mark is then taken as a true mark. This is an approach to the 'true mark' suggested by C. Burt as being the average mark of an infinite number of markers; but even this mark cannot be regarded as a 'true 'mark. It is clear, however, that these techniques of increasing consistency are not generally amenable to administration in schools: they are very time consuming and can be expensive, consequently they are rarely used outside large-scale public examinations.

Another criticism sometimes made of the essay-type question is that it favours the verbally fluent. The question intended to discover how much the candidate knows about a given subject will only succeed in its aim if language is, for the candidate, an instrument of expression and not an obstruction. In some examinations of a practical nature (see above), examiners' reports make it quite clear that language difficulty is putting a barrier between the candidate's knowledge and his conveying it to the examiner. This need cause no concern if ability in the use of language is considered to be part of the examination, but if the writing of an essay-type answer is merely to enable the candidate to parade his factual knowledge, then language difficulties could prevent the examiner from really discovering the true extent of the candidate's knowledge. In all spheres, of course, fluency in the use of language could give an advantage unrelated to the knowledge and understanding of a subject. If we are concerned to discover this knowledge and understanding, we must be concerned to remove the barrier.

On the other hand, examinations in certain subjects set great store on the effective command of language. Such tests would include those demanding the ability to present an argument logically, the discursive philosophical essay, and discussions of an aesthetic nature. In such tests the examiner would be concerned with the command of language and it would enter into his assessment. He should not, however, expect a very high degree of consistency in his marking.

The 'objective' or 'new-type' test

A method of testing which has been used extensively in the U.S.A. for many years and in some spheres in this country has involved the use of the *objective test*. The mark awarded to an essay-type answer tends to be subjective in the sense of its being the expression of a personal point of view; that of one examiner at one particular time. The objective test seeks to avoid this subjectivity by asking questions the answers to which are generally accepted by examiners. It follows that where there is any doubt, the test constructor will consult a number of other competent examiners until he is satisfied that the item is satisfactory. The test can also be objective in that it tests facts which are objectively true or false. For example, the question '$2 \times 2 = ?$' tests an objective fact as does the question, 'What is the longitude of London?'

The construction of objective tests

The fact that the constructor of the objective test is concerned so to arrange his questions that they produce generally accepted answers, precludes his asking such questions as those exemplified above in our discussion of the essay-type test. He cannot, for example, use such familiar opening gambits as, 'Write an account of . . .', or 'Compare and contrast . . .'. Instead he has to structure his questions having in mind a fairly precise picture of the answer expected. This is done in a number of ways and the various types of questions, or *items* as they are often called, are used as the tester considers appropriate. We may now consider the different kinds of items used by the compilers of such tests.

The multiple choice item

In this type of question an incomplete statement is presented, together with a number of alternative answers, for example:

'The main industry of Lancashire is the manufacture of (pottery, machinery, cotton, wool).'

The candidate is asked to pick out the correct answer. The main problem in composing such items lies in the difficulty of providing suitable alternatives. Clearly the alternatives must be feasible or they are valueless, for example:

'The largest county in England is (Yorkshire, Quebec, Belfast, Paris).'

Another problem is that unless six or seven alternative answers are given the chance of the candidate guessing the correct answer could be, in theory, sufficiently high materially to affect the total mark on a test consisting of such items.

True or false items

Here the student is presented with a statement and asked to decide whether or not it is true, for example:

'It is unlikely that learning will be effective without knowledge of results. True/False.'

Clearly if the item is left like this there is an even chance of guessing the correct answer. To avoid this it is advisable to include a third alternative answer: Don't Know. The candidate is told to select 'Don't Know' rather than to guess, since a wrong answer will be penalized whereas a 'Don't Know' will not.

Matching items

In questions of this nature the pupil is given two lists and asked to indicate which items in one list are associated with each of the items in the other list, for example:

'Match the quotation with psychologist. Thorndike, Kohler, Pavlov.

"Learning is connecting" . . . .
"Insight is central to learning" . . . .
"Speech is the second signalling system" . . . . '

The completion item

The type of items so far considered are questions which assess the ability to recognize information, that is, the information is provided and the pupil has merely to identify it. Another class of items makes greater demands on the pupil and in general is more satisfactory: this is the completion, or open-ended item. In these items the pupil is asked to give an answer to a question or may be asked to fill in a blank space in a statement. This is more exacting for the pupil since it is more difficult to recall information than to recognize it. Such items avoid the difficulties of multiple choice questions and restrict the pupil less. They are at times more difficult to mark, since there may be several admissible alternative answers. Here is an example of a completion answer item:

'Changes in the autonomic nervous system associated with strong emotion could be:

1...
2...
3...
4...'

Recently some work has been done with these open-ended items which illustrates clearly the suggestion above, that their value lies in their lack of restriction. Liam Hudson, a Cambridge psychologist, gave sixth form boys a number of open-ended questions. He found that many of the boys, who did poorly on the closed multiple choice type of item, succeeded well when given open-ended questions which gave scope to their imagination and general cultural background.* Here is an example of the type of question used in the experiment and the answer it evoked.

The boys were asked to write down the different uses of a blanket. One of them answered:

'Warmth, stop fires, sick people, fine blanket to jump into, to protect hands when smashing windows, suffocating people with, ladder, rope, hat, cap, trousers.'

The interpretive item

This kind of item could combine two or more of the methods of responding referred to above. Interpretive items enable the tester

* HUDSON, L.: *Nature*, 10 November 1962. See also GETZELS, J. W., and JACKSON, P.W.: *Creativity and Intelligence*, Wiley, 1962.

to assess the child's ability to use his learning in situations which approximate to real-life situations. Questions of this nature present the candidate with information in a given field and the candidate is asked to interpret the information and make evaluations using the knowledge he should have learned. Here is an example of such an item which gives information which is only likely to be interpretable by a candidate who has studied the subject and who is able to use his knowledge in a meaningful way. It tests some of the information given in the next chapter: you might like to attempt to answer the item now and after you have read the next chapter to see whether in fact it is a useful test item.

Answer the questions from the data given:

Child aged ten years
Performance on Terman–Merill revision of the Binet Intelligence Test (1937 revision)

Passed all sub-tests at the 11-year stage
Passed four out of six sub-tests at the 12-year stage
Passed two out of six sub-tests at the 13-year stage
Passed none out of six sub-tests at the 14-year stage
Reading age 14 years
Arithmetic age 10 years

(1) What is the child's basal Mental Age? ....
(2) What is the child's Mental Age? ....
(3) What is the child's Intelligence Quotient? ....
(4) In comparison with his brother age 5 years with the same I.Q. he is more/less/equally advanced or more/less/equally retarded as/than children of his own age ....
(5) What is his achievement quotient in reading? ....
(6) What is his achievement quotient in arithmetic?..........

From the examples of objective test items given, readers will have realized that one question will by no means take the time to answer that one essay type question would. This suggests another characteristic of the objective test; it is possible to ask a large number of questions in a fairly short space of time. This enables the examiner to cover a very wide field in a way that cannot be done with the essay-type test. So, for example, it would be possible to give a test of up to a hundred items in the same time that would be taken by five essay-type questions.

This not only enables the examiner to cover a much wider field but it also increases the reliability of the test. Reliability means the extent to which a test will produce the same pattern of scores from a given group of subjects on different occasions. Thus, in a highly reliable test each candidate would be expected to occupy a similar position in the range of scores from one administration of the test to another. Generally, reliability increases with an increase in the number of questions. An objective test has to reach a very high level of reliability before it can be accepted as suitable for administration as a public examination. Reliability in this sense is quite foreign to the essay-type test.

We can now see that the essay-type test and the objective test have four essential differences:

(1) The objective test consists of items that demand answers generally agreed among examiners. This ensures a very high level of marker consistency. On the other hand the essay-type test has a high level of marker inconsistency. The objective test will also be highly reliable when given on subsequent occasions.

(2) Since objective test items do not demand lengthy answers, a test can consist of a large number of items. This enables the examiner to cover a very much wider area of the field to be examined than would be possible with essay-type questions. A well designed objective test renders 'question spotting' and 'cramming' unprofitable.

(3) Because of the care needed in the construction of the objective test and because of the large number of items, the construction of such a test is a very arduous task. In addition, any test that is more than a casual one to be given in the classroom, is normally given a try-out to spot any ambiguities or faults in construction which can be corrected before final presentation of the test. The composition of an essay-type test is generally a less laborious process and very rarely involves a try-out. Conversely the accurate and reliable marking of essay-type tests is very difficult and time consuming, whereas the marking of objective tests is rapid and reliable.

(4) The essay-type test gives the advantage to the verbally fluent; the objective test is a more accurate assessment of the pupil's ability in the subject being examined.

The scoring of tests

A problem which faces anyone who uses tests or examinations of any type, is the question of reporting the marks obtained in a meaningful way. One method of doing this is exemplified by the school report which gives a mark for each subject and an aggregate mark which sums the subject marks and from which a class position is derived. Such a procedure will almost certainly give an inaccurate picture of the relative attainments of the different pupils. The reasons for this can be seen if we consider the process whereby such marks and class positions are obtained.

Let us consider two sets of marks, one obtained from a test of mathematics and one from a test of English. Typically, the scores in the mathematics test would range from a fairly low mark to a fairly high mark. If we arrange such scores on a diagram we would get a curve of the type shown in Fig. 16. The English

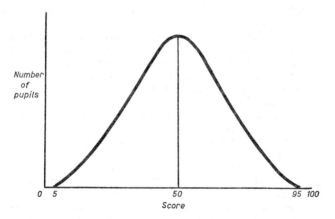

Fig. 16. Distribution of scores on the mathematics test. Note that the scores take up almost the whole of the marks scale.

marks, however, typically have a much narrower spread and tend to cluster around the average. Expressed diagrammatically they would produce a curve such as the one in Fig. 17.

Since our curves are symmetrical it will be clear that the average mark in the mathematics test is 50 whereas the average English mark is 40. Thus a pupil who scores 40 in both would be below average in mathematics and might well need extra tuition, while in English he would be average and cause the teacher no concern. To compare the performance of a pupil on the two tests

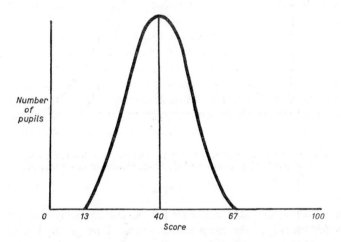

Fig. 17. Distribution of scores on the English test. Note the lower mean than that of the mathematics test and the closer bunching of scores which makes use of only about half of the mark range available.

we need to take account of the difference between the averages and to make such a comparison we must first equate the average scores on the two tests. This can be done by setting the average of both sets of marks at the same figure. In our example this could be done by increasing the average of the English test by 10 marks, which would involve our adding 10 marks to every score on the English test. We should then have a situation where the average marks on the two tests were the same. This is presented in Fig. 18.

From the diagram it can be seen that while the average marks

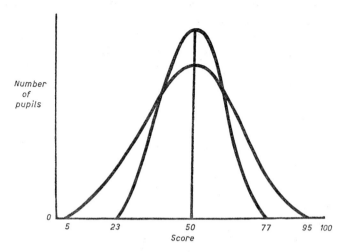

Fig. 18. Pattern of English scores with mean adjusted to 50 added to the diagram of the distribution of mathematics scores.

are equated, the other marks are not comparable because of the wider spread of the mathematics scores. Thus a pupil who scores top marks in the mathematics test obtains 95, whereas the top English mark is 77. To make comparison possible throughout we have to change the shape of one of the distributions to match the other. This technique can be illustrated diagrammatically as in Fig. 19, where the distribution of English marks has been stretched until it matches the distribution of the mathematics marks. The top marks in the tests are now both 95 and the bottom marks are both 5: in addition all the intermediate scores are equated. (Note that the relative positions of all marks on the English test are unchanged.)

The effect of this technique of equating scores can be seen if we first add the original or raw scores of two candidates, one good at mathematics and average at English, the other good at English and average at mathematics, and compare the result with that derived from the addition of the scores which have been equated.

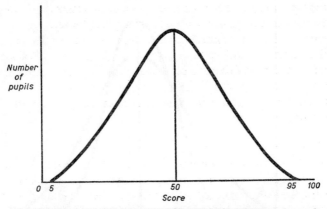

Fig. 19. English scores with the mean adjusted to the mean of the mathematics scores and the spread or dispersal of the marks also adjusted to that of the mathematics scores, now coincide with the pattern of mathematics scores when added to the diagram.

| | Raw Scores | | | Equated Scores | | |
	English	Mathe-matics	Total	English	Mathe-matics	Total
Pupil A	40	95	135	50	95	145
Pupil B	67	50	117	95	50	145

We can now see that in any addition of raw scores, pupils with an aptitude for subjects, tests of which tend to produce marks with a wide spread, will have an advantage over other pupils. In fact, unless marks in all the subjects are distributed in exactly the same way, then error is introduced immediately. In the case of the school report mentioned above, it is most unlikely that the class positions arrived at by adding the raw scores in all the subjects would be accurate. We would probably find, if we were to equate the distributions of marks in all the subjects, that the summed raw scores gave spuriously high positions to the pupils who shone in the science subjects since the distribution of marks in these subjects generally tends to be more spread out than in

262

the literary subjects. It is essential, when it is desired to make a meaningful comparison of two or more sets of marks, to convert them both to a common scale. A suitable scale for use in school is one which gives scores resembling percentages. Unless this is done marks should never be added, nor is it really possible to make meaningful comparisons between them. The technique of converting raw scores to equated or standard scores is explained in the Appendix. Readers wishing to compare sets of scores should use this technique.

Uses of tests

(*i*) *The evaluation of learning.* We have so far considered merely the *methods* of testing used in schools and in public examinations; what is equally important is the *aim* of the test. The test given by the teacher in school generally follows a specific piece of instruction, and school examinations are often intended to assess the extent to which the content of the various syllabuses has been learned. Such tests attempt to evaluate learning, and in theory, if teacher and pupils have both worked effectively, the whole class could get full marks. In practice this rarely happens, largely because the teacher tends to set the level of difficulty of material so that the 'average' child will obtain scores approximating to some rather arbitrarily conceived 'average' mark. However, this does not really affect the aim of the test, and the teacher will be able to assess the efficacy of his teaching and the pupils' learning, provided he has used a reliable test. When he has seen the results of his test he can use the information he obtains from it to determine his future course of action with his pupils.

(*ii*) *Diagnostic tests.* Another use of tests is that of diagnosing educational weaknesses. Many children have difficulty with some aspect of learning. Some fall behind in learning the basic skills of reading and arithmetic, and it may be difficult for the teacher to pinpoint specific difficulties which the child may have. Diagnostic tests are designed to give the child a carefully graded series of sub-tests which deal with the main aspects of the subject so that failure on one or more of the sub-tests will pinpoint the particular difficulty or difficulties which the child is experiencing. For example, a child having difficulty with reading might, through the administration of a diagnostic test, be found to have difficulty in perceiving shapes accurately. Remedial measures could then be taken to improve his visual discrimination and thereby enable him more effectively to distinguish one letter from another. It is unlikely that the teacher would have been able to make such a diagnosis intuitively. Similar tests are available which analyse difficulties in the understanding of mathematical processes; although in view of the findings of modern research into the developmental aspect of children's mathematical thinking and into methods of teaching mathematics, it would seem that there is a need for tests which take such findings into consideration. Some tests make a much more superficial assessment of ability. These do not make an analytical and qualitative assessment of the child's disability, but make a quantitative judgement which states merely that the child is average, above average, or below average. These tests are of some value, but clearly do not help in the same way as the more analytical ones.

(*iii*) *Tests of attainment.* Some tests are designed with no specific group of students in mind. They aim, instead, to be used generally, to sample the level of attainment in the more common subjects of the curriculum. The compiler of such a test would have in mind the general level of attainment in these subjects and would design his test to cover the main aspects of the subjects at that level. With tests of this nature it is possible to derive *norms* from an analysis of the answers of large numbers of pupils. These norms indicate the average performance of individuals or groups in that particular test. They can then be used to assess the attainment of an individual, or possibly a group, in relation to the total population of similar persons. The derivation of norms for a given population is termed *standardization*, and in tests which are given norms, the nature of the population used for standardization is crucial. The basic assumption of standardization procedures is that the population is homogeneous; that is, that the sample used for standardization is truly representative of the whole group from which it is drawn. For example, tests standardized on English children from rural areas would not be applicable to urban English children. Similarly, tests standardized on American children cannot automatically be transferred to English children. Teachers need to be very careful in the use of standardized tests. The process of standardization is so onerous and time consuming that few tests can claim to have really accurate norms. P. E. Vernon recommends teachers to use only recently standardized tests and to scrutinize the standardization details carefully before using them. They could also build up their own norms in their own schools or districts [30].

One difficulty inherent in the construction of attainment tests such as we are considering, is the content of the test. Since these tests are designed with no specific group of pupils in mind, the test constructor has to estimate the possible content of the course which would be common to the groups eventually using his test. This endeavour to be inclusive often means that the test samples only part of the field of study of any one group, and if norms are also used a very misleading picture of the ability of a child or group of children might be obtained. In such subjects as history and geography the difficulty of providing meaningful content is seen clearly. In these subjects, and in many others, there is no commonly agreed syllabus and it is clearly impossible to prepare a meaningful standardized test for such subjects. However, to a less obvious degree, the problem is present throughout, even in the 'basic' subjects. In view of the problems inherent in the use of large-scale attainment tests, the teacher wishing to test his children would do well to construct his own objective test; or if he did use a published test, he should scrutinize carefully the standardizing procedure (see pp. 271 and 398).

(iv) *Selection tests.* Perhaps the most widely known type of test is that used for selection. Selection was the aim of the first public examinations used in England, and from then on such examinations have been used to arrange candidates in order of merit so that the best can be selected for admission to certain professions and certain educational institutions. These examinations are similar in aim to the attainment tests we have discussed, although, in Great Britain, they are mainly essay-type examinations. They differ from the attainment tests mentioned above in that the examiners prescribe the content of the examinations and the schools and colleges adapt their syllabuses to conform to the content of the examinations. However, they are attainment tests in that they attempt to assess the educational level attained by the candidate. That is, although the tests are designed to select candidates for future activity, they attempt to measure past learning. For example, the General Certificate of Education 'A' Level is an assessment of educational achievement at the end of secondary education. But at the same time it serves as a tool of selection for higher education; candidates for entrance to university and other institutions of high education being selected largely on the basis of their performance at 'A' Level.

Consideration of the other most widely used public examinations, the selection examination at ten or eleven, brings us to a test which, while used for selection, has an entirely different basis from that of the tests we have so far considered. It is different in that it does not attempt primarily to assess learning which has taken place, but rather it seeks to discover something more fundamental: the ability to learn. The need to do this arose from the changes following on the 1944 Education Act when fees for secondary education were abolished and when secondary education for all became law. Before this time secondary education had been generally available to those who could pay or those who obtained scholarships from public bodies (such as local education authorities). Since such children were in a minority (about 15% of the population) there were comparatively few secondary school places and most children went to elementary schools. Local authorities, therefore, under the 1944 Act, had the job of allocating about 15% of children at age ten or eleven to secondary schools ('Secondary Grammar Schools' with a few 'Secondary Technical Schools' was the new nomenclature), and about 85% to 'Secondary Modern Schools' (as the senior departments of the old elementary schools were now called). Allocation by length of purse was no longer acceptable: some other, educationally desirable method was needed. The intelligence test provided the answer. Not only was it clearly more equitable than the fee paying system, but, because it purported to assess ability to learn, or more precisely, 'innate, intellectual capacity' (see below), it also ensured that the quality of a child's primary school experience was not the most important contributory factor in the allocation. In other words, in the competition for places in grammar schools, all children, it was suggested, had the same opportunities. If a child were not selected it was because his basic ability did not measure up to the demands of a grammar school education. He was not 'grammar school calibre'. There is in these ideas the assumption that the ability of the child of 'grammar school calibre' is different in kind from that of the non-grammar school child. This assumption has been challenged by many psychologists and we shall discuss their criticisms later together with the techniques and assumptions of intelligence testing.

Attitudes to testing

Despite the widespread use of objective tests and their undoubted value, they have not been taken up by the schools or examining boards (with the exception of eleven plus examinations) to any great extent. There is, indeed, a decided hostility towards them in some educational circles, an attitude which was expressed by the remark made by one high official in a G.C.E. examining board who said that such tests would be introduced 'over my dead body'. American writers have also written very critically about these tests. M. Mayer writes that these tests '. . . move error from the marking process to the test writing process' [31]. Mayer is writing in the context of American education where the objective test is ubiquitous and test writing is almost an industry, with the consequence that there are undoubtedly many poor tests which ask questions of appalling triviality. The constructor of a bad test will give priority to the ease with which the item will conform to the objective pattern, often at the expense of the content: the constructor of a good test will give the content priority and then endeavour to frame the question most suitably for his purpose. There is clearly no merit in asking worthless questions merely because they are amenable to objective marking. Another of Mayer's criticisms links up with the work done at Cambridge with open ended tests; he points out that the 'wrong choices' in some tests are in fact much more insightful than the 'correct' ones.

Jacques Barzun, within the same educational climate, writes bitterly of the stultifying influence of the American addiction to testing on the student's ability to use his own language, with the associated loss of sensitivity. He says:

Taking an objective test is simply pointing. It calls for the least effort of mind above that of keeping awake: recognition. And it is recognition without a shock, for a veteran of twelve years old, the traditional four choices for each question fall into a soothing rhythm. No tumult of surprise followed by a rallying generalship and concentration as in facing an essay question. No fresh unfolding of the subject under unexpected demand, but the routine sorting out of the absurd from the trivial, or the completing of dull sentences by word- or thought-clichés. No other single practice explains as fully the intellectual defects of our students . . . than their ingrained association of knowledge and thought with the scratching down of check marks on dotted lines.*

And later:

Even if the tests were constructed with impeccable draughtsmanship and were free from all ambiguities and errors, they would, in my opinion, still have serious defects as testing instruments, especially when applied to creative persons and to some of those people, who, despite impressive gifts, do not shine at parlor games. For multiple choice tests, by their very nature, tend to favour the pickers of choices over the doers, and the superficially brilliant over the creatively profound. And the use of these tests has a baleful influence on teachers and teaching.

However it is clear that Barzun is concerned only with the multiple choice question which we have considered above. He is also concerned about a situation in which multiple choice tests have a completely clear field and where the essay test is almost a thing of the past. In Britain, however, this does not apply, and it would be unfortunate to reject the objective test merely because it has been used unimaginatively and in ways of dubious educational value. The criticism of both Barzun and Mayer can be met by a well-designed test using a variety of items; but we might stress that the use of objective tests does not preclude the use of

* BARZUN, J.: *The House of Intellect*, Secker and Warburg, 1959.

essays or the teaching of the native tongue and the cultivation of sensitivity and aesthetic appreciation.

It is interesting to note that similar criticisms are sometimes made of the G.C.E. examinations at 'O' and 'A' Level, while recently F. R. Leavis said much the same kind of thing about the work which earns an undergraduate a first class honours degree in English. He considered that the final examinations in the honours school were tests of good journalists and nothing else; that the successful student exhibits merely a facile quickness with no real depth.

The practising teacher will do best to base his assessment of his children on a combination of factors. The ongoing activity of his pupils throughout the year will be one of the best yardsticks of their work. He will see, in the work they produce over a period, whether his efforts are bearing fruit. The essay test may well be useful to encourage the children to crystallize their thoughts and make a succinct statement; it will be well to remember, however, that it has many flaws as a measure of learning. Objective tests will give the wide coverage of a given subject and will have the advantages listed above. As a measure of the children's learning, and also for diagnostic purposes, objective tests are a very great aid to the teacher. They must, however, be carefully constructed and teachers might well bear in mind in this connection the aphorism: 'There are no wrong answers, only wrong questions.'

Summary

Most teachers use some form of test to assess the efficacy of the children's learning. In the main such tests demand that children write short essays in answer to questions designed to test their understanding of a given subject. These essays can be marked analytically on a points basis, or by impression. Research shows that impression marking of English essays is very little inferior to analytical marking and is much quicker.

The essay-type test, however, has certain weaknesses. Since only a small number of questions can be answered in the time usually available, the test cannot cover adequately the full range of the subject to be tested. The essay test also favours the verbally fluent even in subjects of an essentially practical nature. It is very difficult to get marker consistency with essay tests. Public examining bodies are able to get a fair measure of consistency but only through use of techniques inaccessible to most teachers. The reliability of essay tests is also low.

Objective tests avoid many of the problems of essay tests. The objective test consists of questions which demand answers of only one or two words. The answers to the questions are *objective* in the sense that most testers would agree with them, and it is a straightforward matter to say whether an answer is right or wrong. The items (questions) in an objective test can be of different kinds, among them are: the multiple choice item where the candidate chooses the correct answer out of a number of alternatives, the true/false item where the candidate has to decide whether a suggested answer is correct or not, matching items where the candidate has to discern connections between phenomena, and the open-ended or completion item where the candidate has to write in an answer to the question. The interpretive item can combine different approaches and enable the tester to assess the child's ability to apply his learning. The virtues of objective tests are that there is little or no problem of marker inconsistency, they are highly reliable from one administration to another, and since the answers demanded are short, the test can cover a very wide field and it is less easy to 'cram'.

Any test, essay or objective, will produce its own pattern of scores from a given set of candidates. From this it follows that it is incorrect to add scores made on different tests. If aggregate scores are required, the scores on all the tests to be added must be converted to standard scores.

The main uses of tests are for the evaluation of learning as when the teacher tests his class to see if the children have learned what he hopes they have learned; attainment tests, which aim to assess the abilities of children as compared with the general population; diagnostic tests, to isolate any educational deficiencies with a view to remedial action; and selection. The main uses of tests for selection are in the G.C.E. examination, which, although not designed as a selection examination, in fact serves that purpose especially as a gateway to higher education, and the examination at eleven for secondary education. The G.C.E. in the main makes use of essay-type tests, secondary school selection generally uses objective tests sometimes in conjunction with essays. One test used for secondary selection which differs from other tests is the test of intelligence. This aims to discover the underlying ability of a child and not what he may have learned.

Critics of objective tests often argue that they are of a mechanical nature, that they encourage rote learning, and that students brought up on them are unable to argue a case in writing. These criticisms may apply when only stereotyped multiple choice items are used, but not when completion items are used and objective tests used in conjunction with essay tests. Objective tests are much more difficult to set than essay tests and because of this there are some poor tests which make very trivial demands on the student and are far from 'objective'. Objective tests should make the candidates think and not just respond without understanding. Teachers should use a combination of methods to assess children's learning.

This chapter aims to give the reader a general idea of the problems of testing. It does not claim to teach test construction. The reader in search of detailed information on test construction is referred to the texts mentioned on p. 398.

CHAPTER 11

Intelligence and Intelligence Testing

Individual tests of intelligence

The first intelligence tests to be produced were those devised by a French psychologist called Alfred Binet who, with his collaborator, T. Simon, published a scale for the measurement of intelligence. This scale was to be administered on an individual basis by the psychologist and not in a group situation such as many readers may have encountered in public tests of intelligence. The aim of the test was to select those children in Paris schools who were below the normal standards of educability so that they could be sent to special schools. The scale was revised twice until by 1911 it consisted of a number of test items arranged according to the age at which they are usually passed. Thus, for example, the average child of five years of age would be able to answer all the questions on the scale below the five-year-old level, all the questions on the five-year-old scale, but none of the questions above the five-year-old scale. Such a child would be, according to Binet's definition, exactly average. On the other hand a child of four may also be able to answer all the questions on the five-year-old scale. This child would, according to Binet's criterion, be above average, while a child of six making the same score would be below average. Binet then introduced the concept of mental age which is derived by discovering the test level which an individual attains. Thus all three children mentioned above would have mental ages of five. In general, of course, children do not produce such a neat, clear cut, pattern of scores, but generally cope with all the tests at one level (this is termed the 'basal' age) and in addition they answer some of the questions in the tests one or two years above this basal age. An example of a child's score in a Binet test may help to make this point clearer.

Child passes all sub-tests on the five-year-old scale:

Therefore basal age is 5 years:	score =	5 years 0 months
Child passes two sub-tests out of six on the 6-year-old scale	score = $\frac{2}{6}$ year =	4 months
Child passes one sub-test out of six on the 7-year-old scale	score = $\frac{1}{6}$ year =	2 months
Total or Mental Age	=	5 years 6 months

Used on its own, the concept of mental age could be misleading. As we have seen children of different chronological ages can make the same score on the test and this will give them all the same mental age. However, the child who is older than his mental age will be backward compared with other children of the same chronological age, whereas a younger child scoring the same will be in advance of children of his chronological age. The practice therefore developed of presenting mental age and chronological age (M.A. and C.A.) as a ratio. Our three children would, by this procedure, have mental ratios of $\frac{5}{5} = 1 : \frac{5}{4} + 1.25$, and $\frac{5}{6} = .83$. The mental ratio was later replaced by the 'intelligence quotient' which is the mental ratio multiplied by a hundred. We have now the well known term Intelligence Quotient or I.Q., which is $\frac{M.A.}{C.A.} \times 100$. On this rating our children have I.Q.s of 100, 125, and 83.

The concept of mental age and the idea of graded tests was Binet's main contribution in the field of intelligence testing. He saw intelligence as an amalgam of abilities including such things as command of vocabulary, memory span, and number ability. A few examples taken from the American Terman–Merrill revision of the test will illustrate this. At age six the average child is able to define satisfactorily the words: *orange*, *envelope*, *straw*, *puddle*, *tap*. At age eight he will know three more words: *gown*, *eyelash*, and *roar*. The difficulty of the words continues to increase until at Superior Adult II level the requirement for passing is twenty-six words, some of which are: *lotus*, *bewail*, *flaunt*, and more difficult ones, *achromatic*, *homunculus*, and *sudorific*.

Other items test the child's ability to copy geometrical shapes. At age three the average child will be able to copy a circle, at age five a square, and at age seven a diamond.

Some items test the child's ability to remember and repeat sentences. At a later stage a similar test involves the remembering of a short story. A digit span test demands that the child repeat a number of digits after the tester. For example, in the test at age four years six months, the tester says: '4 – 7 – 3 – 1,' and the child has to repeat the digits. Another type of item asks the child to detect the absurdities in certain statements. For example, 'The judge said to the prisoner: "You are to be hanged and I hope it will be a warning to you." ' Other items involve detecting similarities and differences; analogies; rhymes; sentence completion; and coding. It can thus be seen that the Binet test attempts to sample a number of rather different abilities.

Binet emphasized the skilled nature of the administration of the test. Great stress is placed on the relationship or *rapport* established between child and tester, and the essence of the test is the face to face confrontation of the two: the tester must take test conditions into consideration when attempting to assess a child's ability, he does not consider them neutral as is assumed in group tests.

The original Binet test was revised by American psychologists at Stanford University in 1916 and the later version of 1937, produced by Terman and Merrill, has been used extensively in America and Britain. A 1960 revision is now available and on any occasion when an individual intelligence test is required this is the one which is most likely to be used.

Another individual test of intelligence is the Weschler Scale. Originally devised as the Weschler–Bellevue Scale for adults, it was later extended to produce the Weschler Intelligence Scale for children. The mode of administration is the same as the Stanford–Binet test but it has two important differences. One is that the concept of intelligence underlying the test is more comprehensive than the Binet test and includes items of a practical nature throughout, whereas the Binet test has 'performance' items only in the early years where verbal ability is rudimentary. The Weschler Scale consists of two tests, one verbal and the other performance. The verbal test resembles the Binet test having such items as vocabulary, information, arithmetic, comprehension, and similarities. The performance test does not depend upon language to any great extent. It includes such tests as the ability to follow a maze; to assemble, jigsaw fashion, pieces of various objects; to detect the missing part in pictures of incomplete objects (for example, the tooth missing from a picture of a comb); to assemble coloured blocks to form a given pattern. These two tests are scored and standard scores produced from the raw scores giving a standard score for the whole of the performance test and the whole of the verbal test. These scores can be combined to give a global score which gives a more comprehensive picture of a child's abilities than the two separate scores. Since the Wechsler has this performance section it will often produce a different I.Q. from the more exclusively verbal Terman–Merrill test.

Another important difference between the 1937 Terman–Merrill test and the Wechsler test lies in its standardization. Whereas the Binet norms were produced by giving the items to children of all ages and selecting the questions from the answer pattern data of the complete range, the Wechsler Scale was standardized separately on each age group. Thus, whereas a score on the Terman–Merrill test represented the placing of a child on a scale given to children of all ages, the Wechsler score gives his place in comparison only with children of his own age. It is possible to produce I.Q.s from Wechsler standard scores but they are not I.Q.s in the Binet sense, but standard scores converted to a scale with a similar mean and standard deviation to Binet I.Q.s The 1960 revision of the Terman–Merrill test has now introduced a similar method of scoring to that used by Wechsler.

Group tests of intelligence

The Binet test was an instrument for selection or guidance and it was essentially a clinical instrument. Some years later when America came into the 1914–1918 war, the American army looked for a method of guiding over a million recruits into the multifarious jobs of the armed forces. They needed a mass-produced tool and not a specialized delicate instrument such as Binet had used. American psychologists supplied the tool in the form of group tests of intelligence.

Two tests were produced, the *Army Alpha* which was a verbal test, and the *Army Beta* which was a non-verbal test to be used with illiterate and near-illiterate recruits. The results of the tests helped to single out feeble-minded recruits who were then given relatively simple jobs to do. The advantages of these tests in administration over the Binet test were that they could be given by persons without special training, to large numbers at once since they were paper and pencil tests, and the scoring could be done rapidly and without demanding special knowledge. It has, in fact, in recent years, become commonplace for American tests to be marked by machine.

The test items themselves resembled those of the Binet test. They sought to assess such things as arithmetic ability and vocabulary but in construction and administration they resembled objective tests of the multiple choice type.

British group tests have generally been constructed along rather different lines. Instead of following Binet's views that intelligence is an amalgam of factors, British test constructors have tended to follow the ideas of the British psychologists, Spearman and Burt. Spearman saw intelligence as *the ability to educe correlates* and *the power to discover relations*. He reached this definition after the critical scrutiny of many other definitions and after exhaustive statistical analyses of the results of various mental tests. He claimed to have discovered a *general factor* which ran through all mental activities. This was similar to what is commonly termed *intelligence* but Spearman preferred to use the term g hoping to evade the problems raised by the many conflicting definitions. Typical items in a test designed to assess g might be:

   i. Here is a list of words. In the spaces provided write the words that mean the opposite of the words you are given.

     (1) Black ....

     (2) Hard ....

     (3) Mother ....

     (4) Cheap ....

The child here is required to think of the relation given (oppositeness) and to *educe*, or bring out, the word which relates in this way to the word given, i.e. to its *correlate*.

   ii. Shoe is to foot as glove is to ....

Here the candidate is required first to discern the relation between *shoe* and *foot* and then to educe the corresponding correlate to *glove*.

Often the questions in these tests are multiple choice, and often they are considerably more difficult than the example given; however, the majority of the items in most tests are basically of this nature.

Such tests have been constructed in very similar ways to the objective attainment tests already described. They are tried out before use, and in general only items which discriminate highly between high and low scorers are retained for the final version of the test. Probably more effort has gone into the perfecting of these group tests of intelligence since 1945 than into any other field of educational research in Great Britain.

When used for secondary selection these tests are administered to children of about eleven, generally in conjunction with attainment tests in arithmetic and English, sometimes an essay, and occasionally using scaled head-teachers' estimates. From the results an order of merit is drawn up. A line is then drawn across this list and the children above the line will go to the grammar or technical schools, while the rest go to modern schools. In most authorities the candidates just below the line and those just above the line are given special consideration and further scrutiny before a final decision is made. This group of children is the *border-zone* often referred to in discussion of selection. As was suggested earlier, the key factor in deciding where the cut-off line shall be drawn is the number of places the local authority has available in grammar and technical schools.

Non-verbal tests of intelligence

The American *Army Beta* test was, as has been mentioned, a non-verbal test. It was the forerunner of many such tests, the

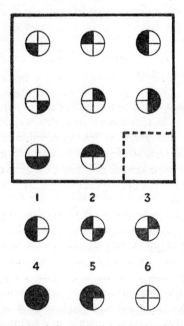

Fig. 20. Example of items from the Daniels figure-reasoning test. The subject has to work out which of the examples from 1 to 6 fits in the space in the right bottom corner of the pattern.

278

Fig. 21. Examples of items from the American Otis non-verbal intelligence scale. In A the child has to point out what is missing from the picture. In B the child has to arrange the pictures in the correct order.

aim of which was to assess the intelligence of pupils who had not learned to read, of adults who were illiterate, or to provide an assessment of intelligence as free as possible of verbal ability. In general these tests attempted to pose in pictorial or diagrammatic terms the same kind of problems posed in verbal tests. This may be seen in the examples of items from American and English tests given above.

The examples from the British, Daniels Figure Reasoning Test, are typical of all the items, and differ from the rest only in the level of difficulty. In the American Otis Test, however, the items are different in kind and include such things as: following instructions, detecting associations, picture completion (illustrated), following a maze, picture sequence (illustrated), similarities, synonym–antonym and *common sense*. To test *common sense*, the tester reads out questions and three alternative answers. The child underlines on his test sheet the number of the answer he considers to be correct.

The rationale of intelligence testing

So far we have considered intelligence testing mainly from a descriptive point of view. Let us now consider some of the basic postulates of the theory of intelligence testing [5].

As we have seen, American and British tests of intelligence have made use of different concepts about the nature of intelligence. This points to one of the most intractable problems in this field: there is no generally accepted definition of what is being tested. Psychologist have grappled with this problem over the years; books have been written arguing one view or the other and many issues of educational journals include discussion and argument about intelligence and its nature.

The extent of the difficulty may be illustrated by an examination of the comments of different psychologists on the subject. Spearman, as we have seen, considered intelligence to consist mainly in the 'ability to educe relations'. Burt considered it to be 'innate, general, cognitive ability'. On the other hand in the 'General Instructions to the use of the Stanford revision of the Binet test' (1955) Terman and Merrill comment:

'*Whatever the nature of intelligence may be* [my italics], its manifestations in the individual are uneven. . . . Abilities are always manifested and measured in relation to experience and training, and the behavioural composite which we call intelligence is of necessity modified and moulded by these factors.'

D. Wechsler in the manual to the *Wechsler Intelligence Scale for Children* (1949) considers that: '. . . intelligence is part of the larger whole, namely, personality itself. The theory underlying the W.I.S.C. is that intelligence cannot be separated from the rest of the personality, and a deliberate attempt has been made to take into account the other factors which contribute to the total effective intelligence of the individual.' He also considers that an intelligence test is a more useful diagnostic instrument '. . . when some attention is paid to the non intellective factors which modify and affect a subject's performance'.

Wechsler thus deliberately introduces heterogeneous items into his test. (The Stanford–Binet is also heterogeneous.)

However, P. E. Vernon, a leading British psychologist, considers:

'. . . the well constructed *group* test is highly homogeneous, each of its sub-tests or types of items involving much the same factor pattern. Spearman would have claimed that it was an almost pure measure of *g*, though we realize now that the content and form of the items, together with the difficulty level and timing conditions, do introduce other factors' [32].

Finally, J. Drever, in *A Dictionary of Psychology* (1962), declares:

. . . many definitions of *what is really indefinable* [my italics] have been attempted by psychologists, of which the least unsatisfactory are: (1) the capacity to meet novel situations or to learn to do so, by new adaptive responses, and (2) the ability to perform tests or tasks, involving the grasping of relationships.

It is not proposed here to add to the list of definitions of intelligence. However, it is of some importance that we avoid taking the attitude that intelligence is a 'thing' or a substance. It is not unknown to see references to the quality and *quantity* of intelligence. Such language assumes implicitly the existence of an entity and (one might think) it may well be that this entity can be observed and measured. The assumption that intelligence is a 'thing' can hardly be sustained. It is different to say that a person behaves in an intelligent way. We might then define an intelligent act as an act which is adaptive in the circumstances existing at the time in the environment. It is true that there would be room for argument as to what constitutes an adaptive act under a given set of circumstances, but in many cases there would be at least as much agreement as is generally found among definitions of intelligence. To illustrate this point we might consider that a lumberjack would behave intelligently if he felled a tree to fall exactly where he wanted it. A university professor would probably behave very unintelligently in the same circumstances and might possibly fell the tree so that it fell on him! Conversely, the lumberjack would probably behave very unintelligently in a university library. It would no doubt be possible to devise a test of tree felling which would discriminate among lumberjacks so that one could give a score and work out a rank order of lumberjacks in the same way as is done with any intelligence test.

While the intelligence test devised for lumberjacks would hardly serve the purpose of selection for secondary education in English schools, it would be difficult to demonstrate that it was a less valid test of intelligence. Given its basic assumption of the nature of intelligence, and this is no less arbitrary than the ones made by the psychologists quoted, the tree felling test is as good a test as any.

This example indicates an important aspect of intelligence tests; that is, that they are built upon views of the nature of intelligence peculiar to the individual test constructor. This means that different tests will probably give different scores and different I.Q.s for the same child. It is therefore important that when an I.Q. is quoted, the test from which it was derived is also given.

Group tests used in this country tend to follow Spearman-type ideas of intelligence and are aimed at measuring general all-round intellectual ability. They attempt to get an estimate of this uncontaminated by capability acquired through education; indeed, this was one of the main points advanced in their favour when they were first introduced on a wide scale. The main use of the group tests used for selection was to pick out those children who had sufficient intelligence to profit from a grammar school education. They were to be used as a once-and-for-all measure of fitness for grammar school. The argument was that the tests were so designed that poor home circumstances and indifferent primary schooling would not affect the issue, but that the tests would see that selection was just and equitable despite the disparity in children's backgrounds.

There are two major points of difficulty here. The first one lies in the assumption that a good test would pierce the skin of acquired scholastic attainment and penetrate to the basic ability upon which all else is built. This view follows the arguments that intelligence is innate. Such a view conflicts with almost everything we know about human learning. We have seen that the young child has very few innate patterns of behaviour. The reflex

282

activities with which he is born are very soon overlaid by socially produced behaviour patterns. Without the influence of society these patterns of behaviour would not be produced. As we have seen, socially deprived children are backward in all spheres of human behaviour, while chimpanzees in a stimulating human environment learn to do intelligence tests designed for children. We should also note that the tests we are considering, being highly verbal, involve a fundamentally social and highly artificial phenomenon, that of language. The concepts involved in the tests have no existence without language, and language has no existence without society. The influence of society on the ability to manipulate these concepts must therefore be very great indeed. The other difficulty arises when we take a measure of a child's intelligence today as giving an accurate forecast of what he will be able to achieve in the future. Such a view makes some very confident assumptions about the precision of testing, but some rather pessimistic assumptions about the ability of educationists to improve 'general cognitive ability', the 'ability to see relationships', or any of the other attributes considered to be inherent in the nature of intelligence.

In fact views about the nature of intelligence have changed a good deal in recent years. Vernon considers that the description of intelligence by many of the standard textbooks as '. . . a general innate capacity, underlying all our abilities, dependent on the genes we inherit, and therefore fairly constant through life', to be 'unrealistic'. He adds that psychologists are unable to measure inherited differences in intellectual capacity, and that the '. . . good or poor intelligence which we observe in everyday life, at school or at work, and which we measure in our tests, is the product of innate factors and environment' [32].

Elsewhere, Vernon states that he disagrees with the assumption that:

. . . intelligence is a single, clear-cut mental power or faculty, or in other words that any one child will get the same I.Q. whatever test he is submitted to. In fact it is only partly true that different intelligence tests measure the same thing. They do overlap or correlate fairly highly with one another, but somewhat different results will certainly be obtained from, say, Moray House and National Foundation [for Educational Research] tests, more different from a verbal group test and individual Terman–Merrill, and still more different from verbal tests and non-verbal ones based on pictures, diagrams, or practical materials. Unfortunately it is far too common for teachers to apply one test and to enter the results under I.Q. on the record card, as though this was fixed immutably, regardless of the test used or the age of testing.*

D. O. Hebb has suggested a view of intelligence which has been taken up by some psychologists. He suggests that we consider intelligence as having two components, intelligence A and intelligence B. Intelligence A he considers as 'an innate potential for the development of intellectual functions'. Intelligence B is the average level of that development at some later date. Intelligence B, which depends greatly upon the influence of the environment, is that which we attempt to measure when we use intelligence tests. However, '. . . the level of intelligence B which we can measure does not necessarily reflect the level of intelligence A, and hence we cannot really measure intelligence A'. The fact that intelligence tests are less than perfect instruments for the assessment of intelligence B is tacitly admitted by Vernon who has suggested the use of another term, intelligence C, to signify the *level of intelligence* indicated by a score of an intelligence test.

With all these reservations about the practice of intelligence testing it seems clear that we cannot really measure 'pure intelligence'. Perhaps the best that we can do is to infer it from the way a person behaves. Even then the important thing is not what the level of hypothetical 'pure intelligence' is, but what a person is capable of when he makes use of all his abilities, innate or acquired. Tests which aim to cover a wide spectrum of abilities, such as the Wechsler test, are more likely to sample a person's abilities thoroughly than a test which is less broadly based. But whichever test is used the behaviour which it samples can only be expressed through the medium of such complex social attainments as speech, writing, the ability to manipulate numbers or symbols, and so on. All of these are acquired abilities which

* VERNON, P. E.: in *Educational Research*, Vol. I, No. I, November 1958.

depend to a very great extent on the social environment and cultural stimulation. Because of this, we can no longer say, as did some of the early testers (but not Binet), that once a person's I.Q. had been determined, we had the measure of his ability which would be unlikely to change.

American educationists are now taking a similar attitude towards intelligence testing. H. Chauncey, president of the Educational Testing Service at Princeton University foresees a radical change in testing practice in American education which is likely to dispense with intelligence tests such as we have discussed. He considers that: 'It has become recognized by most that the so-called intelligence tests never did measure some innate thing called "intelligence" that could be summed up in one number called an I.Q. Actually, the use of the term intelligence tests has declined rapidly, as it became clear that what we are testing is developed ability or aptitude which results from the development of whatever innate ability an individual has.' He goes on to suggest that in future intelligence tests are to be replaced by tests of academic progress and more precise tests of aptitude.*

The achievement ratio

One of the earlier tenets of intelligence testing which still has very wide currency in the schools is that a child will never attain a higher standard score in a test of scholastic attainment than the score he will make on an intelligence test. The argument was that the intelligence test gave his ceiling of ability, whereas the attainment test was a measure of the extent to which he had realized his ability in the given subject, say arithmetic or English. In general a child would have a lower reading or arithmetic age than his mental age. This would follow from the views that the intelligence score represented 'true intelligence' uncontaminated by schooling, whereas arithmetic and reading ability are clearly dependent on schooling. When the attainment score is compared with the score in an intelligence test a ratio is obtained: if we put the attainment score over the intelligence score the ratio will be less than unity if the child scores less on the attainment test than

* *Times Educational Supplement*, 4 June 1965.

on the intelligence test. This, it was considered, will almost universally be the case and the possibility of a child scoring higher on an attainment test than on an intelligence test was very remote.

Teachers and other educationists holding this view naturally concluded that if a child were scoring similarly on both tests, he was achieving up to his limit. If his I.Q. were 90 and he obtained a Reading Quotient (a standardized reading score) of about the same (say 85–90), then it would be considered that he could not really expect to improve his reading. If, however, he had a reading quotient of 75 then the teacher would conclude that his reading could be improved and would arrange to give him remedial reading practice.

The concept of the achievement ratio was never universally accepted, but in 1956 D. A. Pidgeon and A. Yates published the results of an investigation which showed that as many children *over-achieved* as *under-achieved*. That is as many children scored higher on attainment tests than on intelligence tests as vice versa. Many children were therefore educated to a point well above their 'ceilings' under the assumptions of the achievement ratio: the intelligence quotient clearly did not represent a ceiling at all.

These findings call into question the procedure whereby the teacher, who finds that a child with low attainment in the basic subjects has a correspondingly low I.Q., considers that the child is making satisfactory progress, and will consider remedial instruction necessary only when a child achieves less in the basic subjects than in intelligence. This practice is still followed in many schools, but as a guide to educational action by practising teachers the achievement ratio is best forgotten.

The stability of the intelligence quotient

From the early days of testing it has been assumed by many that the intelligence quotient of an individual was unlikely to vary very much from one test administration to another. It was also considered that coaching or giving children instruction in answering tests of intelligence would have little effect on the I.Q. In the years following the introduction of selection for secondary education, many teachers ignored this view and in primary schools all over the country 'Intelligence' found its way into the syllabus: in addition private schools sprang up for the express purpose of coaching children for the selection examination. Children were trained on questions based on the Spearman view of intelligence and 'analogies' and 'opposites' were a staple diet of many candidates for selection. To what extent teachers in primary schools resolved the contradictions in the view undoubtedly held by many, of a relatively fixed I.Q. and the practice of coaching, is an interesting speculation.

In recent years investigations into the stability of the I.Q. have been made which have demonstrated that the I.Q. can by no means be considered as stable. Vernon writes: '. . . the average or median child alters by about 7 I.Q. points on retesting. Many are more stable than this, but a very few show much larger gains or losses of 30 or more points . . . and 17% are liable to alter 15 or more points either way' [32]. Changes of this order could make a considerable difference to children being selected for secondary education. A difference of 7 points of I.Q. could easily bring a child from a fail into the *border zone* for further consideration, while a difference of 15 points could take a child from a position of failure to a clear pass. The reverse could also apply of course. Vernon also discusses the effect of coaching and declares that this can produce an average maximum rise in I.Q. of 12 to 15 points on subjects who have not seen such tests previously; with others the gain is about half as much. In order to allow for the effects of coaching some educationists suggested that all children be coached for the tests. But the impossibility of equating the quality and quantity of such coaching makes this an unreal solution although some authorities have permitted practice tests. Another procedure which has been employed is to forbid teachers to coach. Such regulations could not apply to private schools, and in practice 'illicit' coaching thrives in many state schools.

The changes in I.Q., which come about merely through retesting or through coaching, have considerable bearing on the processes of selection. Implicit in the procedures adopted by many educational authorities when they divide up the children at eleven, is the assumption that once an assessment is made, it will apply throughout the child's secondary school career. Compilers of tests are less convinced about this than they were formerly and although they would still argue for the intelligence test as a tool of selection, it would be, as Vernon says, because 'General thinking skills as well as attainment . . . are highly relevant to grammar school success'.

The distribution of intelligence

Intelligence, it is suggested by some psychologists, is distributed among the population with a statistically *normal* distribution. *Normal* in this context is a technical term and has different

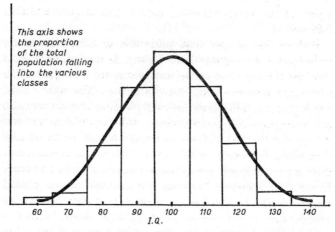

Fig. 22. Diagram of the normal curve fitted to I.Q. data.

connotation from its everyday use. A normal distribution of intelligence scores of the general population if plotted graphically would assume the form shown in Fig. 22. In general terms this means that the pattern of test results would yield a few high scores, a few low scores, and a large number of scores would be clustered around the average or *mean* score. The curve which can be drawn from these data is considered similar to the Gaussian curve of error which can be expressed as a mathematical equation. The argument which underpins the idea of the normal distribution of intelligence is that many physical characteristics are distributed in this way (height is the one most usually quoted), and by analogy we might reasonably expect intelligence to be so distributed. Reasoning by analogy can hardly be held to be scientific but it is even more doubtful when we apply the analogy to such an intangible as intelligence. But the most curious feature of all is that hardly any physical characteristics are distributed normally and if we were to reason by analogy we could only conclude that intelligence is not distributed normally.* Despite this, a very large number of authors continue to assert that intelligence is distributed normally. The truth of the matter is that tests are often designed to produce scores which conform to a normal distribution, and, in the construction of such tests, questions which distort this pattern are rejected in favour of the ones which are calculated to produce the required distribution. This procedure is somewhat analogous to a scientific experiment where the scientist tests a hypothesis and then proceeds to modify his experimental technique until he obtains the results he projected in the first place. If we then imagine him making generalizations from the results of his 'successful' experiment we have a picture comparable to the compiler of an intelligence test who tailors his test to suit his hypothesis. Vernon comments on this topic: '. . . it is practically impossible to prove that mental abilities are normally distributed. But there is no logical reason, nor any strong evidence, for suggesting any other type of distribution. Psychologists have accepted this dogma, since it provides a convenient basis for test construction and for statistical analysis of test scores' [32]. He goes on to point out that tests are sometimes designed to give a particular type of distribution for a particular purpose. Thus, for example, for purposes of selection, a rectangular

* WECHSLER, D.: *Range of Human Capacities*, Williams and Wilkins, 1952.

distribution might be aimed at to cut down the number of 'borderline cases'.

What are the implications of this for the educator? It is not unlikely that if he accepts the idea of the normal distribution of intelligence he will be inclined to expect the educational achievement of his children to approximate to this pattern. Probably he will even construct his tests with this in mind. If his children all got full marks he would probably consider his test faulty. If, on the other hand, he had no preconceived ideas about the distribution of intelligence, he would view with equanimity, if not with delight, the sight of all his children getting full marks if the marks were awarded for achievement in something which he had tried to teach.

In this connection the work that has been done on programmed learning raises some important issues. When children use a programme, the pre-test decides whether a child is equipped to work through the programme. But once he starts the programme he will be expected to work through it and score well in the terminal test no matter what his measured intelligence might be. All children working the programme will be expected to score highly because in the preparation of the programme it will have been rewritten and revised until any group of children for which it was written will produce a large proportion scoring highly on the terminal test. As we have seen, some programmers have set their objectives as high as 90% of the target population scoring 90% in the terminal test. Not all programmes will have such a stringent specification but the general approach will be similar. In such cases the distribution of scores will have no resemblance to the *normal curve*. Such distributions will show a close bunching of scores at the top end of the scale. Experience has demonstrated that in practice there is little correlation between I.Q. and performance in the post-test of many programmes, whereas in general, 'orthodox' teaching shows a much higher correlation between I.Q. and test performance. This seems to suggest that 'orthodox' techniques of teaching rely more on the student's own ability than do programming techniques which place the onus for teaching efficiently squarely on the teacher/programmer.

Skinner contrasted the outcomes of the two techniques when he said: 'In traditional practice a C means that a student has a smattering of a whole course. But if machine [i.e. programmed] instruction assures mastery at every stage, a grade will be useful only in showing *how far* a student has gone; C might mean that he is halfway through a course. Given enough time he will be able to get an A.' With such a view of teaching a teacher will, indeed, be hoping for anything but a normal distribution in the scores of his children when he tests whether in fact he has taught them what he set out to teach them.

The validity of intelligence tests

The problem of the validity of intelligence tests is one of the most vexed questions in the whole field of testing. Validity in this context might be said to be the extent to which a test does what it is designed to do. With tests of attainment, and especially those which attempt to assess what has been taught, the problem is more or less manageable: the content of a test provides its own validation. But in the case of intelligence tests the situation is entirely different. Vernon illustrates this difficulty: 'The validation of intelligence tests, or of tests of capacities such as practical ability, verbal ability, and the like, is particularly difficult, since we possess no objective criterion of intelligence, etc., with which to compare them' [32]. Methods which have been used in attempts to check validity have been to compare test results with teachers' ratings; to check with another intelligence test; to compare the results on a test with examination results; and by a statistical technique termed 'factor analysis'. The first three of these methods are clearly no answer to the problem. Teachers' ratings will be subjective and suspect in the eyes of testers. To use another intelligence test is to check one unknown against another; and to use school or public examinations is to introduce a variable which does not purport to measure intelligence and which is subjective in addition. The fourth method, of factor analysis, involves the adoption of a technique which depends on the statistical scrutiny of the test to see if its different sub-tests are mutually consistent. It is common for psychometrists to discover 'a general factor' common to a number of different sub-tests; that is, the sub-tests are consistent with each other. The next step is to assume that this factor is intelligence. It is this crucial step which is so unsatisfactory and unacceptable to some psychologists. Assuming all are agreed on the Spearman version of intelligence (and this is by no means so) then to equate the general factor with intelligence is an assumption only.

In fact the problem of validity as applied to group tests of intelligence, has no real answer. Such tests, by definition, attempt to assess something inaccessible to other techniques. In the absence of any external criterion, validation inevitably leads to circularity of argument, either external as in making comparisons with other tests, or internal by scrutiny of the consistency of sub-tests.

In the course of our discussion on intelligence testing we have considered some of the issues about which there is some disagreement and I have tried to show that some previously held views are no longer so widely held. S. Wiseman of Manchester University, however, is one of those psychologists who are still convinced of the usefulness of intelligence tests for selection. He says:

... it is relatively easy to mount a plausible attack by careful selection from among the vast mass of technical data available in textbooks and research reports. Hence the discussion of such things as the definition of intelligence, the constancy of the I.Q., the normal curve of distribution, and so on.

He goes on to make a further most important point:

Notice that from one point of view all these criticisms are irrelevant. The *selector's* purpose is to produce tests which will select those children who are likely to profit from grammar school education. By following these children through the grammar school he can discover how well his tests predict their later success. If any test predicts well, then it is worth using, whatever the label may be on the front. The selector is not immediately concerned with any hypothetical innate ability; he does not rely upon some ability or other being normally distributed; he has no concern with the constancy of the I.Q. He finds that tests called 'Intelligence

Tests' predict very well indeed – and often better than the tests of English and Arithmetic – and so he will continue to use them.*

This pragmatic view is somewhat different from that of the early testers who considered that the intelligence test was a 'true' assessment of a child's innate capacity. It might well be, one could argue, that other methods of selection would 'work' in the sense that children chosen by these methods would do well at grammar school; the difficulty is that one can never tell what would have happened to the unselected had they been given the same kind of education. In most places the main factor in deciding how many children shall go to selective schools is administrative rather than psychological since it depends upon the number of selective places available, the intelligence test is used only to allocate those places as equitably as possible. Even though the intelligence test 'works' in this situation it tells us nothing at all of an absolute nature about the number of children who could benefit from attending a school such as the present selective schools. Wiseman considers that the administrators should decide what kind of grammar schools they want and let the psychologists select for the schools. In other words the administrators should decide the percentage to be selected. I personally consider that the psychologist should take a more positive role and suggest to the administrators what he considers to be the best educational treatment for children.

With regard to the question of selection, however, it seems to me that the essential thing is not whether intelligence tests 'work' or not when used for selection. Given the need or the desire to select there is little doubt that the tests 'work'. But as Wiseman says it is one thing using them to uncover unsuspected ability, but it is another thing to use them to 'prove' that low-scoring children can never be expected to reach a normal level of education. How we define a 'normal level of education' is yet 'another thing'. The 'normal level' for America or West European countries is the very 'super normal' level of the very

* WISEMAN, S. (Ed.): *Examinations and English Education*, Manchester University Press, 1962.

much poorer 'emergent' countries of Asia and Africa. Our own views on what is normal change with the years as we acquire knowledge and wealth to provide educational opportunities at a higher level and for more children. From what we have seen of the effect of the social environment on learning and development it seems highly likely that given a considerably richer educational environment (and this includes the continuous development of teaching methods and of our understanding of how we learn) all children would be capable of developing much more complex mental skills than they are capable of now.

The dust of controversy has not yet settled over the various issues concerned with the practice of intelligence testing. The atmosphere is, however, considerably clearer than it was a few years ago. While, as may be seen from the remarks of Wiseman, the point of view taken by the author in this chapter is not one which would find universal acceptance, there is little doubt that views held until quite recently about such things as the fixity of the I.Q. and the validity of intelligence testing have changed considerably.

In this chapter the nature of intelligence testing and some of the difficulties involved in the practice have been discussed. Some of these may be of little direct relevance to the teacher in the classroom. However, the general theoretical position which follows from some of the practices could well have an adverse effect on the teacher's approach to his task. The most important general point for the teacher to bear in mind is that contrary to the declarations of some of the early testers, a low score on an intelligence test is not necessarily a bar to educational achievement. A good, well administered, broadly based intelligence test may give an indication of a person's present status in relation to other people, but it says nothing of an absolute nature about his abilities. Nor, in school, where the teacher's purpose is to bring about change, can the intelligence score be regarded as being authoritatively predictive of a child's future achievement.

Intelligence tests such as the Wechsler provide useful samples of the current behaviour of an individual. They help us to discern his present strengths and weaknesses; they may help us to isolate the results of past educational neglect or current deficiencies. Provided we use the information gleaned from these tests as a guide to action rather than an excuse for inaction, then they can be useful tools of the educational psychologist.

Summary

The first intelligence test was devised by Binet in 1905. Revised versions of the test at the moment consist of items intended to sample different features of a child's abilities. The test items are selected by try-out on a large number of children and the whole test is then standardized. The score made on the test gives a *mental age*. When *mental age* is compared with *chronological age*, an I.Q. may be obtained. If a child's M.A. is the same as his C.A. he will be considered average and will obtain an I.Q. of 100. The I.Q. is calculated by the formula $\dfrac{\text{M.A.} \times 100}{\text{C.A.}}$.

The Wechsler test is another widely used individual test. The view of intelligence underlying this test is somewhat wider than that of the Terman–Merrill revision of the Binet. The Wechsler test has a verbal scale and a performance scale. The performance scale is intended to assess non-verbal behaviour. The Wechsler test uses standard scores rather than I.Q. Standard scores are more meaningful than I.Q.s since they are directly comparable from one age to another whereas I.Q.s are not. The 1960 version of the Terman–Merrill test uses a similar type of scoring.

Group tests may be given to large numbers at a time and do not demand skilled administration as do individual tests. They were originally devised by the U.S. army and have since been widely developed in America and England. In England, they have been used most widely in selection for secondary education.

Although intelligence tests have been used for many years it is difficult to get a universally agreed definition of intelligence. It is suggested that intelligent behaviour rather than *intelligence* is a more useful term since it avoids the danger of regarding intelligence as an entity. Intelligent behaviour will be behaviour which is adaptive in a given situation.

Some psychologists have considered that an intelligence test can provide an assessment of the innate ability of a child, and the score obtained on such a test will predict his future scholastic performance. These ideas formed the basis of the theories underlying the practice of selection for secondary education. Of recent years, however, it has become generally accepted that *true* intelligence is inaccessible to testing since it can only be expressed through the medium of cultural acquirements such as speech and writing. The concepts of intelligence A, B, and C have therefore arisen. Intelligence A is *pure* intelligence and cannot be measured. Intelligence B is the extent to which the potential of intelligence A is realized and manifest in acquired abilities. Intelligence C is that part of B which is measured by intelligence tests. The outcome of these views is that, whatever it is that is measured by intelligence tests, it is not fixed and unchanging. It will depend upon training.

An individual's intelligence test score does not remain fixed. It is possible for it to change merely through retesting. Practice and coaching can also produce changes. The changes produced could often have a great effect on the educational provision recommended for the child. A low score on an intelligence test does not mean necessarily that low achievement in the basic subjects is inevitable. As many children *over-achieve* as *under-achieve*. Teachers should not regard the I.Q. as a ceiling. Intelligence scores will not inevitably fall into a normal distribution and a teacher should not have preconceived ideas that his tests will produce a normal distribution. Good teaching might well produce a distribution where most of the scores were at the top of the scale.

It is extremely difficult if not impossible to prove that intelligence tests are valid; that is, that they do what they purport to do. It is sometimes claimed that the use of intelligence tests for selection is justified 'because they work'. This is a statement which cannot be proved or disproved. There is no way of testing it. However, on the basis of learning theory it seems that it is unlikely to be true, since the treatment of the child after selection produces the qualities which the test was supposed to assess.

One of the most valuable approaches to intelligence testing would seem to be in the use of such tests as the Wechsler, which samples a wide range of abilities, for use in diagnosing educational difficulties with a view to providing remedial teaching.

CHAPTER 12

Backward Children

The problem of the child who lags behind in his school work is one of the most difficult that teachers have to face. It is a problem which can arise in almost any school. Selective secondary schools may have pupils who have difficulty in reaching the academic standards set, but the non-selective secondary schools and the junior schools have problems of a different order. In these schools are children who are retarded in their educational capabilities to such an extent that they may be seriously handicapped in their relationships with society. At the secondary level it is particularly obvious and acute when a child who is about to leave and find a job is still unable to read or to cope with anything more than the simplest computations. These deficiencies are built on a foundation of persistent failure to achieve what other children are achieving, and, while we may be able to assess with some measure of accuracy how far behind a child might be in reading, we can only guess the extent of the negative feeling caused by this history of failure.

The question that the student and young teacher will probably ask, is to what extent the backwardness he encounters in school is due to factors beyond our control and to what extent they are caused by factors which the teacher can manipulate. From what we have seen in previous chapters we might surmise that backwardness may well, in part at least, be caused by deficiencies in the life experience of the child. We think of the animals who have been deprived of normal experiences. The dogs reared in an unstimulating environment behaved less intelligently than normally reared animals. We may think of the children in Spitz's investigation in the foundling home, or the twins investigated by Luria who had developed their 'private speech' which acted as a barrier between them and normal human intercourse and thus produced backwardness. Or we may remember the work of Oléron who found that deaf children coped less well because of their lack of linguistic experience. All these examples point to important aspects of the problem of backwardness and suggest methods of therapy. They also suggest that to a great extent the causative factors of backwardness are within the control of parents and teacher. This is not entirely the case as we shall see, but is more so than was once believed.

The young teacher often has a particular difficulty in dealing effectively with children who are backward because his own educational experience will have been entirely different from theirs. He will almost certainly have had a successful junior school experience followed by secondary education in a selective school. He will not even have come in contact with slow-learning children and when, after a highly specialized secondary education followed by an academic higher education, he comes into the schools, he will find the mental adjustment necessary to understand the problems of the backward child very difficult indeed. In order to give the reader some insight into the difficulties of backward children he might meet in the classroom, we consider some of the factors involved in the causes of backwardness.

To lend perspective to our discussion of backwardness we consider first the whole field of mental subnormality. In this way it will be possible to get a clearer picture of backwardness as it affects the teacher in the ordinary school.

The term *mental subnormality* covers a number of different categories. It is not a disease but a condition of subnormal mental development whose chief characteristic is a low level of intelligence. Nor is it the same as mental illness, a term which applies to other forms of mental disturbance which arise later in life.

In the Education Act of 1944, Local Education Authorities were made responsible for ascertaining which pupils needed special educational treatment. Subsequent regulations defined ten categories of handicapped children. They were: blind, partially sighted, epileptic, physically handicapped, deaf, partially deaf, educationally subnormal, maladjusted, pupils suffering from speech defect, and delicate pupils. The largest of these categories is that of educational subnormality (E.S.N.) which accounted for over half of the total of handicapped children in 1960. Teachers in ordinary schools are unlikely to meet many children suffering from handicaps other than subnormality but most will come across educationally subnormal children or children with very similar problems sometimes referred to as slow-learning children. In this chapter we shall therefore confine our attention to problems of educational subnormality.

Some children are so severely subnormal that they cannot benefit from the education given in ordinary schools or schools for E.S.N. children and these children are now referred to the health authorities as children 'unsuitable for education'. The Health Department then has the responsibility for placing such children in a training centre where the approach emphasizes the learning of practical and social skills rather than the academic ones.

Prior to the Mental Health Act of 1959 mental subnormality covered a number of categories such as feeble minded, imbecile, mental defective, and idiot. These terms are no longer used. Instead we use the classifications of subnormality, severe subnormality, and psychopathic disorder. Severe subnormality has a physiological basis. The largest group of severely subnormals is that of the mongols. These children have one extra chromosome in their body cells. Other children in this category are likely to be suffering from fairly severe brain damage. Subnormality, on the other hand, is associated with minor brain damage or no damage at all. Thus the problems of subnormal children are different in kind from those of the severely subnormal. Whereas the main causative factor in severe subnormality is organic, in the case of the backward child in the ordinary school, the important causative factors are likely to be environmental.

Educational subnormality

Educationally subnormal children are deemed to be capable of being educated either in ordinary schools or in special schools for the E.S.N. On the other hand children who are classified as severely subnormal are considered to be ineducable in such schools and are often sent to special training centres. Such children are likely to be those who suffer from organic defect. This will mainly be minor brain damage and most of the children in this category will be excluded from the schools. A few will be found in the schools for the E.S.N. H. Tansley and R. Gulliford estimate that between 3% and 5% of children in special schools (E.S.N. schools) are likely to suffer from brain damage [33].

Since the 1944 Education Act the term *educational subnormality* has been applied to those children whose attainments were lower than 80% of the attainments of average children of the same age. A child aged ten whose attainments were below those of an average eight-year-old could be considered E.S.N. (Although generally the term tends to be reserved for children in special schools or classes.) It is generally estimated that about 10% of the school population would come into this category: and between 1% and 2% are likely to be children who would be considered best in a special school; the rest would be best taught in special classes in the ordinary schools.

The intelligence quotient and educational subnormality

So far the I.Q. has been excluded from our discussion of subnormality although it has, in the past, figured large in its ascertainment. Ascertainment is the term applied to the procedures adopted for diagnosing educational subnormality. It should be remembered that educational subnormality is essentially an educational definition and the tests given in the course of diagnosis are aimed at assessing the extent of the child's educational retardation. It is not intended to say anything more about the child. The question of the I.Q. is raised now in this connection since it is often referred to in discussions of backwardness and is still used as part of the total appraisal of the child suspected of being E.S.N.

Textbooks dealing with the problem of backwardness in the past often included tables setting out ranges of I.Q. from zero to some figure at the top end of the scale such as 150 or 160. This scale would be divided into sections and each section would be named in such styles as *superior*, *normal*, and so on. Idiots were commonly regarded as those children having I.Q.s of below 25. Between I.Q. 25 and I.Q. 55 would be imbeciles. I.Q.s between 55 and 70 would be classified as feeble-minded. Over 70 and under 85 would be dull. Although it was usually stressed that the lines of demarcation were by no means rigid, and were only part of the total assessment of a child, many students and teachers have come to regard I.Q. 70 as a kind of watershed on one side of which go the children who can be educated in the normal schools and on the other side go the children who need to go to special schools. Undoubtedly these ideas squared with reality in the past since they were in fact used in the classification of E.S.N. children. The increasing dissatisfaction with intelligence tests which we have already considered: such things as scepticism with regard to their prognostic validity and the fact that the I.Q. can change, have made it evident that the use of the I.Q. as a sole criterion, or even as the major factor in a number of items, is to be avoided. Tables of I.Q.s corresponding to categories of children give an air of spurious accuracy to the diagnosis of educational subnormality quite at variance with the reality of slow-learning children all with different problems that cannot be put neatly into convenient pigeon holes. As was suggested at the end of Chapter 11, individual intelligence tests used diagnostically are the tests which are likely to be of most use in the ascertainment of subnormality [34]. Students and teachers should be aware that while the I.Q. may be considered in ascertainment it is *only one factor* and it can by no means be regarded as a precise instrument for diagnosing educational subnormality.

Since the 1944 Act, then, the criterion of the E.S.N. child has been a level of attainment not more than 80% of the ability of average children of the same age. This means that a child capable of obtaining a high score on a non-verbal intelligence test but who had not learned to read or write by the early years of the junior school (7–11 years) could be classed as E.S.N. This would not have happened previously when the I.Q. was the main arbiter. To a degree this is probably a good thing. No longer can it be thought that all E.S.N. children are doomed to very low achievement even if we accept the I.Q. as truly predictive. This helps to overcome the attitude, unfortunately still prevalent, where teachers dismiss the possibility of teaching a child, with the remark: 'Oh, he's E.S.N.' It should be noted, however, that this definition of educational subnormality necessarily means that 10% of children are bound to be E.S.N. no matter how much the general level of ability rises. This is because there are always bound to be some children who are below the average; the very concept of average implies it. In this sense the backward child will always be with us. Our statistical techniques create him.

Children in schools for the E.S.N.

To some extent the more flexible definition of educational subnormality has created problems. There is a tendency for the naughty child, with low attainment but relative high intelligence score, to be recommended by head-teachers for special school, not primarily because of his backwardness, but because he may be a nuisance in the classroom. This solves the problem for this particular teacher and possibly helps the child referred, but it does little for the special school, and it may well deprive a more docile but more handicapped child of a place.

It is possible, therefore, for children to find their way to a special school, not always for the best reasons. The special schools, however, will have mainly those children who are very immature intellectually and often have other handicaps. They take just over 1% of the school population and a small percentage of children in them have slight brain damage. In addition, a large number of children who have been recommended for special school are unable to get in because of the lack of provision.

Provision in ordinary schools

E.S.N. children who are not referred to a special school are, according to Ministry recommendations, to be catered for in special classes of the ordinary schools. Often, teachers in ordinary schools tend to consider these children as backward and reserve the term E.S.N. for children who have actually been recommended for special school. This is a question of terminology which may do little harm unless, as has been mentioned, teachers regard the children who are recommended for special school as beyond the educational pale. The obverse can happen. Teachers may regard the children who are backward but in the ordinary schools, as children with no special difficulties who can be treated in much the same way as other children, thus ignoring an important educational problem.

One of the difficulties involved in provision for the backward child in the ordinary schools, is the varied nature of *special classes*. The term has been interpreted in many ways and the quality and extent of provision varies greatly according to the authority concerned and even the individual school. Whereas the responsibility of the E.S.N. school is clear, the situation in the ordinary schools is not.

In schools for the E.S.N. will be found some teachers who are especially interested in the teaching of backward children. In some cases these teachers will have had special training in methods appropriate to the teaching of such children. Sometimes these teachers will be found in the ordinary schools but this is very often fortuitous rather than by design. In the ordinary schools provision for the backward children in a special class as is recommended is not always possible. This may be because of the insufficient numbers involved, coupled with high staffing ratios, but often it is because there is no member of staff sufficiently interested in the work to establish such a class. There is also the major problem of knowing exactly what the special class is supposed to be. Some schools, while making provision for a class for the backward children, give much the same treatment to the children as that given to the rest of the school, when of course what is wanted is 'special' treatment. We shall consider later the nature of the treatment most suitable for children in special classes. Let us now examine the nature of the difficulties of the children in these classes.

Retardation and dullness

Children who do not come into the category of severely subnormal are traditionally thought of as retarded or dull. These concepts were derivative of the ideas of intelligence as a fixed trait which would give a reliable and objective estimate of a child's innate educational potential. As we have already seen, this view of intelligence is no longer tenable and this fact brings the concept of retardation under scrutiny. A child who was retarded was considered traditionally as a child whose educational attainments lagged behind his intelligence. If, for example, a child of I.Q. 90 had a reading quotient of 80, he would be held to be retarded. This is the situation we considered previously when we discussed the concept of the achievement ratio. As we have seen, this concept is no longer viable, and this being the case, the use of the term *retarded* in this sense has little meaning and adds nothing to our understanding of the backward child. It is mentioned here because, although the point is generally understood by those teachers who are concerned with the education of backward children, many teachers in ordinary schools make use of the ideas of retardation and the achievement ratio.

The idea of *dullness* is a different matter. Children in this category were generally those who registered low on intelligence with I.Q.s of 70–80 or 85. It was considered that such children were limited because of their low intellectual capacity and in fact teachers were often satisfied if the educational attainment matched the I.Q. Some consideration has already been given to this point, but in relation to the concept of dullness we should remember not only that rises in I.Q. are not uncommon, but also that the educational difficulties of two children with the same low I.Q. are almost certain to be quite different. This is because the children will inevitably have different score patterns on testing. For example, one child may fail on the verbal items of a test while the other might fail on the performance side. Other different combinations of failure could occur so that each child will have his own characteristic pattern. The overall I.Q.s may be the same but the way in which they are derived will be different. It should also be borne in mind that few people would now accept the premise that the I.Q. is mainly a measure of innate ability. Most would say that it reflects to a very great extent the cultural and educational history of the child, and yet the idea of dullness really rests on this foundation. Once we admit that intelligence is even in part culturally determined, then we can no longer use a term such as dullness measured as an I.Q. level to set a ceiling for any child's attainment. Stott doubts that 'just dull' children exist. He found in an investigation of 188 'dull' children in the west of England, '. . . that in every case there was at least one feasible reason, in pre-natal or post-natal development, or in the environment, for the backwardness'. In other words he was unable to find one case of backwardness (in special schools and occupation centres) that could be ascribed to 'just dullness' that is, merely to having a measured I.Q. below 85.*

In practice, as in the case of retardation, many schools view the I.Q. as a ceiling which limits the potential educational development of a child. Unfortunately the low I.Q. has far too often been the justification for the teacher's ceasing to try to increase the child's educational abilities on the basis that you cannot go beyond the child's 'natural' limitations. In fact, the I.Q. is neither 'natural', in the sense of being innate and unchanging, nor is it necessarily a limitation. A low I.Q. represents a challenge to the teacher, not a let out. As has been suggested, in one sense the problem of backwardness will always be with us. So long as we talk in terms of 'average', 'below average', and 'above average' we cannot avoid it: someone will always be 'below average'. As we have seen, this situation is also inherent in the concept of the I.Q. so that there will always be children of low I.Q. as long as we continue to use the present techniques of mental measurement. In this sense 'dullness' is an artefact of the practice of intelligence testing and given a generally high level of educational achievement of the school population we should find that then even the backward children would be capable of coping adequately with the basic subjects according to our present criteria. The fact remains, however, that despite this theoretical point, teachers at the moment will find children in their classes who have difficulty in mastering the basic skills; particularly, and of prime importance, reading and writing.

We have seen that children with severe brain damage are unlikely to be found in the ordinary schools. We have also seen

* STOTT, D. H.: in *Forward Trends*, August 1960.

that we cannot explain away failure to achieve the fundamental skills of reading and writing by declaring the failing children are lacking in intelligence. We might now ask what factors are at work producing the inability of some children to master the basic elements of the three r's.

Minor physical defects

Children with major physical defects are generally noticed early in life and provision made for them. Children with less severe defects are sometimes unnoticed and are consequently handicapped in their learning by these defects. For example, a child who suffers from acute hearing loss will be discovered and probably sent to a school for the deaf. On the other hand a child with only slight hearing loss may not have his defect detected. He may suffer from the inability to hear sounds of certain frequency and consequently will not be able to discriminate among different words incorporating these sounds when the teacher is beginning to teach reading. Consequently the child will have difficulty right from the start with his reading. Having made a bad start, he will probably drop further and further behind the other children and, unless his disability is discovered and remedial treatment given, he is quite likely to suffer from a quite serious degree of backwardness.

Teachers will often have difficulty in detecting partial hearing loss in a child, and in the case of any child who is having difficulty, especially with the early stages of reading, it would be worth while to arrange for an audiometer test through the school health service. This will reveal any hearing loss and the teacher will be able to take account of it.

Speech defect is also associated with backwardness. A number of researches have shown that such defects are far more common among backward than among normal children. Poor speech interferes with the child's learning to read, with his relations with the teacher and the rest of the class; and according to the extent of the defect, his linguistic development will be adversely affected and with it his whole intellectual development.

Inadequate vision may also be instrumental in causing a child difficulty with his learning. It is more likely to be noticed than slight deafness, but any child who has not been recognized to suffer from defective vision and who shows signs of eye strain or visual difficulties in early reading activities, should be given an eye test.

Generally poor health, recurrent illness, inadequate diet, and unsatisfactory home conditions, all contribute to rendering the child insufficiently alert and receptive in the classroom. These factors also have other effects such as producing irregular attendance which is cumulative, making the child lose more and more ground as compared with the rest of the class.

One aspect of minor physical disabilities that teachers need to be aware of, is the fact that children are very often extremely sensitive about them. Children with defective vision will refrain from wearing glasses because they feel selfconscious about them and there is no doubt that they are sometimes baited by other children. One boy in the 'A' stream of a secondary school had a slight hearing loss but didn't like wearing his hearing aid because other boys made fun of him. As soon as he left home to go to school he would remove his aid and keep it in his pocket until he reached home later in the day. He had a certain skill in lip reading and this helped him along until he came to learn French. He soon began to drop behind because his lip reading was of no use to him with spoken French. It was then the teacher discovered his disability and encouraged him to wear his aid.

Environmental deprivation

Under this heading are subsumed both the actual physical conditions of the home and the quality of the intellectual stimulation from the family. The actual physical conditions are clearly linked with the physical deficiencies we have just considered. Children from slums are likely to suffer from the effects of neglect to a greater degree than other children.

Burt, in a survey of backwardness in twenty-nine London boroughs, found that the backward children were to be found in greatest numbers in poor and overcrowded areas.* The more

* BURT, C.: *The Backward Child*, U.L.P., 1937.

recent report of the Manchester University School of Education found poor social environment to be closely correlated with school attainment and with measured intelligence [35]. The Newsom Report recently also drew attention to this fact and since then the Department of Education and Science has given support to a number of research projects to investigate the effect on children of an unfavourable social environment. The Department has also published a leaflet in its series of Reports on Education (No. 17, December 1964) in which a group of head-teachers of schools where this problem is particularly acute, discuss the problems of social deprivation and suggest ways in which the school can help. The picture which emerges from studies such as Burt's and subsequent investigations is that children from such social conditions suffer severe educational handicap and, although the general standards of living have gone up since he made his surveys, the crucial difference between good and poor homes remains. Children from poor homes are likely to show to a greater extent the effects of undernourishment, illness, and lack of sleep. There is also likely to be a negative attitude to school which manifests itself in truancy. But the physical aspect of environmental deprivation is only one aspect: added to the disabilities flowing from these unsatisfactory physical conditions are the effects of cultural deprivation, and the two conditions interact and are to some extent, mutually reinforcing.

Problems of this kind are sometimes to be found in the homes of higher cultural and social levels. In some professional families the parents are sometimes so absorbed in their work that the children are neglected. Such children may well have educational difficulties even though they come from fairly privileged homes. The point to note is that it is not merely the low economic circumstances that cause trouble, but the things that are often (but not exclusively) associated with it.

We may get some insight into the probable effect of cultural deprivation if we think back to the work we considered earlier when we discussed development and learning. We saw there how dogs, which had been deprived of environmental stimulation, were 'backward' when compared with other dogs which had been reared under more normal conditions. Animals such as rats have been shown to exhibit more intelligent behaviour when reared in highly stimulating environments than rats reared in cages. Chimpanzees reared in human families performed better at problems than have more orthodoxly reared animals. If we consider the children reared in the foundling home referred to in Chapter 2 we see in a most striking way the effect of such cultural neglect. The work of Luria has shown us how inadequate cultural stimulation led to linguistic deficiency with all the marks of severe backwardness. In older children the work of Bernstein has suggested that linguistic disability springing from restricted cultural experience depressed the verbal intelligence scores of working-class children.

The question of linguistic disability is one of the key problems in the field of backwardness. As we have seen from our study of learning, language performs a supreme function in the development of the child's ability to cope effectively with his environment. The experiments of Luria demonstrate how the speech of the adult helps the child to build up patterns of visual discrimination; to isolate an object from its surroundings; and gradually to help the child to regulate its own activities effectively. Vigotsky has shown how fundamental the processes of language are in the development of conceptual thought. Indeed, it seems likely that, although conceptual thought may be possible without language, the level of conceptualization expected of school children is bound to be dependent upon language. Competence in abstract thought, that is, depends upon competence in language usage. Thus deaf-mutes without special training do not readily achieve concept formation and stay at a very low level of cognitive development.

It should be stressed that children with poor linguistic skills do not merely lack vocabulary, or do not speak 'correctly'. The problem is that the speech they use is poor and thin; lacking in abstractions; and linked to the concrete situation as was the speech of the twins in Luria's investigation. If complex relationships and ideas are not presented to the children by the parents through speech, the children are in no position to build up the habits of abstract conceptual thought. To take a simple example; unless children are helped to acquire the idea of *left* and *right* by their parents through the use of language, they will be unable to make the distinction. It would be very difficult, if not impossible, to convey the idea of *left* and *right* without language. The ideas of *left* and *right* are relationships and the ability to perceive relationships is, as has been seen, considered to be one aspect of intelligent behaviour. The lack of intelligence of backward children is sometimes manifest in the inability to make this kind of distinction and such children are unable to tell right and left until later than children of the same age. More complex abstractions need correspondingly more experience linked with language if they are to be acquired effectively by children. (It is a fact, however, that some highly educated people with great verbal ability who are quite clear about the concept of left and right, have difficulty in distinguishing between them in practical situations such as, for example, when they are asked to turn left or right. This difficulty may well be due to an unusual dominance of the relevant centres in the brain and does not mean that the person has not achieved the concept.)

In a home where the cultural level of the parents is depressed, the parents themselves will be unable to give the children the linguistic experience necessary for the development of a high level of conceptual thought. This, it is almost certain, is a very potent cause of backwardness in the ordinary schools. This fact has recently been recognized in the report of the Newsom committee which has recommended that research into the question of linguistic disability be carried out. Bernstein has suggested in this connection, that children of this type should be taught in smaller classes than usual so that the teacher might be able to give the children the linguistic experience they need but which they are unlikely to get in classes of normal size.

Some evidence is available that given special linguistic training, backward children will not only increase their ability with language but also their I.Q. Dawe reported in 1942 on an experiment in which orphanage children aged from three and a half to six years, with I.Q.s ranging from 65 to 92 (mean 80), were given an intensive programme of language experience and training. At the end of this time the children had made considerable progress in language ability but also the mean I.Q. of the group had risen to nearly 95. A control group (that is a similar matched group of children who were given no special training) showed, on the other hand, a slight drop in I.Q.* Gulliford points out that the children in this investigation were originally in an environment much less stimulating than that of normal homes so that it is not surprising that the gains were made. In the same place he alludes to an investigation made by Kirk who studied eighty-one mentally subnormal children from three to six years old living in their own homes. This observation went on for several years and in this time he gave to forty-three of the children the equivalent of a good nursery school experience involving the stimulating of intellectual and verbal ability. He claimed that the treatment had the effect of raising the standard of development and that the children who were most deprived of environmental stimulation at the beginning, made most progress. The work of Luria (p. 184) is also evidence of the beneficial effects of special linguistic training. The twin who received special linguistic training made more rapid all-round progress than did the other twin.

Emotional difficulties may be a potent factor in backwardness. Broken homes, homes where there is conflict, and homes where there is lack of affection and insecurity, will all create the conditions in which backwardness may develop. As we have seen in the discussion on learning, stimulus situations which create excessive anxiety inhibit learning. Learning may be inhibited in the home or in school. Homes which engender anxiety and insecurity will almost certainly be homes which provide the children with the minimum of stimulation that we have just considered. The child will thus be under a double handicap. Not only will he lack the stimulation necessary for his healthy development, but his emotional problems will interfere with what learning he may be making. Emotional difficulties caused by anxiety at school are not peculiar to the backward child, but such school-generated anxiety will be more serious for the backward child than for the

* GULLIFORD, R.: in *Educational Research*, February 1960.

normal child. Harsh discipline, unreasonable demands on the children and, with the E.S.N. child, lack of understanding of his particular problems, are all likely causes of emotional difficulties.

Streaming

Recent research has suggested that one factor which must be considered in any discussion of educational retardation is the practice of 'streaming'. This involves the placing of children in 'homogeneous' groups according to their intellectual capabilities: the 'A' stream, the 'B' stream, the 'C' stream, and so on. In actual fact, the homogeneity hoped for in this procedure is very often more apparent than real in view of the difficulties involved in assessing intelligence and achievement; and, of course, such measures take no account of emotional factors which are clearly of importance. The point at issue is that such measures result in the creation of a limited educational environment for the children in the bottom stream, since the bottom class will consist of children who have had difficulty with learning, who have probably come from unstimulating home backgrounds, and who will have little to contribute to the class. The grouping together of such children tends to create an unstimulating classroom situation, while at the top of the school the more able children will be formed into a different kind of group where the children, being educationally and probably emotionally more mature, will be creating an atmosphere of mutual enrichment. In addition to this, all too often, the young inexperienced teacher is given the lowest class in a streamed school; or, in the case of staff shortage, this will be the class given to the temporary teacher. Such teachers, lacking experience and understanding of backward children, are often unable to give them the special educational treatment they need which, of course, exacerbates the situation.

An investigation carried out by J. C. Daniels and reported in the *British Journal of Educational Psychology*, 1961, gives some evidence about the effects of streaming in the junior school. He studied the development of children in four junior schools over a period of four years. Two of the schools were streamed and two were unstreamed. The streamed schools were quite ordinary junior schools, the unstreamed schools had adopted non-streaming as deliberate policy. He compared the performances of matched groups of children from the streamed schools and the unstreamed schools. At the end of four years in the junior school it was found that the unstreamed children had made more progress than the streamed group. The average I.Q. of the unstreamed group had gone up by three points and attainment in arithmetic was also higher in the unstreamed group. There was no noticeable 'holding back' of the brighter pupils, but the dispersion of the marks in the unstreamed schools was lower than in the streamed schools. Daniels suggests that the main effect of non-streaming is '. . . a radical "pulling up" of the more backward children' [36].

One further point suggested by Daniels' work is that the improvement made by backward children in the unstreamed school is greater in the early years. This has some bearing on the attitude of the secondary school to the problem of backwardness. If children arrive at the secondary school unable to read, and very many do, the handicap may be so great that a special class is the only answer to the problem; possibly until the children have made sufficient progress to move to an ordinary class.

J. W. B. Douglas, in an investigation of streaming, concluded that streaming by ability tended to depress the attainments of the children placed in the lower streams. He found that, in general, children who came from good homes and who were well dressed and clean, stood a greater chance of being placed in a high stream than did the child from a poor home lacking the external evidence of parental care. Children placed initially in the higher streams tended to remain there and improve their performance, while children of similar initial attainment placed in lower streams deteriorated in their performance [37]. Both Douglas and Daniels point out that the very act of segregation seems to prove self-justifying. Once the children are streamed the circumstances are created for the accentuation of the differences which existed at the outset, and probably for the creation of differences which did not exist.

So far the question of non-streaming has been posed largely

in terms of the junior school and at the present moment many junior schools are turning to non-streaming. As the junior schools gain experience of non-streaming, and as 'unstreamed' children come from them, the question of the non-streamed secondary school is likely to be considered more and more.

More evidence is needed to give us an authoritative picture of the effect of streaming and at the moment of writing the National Foundation for Educational Research is engaged on a programme of research to investigate the question on a larger scale than investigations reported so far. It does seem, however, that the evidence so far available, points to the fact that streaming, which teachers generally think advantageous to the backward child, in fact operates to depress his level of attainment. The Newsom report recommends that rigid grouping by ability be discontinued so there is a possibility that more evidence will be gathered concerning the effects of streaming on the development of the backward child.

Problems of ascertainment

We have discussed some of the main causes of educational subnormality and some of its more important manifestations. We now examine the methods by which backwardness can be diagnosed.

Whether a child is being considered for referral to a special school or for special treatment within an ordinary school, the most important thing about the diagnosis of educational sub-normality is that it be made as early as possible. To an extent, of course, this is difficult, since the younger the child the lower his level of attainment and this makes it difficult to say whether the child is lagging behind his peers or not. However, any teacher who has reason to think that a child may be having special difficulties in class, should take steps to ascertain the nature of the difficulties and whether the child is in need of remedial treatment in an ordinary school or special education in a special school or class.

An important part of the diagnostic examination which will be made to ascertain whether a child is E.S.N. and to discover the nature of his disability, is the medical examination. Tansley and Gulliford suggest that this should include examination of eyes, ears, throat, speech organs, and central nervous system. This is more than the ordinary school medical examination normally does and will necessitate the consultation of ear, nose, and throat and other specialists such as the neurologist to see if there is any brain damage.

The medical examination will be supplemented by a psychological examination given by the educational psychologist attached to the local authority. From what has been said previously when the question of tests was discussed, it will be clear that an individual test such as the Wechsler will be the most useful guide since it has both verbal and performance sub-tests with a number of sub-sections which will not merely give a quantitative score but a qualitative diagnostic picture of the areas of the child's possible difficulties.

The level of the child's educational attainment will be needed: his performance in the school subjects, his speech ability, his emotional and social adjustment, his interests, and history of full-time schooling.

In view of what has been said about the effect of home background on development, it will be important to have a picture of the kind of home the child comes from. Is there a history of neglect or deprivation, physical or cultural? Is there any history of disturbances in other members of the family? And what is the child's pre-school developmental history? Teachers and psychologists sometimes use specially prepared guides which aim as far as is possible to obtain a comprehensive and meaningful picture of the child's behaviour and character and to help in the detection of emotional instability. The Institute of Education of Bristol University has developed a set of these guides for the observation of children in different circumstances such as in school or in residential care. Essentially they consist of a number of sections covering such things as 'Attitudes to the Teacher', 'Attitudes to School Work', 'Attitudes to Other Children', 'Personal Ways', 'Games and Play'. Each of these sections contains a number of divisions covering different aspects of that section. For example, under 'Attitudes to Teacher' we find such divisions as *Greeting Teacher*, *Response to Greeting*, *Liking for Attention*, and several others. Each of these divisions has a number of alternative comments. Thus under *Liking for Attention* we find: 'Appreciates praise: tries to monopolize teacher: put out if can't get attention: wants adult interest but can't put herself forward: suspicious (on the defensive): unconcerned about approval or disapproval.'

The teacher is asked to underline the phrases which describe the child's behaviour or attitudes over a term or so. The idea is to provide a framework within which teachers can work and give a picture which to some extent may be considered a standard picture. As may be seen from a scrutiny of the alternatives, they provide a fair range of possibilities into which it will probably be possible to fit the child under consideration.

Another guide which may be of assistance in assessing a child, is the Vineland Social Maturity Scale. This is a scale of levels of social adaptation ranging from babyhood to adolescence and beyond. It consists of a number of items appropriate to various ages. For example, at age seven to eight the average (American) child will:

Tell time to quarter hour.
Use table knife for cutting.
Disavow literal Santa Claus.
Participate in pre-adolescent play.
Comb or brush hair.

The examiner obtains the information about the child from the parent or some trustworthy person who knows the child well, and a level of social maturity is calculated for the child in a similar way to the way one might calculate his mental age.

When as much data as possible is assembled, the staff concerned will decide on the course to be taken. Is the child to be recommended for admission to a special school, or will he be better off in a special class in the ordinary school?

While these procedures are really necessary for all children suspected of serious backwardness, in practice the acute shortage of staff in the school medical and psychological services leads to the position that only the worst cases are dealt with in this way. Other cases may be given part of this diagnosis with the possibility of considerable errors of assessment, especially if group tests of intelligence are used. Children who are not likely to be recommended to a special school may possibly not be referred to the child guidance clinic and often the child who is educationally subnormal, but docile, is passed over while the troublesome child with more ability is referred. Children in the bottom streams of junior school or the remedial classes of secondary schools are rarely given the type of examination outlined. In secondary schools often the only measure of assessment for remedial education is the results of the eleven-plus selection examination.

The task of ascertainment is thus a complex procedure. But once a diagnosis is made it is not always simple and straightforward to recommend a course of action. According to Stott, who has studied the subject intensively and over a long period: '. . . there is no quick and certain method of sorting out the children who merely need remedial tuition from those needing long-term treatment. The children's actual progress in remedial groups is the best means of such classification.'

In the next chapter we consider the nature of the treatment which children who are backward should receive.

Summary

The average teacher in training, or young teacher in the classroom, will probably have difficulty in understanding the problems of backward children. He is likely to have little, if any, experience of educational failure; the children are likely to have experienced little else. This should be borne in mind by any teacher who takes charge of backward children.

Backwardness, or educational subnormality, differs from some other categories of mental subnormality in that no major physiological defect is associated with it. An E.S.N. child is defined as one whose attainments are lower than 80% of the average for children of the same age. (This definition has the weakness that for statistical reasons it necessarily implies that there will always be a proportion of children who must be considered E.S.N.)

Previously ideas about backwardness led teachers to believe that a low I.Q. was often the *cause* of educational subnormality, whereas it is more correctly regarded as a *descriptive* statement about the child's present level of ability as compared with children of his own age. This new attitude has led to a modification of former views about 'dull' children and it is now no longer held that a child's attainments are rigidly limited by a low I.Q. Thus a low I.Q. presents the teacher with a challenge and not an excuse for a child's failure.

Minor physical defect is a major factor in causing backwardness. Poor vision, defective hearing, defective speech, poor health, and recurring illness are all involved. Other important factors derive from unsatisfactory environmental conditions. Economically and culturally poor homes do not provide the stimulation necessary for the development of the intellectual abilities involved in school-learning. Cultural deprivation also leads to linguistic disability which adversely affects children's ability for conceptual thought.

The practice of streaming probably exacerbates the problem of backwardness in the ordinary schools, although it is often justified on the grounds that it gives backward children a better chance. The unstimulating atmosphere of the bottom streams of junior and secondary schools tends to confirm existing backwardness. The practice of giving the bottom streams to inexperienced or temporary teachers often makes the problem worse.

Some children who are ascertained E.S.N. are in special schools (just over 1%) but many are in ordinary schools because of lack of provision in the special schools.

Ascertainment of educational subnormality usually involves medical and psychological investigations. The medical inspection will aim to discover any physical disabilities, the psychological tests will seek to discover the child's level of attainment in school work, his abilities of a more general nature, any specific educational difficulties, and any emotional problems. Tests of social maturity and social adjustment are sometimes used in conjunction with other tests. The general aim of all these investigations should be diagnostic so that realistic remedial measures can be taken.

CHAPTER 13

The Treatment of Backwardness

Most research in the field of backwardness nowadays, indicates that given the appropriate treatment and attention backward children can make progress not previously thought possible. Binet himself made this point many years ago:

Some recent philosphers appear to have given their moral support to the deplorable verdict that the intelligence of an individual is a fixed quantity, a quantity which cannot be augmented. We must protest and act against this brutal pessimism. We shall endeavour to show that it has no foundation whatsoever. . . . A child's mind is like a field for which an expert farmer has advised a change in the method of cultivating, with the result that in place of desert land we now have a harvest. It is in this particular sense, the only one that is significant, that we say the intelligence of children may be increased. One increases that which constitutes the intelligence of a school child; namely the capacity to learn, to improve with instruction [38].

Half a century later the New York Board of Education set out to see what could be done about backwardness caused by general cultural deprivation [31]. Taking a slum school with a high rate of truancy, a high turnover of both staff and children, and drawing children from homes where the majority of parents were unemployed, the Authority embarked on its 'Higher Horizons' plan. The plan involved giving the children enriched social and educational experiences. About half the children at the school were included in the plan and were selected on the basis of an average score on six of ten criteria which included several tests, the teacher's recommendation, and the child's school attainments. Provision was made for children who did not make the grade to be included if there was any reason to think that the criteria involved did not give a full picture of their abilities. This procedure is a form of selection but since the average measured

I.Q. of the children was 82, it can be seen that it scarcely involved 'picking the winners' or 'skimming the cream'. In fact of course, the average measured I.Q. of the children was below the limit of 85 which was formerly used as the upper limit of the English category of 'dull' children.

The children's cultural horizons were raised by an ambitious programme of school visits to plays, to concerts, and to places of historic and cultural importance. They were taken round their own city to see parts they had never known existed. They visited institutions of higher education, sports occasions, and in general their cultural environment was expanded enormously. At the same time more emphasis was placed on academic courses and a concentrated effort was made to clear up reading difficulties.

The results of the programme have been quite phenomenal. The number of students from the school passing out from the high school fed by the school, rose from five passing all their subjects in 1953 to fifty-eight in 1960; and whereas only two got average grades of 80 or better in 1953, twenty-eight had grades of 80 or above in 1960. Some individual cases provide striking evidence of the efficacy of the programme. One boy, with a measured I.Q. of 97 on entry to the school, reached the top of the scale on one test of intelligence with an I.Q. of 139 before he left high school. He also won a scholarship and got a job at Columbia University. Another with an initial I.Q. of 74 got a scholarship to New York University. Many other children from the school who made less startling progress won scholarships to various forms of higher education. The plan was started in 1956 and has now spread to other slum schools in New York with very encouraging results.

The main administrative innovations which underpinned this programme were an increase in the number of staff in the school and the expenditure of more money per child. In terms of cash this amounted to 50 dollars per child per year. In terms of gains to society and to the individual the returns on the increased expenditure are immeasurable.

The importance of this experiment is that it demonstrates in practice that backwardness is not an intractable problem; that environmental enrichment can produce drastic changes in intelligence and in the general level of achievement. It also suggests that cultural deprivation in early life need not necessarily depress ability and attainment permanently.

One aspect of the Higher Horizons project which should be especially noted, is that as part of their schedule of visits, the children were taken to places where they saw Negroes and Puerto Ricans (many of the children were of similar stock) getting a higher education. This was part of the first task of the programme which was to give the children the idea that it was possible for them to achieve what they had grown to believe was the prerogative of the more privileged members of the community. This is a problem common to all who teach children who are backward. A prolonged period of failure and discouragement by itself will act as a negative reinforcer of the child's efforts in school. The restricted environment and probable emotional difficulties will most likely result not only in lack of achievement, but a built-in tendency to under achieve.

The training of the severely subnormal

Work with children and adults who are classified as severely subnormal is not likely to be the province of the teacher or the teacher in training. Nevertheless a short consideration of the approach to the training of low-grade mental defectives illustrates some of the problems and possibilities of work with backward children even though they are of a different order. Until recently the most common approach was to place the child in an occupation centre where he would be kept occupied in such things as rug and mat making. The emphasis was, that is, more on keeping him 'happy' than in training him, and it was generally considered that the ability of imbeciles was so low that there was little if any possibility of their acquiring even the simplest skills.

A number of workers concerned with the training of the severely subnormal have found that the traditional view of their potentialities and the accepted methods of dealing with them, are by no means well founded [38]. The traditional clinical view of the severely subnormal is that they find it extremely difficult to concentrate and to generalize; to appreciate the difference between cause and effect; to adapt to anything out of the ordinary; to perform anything but the simplest routine tasks and then under supervision; and because of all these factors they are incapable of contributing to their own support. In a study of learning in these children N. O'Connor found that they did in fact generalize learning of a problem type, in addition to making improvements in speed and quality of solution.

Experiments involving severely subnormal adolescents and adults resulted in the demonstration that, under the proper training conditions, they could learn to carry out simple industrial processes such as assembling bicycle pumps, or soldering wires to the correct terminals of a television component. From the experiments it was deduced that, while initial ability on industrial tasks was low, it was no indication of the eventual level of competence of severely subnormals although they took longer in the training than normals.

The methods of training which in experimental situations proved effective are likely to be relevant to some degree in the teaching of backward children. Experienced teachers will have evolved some of these principles themselves but as they are now presented they were arrived at from carefully controlled experimental situations. In summary, from the list given by A. D. B. Clarke, they are:

(1) *Incentives* As with normals, learning is very much affected by the presence or absence of suitable incentives. The most effective approach seems to be to set a realistic goal to work to slightly higher than the previous day's. Visual indication of the extent of the previous day's effort is very important. Encouragement reinforces learning.

(2) *Breakdown of work* In the teaching of skills the task to be learned should be broken down to its smallest components and the parts taught separately but in the right sequence so that the whole job from start to finish is tried at each attempt.

(3) *Correct movements* It was found important to teach the

correct movements in the teaching of a skill, right from the beginning because the correct movements are by definition the easiest.

(4) *Learning should be spaced* In common with many other experiments into the learning process, it was found better to learn in fairly short sessions, say three of twenty minutes rather than long session, say one of one hour.

(5) *Need for overlearning* As we have seen before, it is necessary to go beyond the stage at which the responses are first made correctly to ensure that the learned behaviour persists.

(6) *Verbal reinforcement* The work of Vigotsky and Luria will help us to see the relevance of verbal reinforcement. With the actions made by the young child or the low-grade defective goes a spoken commentary which acts as a regulator of the actual activity. Building up a verbal chain to go parallel with the actual activity helps in establishing the required behaviour. This is particularly difficult to do with severely subnormals but it will be easier and doubtless of value with the less severely retarded.

(7) *At first, accuracy rather than speed should be stressed.*

(8) *Material should be arranged (in the training of skills) so that muddle or fumbling can be minimized.*

The second and third points in this schedule are similar to the principles of programmed learning. The breakdown into small steps and the need for the avoidance of errors are common to both. And indeed a 'programmed approach' by the teacher of backward children will be a very fruitful one. Many of the other points are of quite general application and certainly carry over to work with children in special schools and retarded children in the ordinary schools.

The work of the special schools

The special school for the E.S.N. is generally a small school; in the main the number of children does not rise much above 100. The classes in such schools are smaller than those in the ordinary schools and the Ministry of Education suggests a maximum of twenty. In the case of children who have other handicaps, perhaps of a physical nature, the classes should be smaller than this. The organization of the school will be much more flexible than that of the ordinary school and children will tend to be placed in the class most appropriate for their current stage of development, rather than strictly according to their age. In general, teachers will stay with one class rather than have the children moving from one group to another. Within the classes it is desirable, where possible, to depart from the traditional organization with rows of desks and to introduce a much more flexible organization of work, including departing from the idea of different lessons following on in a set sequence. Tansley and Gulliford make a number of suggestions for the running of classes in special schools. On the basis of the flexible timetable and classroom organization they suggest the following:

(a) Have available a variety of alternative activities; e.g. a wide range of supplementary readers, free access to art and craft materials.

(b) Pay particular attention to preparation and planning.

(c) Allow the brighter children to help the others.

(d) Encourage the children to help in class organization and planning activities.

(e) When the children's interest flags in one activity replace it by another.

(f) Have several periods a week when the class is engaged as a whole, e.g. story, drama, or music.

Special classes

Ideally the special class should be very similar to the classes in the special school. The suggestions made above would apply to the arrangement of such classes; indeed many of the principles expounded would carry over into normal classes with advantage. The curriculum should not be a watered-down version of the normal curriculum but should be run on lines similar to those suggested above. Especially is this the case in the secondary school. It is quite pointless to timetable a special class in the same way as the rest of the school. The class should be allocated blocks of time within which the teacher responsible may apportion his time as he thinks best, maintaining the fluidity to which we have referred.

In some schools the special class includes children of all ages. In a small school there may be one class for all children who are retarded no matter what their ages. Larger schools may have two such classes but, as M. F. Cleugh points out, often the larger schools have only one class because teaching the backward children is not a popular job and unfortunately the reason for there only being one class is to avoid the need for having two teachers of backward children. This means that there must inevitably be some children in the ordinary classes who could benefit from special instruction.*

Where the school is streamed it is desirable that, where possible, there should be more than one 'omnibus' special class. It is desirable that the children should feel themelves in as 'normal' a class situation as possible, and if they see their peers in other classes transferring year after year, while they remain in the same class, they may feel they are being passed by and probably become more conscious than otherwise of their disabilities. It is also a considerable problem to organize a class with a wide spread of ages effectively and, as has been said previously, the organization should be very thorough in such a class.

In the secondary school it is generally more common for there to be special, or remedial, classes for each year. In some schools these classes are just the bottom streams in the school with no difference in curriculum or timetable and with no special teachers alloted to the classes. In other schools these classes are organized as special classes in the way suggested above, with a fluid timetable and teachers who are interested in the problems of backward children. In recent years the development of large non-selective schools has resulted in the setting up of increased numbers of such classes, sometimes staffed by teachers who have had special training.

The teacher in the remedial class in an ordinary school should

* CLEUGH, M. F.: *The Slow Learner*, Methuen, 1959.

aim to get as many of his children as soon as possible, back into the mainstream of normal classes. Teachers do not always have this in mind. The two extreme attitudes on this question may be exemplified by two headmasters of secondary schools. One head has an intensive course in the basic subjects in the first year. The overwhelming emphasis of the course is to teach the children in the remedial class to cope with the basic subjects so that in their second year they may all be absorbed into the normal class. The other headmaster in a large non-selective school thought of the Remedial Department in the school in a similar way to the way he thought of the English or Mathematics Department. In this case there was never to be any absorption; the more children stayed on at school, the bigger would be the remedial department. In theory there was nothing to preclude a remedial sixth form!

Remedial services

One other method of providing remedial teaching for children in the ordinary schools is through the remedial services of the local education authority. Often the remedial service is organized by the school psychological service and is often linked with the child guidance clinic. Some authorities have special remedial teachers who visit the schools giving tuition in the basic subjects to the children who are backward. Sometimes it is possible for a large authority to have remedial centres to which numbers of children from different schools can come to special classes, and in certain cases, for example when backwardness is combined with maladjustment, the child may visit the child guidance clinic for his instruction.

In another approach to remedial teaching of reading, temporary remedial groups of twelve to fifteen children were formed in large primary schools. A remedial teacher was responsible for these groups in four neighbouring schools so that he could move from one school to the other during the day. In this way the problem of non-reading was largely solved within one year. Subsequently the teacher moved on to another area and returned to the original one in three years' time.

Psychological factors in the teaching of backward children

Our consideration of the treatment of backwardness has so far centred on the more practical aspects of remedial treatment. This has involved an implicit linkage of practical considerations with the psychological factors we have discussed in previous chapters. We now turn more explicitly to consider the way in which our practical activities are related to the underlying psychological considerations.

One of the more important aspects of our remedial treatment will be the deliberate attempt to extend the child's environment. The results of deprivation in animals and in children to which we have alluded, are being compensated for in the 'Higher Horizons' project with the emphasis on the enrichment of the children's experience, not only through the classroom set-up, but through contact with the outside world. The suggestions to the teacher for the enrichment of the child's experience within the classroom by getting away from the rows of desks and the traditional subject-bound curriculum, are also providing that environmental stimulation. The net result of such educational measures will generally be to facilitate the children's ability to come to grips with the world in a more effective way. In the terms of learning theory, we could say that they adapt to the social environment at a higher level.

The fact that backward children are often suffering from emotional problems presents difficulties in treating them. Thus, although the children need new experiences and a richer environment to stimulate them intellectually, they may well need stability and a protected environment for their emotional difficulties. An unstable home with emotionally disturbed parents may produce unsatisfactory emotional attitudes in the child and interfere with his learning. As we have seen earlier, negative affect will act as a powerful inhibitor of learning, and if the family combines instability with a restricted environment, as it often will, the child is doubly handicapped and the remedial teacher has a more difficult job. Children who have suffered from this twofold affliction will have a negative attitude to learning. Having probably had little, if any, encouragement before school, and having been subjected to more than usual inconsistency in the schedules of reinforcement by parents, such children will lack confidence, will shrink from the unknown, whether it be a new situation or a problem in learning. Lacking experience of consistent reinforcement they will tend to abstain from any new activity which, so far as they know, will be punished.

The treatment for such children is not unlike that for children with neuroses and acquired patterns of maladaptive behaviour to which we have referred earlier. In the case of the child with negative emotional attitudes towards learning, the careful devising of learning gradients is essential. As far as is possible the classroom should generate a sense of security so that positive, and not negative affect predominates. From this situation the teacher will introduce problems, that is, disturb the existing equilibrium, so that the child in the act of adapting will acquire the new patterns of behaviour which we wish to develop. This is what the teacher in the normal class in fact does, but with the children we are considering here, the disturbances of the state of equilibrium will be carefully graded so that children are capable of adapting to the changed situation without arousing negative affect. The teacher presents very slight changes at first in a situation charged with positive affect. A simple problem with a maximum of encouragement leads the child to attempt a solution. The easy achievement of the solution and the reinforcing approbation from the teacher begin the process of setting up positive attitudes towards learning. If steps are too big at the beginning no progress can be made, the effect is merely to increase the negative feeling towards learning. Other factors which could interfere with the satisfactory acquisition of a balanced emotional attitude towards learning could be extraneous to the classroom. If the child is bullied, or baited by children, or treated unsympathetically by teachers, the negative affect generated will operate against the best efforts of the remedial teacher. This may be a sound argument for providing special classes for these children where they can be gradually 'weaned' to cope with more 'normal' situations.

Children such as these will also have had relatively little experience in the solving of problems as compared with normal children. They will thus have had little opportunity of learning how to learn in the way that the monkeys and children did in Harlow's experiments on learning sets. In the course of remedial education they should be given the opportunity of developing the techniques of learning through an adequate amount of practice. In practical terms this means that the backward child will need more practice in problem-solving activity than the normal child.

The nature of the activity the teacher arranges for backward children is of great importance. Backward children are by definition limited in their ability for abstract thinking. It is easier to get through to them through the visual and the concrete. From this point of departure it is sometimes argued that such children should be taught using visual and concrete material and abstraction should be kept to the minimum. This attitude is, as Vigotsky put it, teaching to the child's yesterday when we should be teaching for his tomorrow. It springs from the acceptance of an outlook which considers that the child's performance today mirrors what it shall be in the future. The teacher of children who lack the ability to think in abstractions should use the concrete and visual skilfully to develop their ability for abstract thought. If we think of the way young children develop we can see that there is nothing unusual in this proposition, it is merely the way that all children learn. Backward children in the ordinary schools lag behind children of the same age but they are on the same developmental path. If no attempt is made to lead them forward from visual methods of learning to abstract thinking they become more and more dependent upon these methods and their backwardness may well be reinforced. In brief, the use of the visual and the concrete in the teaching of backward children should be viewed as a means and not an end.

Language and backwardness

As we have seen in previous chapters, language is of key importance in the development of human abilities. Through language children progressively develop the capacity for abstraction and generalization. That is, they learn to think in more and more abstract terms. It is quite clear then, that language will be of great importance in the remedial treatment of backward children. The comments made on the use of language in the normal class will apply equally to the class of backward children, the main difference being that the teacher will need to be much more systematic in introducing new words and concepts to the children.

In a discussion of different methods of tackling the problem of poor linguistic ability in backward children, Gulliford gives a summary of suggestions made by McKee for the development of vocabulary and comprehension which may be regarded as a typical approach. These are:

(1) Rich, varied and meaningful experiences.
(2) The use of pictures and drawings.
(3) Opportunity for informal discussion for the exchange of experiences and ideas, for questioning and simple explanations.
(4) Much simple explanation by the teacher of new and partially formed concepts.
(5) Determined effort to make the child feel dissatisfied with lack of meaning concerning anything he encounters and to encourage him to ask frankly for such meanings.
(6) Much oral reading and story telling by the teacher in which new concepts and meanings are presented in sufficiently familiar settings to ensure clear understanding.

We see running through these suggestions the theme, which has been stressed repeatedly, that richness of experience is essential to satisfactory development. The work of Luria and Bernstein suggests to us that children in restricted linguistic environments do not develop satisfactory conceptual thinking. They also indicate that discussion among children themselves while being of some use, is not in itself enough. The teacher of children with inadequate linguistic ability has the onerous task of being the main agent in the development of adequate linguistic skills. The teacher needs to provide experiences which will stimulate children to talk; to see the limitations of primitive speech; and to help them to acquire more adequate speech abilities. As has been stressed before, in discussing normal children, this is not merely a question of developing 'correct speech', or even of increasing vocabulary, although that is part of the process; what we should be aiming at is the development of more complex linguistic patterns. This should aim at unlocking the word from the actual situation. Children should be encouraged to talk about things outside their immediate environment. This at once makes greater demands on them. Furthermore, the children should be helped to develop their command of the different parts of speech as was mentioned in the discussion of the linguistic training of normal children. This will enable them to be at once more precise in what they say, and at the same time they will become capable of wider generalization. The quality of their thought, that is, will improve.

The great difficulty at the moment, is that much more research is needed in how best to promote the development of linguistic ability. Most work on language training centres about the development of vocabulary. A more important present requirement is systematic investigation into how children, and particularly backward children, can be helped to develop more complex linguistic skills.

Specific difficulties

Extending the range of experience of children who are backward will not automatically remedy existing difficulties. What is needed is a systematic attack on the specific deficiencies underlying failure to learn. These specific difficulties may have arisen for a variety of reasons, but absence from school at a critical point in the development of one of the basic skills will be one of the most common causes.

To illustrate this point let us consider an actual case of backwardness in reading in a class of first-year secondary boys. These children had reached various levels in their reading ability and their reading ages ranged from 5 years to about 8·5 years with the bulk of them scoring at about 6–7 years. Before putting them on a systematic reading course, diagnostic tests were given and exploratory lessons were given to assess the main causes of difficulty. It soon became apparent that most of the boys at the lower end of the reading scale had little or no idea of the sound values of the vowels. Lacking this basis they had never been able to generalize what little reading skill they had, which was almost entirely of a rote nature. Clearly, giving these children the extended experience of which we have spoken, would not by itself improve the reading of these children. What was needed was systematic instruction in the sound values of the vowels (in a meaningful context of words), so that they would have a basis on which to build the more complex combinations necessary to analyse and synthesize more difficult words. In this case, it should be noted, it was not sufficient merely to instruct the boys in the correct vowel sounds. Because they lacked understanding at such a crucial point they had been unable to develop the reading skills which are based on the knowledge they lacked. Remedial measures had to go back to the point where the boys had failed, to build secure foundations for subsequent learning.

An example of failure in arithmetic makes the same point. In this case, the investigator (A. N. Leontiev) was interested in the way the children in a special school coped with mental arithmetic. He noticed that when they were asked questions they attempted to work out the answers by counting on their fingers [8]. He then gave the children each two plates and told them to hold them above the desk when they were doing their mental arithmetic. He found that in the majority of cases the operation of adding just disintegrated. The children had no idea how to answer. The remedy to this situation was not to give the children more practice in mental arithmetic, but to take them back to the stage where they had failed. In this case they had not made the transition from adding in ones using objects, to adding 'in the mind'. The children were, therefore, taken back to the stage of counting using objects and then taken forward gradually and systematically so that this counting was condensed, first into the spoken word, and then internalized so that they were then really 'counting in the mind' and not secretly reverting to a previous stage by counting under the desk.

These two examples of specific difficulties of failing children, remind us of Galperin's researches referred to earlier (Chapter 8).

Essentially, the point is that children build up their grasp of the basic skills in a series of stages each of which rests on the foundation of the previous stage. The teacher who tries to build on shaky foundations will be wasting his time.

In concluding this section we should give some thought to the fact that the Higher Horizons project referred to at the beginning of the chapter, involved not only a very greatly enriched environment for the children, but also a systematic and rigorous approach to teaching. The most potent factor in enlarging the child's environment should be the teacher.

In this chapter methods of dealing with the problem of backwardness of varying degrees of severity have been discussed. Some of these dealing with brain-damaged children are not perhaps of immediate import to students and teachers of normal children but it is instructive to see how the methods worked out for the severely subnormal have considerable application to the backward class in the normal school. In all degrees of retardation it is clear that skilled teaching is necessary and in matters of method there are no clearly defined boundaries. The success some workers have had with the training of children once declared 'ineducable' is of considerable significance for the teachers of backward children.

The present position with regard to the education of the backward child in the ordinary school is somewhat more optimistic than formerly. Whereas until fairly recently it was considered that children with low measured intelligence, i.e. those considered 'just dull', were destined to make very limited progress no matter what the teacher did (Burt, *The Backward Child*, 1937), many workers in the field of remedial teaching are taking a different view very well summed up by W. D. Wall and quoted by S. S. Segal [34].

Human nature could be changed. . . . Intelligence could be changed. Environment could be changed and organized to create intelligence and personality. Change was the purpose of education.

Summary

Recent views on the treatment of backwardness reflect the results of investigations into the effect of deprivation of experience. Retardation previously attributed to innate lack of ability, is now seen as to be very often the result of an unstimulating environment. One of the key methods of attack on backwardness in the ordinary schools is therefore the enriching of the environment of backward children. In New York striking results were obtained when more money and more staff were made available to slum schools thus enabling the teachers to provide the enriched environment. Enrichment on its own, however, does not solve the problem. A systematic approach to teaching and learning must go hand in hand with enrichment.

Systematic approaches to the teaching of severely subnormal children have demonstrated that they can learn far more than was formerly considered possible. The teaching methods evolved for imbeciles is of value for teachers of ordinary children. Points stressed in these methods include:

Realistic incentives; encouragement.
Breakdown of work.
Teaching the correct movements in a skill carefully.
Spaced learning.
Need for overlearning.
Verbal accompaniment by the learner as reinforcement.
Stress accuracy rather than speed at first.

Some backward children are in special schools. Classes in these schools are generally small, the schools also are generally small. Classes in the school should be run with a flexible timetable.

Backward children in special classes in ordinary schools also need a flexible timetable. There is probably too little provision of special classes for the children who could benefit from special attention. An important aim of the teacher in remedial classes should be to help as many of the children as possible to return to the ordinary classes.

Many local authorities make provision for peripatetic remedial teachers to give special instruction to backward children. Some remedial clinics are also run in conjunction with the child guidance clinic and the school psychological service.

Teachers of backward children need to be aware of their special psychological difficulties. Along with the effort to enlarge their experience and to systematize their learning, must go care to build up a positive feeling towards learning to replace the negative attitudes they have acquired through persistent failure. Care must be taken not to attempt too much at once and the children must be given plenty of practice to consolidate learning and to build up confidence. At the same time the teacher must beware of 'teaching to the children's yesterday': once a skill has been acquired he must move on.

Backward children will have poor linguistic ability. Because of the importance of language in conceptual thought the cultivation of the children's speech is extremely important. The teacher should therefore attempt to develop the children's ability to use complex speech forms.

Specific difficulties may be disclosed by diagnostic tests and should be treated by tackling the stage at which the children first experienced difficulty. This may mean going back several stages in a process to rectify a specific disability before moving forward again.

In general, there is more optimism with regard to the possibility of treating backwardness now than there was formerly. A stimulating educational environment, a systematic approach to instruction, and careful diagnosis and treatment of specific difficulties can do much for children who were formerly considered to be 'dull' by nature and beyond the scope of the remedial teacher.

CHAPTER 14

The Social Psychology of the School

Throughout this book stress has been laid on the importance of society as the key educative influence in man. Man becomes man only when he is in society. Man isolated from society is an interesting fiction, but children brought up outside society are unlikely to be recognizably human. The wild boy treated by Itard mentioned in the first chapter, was such a child, and, as we have seen, the more removed children are from normal human company, the less adequately human they are likely to be.

We can see why this is necessarily so if we consider again the factors which so sharply differentiate man from the lower animals. Huxley in 1863 stressed the main points when he said that man alone of all the animals possessed the power of rational speech whereby '... he has slowly accumulated and organized the experience which is almost wholly lost with the cessation of every individual life in other animals'. Speech, thought, and culture are the touchstones which single man out from what Huxley called 'the brutes', and these three can exist only in society. Any child brought up outside society (assuming that this were possible) would be in the position of the lower animals: all the characteristic features of humanity would be denied him. He would, like other animals, build up patterns of behaviour based on conditional reflexes set up in the actual concrete situation. There would be virtually no abstraction or symbolization; no past; no future.

But as soon as we have society we have the conditions appropriate to the transmission of habits, of skills, of methods of coming to grips with nature, from one generation to the next. The more primitive the society, the more primitive will be the modes of transmission and the skills which are transmitted. It might well be said, however, that education and society develop hand in hand: there can be no education without society; there can be no society without education.

The quality of the education given by a society to its children will depend on the nature of that society. The content of education will inevitably depend on the level of technological development of a given society. Less obviously the psychology of children will in many ways reflect the currently held social attitudes and values. As we have seen in previous chapters, the new-born child is in a way only potentially human. He will become fully human only through social living, through making part of himself the patterns of social thinking and feeling which are characteristic of his particular cultural group. His psychological make-up will therefore approximate to that of his home, his school, his society at large.

Anthropologists and sociologists have shown through their investigations how this works out in practice. Margaret Mead, in her studies of South Sea Island tribes, showed how children brought up in one society grow up to be cooperative and mild in temper, whereas those from another tribe grow up to be assertive and belligerent. The Mountain Arapesh tribe in New Guinea are responsive and cooperative. They have developed a society '. . . in which, while there is never enough to eat, each man spends most of his time helping his neighbour, and committed to his neighbour's purposes'. On the other hand the Mundugumor people, also from New Guinea, have very different social attitudes. These people '. . . devote their time to quarrelling and head hunting, and have developed a form of social organization in which every man's hand is against every other man. The women are as assertive and vigorous as the men; they detest bearing and rearing children and provide most of the food, leaving the men free to plot and fight' [39]. Other tribes brought up their children in other ways, so that in these tribes could be found children with patterns of behaviour which differed markedly from tribe to tribe. Similarly, children in advanced technological countries develop the patterns of behaviour of their society.

Whilst the psychological development of children in primitive society may be fairly clearly linked with the social customs of the tribe, the position is not so clear in societies such as our own. Here there are so many influences at work that it is impossible to consider any one of them to be the major factor in determining how children will develop psychologically. The school, however, will be a major factor for most children, since the school is society's expression of the deliberate attempt to transmit its culture in a systematic way and as effectively as possible. The environment which the school provides will naturally itself be socially determined, nevertheless it is possible to consider what conditions within the schools are likely to provide the best environment for the upbringing of the children.

The individual and the group

Every child in school is a member of a very important group; his class. How he gets on with the members of the class will affect his educational performance. In particular the general atmosphere of the group is surprisingly important. This general atmosphere is very susceptible to influence by the teacher. Let us consider some of the implications of that influence.

In the classes of some junior schools the teachers give a weekly test in various subjects. Children are placed in rank order on the results of these tests and are then allocated to a seat in the class which corresponds to their rank position. The seating at any one time will thus indicate the 'order of merit' of the children, and this will be changed weekly according to the test results.

This is an extreme example of a fairly common practice which most schools indulge in. It is quite customary for schools to draw up rank orders at the end of each term, to promulgate these in class lists, and to record them in the children's reports. We have seen the fallaciousness of this procedure from the statistical point of view (p. 262), let us now consider its psychological implications.

Whenever children are placed in rank order the success of one child is dependent on the failure of another. The positive reinforcement and corresponding affective state of the child at the top of the list has its obverse in the negative reinforcement and adverse emotional state of the child at the bottom. Only one child in the whole class can possibly experience an unalloyed feeling of success; every other child in the class will have failed in some degree. In such a set-up the key reinforcer is no longer the successful achievement of a task but rather the act of doing better than other children in the class. Because the reinforcement is no longer linked directly to the learning process a child could well be satisfied with a mediocre performance so long as the rest of the class has done badly. Instead of reinforcing behaviour which leads to the successful accomplishment of educational tasks, we reinforce the act of doing better than other children. It is thus impossible to reinforce the learning of all children in the class in the way we have seen to be necessary if the learning is to be successful. In one experiment, Skinner reinforced belligerent behaviour in pigeons until the pigeons would fight each other to the death if not stopped by the experimenter. The pattern of reinforcement in the class geared to the order of merit is not dissimilar.

It is sometimes suggested that the competitive striving to be 'top' is inherent in human nature, and that competition in the class is healthy. In view of what we have seen of the way in which children develop, and the findings of the anthropologists, this view can hardly be sustained. W. J. H. Sprott gives an interesting example which suggests that competition is by no means the natural order of things. In China, he says, deliberate use is made of cooperation in the schools and when English children who had been educated in a Chinese school came to England they found the atmosphere of competition quite bewildering. Sprott also instances the case of a group of Chinese students who stayed in the university for part of their holiday in order to coach one of the group who had been ill, so that the whole group would be sure to pass the examination. The failure of one of the group would have meant disgrace for the whole group, not just for the person who failed [40].

Investigations have been carried out into the relative merits of competition and cooperation. M. A. Deutsch divided the members of a psychology class into two types of group, one group was told that:

... the group score obtained by solving problems in human relations would count towards their grading in the course, and the other, that individual contributions would count towards the grading of the individuals who made them. The results bring out the virtues of cooperation. The cooperative groups produced more, the members had a greater sense of responsibility, produced more diverse contributions, were more attentive to one another, more friendly, and enjoyed themselves more. The competitive ones were obviously anxious to restrict communication in the interests of personal victory, and less interested in what the others said because they were intent on their own success [40].

The methods used in this experiment are readily applicable to to the classroom. Instead of having the educational success of one child contingent on the educational failure of another, success is linked to other more socially and educationally desirable ends. This can be done by the teacher setting realistic educational goals, the achievement of which will provide the necessary reinforcement. If the class is also organized on cooperative lines, the success of one child will be positively reinforcing to the other children and the positive affect of the group, accompanying the group success, will, in turn, produce a more favourable situation for future achievement.

Such an approach to class teaching involves an attitude towards teaching and testing such as we have considered in earlier chapters. In very many schools and in other educational circles the hallmark of excellence is equated with the ability to come at the top of the order of merit; the average child comes about halfway down. The marks awarded sometimes parallel this pattern with the top child getting roughly top marks and the average child getting roughly half marks. More commonly, however, the top child will receive about seventy to eighty 'per cent'. (We should remember here how arbitrary and subjective this 'percentage' is.) Many teachers have a strange reluctance to award full marks. Instead of this approach, under a non-competitive system the teacher aims to make it possible for all the children to get high marks because their marks are awarded for successful accomplishment of the task set. This is very similar to the attitude of the programmer who revises his programme until a very large proportion of children working through it is able to obtain high marks on the terminal test (not by making the test easier, but by teaching more effectively and by setting realistic educational goals). In this way the teacher can introduce the cooperative atmosphere described by Deutsch. Through some such class organization the teacher can arrange things so that the interests of the group are the interests of each individual within it rather than these interests being mutually antagonistic.

Sociometry in the classroom

Certain techniques have been developed which help the teacher to exercise his influence in the classroom in a more objective and informed way than might otherwise have been the case [41]. Social groupings often form on rather arbitrary bases regardless of individual preferences. In school, children are allocated to classes on various criteria; generally this will be done on the basis of scholastic attainment, although in unstreamed schools it could be done on the basis of age or by alphabetical order. Allocation to such school groupings as houses could be purely random. And yet as we have seen, the nature and composition of the social group in which a child finds himself can have quite important effects on his development.

Sociometry is a technique which has been developed to make the allocation to small groups less arbitrary in the hope that it will result in better group morale leading to more effective group work. The technique was invented by J. L. Moreno in America and was originally used in the New York State Training School for Girls. The girls lived in houses under the supervision of 'house mothers' and the technique was used to make the social relationships in the various houses more harmonious.

Sociometry aims at forming groups on the basis of individual preferences rather than on arbitrary criteria external to the group. Most teachers will be familiar with the way which children will ask to sit next to their friends; sociometry in school systematizes these preferences in order to improve class morale and the children's work. It would be possible to arrange the class in groups on the basis of the casual requests of children. It would, however, be a rough and ready way of doing it and would probably be inaccurate. The sociometric approach involves asking each child in the class to state a social preference in private and to a specific criterion. Thus the child is not asked whom he likes best, but is asked with whom he would like to sit, with whom he would like to go on holiday, with whom he would like to play football and so on; the questions relate to specific situations. The children are

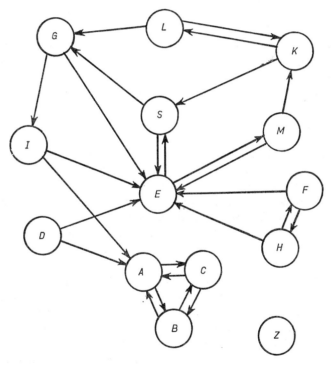

Fig. 23. An example of a sociogram showing the various choice patterns referred to in the text.

given one or a number of choices of this nature and their socio-metric status is calculated by adding up the number of preferences each one receives; the popular ones will probably receive a large number of choices whereas the isolates or rejected will receive few or possibly none.

The sociometric structure of a group can be represented diagrammatically in a *sociogram*. In the sociogram, individuals are represented by small circles and their choices are represented by lines. In the example shown the popular child, E, can be identified by the large number of choices forming a characteristic 'star'. Other typical patterns are the pairs making mutual choices as may be seen in the cases of F and H. Cliques emerge from the overall pattern as in the case of A, B, and C forming small stable groups within the main group. The isolate receiving no choices is shown by D who chooses but is not chosen. Sometimes members of the group are asked to indicate those they would not choose. In such cases an isolate may not only not be chosen but might also be rejected. It is also possible that what is sometimes called the 'true isolate' not only is not chosen, but does not exercise a choice himself. In the diagram he is represented by Z.

The use of such a diagram enables one to see fairly readily the pattern of preferences in a group. The starred members stand out clearly, as do the isolates and cliques. The pattern which emerges from the sociogram very often confirms much of what the observant teacher will have noticed but it will also very often uncover relationships and groupings that he had not suspected. This is especially so if children are asked to make their selection on the basis of criteria which are outside the normal classroom conditions: for example, such a criterion as whom they would select to go on holiday with. The sociogram also shows preferences which would otherwise be hidden because the children in question may be too shy to exercise in real life the choices they would like to make.

Sociometric techniques may be used by the teacher to arrange classroom groupings to the best effect. If the children are to work in groups at any time the groups could be formed on the basis of sociometric analysis. The teacher could also use the information to arrange the class or the groups within the class so that the isolates might be more readily assimilated. Moreno considered it essential to follow up a sociometric test with an actual regrouping such as has been suggested, otherwise choices made would not be taken seriously by the children. For experimental purposes it may be permissible to give a sociometric test and not to act on it, but only if no further tests were to be given to the tested groups. Moreno called such a test a *near-sociometric* test. Although the teacher may not follow such a test with the physical regrouping of the class, he could use the information to help the isolates, to select group leaders, or to put mutually chosen children together on tasks which demanded the cooperation of two or three. The near sociometric test is also used for research purposes so that the effects of such things as the promotion or demotion of individuals on the group might be studied. There is always the danger, however, with children, that unless the test is to be acted upon in some way they will not give real choices.

While the use of sociometric techniques can be of undoubted value in promoting desirable social relationships with a corresponding influence on the emotional state of the individuals within the group, there are certain possible disadvantages. One disadvantage may be illustrated by the reaction of one experienced teacher encountering the ideas of sociometry for the first time. She declared that she would want to separate those children who wished to be together! This is a not uncommon attitude but it seems to spring from an essentially authoritarian approach to the children. The assumption would seem to be that the children grouped with their chosen companions would be up to no good and such groupings would be deleterious to class order. This teacher would presumably be working on the principle of 'divide and rule' rather than on Moreno's theories. Such attitudes do serve to illustrate the difficulties of implementing sociometric techniques. Essentially sociometry assumes a non-authoritarian régime and where the classroom set-up is authoritarian there will be a conflict between the theory and actual practice.

But one aspect of the technique which is related to the objections raised by the teacher just mentioned, is of general application and is an important issue. When a sociometric test is given, it produces a sociogram which represents the pattern of social relationships at a given time. It does not consider the circumstances which led up to the choices which emerged. It is conceivable that children would make choices for what would be anti-social reasons. It is also possible that the groups which already exist came into being for undesirable reasons. By allocating children to groups within the class on the basis of a sociometric test, the teacher would be tending to perpetuate such groupings, whereas it might well be better for the class were the groupings to be altered. The teacher might well consider, also, whether it is desirable to take groupings, which have come into being often fortuitously through force of circumstances, and to crystallize these groups deliberately. If the teacher merely groups the children on the basis of their preferences he is adopting an essentially passive role. The skilled and experienced teacher will most likely feel it his duty to play a more active part. He will certainly not react to the findings of a sociometric study by arranging for the isolates to be put in isolation to conform with the sociogram: it might well be that informed manipulation of all relationships uncovered by the sociogram is the most fruitful way for the teacher to use the technique. The difficulty here, of course, is that the tests used in this way tend to become 'near sociometric' rather than really sociometric since the children will not necessarily be regrouped on the basis of their expressed preferences. One way of coping with the problem that a sociometric test as used in schools must almost inevitably be 'near sociometric' is to put the questions to be asked in a heterogeneous collection of items unconnected with the sociometric analysis. This does not make the test really sociometric in its purest terms, but it probably provides the teacher with information of reasonable accuracy and the test can be repeated.

One other important point needs to be considered in the use of sociometry. While it is aimed at producing the most fruitful and satisfactory social groupings, it could well have a divisive effect. Whereas the key grouping is the class as a whole, the groups emerging from a sociometric study may tend to break down the idea of class unity in favour of the unity of the small group. It may well be that the teacher should concern himself with blurring the boundaries of the small groups within the class in order to draw all the children into an integrated larger class group.

The effects of streaming

Our discussion so far in this chapter has dealt chiefly with the effect of attitudes and feelings on performance. In addition it must be remembered that a class develops an intellectual energy as well. The bright questions of some members of the class draw out others. Recent research suggests that the performance of individual children is very open to influence by other children in the group.

The practice of allocating children to different classes according to their ability is one very common practice which bears closely on our question. Streaming occurs in some infant schools, in many junior schools, and nearly all secondary schools. Until recent years the great majority of junior schools were streamed, and, indeed, the practice of streaming was recommended by the Board of Education. And yet, if we consider the practice in the light of our discussions of learning, we can see that it is of doubtful efficacy.

All the evidence points to the fact that children's learning is closely dependent on their experience and particularly on their social experience. Contact with adults is very important but so also is contact with other children. As was suggested in Chapter 12, streaming is likely to produce a restricted social environment within the school which mirrors the restricted cultural backgrounds of the children. This has the effect of depressing the *general level* of achievement of children. As the report of the British Psychological Society in 1955 put it: 'Children who are relegated to a low stream to suit their present level of ability, are likely to be taught at a slower pace; whereas the brighter streams, often under the better teachers, are encouraged to proceed more rapidly. Thus initial differences become exacerbated, and those duller children, who happen to improve later, fall too far behind the higher streams in attainments to be able to catch up, and lose the chance to show their merits.'* This argument has been substantiated by the subsequent researches of Daniels and of Douglas already cited (Chapter 12). On the results of recent research into the question, therefore, it would seem highly probable that streaming works against the best interests of the children.

The most important part of the child's environment in school is, of course, the teacher. If the teacher is of the opinion that children in the bottom stream are in some way limited by nature to a very low level of attainment, he is likely to assume the attitude that, 'You can't make a silk purse out of a sow's ear.' The teacher who holds such an attitude is unlikely to work consistently and systematically to raise the level of the children's ability. He will tend to be satisfied with a low level of achievement. Provided that there is no 'hidden streaming' by grouping in the unstreamed class, however, the teacher must adopt a very different approach to the children. He will probably give more thought to the planning of his work in order to keep the class moving along together. He will be more likely to look for means of bringing up to scratch those children who are behind because of the factors we have considered before: such things as absence, change of school, ill health, or poor home background. If the child cannot be 'sent down' to the bottom class some means will have to be devised for keeping him as nearly as possible at the level of the other children.

The experience of unstreamed schools suggests that there is in fact a different attitude among the teachers. There being no A, B, or C streams, there are no A, B, or C teachers. In streamed schools it is not uncommon for the lower streams to be unpopular with teachers so that newcomers to the staff, often straight from college, and part-time and supply teachers, even unqualified teachers, are given these classes. In a discussion of this practice, B. Jackson reports the case of an A teacher who resigned after she had been given a B stream class to teach [42]. A discussion of teachers'

* VERNON, P. E. (Ed.) for the British Psychological Society: *Secondary School Selection*, Methuen, 1957.

attitudes towards streaming may also be found in the symposium on the junior school edited by B. Simon [43].

The emotional effects of streaming should also be borne in mind. Children in the bottom streams are more likely to suffer from emotional disturbances than other children mainly because they are more likely to come from unsatisfactory homes. The result is that lower streams will probably contain an unduly large proportion of these children, which in turn produces a less healthy psychological atmosphere than exists in other classes. There is therefore a tendency for an emotional vicious circle to be set up which is very difficult for the teacher to break. The position is made worse by the fact that the children are generally aware that they are in the 'bottom' class. Traditionally, being bottom is associated with rejection. We no longer use the dunce's cap but the social attitudes it symbolizes are still with us. Rejection evokes complex affective states which act to inhibit learning besides contributing to the mental unhealth of the children.

Evidence that children in the lower classes of streamed schools are less well adjusted psychologically than children in unstreamed schools is provided by a number of studies. C. J. Willig found that there was '. . . a tendency, in some cases a strong tendency, for children in unstreamed classes to be superior in social adjustment as defined by Stott's Scale, and superior in social attitudes to children in streamed classes'.* R. A. Pearce found that classes composed of friendship groups suffered less from the 'ordinary frustrations of adolescence' than did children in streamed classes. He also found a sense of failure in the lower streams of streamed schools and considered a decline in morale, effort, and attainment 'inevitable'.†

Although more evidence is needed to prove conclusively that unstreamed classes are superior to streamed classes, there is a growing body of research information which suggests this. There is, on the other hand, virtually none to indicate the opposite.

* WILLIG, C. J.: 'Social Implications of Streaming in the Primary School', in *Educational Research*, Vol. 5, No. 2, February 1963.

† PEARCE, R. A.: 'Streaming and a Sociometric Study', in *Educational Review*, Vol. 10, No. 1, June 1958.

Educational developments which we discuss in the next chapter may well lead to changes in school organization which will render the question an academic one in the future. Such developments are likely to introduce a much more fluid grouping of children allowing for large groups for some activities, very small groups for other activities, and individual work both supervised and unsupervised. The accent will then be placed more heavily on the children's learning than the teacher's teaching; and this means that instead of thinking in terms of 'homogeneous groups' of children, the teacher's attention will be focused more clearly on the needs of the individual child.

Much that has been said about streaming can be said about selection for different types of schools. By dividing children up into categories and giving them different educational experiences we tend to create differences among them. This has not always been appreciated by educationists who have occasionally confused cause with effect. An example of this may be seen in the views put forward in the Norwood Report of 1943 and stemming from the Spens Report of 1938. The argument was that there are three different types of children; the academic type, at home with the use of books and learning best by abstract thinking; the technical type, children with a mechanical bent; and the rest, i.e. children who lacked these attributes and learned in practical ways. The terms 'hewers of wood and drawers of water' have been used more than once in connection with this group of children. This typology was a direct reflection of the situation existing at the time. There were, in fact, three types of school catering for the child of eleven plus. The education provided by these schools precisely matched the three types of children identified by the reports. Since the three kinds of schools had educated children in three different ways, it was not surprising that the investigators found differences among the children from different schools. Few psychologists would now accept the Norwood typology, nevertheless its effects linger on in the organization of secondary education over much of England and Wales into the three divisions of Grammar Schools, Technical Schools, and Secondary Modern Schools, allegedly corresponding with the typology.

What has been the effect of this division of secondary education into three strands? Much has been said and written for and against such a division but there is little reported research into the comparative merits of a selective or a non-selective school system. From what has been said earlier the reader will realize that the methods of selection are now considered to be less efficacious than was once thought. He might wonder whether children in non-selective education fare better or worse educationally than children in selective schools.

One research carried out by T. W. G. Miller and reported in 1961 investigated some of the important issues involved in secondary education in selective and non-selective schools [44]. On the basis of facts and figures from existing schools he came to the conclusion that there was no basis for the assertions that academic standards are bound to fall in a comprehensive school, and that the comprehensive school will be so large that it will become a 'soulless educational factory'. Miller went on to investigate experimentally a number of important aspects of the social psychology of the secondary school. He investigated the claims made on behalf of the comprehensive school that it:

- (a) fosters cultural unity and a general improvement in cultural standards;
- (b) helps to overcome the problems associated with disparity of esteem for the different kinds of secondary education;
- (c) contributes to the development of social unity; and
- (d) encourages children to remain at school longer and gives greater purpose to their secondary education.

From his investigations Miller was able to show that the comprehensive school did indeed help to overcome the problem of disparity of esteem for the different types of secondary education. He found also that compared with the secondary modern school the comprehensive school offers an education which is more purposeful, and which encouraged the children to stay on longer at school. The beneficial effects of the comprehensive school for the 'modern school' child, may, he suggests, be due among other things to the stimulus afforded by the presence of the more able pupils and the fact that the school is held in high esteem by the community. The comprehensive school also, it seems, may well contribute to an improvement in general cultural standards. The general effect seems to be a levelling up rather than a levelling down. With regard to the question as to whether the comprehensive school contributed to the promotion of social unity little evidence one way or the other was produced. Finally, the point was made that not all comprehensive schools are equally effective with respect to the findings outlined.

The last point made by Miller is an important one. Bringing children together into one school is no guarantee that an integrated educational community will *of necessity* develop in a comprehensive school. The attitudes derived from the tripartite system, and especially the idea of the different types of children, can carry over into the non-selective schools, which can be rigidly streamed with the staff thinking in terms of the 'grammar stream' and the 'modern stream'. If this kind of attitude prevails it is likely to affect adversely the influence of the school on the children in it.

Authority in the classroom

We have seen that group attitudes affect children's behaviour and that these attitudes can be influenced by the teacher. Now the way in which the teacher influences these attitudes is important. In particular the way in which the teacher uses his authority in the classroom is a very important factor in the efficacy of the children's learning. In a celebrated experiment the Americans Lippitt and White investigated different ways in which the teacher might fill his role as wielder of authority in the classroom.

In this experiment four groups of eleven-year-old boys were subjected to three different régimes: an 'authoritarian' régime in which the adult leader of the group ordered the boys about and told them what to do; a 'democratic' régime in which he consulted the boys and discussed the problems with them; and a *'laissez-faire'* régime in which the leader left the boys to their own devices. The results of the experiment were that under the authoritarian régime one group was rebellious under authority and the others were cowed into apathy but under the other régimes they let themselves go. All groups were well integrated and worked well under the democratic régime while under the *laissez-faire* treatment they were frustrated and bewildered. When the leader left the room the groups reacted differently according to the régime they were under. The democratically run groups carried on working, those under the authoritarian régime did nothing.

The results of this experiment complement those concerned with the investigation into cooperative and competitive régimes. Similar forces are at work in both cases. The authoritarian teacher becomes associated with punishment and the generator of negative affect for the whole class. The learning which goes on in his classroom will be more likely to be rote learning with the minimum of generalization, since he is more likely to try to 'drill it in' to the children rather than to arrange the appropriate learning situations. In general, learning in such classes will tend to be avoidance learning; that is the children will attempt to learn to avoid the displeasure or punishment of the teacher. This is Skinner's 'aversive control' which almost all psychologists agree is inefficient in these circumstances. Furthermore, the children will probably work only under surveillance, and when coercion is removed will lapse into inactivity.

The extreme case of the authoritarian régime is one which relies on corporal punishment. The majority of English schools today use some form of corporal punishment as an ultimate sanction and most teachers think that it is necessary. Yet the experience of teachers who have abandoned corporal punishment completely (and its threat) and attempted to introduce more democratic and cooperative ways of working in school, suggests that schools are better places without corporal punishment. Conversely many educationists would agree that discipline is often worse under a repressive régime.*

Some recent evidence lends support to this suggestion. An inquiry among the secondary schools in the West Riding showed a positive association between corporal punishment and juven-

---

* See CASTLE, E. B.: *People in School*, Heinemann, 1953, and HIGHFIELD, M. E. and PINSENT, A.: *A Survey of Rewards and Punishment in Schools*, Newnes, 1952.

ile delinquency. In order to check whether both corporal punishment and delinquency were caused by 'the concentration of "caning" schools in the poorer areas – where, it is claimed, corporal punishment is necessary' data were obtained on the average rateable value of property, and on the percentage of homes with an occupancy rate of more than two per room. This established that there was little connection between quality of neighbourhood and delinquency or caning. It was thus not true that corporal punishment is necessary in these districts. Commenting on these findings, Wiseman suggests that, far from *reducing* delinquency, caning might well be increasing it [35].

The results of the West Riding survey were subjected to detailed statistical scrutiny by the researchers in the Manchester University Research Committee. They found an association 'of undoubted significance' between school behaviour and juvenile delinquency and corporal punishment. This association, however, Wiseman points out, does not *prove* that corporal punishment *causes* bad behaviour and delinquency. He does consider, however, that:

> The total pattern of this analysis is one which offers no shred of opposition to the hypothesis that corporal punishment encourages bad behaviour and juvenile delinquency, but does offer evidence *against* the alleged association of caning and poor school neighbourhood. Taken in conjunction with other evidence, and with our results from the Salford analysis [where 'progressiveness' was found to be an important factor affecting attainment and intelligence test score], the balance of judgement lies heavily *against* corporal punishment as a device for improving behaviour, raising moral standards and improving children's attitude to authority.

It might be asked why the practice of corporal punishment persists in view of its doubtful efficacy. The main answer, it must be admitted, is that the majority of teachers believe that it is effective. The forces of tradition die hard and the cane has been the main teaching aid in many schools for centuries. For those who believe in its efficacy, the use of corporal punishment seems to deal with a problem quickly and conveniently, whether the problem is one of a disciplinary misdemeanour or the failure to learn. Perhaps the most disturbing of all explanations is the one suggested by Skinner, which he applies to punishment generally. The parent or teacher who punishes a child is often himself positively reinforced. The discharge of anger or frustration which accompanies the punishment is the reinforcement in this situation. Corporal punishment would be the extreme case here. Whichever way we consider it, there seems little to be said for punishment in the classroom and the teacher would probably be well advised to avoid its use.

Theory and practice

In this chapter we have discussed some of the most important ways in which the nature of the group powerfully influences the psychology of the individual. Certain suggestions have been made which should help the reader to see how the teacher can arrange his class and attempt to influence his school so as to produce the best conditions for his pupils. The topics we have considered have been based on the findings of investigations, some in schools and some in other social groups. There is little doubt, however, that the majority of readers will have attended schools where few if any of the practices suggested are to be observed. Readers may well wonder if any schools have adopted the practices.

In fact a number of schools have adopted such methods, and have contributed to our knowledge of their efficacy. Especially is this the case with regard to unstreaming and the setting up of comprehensive schools. However, some of the other topics we have mentioned are by and large still not generally considered. Even here, there is evidence of the practical value of the approach to classroom and school organization which takes careful note of group influences on the individual child, and there are, undoubtedly, many schools working along the lines suggested in this chapter, whose work is not reported. Among the schools which have recorded their experiences, the 'Independent Progressive Schools' have been particularly prominent. In many of these schools, school councils take the place of prefects and the whole ethos of the school is aimed to create a corporate spirit where competition is replaced by cooperation [45]. Schools in the public sector of education have also recorded their experiences of introducing similar methods of organization. A brief consideration of one such school may help to give a more positive illustration of the practical working out of the ideas we have been discussing.

W. Pattinson has described one school which, in its organization and educational outlook, embodies most of the ideas with which this chapter has been concerned. The school is a selective technical school for boys and girls. It is by policy unstreamed. The children are grouped at random on entering the school and each class has a wide range of ability (and, one might assume, a similar range in attitudes and personality). The aim of the school is to foster cooperative effort rather than competition. There are, therefore, no subject or form lists, no promotion or demotion and formal examinations are kept to the minimum. The School Report has no provision for marks or positions, but gives credit for effort and highlights success. There are no order marks, no merit marks, and no detentions or allied methods of punishment. The school has no house system, no corporal punishment, and no prefects. On the other hand there are form and school councils which meet regularly [46].

Pattinson claims that the school has been 'singularly free from behaviour problems and delinquency', and visitors have commented on the atmosphere and enthusiasm. The children have joined in school activities with enthusiasm and there have been no cases of early leaving. Academically the school has done well and it is interesting that children who came in at the 'bottom of the list' in the selection examination have done as well in G.C.E. as the ones at the top. In a questionnaire on streaming the children showed that they overwhelmingly preferred unstreamed classes. Pattinson gives a specimen response which indicates that one child at least had detected some of the key issues involved in streaming. She said in her reply:

I think it is better without streaming because with it,
  (a) there is jealousy;
  (b) usually those in a lower class are not encouraged much;
  (c) people who are not clever yet try hard are discouraged if they are put into a lower class; and
  (d) the people in the top class become snobs.

The author stresses that unstreaming was only one part of the total approach to making school a more friendly, cooperative place calculated to build up the children's confidence and to encourage their personal effort as good in itself, rather than as good to the extent to which it was better than other children's.

The school referred to here was a selective school, but the author also refers to his experience in a secondary modern, non-selective school. Over a period of five years, during which the school changed from rigid streaming to unstreaming he found improvements in every way. The standards of behaviour and cooperation improved greatly and achievement also improved throughout.

This particular example of one school does not establish a general case, and, of course, the statements of individual children cannot be taken as evidence although we must pay attention to their collective views. However, taken in conjunction with the evidence from other sources there seems a good case for holding that the practices in use in this school are to the benefit of the children.

The results of the Salford survey referred to above substantiate this suggestion. In this survey schools were rated by the local education authority for *progressiveness* ranging from the 'extremely formal, rigid, and orthodox to the most informal, free, and progressive, with a curriculum organized through activities related to the interests of the children'. The survey showed that progressiveness, as defined, was the most important factor influencing attainment and intelligence test score. The more progressive the school, the higher the attainment and the intelligence test score. Especially is this so in the case of reading and arithmetic.

While the evidence points to the superiority of progressive methods, the young teacher might well take note that progressive methods make more demands on the teacher. Wiseman considers that for the very weak teachers 'such methods may be beyond their capacity, and they are perhaps safer with the formal methods which they understand and to which they themselves have been conditioned in their own education'. A young teacher in a formal

357

school would, if he accepts Wiseman's point, be very cautious about introducing progressive methods until he was quite sure of his ability to cope with them effectively.

Summary

Man as we know him can exist only in society. Education is one of the most important social phenomena and society and education are interdependent. The most important human attributes such as speech and thought are almost entirely dependent upon society. Because of this, the type of society in which a child is brought up will have a profound influence on the nature of the child's development. Studies of other cultures have shown that different cultures produce different human beings.

The school is a microcosm of society and the nature of the school will influence the nature of the children in it. Schools which fail to provide a stimulating atmosphere will fail to develop satisfactory patterns of emotional and intellectual behaviour in the children. Schools which put children into different streams are likely to produce a less stimulating environment for the children in the lower streams. Streaming also seems to accentuate the emotional problems of the children in the lower classes. Schools which are not streamed have provided evidence which suggests that unstreaming alleviates some of the emotional and social difficulties of the lower stream children.

The streaming of children of secondary age into different types of school was originally closely linked with the view that there were, psychologically speaking, three types of children. This view is no longer held and there is more flexibility in secondary school organization now. A comparison of comprehensive schools with grammar and modern schools showed that the 'morale, interests, and sense of belonging are all enhanced in the academically less able pupils in comprehensive schools . . . without lowering the feeling and standards of the abler pupils' [44].

The atmosphere of most English schools is competitive. Through a system of class and subject places and the frequent arranging of children in rank order within the class, the measure of success is the extent to which one child has done better than another; one child's failure is the condition of another child's success. This is not the only way of running a class. Nor is it necessarily the best. Schools and classes can be organized to work cooperatively. Cooperation has been found to be more effective for scholastic achievement and in the generation of a satisfactory emotional atmosphere.

Research into the way in which authority is exercised in the class indicate that a 'democratic' régime is more efficacious than a '*laissez-faire*' or an 'authoritarian' régime. Many teachers think there is a place for corporal punishment in schools, yet there is no experimental evidence in its favour and there is a good deal to indicate that no benefit accrues even in the 'toughest' schools through its use. The indications are, in fact, that corporal punishment might exacerbate disciplinary troubles and increase delinquency.

The techniques of sociometry may be used to investigate the pattern of relationships of the individuals within the class. Children's preferences for other members of the class are investigated and the teacher can then take action on the basis of the relationships discovered. He may attempt to integrate the isolates and to make use of sub-groupings for the organization of group work. The teacher using these techniques should, however, consider whether it is necessarily advisable to solidify the social groupings, exposed by the sociometric test, by arranging his class on the basis of children's preferences. It might often be more suitable to use the information in an attempt to strengthen the unity of the whole class rather than the sub-groupings within the class.

The progressiveness of schools has been found to be positively correlated with the attainment of their children and their measured intelligence.

The experience of one school run on progressive lines was referred to as a practical example of some of the points discussed in this chapter.

CHAPTER 15

The Teacher's Task

In this chapter I shall attempt to bring together the topics we have discussed and to focus them on the classroom situation. The primary aim will be to relate the principles of learning and development to the job of the teacher.

A useful point of departure might well be that made in Chapter 1. Here it was stated that at least 50,000 years ago there were men who were capable (under appropriate conditions) of conducting a symphony orchestra, or of reading a paper to a learned society. There were no symphony orchestras or learned societies, not because of any purely psychological reasons, but because the processes of cultural accretion were at an early stage. That is, social and technological developments were too primitive to provide the appropriate conditions to nurture the psychological processes involving the very high levels of symbolic activity, necessary in such complex skills as conducting or discoursing before learned societies.

This argument faces the teacher with a fundamental question which cannot but influence his approach to teaching. Are we to consider that mankind has now reached a pinnacle of psychological development? Or that it is impossible for the general run of children to master increasingly complex mental skills? History would suggest that this is not so, but rather that in the past the potential was probably there but unrealized because the contemporary environment was inappropriate. It would seem, therefore, a reasonable assumption that children's educational attainments will be very greatly dependent upon the current level of knowledge in the psychology of education and its practical application.

There is an obvious link here with the way in which experience has been shown to affect development. Children who, for some reason, have suffered adverse environmental conditions, have fallen far short of the level of development of the average child. These children can be helped if the conditions are changed and suitable therapeutic measures taken.

A teacher who is aware of the influence of environmental stimulation on development will not just wait for the abilities of his children to appear; he will realize that the quality of their learning depends very largely on the quality of the experiences he provides for them in the classroom. He will therefore not wait on maturation for development but will anticipate it in his teaching in the realization that he is creating the conditions for that development. Should he use tests to determine the children's level of attainment he will not then teach to that level otherwise he will, in Vigotsky's words, be teaching to the yesterday of the child's development. Good teaching, he will remember, is that which outpaces development. In practical classroom terms this means that, while the children are mastering one stage, the teacher is looking to the next and at the same time preparing the ground for the children to move ahead. He will not wait until the children are 'ready' to move ahead but will seek to provide the conditions to get them 'ready'.

The teacher will adopt a similar approach to the question of intelligence. He will be able to use the I.Q. obtained by an individual intelligence test as a useful diagnostic guide, but he will not regard it as a natural ceiling of a child's ability. He will bear in mind Binet's remarks when he protested against the 'brutal pessimism' which considered intelligence to be a fixed quantity which could not be augmented. He will understand that an I.Q. is a measure of current performance which can be improved by good teaching. With such an outlook the teacher will avoid the practice of 'explaining' educational failure as being due to 'dullness'. He will understand that putting a name to the problem does not solve it; an attempt at diagnosis and remedial treatment might.

While the level of cultural development of society at large will determine the overall pattern of child development and education, the teacher will need to consider the influence of smaller social groups on the way in which the children learn, and on the way he teaches.

To consider the children first; it would be well to bear in mind that in the early years the prime social influence will be the family. To a great extent family influences will be beyond the scope of the teacher even though he may consider them to be unsatisfactory. It is highly desirable, however, that he be aware of the social background of his pupils. Only by being so aware can he really come to grips with the problems and possibilities of his pupils in the classroom. In concrete terms, the child who, at home, is treated with affection, given ample intellectual stimulation, and helped to develop complex forms of speech, will need very different treatment from a child who is starved of affection and given little stimulation.

The school and the class are the two most important groups that influence children in the field of formal education, and the degree to which children with their varied home backgrounds realize their educational potential will depend on the intellectual and emotional atmosphere of these groups. Ultimately, of course, this depends on the educational outlook of the staff. Let us now consider what are the concrete aspects of the job of the teacher in school and in the classroom which will help him to create the optimum intellectual and emotional environment for his pupils.

It will be convenient to consider the emotional and intellectual aspects separately. That this is an artificial distinction will be clear to the reader, but it will help to give our objectives precision.

The optimum intellectual environment

From all that has been said in this book it will be clear that the optimum atmosphere for learning will be one which provides adequate intellectual stimulation. The traditional classroom set-up where rows of pupils confront the teacher and blackboard in a room which contains little else, is unlikely to meet the requirements. If, on the other hand, we consider the conditions which obtain in many contemporary primary schools we have the opposite picture. In such a classroom the traditional confrontation is abandoned. Instead of rows the desks are arranged as work tables or in specific groups and the teacher is part of the class, not in opposition to it. The emphasis in such a classroom will be on the active learning of the children and the providing of a wide range of materials which will form the concrete basis for subsequent generalized learning of a conceptual nature.

Merely providing the materials is of course not enough. In some cases it could militate against learning. A heterogeneous clutter of materials is likely to present difficult problems of stimulus discrimination to children. An example from life, which illustrates this point, concerns learning to read. A class of infants was using a reading scheme which made use in its early stages of the name *Dora*. Around the room at the same time as the scheme was being used were labels picking out such things as *desk*, *window*, and *door*. The intention of the teacher here was unexceptionable and yet she had presented two stimuli which at this early stage are at a too high level of difficulty in discrimination. 'Door' and 'Dora' have great phonic similarity, but orthographically they are different. To have them both in use in the early stages of reading was to complicate matters unnecessarily. The proliferation of such labels round the classroom needs careful thought if the teacher wishes to avoid making the children's learning unnecessarily complicated.

Similar problems arise in other subjects. A superabundance of mathematical models or practical apparatus which are not of immediate relevance could act as distractors from the main focus of learning at any one time.

In essence, the teacher should play an active part in assisting the children in their discriminative activity. He should do more than provide the necessary apparatus and experiences for learning, he should control their presentation both in sequence and in gradient of difficulty; he should, in fact, 'programme' the learning situations which he arranges. In addition to this, it is necessary for him to examine the concepts he wishes to foster in the children and to arrange for them to have the practical experiences relevant to those concepts. In most cases he will need to decide on ways of appropriately simplifying the tasks so that the children will be helped to grasp the basic principles; but at the same time he will need to ensure that when the children have acquired an understanding of the principles they have sufficient concrete experience to enable them to grasp the practical applications of general principles.

In specific terms we may instance Dienes's argument about arranging for a variety of *controlled* mathematical experiences to help build principles of general application, and the work of Fleshner who points out that the typical textbook problem is often considerably easier to the pupil because the author has greatly simplified the problem by abstracting it from the real world. To ensure effective learning the pupil needs the experience of reality underpinning his grasp of general principles; but equally, he needs to see how the general principles can be applied to real life situations. Mathematics or science lessons conducted using traditional textbook learning in classrooms without aids or practical apparatus, are unlikely to achieve either. This, of course, applies to junior and secondary schools.

Thus, the teacher should not only make use of apparatus in the classroom and outside, but he must ensure that the children are able to make use of the concepts they have acquired in the relevant practical situations. In mathematics, for example, children should not be asked merely to answer textbook questions, but should be given tasks which demand the practical application of, say their grasp of the concept of weight, or speed, and so on. In geography the children might be given real problems to test their ability to apply their concepts of, say scale or of contours. In science they could be asked to apply their knowledge of, say the properties of lenses, or of magnets. Such methods of teaching undoubtedly demand more effort and ingenuity from the teacher, but they are essential to the formation of satisfactory concepts. It is not merely a question of *proving* that the concepts have been grasped, the very act of applying them makes the child's understanding more profound.

Closely connected with the need for careful planning of the experiences we arrange for children in the building up of concepts, is the need for adequate feedback. The value of many work schemes which provide a practical foundation for the formation of abstract principles is greatly reduced because the children do not get adequate knowledge of results. Thus, while they may be working actively through the material, there is no provision in the scheme to inform the children whether they are right or wrong. It is most essential, particularly in new learning, that feedback comes after each critical response the child might make. While this may be impossible in existing classroom conditions, the teacher should provide as much feedback as humanly possible. He may well be helped by the adoption of programmed learning in certain spheres. He could also probably use group learning situations so that the group response is the response which demands knowledge of results. He might, also, arrange for other children to provide feedback, that is, children would help each other. Help, here, means not that children would *teach* other children, but that a child competent in a particular field would be able to tell another child whether a particular response was correct or not, and could probably explain if mistakes were made. If the teacher has planned the instructional sequence carefully he should have no difficulty in breaking down the main learning task into subtasks. If a child is then told the aim of each subtask before he starts it should be possible for him to monitor his own performance as he goes along. This could be helped by providing appropriate problems after each subtask, which the child could work and check himself. However, the problem of providing adequate feedback is a difficult one. The suggestions made here may help, but much more needs to be known before we are likely to solve the problem satisfactorily. It is perhaps worth noting that feedback may be considered to have two aspects. It may be considered to be knowledge of results which enables error to be minimized. It may also be considered a reinforcer. The latter will presumably usually apply when the learner is succeeding and when his success induces him to keep working. This view is very close to Skinner's view of reinforcement. We will take up this point later. In the meantime the point should be made that unless children are informed of the results of their work fairly soon after they finish it, feedback will be of very limited use.

Telling and teaching. The layman commonly confuses 'telling'

365

with 'teaching'. For him the teacher's task is to expound, the student's task is to assimilate and be prepared to regurgitate later in examinations. The lesson or lecture which uses these techniques assumes an essentially passive student. Such a student may or may not be attending; he may or may not understand; and he may or may not actually learn anything. The teacher has no knowledge of the real state of the student unless he actually sees him asleep!

Any teacher who arranges the learning situations of his children in the ways we have so far suggested, will avoid this problem. His pupils will of necessity be *actively* involved in learning. Educational investigations into active and passive learning have shown repeatedly that active learning is more effective. It is important to realize, however, that aimless, unorganized activity in which there is no real attempt at a systematic attack on a problem will not automatically guarantee successful learning.

Nor will the introduction of aids automatically guarantee a more effective teaching technique. R. Gal makes this point very well when he says:

There is also the merely passive observation of the concrete, or its use by the teacher, either to illustrate what he wants to say, or so that he may dictate to his pupils what they ought to see in real life! *Ex-cathedra* teaching and the most passively receptive pupils are in no way altered by the presence of a concrete object. At least do not let us pretend that to have an object under one's eyes is the same thing as to observe and understand. Experience proves . . . that if we do not go to Nature with questions, if we do not interrogate her, she does not reply, and we content ourselves with the illusion of having understood, while in reality our minds remain vague and in flux.*

In other words the teacher's task is far more complex than 'just telling them': he must draw on his knowledge of the way in which children learn so to arrange the classroom situation that the best possible conditions for children's learning obtain. Whereas the traditional stereotype of the teacher sees him as the oracular dispenser of instant information and the children as passive recipients, his real job demands at all times a two-way process and

* GAL, R.: in *New Era*, March 1961.

more often a multilateral one involving the active participation of the whole class.

This is not to say that there is no place for expository teaching. While the actual experience of reality is essential for the young child to construct accurate mental models of the world, once he has had that experience, the teacher can base his future teaching on it. The important thing is for the teacher to ensure that any new learning, be it guided discovery or expository, can be integrated in the body of concepts the child already possesses. It will be integrated if the child is able to see its relevance to his existing frameworks of understanding, and if the child is unable to do this it will not be integrated. When it is not integrated in his framework of understanding any learning which takes place will be of an arbitrary nature like Skinner's *superstitious* behaviour; that which we have called rote learning. The teacher's job here is to ensure, whether he is explaining to the children or helping them to find out for themselves, that it is possible for new learning to be integrated into the existing framework of understanding. At the same time it must not be so much like previous learning that no effort is required of the children to move on. It is this careful planning of new learning that can ensure that the children are active even though they are not necessarily moving around the classroom or using materials; activity does not invariably mean physical activity. (This is not to say, of course, that expository teaching makes no use of aids. Where necessary aids and other apparatus should be used by the teacher.)

One value of expository teaching is that given a basic foundation of abstract understandings such as one would expect of children in secondary school who will for the most part have reached the stage of Piaget's formal operations, it is possible to build up a more abstract superstructure by verbal instruction. This superstructure can be extremely valuable since the teacher can build into it general principles concerning a given field of learning. The children will then have a grasp of the whole of a given field which they would otherwise acquire more slowly by intuitive discovery using concrete apparatus.

It is necessary, of course, to use techniques in conjunction with the exposition which will ensure that the children really have understood, and will give them adequate feedback. This might take the form of Socratic questioning rather like that used in some teaching programmes with the teacher aiming to help the child to see any flaws in his reasoning and to help him to a deeper understanding. It might take the form of the child's explaining the matter to the rest of the class. Or it might involve a class discussion on the subject to attempt to clarify the issues. Teachers develop their own techniques which are very often based on those mentioned, but there is little doubt that the development of a *systematic body of techniques* in this field would be of great value to teachers generally.

Before leaving the question of the child's active involvement in the learning process, the attention of the reader is drawn to the findings of Galperin set out in Chapter 8. He found that children learned better when they received a good deal of support from the teacher in the early stages of learning. In fact the teacher demonstrated at the beginning, while the child prompted or helped. The child here is, of course, still active although not actually grappling with the material. The reason for the superiority of this method seems to lie in the fact that the child is relieved of the motor part of the task and is able to give his undivided attention to the actual problem. Later, of course, he tackles the problem himself.

Learning to think. The most useful kind of learning is not the memorizing of gobbets of information such as the dates of kings and queens, nor is it the learning of the tricks which win prizes on television quizzes. This learning is at a very low level and has little if any relevance or application of a general nature. It is, indeed, highly specific learning. It is almost a one-for-one stimulus response link, with virtually no stimulus generalization. It has, we may say, little possibility of transfer to new situations. Unless we think the memorizing of dates or quiz answers is important *for itself*, then we should spend time on other forms of learning which will be applicable to a variety of situations. What we need, in effect, is to build up in children strategies of attack on problems and frameworks of understanding of phenomena which will be of general utility.

The work of Harlow (Chapter 4) is relevant here. Harlow claims that the process of acquiring a learning set is analogous to learning to think. Learning sets and concepts are very similar, and in view of the potential for transfer in conceptual learning, it seems logical that children should be encouraged to acquire learning sets. However, the teacher might well consider whether he should follow Harlow's method in the classroom and just give the pupils a great deal of unguided experience in solving different problems of the same general type, or whether he should intervene more directly. Experiments by A. A. Liublinskaya may suggest that he should intervene more directly [16].

Liublinskaya studied learning in infants (approximately 1–3 years). The task was to find a sweet under a paper hat which was distinguished by being of a different size or colour from other hats. When children in the experimental group found the sweet the experimenter named the distinguishing feature (e.g. *red* or *small*). With the control group the experimenter said nothing. Learning was complete when the child could find the sweet every time. Liublinskaya found that the verbalizing reduced the numbers of trials needed drastically. The experimental group acquired the correct responses after about twelve presentations, the control group took about three times as long. Retention in the control group was poor. Few could cope with the problem on the following day, whereas the experimental group could cope well after a week. The experimental group also generalized to other problems more quickly than the control group. But of particular interest was the fact that while the learning of older children in the experimental group was quicker and more stable than with the younger ones, children in the control group improved little with age.

This experiment with young children certainly shows that an adult's verbal cueing can speed up learning set formation (see also pp. 121–2). It also illustrates a very important fact to which I have referred earlier. It is that children do not think about the world as adults do. The control group in the experiment behaved throughout in much the same way as the monkeys in Harlow's experiments. The experimental group, however, were forced into an adult mode of thinking by the adult's verbal prompts. The children's naïve unprompted discriminations, based on simple response learning, were most inefficient. As soon as they were cued by the adult's language they began to think more in adult terms.

Bruner and his associates have recently published impressive experimental evidence from studies of cognitive processes in children from different cultures, which points in much the same direction.* These studies suggest strongly that the use of language in an instructional situation shapes a child's thinking until it approximates to adult thought with its greater economy and power of generalization.

The teacher's guidance, I have suggested, can help children to think in ways which approximate to adult thinking. This implies the more economical organization of concepts. Once a child has acquired an organized body of concepts and a set of mental schemas relating to a particular body of knowledge it becomes possible for him to plan his activity in that field and to investigate phenomena logically. He is able, that is, to formulate hypotheses and to test them in practice with some possibility that his hypotheses will be correct. Without this cognitive framework any exploratory activity he may engage in will be random trial and error. We might recall, here, the work of Bruner and associates on the effect of language on the ability of children to solve problems, and note the great increase in problem solving skill when the child progresses from iconic to symbolic representation. A child who has not yet reached the stage of symbolic representation is likely to try to solve problems by trial and error whereas a child who has reached the stage of symbolic representation will be likely to adopt a more logical approach. A child left to construct cognitive frameworks by unaided discovery as is sometimes advocated, will probably waste a lot of time in such trial and error and may not in the end learn the most economical way to cope with a given problem if he ever succeeds at all. It is also possible that learning by discovery could be arbitrary and meaningless if the child's learning cannot be integrated with existing frameworks of understanding. The planned intervention by the teacher to guide the child most economically in his learning, should be the most

---

* BRUNER, J. S., OLVER, R. R. and GREENFIELD, P. M., *et al*: *Studies in Cognitive Growth*, Wiley, 1966.

potent factor in avoiding redundant activity and in leading him to acquire the most general cognitive structures.

Although there is no royal road to do this and, indeed, it is a field which badly needs investigating, the suggestions made in earlier chapters should help the teacher in some degree. Specifically, attention may be drawn to the chapters which discuss the principles involved in programming, the approach made to instructing backward children, and the examples of the approach to the teaching of specific subjects.

An important common factor of the methods mentioned is the detailed analysis of the problem materials by the teacher. Before attempting to introduce the children to a new type of problem the teacher must scrutinize the concepts involved, attempt to analyse them and isolate the essential components. The components are then presented in a graded sequence so that the pupil can see these basic units clearly and work with them. The teacher should also make clear to the pupils the way in which the sub-units of the problem are interconnected. That is, he so arranges the material that its structure is clear to the pupil. When he does this the pupil gets an overall view of the problem and through seeing its structure is able to work more rapidly and accurately than if he were left to grapple with different aspects of the problem presented in an apparently arbitrary way.

We may illustrate this point by reference to the maze experiment in Chapter 3. Using the experimental method suggested, the subject would be asked to find his way through a maze seeing only one section at a time. His learning would be trial and error learning. If, however, he were allowed a glimpse of the maze before it were covered over, he would have a general picture of its structure and would probably solve the problem more easily. However, the amount of help he got from seeing the maze in plan would depend on the structure of the maze. If the maze were complex and random, even a fairly lengthy look would probably help the subject little. If, on the other hand, the maze had a well defined pattern, say an obvious sequence of left–right turns, it would be possible to solve the problem at once. The teacher in this case differs from the experimenter, in that he deliberately intervenes and imposes a pattern upon the maze so that the pupils will see its structure and learn more readily. That is, he presents his material so that the children will learn not the specific individual turns but a general strategy of attack.

The value of such an approach to teaching is not only that the child is able to reach a successful conclusion more easily, but that the general strategies which the child acquires will be readily applicable to new material, whereas simple linkages between individual items will not. This is because the individual items are likely to be different from one problem to another, whereas the general principles will be applicable in part at least to different problems. (Readers are referred here to Piaget's *anticipatory schemas*, p. 146.)

The Russian psychologist, D. B. Elkonin, has conducted experimental investigations which throw some light on the way in which the teaching of general strategies of attack on problems improves the problem solving activity of children. In his experiments Elkonin taught children in the first grade (seven-year-olds) to analyse the general strategy of arriving at an answer or a conclusion and to analyse any errors which arose to discover what had led to the errors. He also attempted when teaching children to analyse new tasks by themselves, to get them to look for components of the new task which were the same as the components of tasks learned earlier. In other words, the children were encouraged deliberately to investigate the possibilities of positive transfer of learning [47].

As an example of his experimental techniques we may consider the way two groups of children were taught simple skills. These first-grade children learned to make paper chains, woven paper mats, and woven paper baskets with handles, in that order.

One group, the experimental group, was required to make a 'job analysis' before starting work on the paper chains, and a 'job and transfer analysis' before they began the second and third constructions. Specifically, the experimental group was asked to analyse the first task, before starting it, into its component skills, e.g. using a ruler to mark off paper strips of equal width, drawing straight lines with a pencil and straight edge, cutting with scissors, gluing, and so on. The second task had to be analysed in terms of its operational requirements and, in addition, these operations had to be compared with the operations of the first task in order to sort out the operations which were the same in the different tasks from those which were new and still to be learned. By the end of the third task the experimental group was much more competent than the control group. The children who had been trained to investigate the structure of the problems and to look for common elements produced results of a much higher quality and needed less assistance from the teacher than the control group.

Using similar techniques, comparable results were found in the training of early reading and arithmetic. For example, after both groups had been taught to add numbers up to 10 during training, a transfer test, involving the addition of numbers between 11 and 100, showed almost no transfer in the control group, but a considerable amount in the experimental group.

Thus, for children to 'learn to learn' effectively, that is, for them to acquire generalized strategies of attack on problems, it is probably more fruitful if the teacher does more than provide the problem situations. He should show the children that problems can be analysed, their main structure can be observed, and the skills acquired in dealing with one problem can be transferred to different problems.

However, the reader needs to guard against the mistaken argument that certain learning activities transfer very widely. The idea of the 'formal discipline' of the classical languages is still held in some parts. In this view the learning of Latin 'strengthens the mind' or 'develops reasoning ability'. From our current discussion it will be clear that this is nonsense. Learning Latin will carry over into fields other than Latin only to the extent to which the two fields have common content or common principles. Similarly the Spartan activities employed in some spheres of education to 'strengthen character' will have little effect outside the situation in which they are used. Climbing mountains will certainly be valuable experience for climbing other mountains but it is not likely to develop character traits such as integrity, reliability, and initiative, as is sometimes claimed.

The American psychologist, R. Gagné, has also made an analysis of the processes involved in problem solving which has much in common with that of Elkonin [17]. He considers problem solving to be the paramount type of learning in a hierarchy which goes from simple conditioning through concept learning and principle learning to problem solving. Problem solving is in itself a form of learning because once a satisfactory solution to a problem has been reached something has been learned: the capability of the individual has been more or less permanently changed.

According to Gagné problem solving involves the combination of learned principles to achieve some goal. The combination of learned principles which achieves the goal, i.e. the solving of the problem, is itself a higher order principle because it subsumes the principles which the child already knows when it tackles the problem. Problem solving differs from some types of learning lower in the hierarchy in that the actual response (the successful solving of the problem) is not practised until the very end of the problem solving activity; to this extent it resembles concept learning. However, once the problem is solved the higher order principle which is achieved is immediately transferable to many situations and is highly resistant to forgetting.

On the basis of an examination of different types of problem solving, Gagné suggests a number of conditions relating to successful problem solving. In the first place the learner must be able to recall the relevant principles that he has previously learned. The learner, that is, never solves problems in a vacuum. Second, the principles which the learner is to use in solving the problem must be *contiguous*. That is, the learner must be able to hold the relevant principles 'in mind' all at once so that they can be deployed at much the same time. This contiguity may be facilitated by recent recall of the relevant principles. Verbal instruction is a powerful tool in calling principles to mind. Third, verbal instructions may guide the learner into thinking in certain directions. This guidance may vary in amount or completeness but must never describe the actual solution. It should be noted that the verbal instructions may be given by the teacher or by the child himself.

Gagné considers that, generally speaking, the fact that the learner discovers the higher-order principle for himself is the key to the efficacy of problem solving as a type of learning. He does not discount the fact that under certain conditions problem solving could take place where the correct solution is given verbally. However, he suggests that the generation of the higher-order principle by the learner himself is a very potent factor in producing a capability which is highly effective and well retained. This is not to say that the learner is presented with the problem and then left to himself. Such a situation may be considered to be the extreme position of the 'discovery method'. When students have been asked to solve problems without previous knowledge of principles and without guidance they have been markedly unsuccessful.

How should the teacher apply the findings on problem solving in the classroom? The answer seems to be that he should steer a course somewhere between the two extremes of a complete 'discovery' method, where the children are left to find things out entirely for themselves, and a method which gives the children all the answers predigested and merely builds up reflex verbal chains devoid of real understanding. In the problem situation the teacher should come in with cues and guides where necessary, and here verbal cues are of particular help, but he should ensure that the subordinate principles are finally fused into the higher-order principle and the solution reached by the child's own efforts. Looked at in this way it is possible to envisage problem situations which embody large differences in the amount of guidance required by the children. If the subordinate principles are lacking, of course, it will be pointless expecting the children to achieve a solution. It, therefore, behoves the teacher to ensure that his children are 'ready' in that they have the prerequisite subordinate principles before he faces them with a problem.

Gagné makes one further point about problem solving. He points out that the teacher cannot teach problem solving strategies without regard to the content of instruction; that is, facts. Children cannot be taught to 'think' unless they are thinking about something. Thus to be an effective problem solver the learner must have acquired somehow an appropriate body of knowledge and this body of knowledge is what we commonly call 'facts'.

Language and the teacher. Almost everything we have discussed so far in connection with the job of the teacher, rests on the foundation of the child's use of language. Most teachers, coming as they do from a section of the population which is extremely sophisticated in the use of language, do not realize its tremendous complexity. Because of their education, and probably because of their upbringing, teachers will be at home manipulating the complex abstract relationships which spring from language, and will often find it difficult to make adequate contact with children who lack the body of concepts which teachers use automatically. Whether or not the teacher develops methods of helping children to overcome the problems of inadequate linguistic ability, it is most essential that he realizes that the problem exists.

The teacher's task will certainly involve his seeking to improve the quality of the children's language, and here it should be stressed that speech is of very great importance. Whereas, in general, much attention is paid to the written word, often the spoken word is neglected. And yet speech is an essential instrument for building up conceptual thinking and for developing the planning activity of the children. We have seen that children with retarded speech lack the concepts of the more linguistically able children, while severe linguistic retardation like that of the twins studied by Luria, limits their constructional activity. Such children, lacking speech, lack the instruments of abstraction and conceptualization.

They are therefore unable to visualize more than their immediate situation. Like the lower animals their activity can be related only to the concrete and to the here-and-now and it is thus impossible for them to develop forms of imaginative play. Lower animals cannot plan their activity but can only react to the concrete circumstances existing at the moment. They are at the whim of the current stimulus situation. On the other hand, human beings, possessing speech and the concepts which develop along with it, are able to do more. Because of the enormously complex world of concepts and symbols, we can look ahead and *plan* what we are going to do *soon*, or *tomorrow*, or *next*. We can bring the past into juxtaposition with the present or the future. Because we are able to manipulate symbols or concepts instead of the actual thing, we are able to manipulate the environment in imagination which makes our activity infinitely more flexible than that of the lower animals. A child lacking language will probably have little power for conceptual thinking, and will be unable to plan his activity, will be unable to construct anything but the most elementary structures with his toys, and will be incapable of imaginative play.

The lack of constructional and imaginative activity seen in severely linguistically backward children is the extreme case of a phenomenon which seems to apply to linguistic ability generally: the more primitive the speech forms of the child, the more primitive will be his conceptual ability; in brief, his ability to think.

The teacher will not remove children's disabilities by teaching them to elocute or to learn grammatical forms by heart. He will, however, achieve something if he can help them to build up the complex relationships and conceptual forms through guided experience in the use of language.

What does this mean in classroom terms? It means that the traditional textbook of English needs very careful scrutiny by the teacher. It also means that the teacher needs to scrutinize his own procedures. Textbooks (and often lessons) become stereotyped and traditional and in any case are rarely based on psychological principles. They may 'work' but the question is: can we teach more effectively? Or perhaps even: are the books doing the right job? Many such books which are used in schools give formal definition of the parts of speech, e.g. *a noun is a naming word* followed by exercises to discover whether the children are able to pick out the correct words. Apart from the enormous time spent often in merely writing out the answers it is very likely that this learning is so highly specific as to be verging on rote learning. It is certainly very doubtful that such an approach will foster conceptual learning or planning. On the other hand, if the children are given *graded experience* of the parts of speech and encouraged to adopt a problem solving approach to linguistic difficulties they are more likely to acquire skills of general application.

Such approaches to this problem could range from getting young children to explain the difference between the singular and plural of specific words presented by the teacher and gradually building up set of rules, to the presenting to older children of sets of related words so that they acquire an understanding of the basic functions of roots, prefixes, and so on. This could be done without any attempt at formal definitions of the parts of speech. During this process the children will be gradually increasing the complexity of their thinking since they will be constantly introducing new categories of abstraction and classification. These more complex habits of thought cannot be 'dinned into' the child, the child can best acquire them through a great deal of guided and planned speech activity.

In Chapter 8 some specific methods were suggested whereby the teacher might foster the children's linguistic ability. As a general principle it might be said that any activity which involves the children in using their own speech to express abstractions, relationships, and systems of classifications will be valuable.

Such activity could be of great variety and could include imaginative story-telling as well as more straightforward discussion. Merely to give children practice in such activity will be useful, but, if the teacher does this systematically and helps the children to acquire habits of speech which will be of general application, it will be more useful still.

Although language is of supreme importance in human learning, there is an inherent difficulty of which the teacher needs to be aware. As has been indicated in previous chapters on concept formation, it is possible for the child to learn the verbal expressions of concepts without having a grip of the concept itself. This problem is particularly liable to arise when the teacher relies too heavily on the textbook or other verbal material. When children lack the practical experience to help them to build concepts, they may be still able to learn the verbal forms set out in the textbook without having any idea of the real thing. Earlier chapters have given examples of this kind of difficulty in a number of subjects; in general the teacher needs to be very careful to ensure that when the children produce the 'correct' answer their responses are not 'mere verbalizing'; or as Vigotsky puts it, he should beware of the verbal form that covers the conceptual vacuum.

Reinforcement and punishment. Reinforcement has already been mentioned when we were discussing the need for the teacher to ensure adequate feedback to the children. We also discussed the fact that feedback can be considered as providing knowledge of results and as reinforcement. To complete our study of the optimum learning conditions, let us now consider the question of reinforcement in rather more general terms.

Research in the laboratory and classroom investigations have shown the truth of the saying that success breeds success. If a child is punished whenever he makes a mistake in a given learning process, the effect will be to decrease his overall motivation. Should punishment be excessive the child will eventually withdraw and cease to try. This is natural enough since the whole problem solving activity becomes associated with failure and a negative emotional state and the best way to avoid these is to avoid the situation. The reverse applies in the case of positive reinforcement. A child who experiences success in his work, and whose efforts are encouraged, will want to go on working, and will develop a positive emotional attitude towards his work.

In a survey of a considerable amount of research into the effects of praise and blame as motivators in children's learning, the Americans, Kennedy and Willcutt, found that blame was ineffective. They found that praise acted almost universally as a reasonably stable incentive to learning while blame was an equally consistent inhibiting influence on learning.

We must not, however, close our eyes to the fact that the problems of providing satisfactory schedules of reinforcement in the classroom are very great. We may recall Skinner's comment that as a 'reinforcing mechanism' the teacher is out of date. Even if the teacher were able to take care of all the problems of

* KENNEDY, W. A. and WILLCUTT, H. C.: in *Psychology Bulletin*, Vol. 62, No. 5, Nov. 1964.

reinforcement that occur with every pupil in his classroom, the resultant activity of his pupils would probably overwhelm him. Reinforcement provided by the teacher's encouragement is not the only form of reinforcement. One of the most powerful re-inforcers of human behaviour is successful achievement, which probably depends upon the exploratory drive and the tendency to restore equilibrium which we discussed earlier. Learning which is reinforced in this way can be encouraged by the teacher's setting goals which the children can attain and by emphasizing the value of successful achievement. The motivation for such learning is then intrinsic to the learner and the task. The child learns because he finds learning satisfying. However, if the desire to learn is always associated with competition to be 'top' or for prizes, or to avoid the teacher's disapproval it may be difficult to maintain in strength and may well be short lived. This trend is reflected in the lack of interest in learning observed in some children as they move up the school.

The optimum emotional atmosphere

Our discussion of reinforcement is very relevant to the question of producing the most favourable emotional atmosphere in the classroom. As we have seen, reinforcement is connected with affect. Negative reinforcement and punishment are linked with negative affect and positive reinforcement is linked with positive affect. A classroom régime based on negative reinforcement will be a classroom with an unsatisfactory emotional atmosphere. Similarly, in a clasroom where, for reasons outside the actual learning situation, there is an unsatisfactory emotional atmosphere, the conditions will militate against effective learning. The teacher needs to be conscious of any factors within and outside the classroom which may produce unsatisfactory emotional attitudes because such attitudes will not only be undesirable in themselves, but also because they will interfere with the children's learning.

The distinction should be drawn here, between the use of punishment as a method of teaching, and its use in keeping order and general school discipline. As a teaching aid, punishment is extremely ineffective. The teacher who punishes children for failing to learn is almost inevitably making things worse for himself and the children. This applies whether the punishment is mild reproof: 'Have you only got four out of twenty!'; or an imposition such as lines or a detention; or corporal punishment. On the other hand, punishment might be effective in preventing undesirable conduct. But while it might work, it is not necessarily the most effective technique, as the investigations referred to in Chapter 14 indicate. Whether punishment is used in an attempt to teach the children, or to prevent them misbehaving, the negative emotional states engendered will be undesirable. In neither case can punishment in the classroom be regarded as psychologically desirable. If at all possible the teacher should ignore behaviour which he would like to see disappear and reinforce behaviour which he wishes to persist. This applies even if the first few reinforcements are given for seemingly trivial pieces of correct behaviour. Once a start has been made progress can be quite quick. Sometimes reinforcing these minor actions in a predominantly uncooperative child may go against the grain and punishment may seem the obvious method to employ. However, before punishing, even mildly, the teacher would be well to ask himself whether he is punishing as a deterrent to the child, or a positive reinforcement to himself.

It would be unrealistic, however, to expect the techniques suggested to act as a universal panacea for all problems of class control. The class is part of the school and if the school is run under harsh discipline, the problems of the teacher who wishes to adopt more effective techniques are increased. In such a situation the teacher might do his best to put his ideas into practice in the classroom and at the same time try to change the situation in the school. But he should not forget that his class is not isolated from the rest of the school, that his best efforts may be frustrated by factors outside his control, and that he may have to introduce his ideas very gradually.

We considered some of the most important factors involved in the creation of suitable emotional states within the classroom, in the previous chapter. Such things as a democratic atmosphere, cooperation among the children, and the careful consideration of the way group influences are working or could be made to work, are factors the teacher can manipulate so as to foster positive affective states in the classroom.

Outside the classroom the teacher may have limited influence, but what influence he has should be used to try to produce circumstances similar to those he aims for in his classroom. He may be to some extent successful in his own school, but he will probably find it difficult to affect conditions outside the school such as the home and the neighbourhood. He may, that is, find that children develop negative attitudes towards school because of the set-up in the school itself, or because of the attitude of the home. He may have some influence in changing the former but he will probably have little influence in the latter. However, in the classroom he can be constantly aware of the problem of the child who has an unsatisfactory attitude towards school and do his best to encourage such a child, realizing that he will need very much more positive reinforcement than the other children if he is to learn at all effectively.

Some educationists consider that slight anxiety in the classroom is useful in motivating learning. The use of the word *anxiety* here is perhaps a little misleading since it does not refer to the state of negative affect produced by punishment and negative reinforcement, or an unsatisfactory classroom régime. It refers to the anxiety generated by the unfulfilled task. We might express it another way by saying that the teacher, by presenting the class with a problem, upsets a state of psychological equilibrium. To restore that equilibrium the children have to solve the problem. So long as the problem is unsolved the state of disequilibrium exists and this is accompanied by very mild negative affect or anxiety. Solution of the problem ends this state and is satisfying to the children. This suggestion takes a clearly cybernetic attitude which is very close to Pavlov's views of organisms maintaining a state of dynamic equilibrium.

The reader should note, however, that this state of anxiety is mild and highly specific, being related only to the task. Anxiety produced by other factors will have very different results. Anxiety caused by fear of the teacher or even by being in unusual circumstances such as in a strange room for an examination will tend to act as an inhibitor of a child's activity. The teacher should, therefore, to the best of his ability, ensure that any specific anxiety, generated in connection with the solving of problems in children's learning, should take place within a generally positively charged emotional situation.

A note on specific emotional problems. It is impossible to go into much detail about the emotional problems which individual children may have, but it is important that the teacher realizes that they exist and is able to identify them. Children who are of a nervous temperament, popularly described as 'highly strung', need sympathetic treatment by the teacher. His aim should not be to reinforce their nervous behaviour by giving them attention because of it, but rather to help them to acquire confidence. Such children will need more encouragement than the average child and will react more strongly to failure. Encouragement and success in their school work, the sympathetic understanding of the teacher, and a friendly cooperative atmosphere in the class will help them to develop more confidence. Other children may have irrational fears or phobias which lack of understanding by the teacher might aggravate. These fears are probably more common than is generally realized, and although many of them are slight and may cause little inconvenience, they are all undesirable.

Many children, particularly girls, develop irrational fears about 'creepy crawlies'. These fears are not inborn but are acquired from adults or other children (adults are ultimately responsible of course), although it may be possible for such a pattern of behaviour to be acquired from an unpleasant experience with small animals. Often these fears are minor, but even minor fears can be inconvenient in lessons dealing with these creatures. Sometimes these fears can be incapacitating. One student teacher became completely helpless when a flying insect came into the room. She had no control over her fear, realized it was irrational, but was powerless to do anything about it. Sometimes seemingly bizarre patterns of behaviour develop in children. One child was terrified to change into shorts because he had an irrational fear of exposing his knees. A 'no nonsense' approach with threats and punishment had only the effect of reducing him to a state of even more abject fear. Another boy had developed a fear of anything connected with hospitals. Even pictures of ambulances made him anxious.

Teachers who treat such children with impatience and assume that they are being 'silly' or 'trying it on', are making a very serious mistake. There is not much difficulty in distinguishing between the cheerfully mischievous child and the one with genuine emotional disturbance. The teacher faced with such a child should treat him with extreme patience and never force him into the fear-producing situation. He should realize that the child has little or no control over his emotional state and would be only too pleased to 'snap out of it' if he could. The teacher should do his best to encourage the child, perhaps thinking of ways of making the phobic situation pleasant. The teacher is not a psychiatrist, however, and he should refer any difficult case to the child guidance clinic. The important thing is to realize that the child has a real emotional difficulty and to do nothing to make it worse. If a child has gross difficulty in the emotional field the staff of the child guidance clinic may recommend him to a school for maladjusted children.

Guidance and the teacher

In addition to trying to arrange the optimum learning conditions for his children, the teacher will need to ensure that they are all doing the things they are most suited to. On the negative side he will have to be conscious of the fact that some children may have difficulty with learning which he cannot overcome. Or there may be an emotionally disturbed child in his class who needs special treatment. Such cases would be referred by the teacher to the child guidance clinic where they would receive specialist treatment.

The child guidance clinic which is run in conjunction with the school health service is staffed by professional educational psychologists, psychiatrists, and psychiatric social workers. The staff of the child guidance clinic diagnose the difficulties of children referred to them and recommend a course of action. This may be therapy at the clinic in the case of a psychologically disturbed child, or possibly special remedial instruction in the case of a very backward child, while delinquent children might be recommended to a classifying school. These are just examples of possible treatments; the point is that the clinic may provide remedial measures itself or recommend the child to another institution for treatment. In the diagnosis, all relevant factors are considered including the child's medical history, the home background, and so on, in the way outlined when we considered the treatment of backward children.

Teachers are concerned to recommend children to the child guidance clinic when there is clearly need for expert help, but they should also be concerned with the educational guidance of children who never experience any educational difficulties. As the child goes through the school he encounters at times situations when he needs help from the teacher to enable him to take the correct educational decision. This is more likely to happen in the secondary school when the pupil has to make a choice of subjects from a number of options, when he wishes to find out if he has any undisclosed talent which might make it worth his while taking up a new course, or when he reaches the time to leave school and needs advice in a career.

But the most fruitful approach to guidance involves more than giving the pupil advice at critical points in his educational career. Ideally guidance should be continuous. American experience has shown that when guidance is continuous and systematic the pupils benefit both in school and when they leave. Guided pupils have been found to do better than pupils who were not systematically guided, in a number of ways. Guided pupils achieved more, made fewer changes of curriculum, fared better in higher education, made better adjustment in employment after leaving school, and were less given to delinquency than non-guided pupils.*

American schools sometimes have full-time professional

* YATES, A.: in *Educational Research*, June 1959.

counsellors attached to them. Sometimes a teacher is released from part of his teaching duties to act as counsellor. These counsellors have access to full details of each pupil's scholastic records, diagnostic test results, information about the child's background, his personal qualities, his interests, his out-of-school experience, and all these factors are correlated in order to advise the child on his way through the school. The word 'advise' should be stressed here since there should be no attempt to force a child into any particular course but rather to give him a realistic picture of his abilities so that he is able to make the best choice of the opportunities available. A keen interest is often sufficiently powerful to overcome an apparent lack of ability and this should be considered by the counsellor.

In England there has been little systematic attempt at guidance in schools. What there is is often of an *ad hoc* 'amateur' nature. In fact in England the main act of guidance takes place outside the school. This is the selection for secondary education. This has been discussed before and little need be added here except to say that this is by no means guidance in the American sense but quite definitely 'direction'. The other main form of guidance practised is streaming by ability which, as we have seen, is another form of direction which is of doubtful educational value.

One of the most important aspects of guidance is that given to children when they leave school; that is vocational guidance. This should be the culmination of the educational guidance given by the school and should help the pupil to find the most appropriate job for his interests and abilities. Sometimes schools have careers masters or mistresses on their staffs but these teachers are often doing a full-time teaching job as well and are very unlikely to have had any special training in guidance. Many schools, and this may apply particularly to girls' schools, ignore the question altogether. Many grammar schools see their one aim as preparing pupils for university and the staff have little knowledge or interest in careers in other fields, despite the fact that most of their pupils will eventually enter these fields.

If there is a member of staff responsible for vocational guidance, he should work with the youth employment officer in advising children leaving school on their choice of career. Ideally the teacher working with the youth employment officer should have some knowledge of industry and especially of local possibilities of employment. The youth employment officer will have the detailed experience and also some idea of current opportunities. Guidance will, in such cases, consist of the marrying of the youth employment officer's knowledge of employment possibilities and the requirements of different jobs, with the careers master's knowledge of the school leaver. The careers master will draw his information from school records together with reports from teachers who have knowledge of the child. A few youth employment committees use tests to help in the diagnosis of the children's aptitudes. The advice of the careers master and the youth employment officer, the interests of the child and the attitude of the parents are brought together in an interview and the child may be placed in employment on the result of this interview.

In most English schools it is unlikely that there will be a careers master. Possibly the head-teacher may take on the job of counselling, but in the main this is unlikely to be very satisfactory, since the head is probably unable, through other commitments, to be able to spend the time on the job that is necessary to make it of value. It is very difficult in such a situation to provide worthwhile vocational guidance. The teacher in the secondary school who wishes to do his best under the circumstances should try to ensure that he keeps careful records of the progress of the children he is concerned with, bearing in mind the imprecise nature of some of the tests and examinations that may be used. He will need to note the interests and any special aptitudes of the child and the nature of his personality. (Here, again, the teacher needs to be cautious, since much subjectivity enters into such assessments of personality.) Where continuous school records are used, which follow the children through school, the teacher should endeavour to make meaningful comments on the record cards. It is important that he prepares his remarks about the children *before* he sees the record cards so that he is not influenced by what the person who made the last entry said about the child. Since these records are often made up at a time of the year when there are reports to be made out, school sports to organize, the swimming gala, external examinations, and all the other activities which crowd into the end of the school year, the teacher very often has little or no time to spare for the record cards. In such circumstances it is very natural for him to work through the cards quickly and in such circumstances he is very open to influence from the remarks made by colleagues on past occasions. It takes thought to follow an earlier comment of 'morose and anti-social' with a remark such as 'cheerful and cooperative' which is what the teacher may have had in mind. The chances are that the first few entries on a card will have a stereotyping effect: give a dog a bad (or good) name, etc. A. Makarenko, a famous Russian educationist, used to throw away the records which his delinquent children brought with them to the camp he ran, so that he could take the children as they were and not as others said they were. There is a moral here for every school teacher.

One other important point about guidance needs careful thought by the teacher, the careers master, and all concerned with the training of young workers. Vocational guidance and in some circumstances, educational guidance, emphasizes matching the person to the job. That is, the emphasis is on fitting square pegs in square holes. Such practices make the tacit assumption that abilities and other personal characteristics are relatively stable. The stress is, therefore, placed upon vocational selection rather than upon vocational training. It is highly likely that in practice aptitudes and abilities can be changed given the appropriate educational approach. In a rapidly changing world such as ours this is all to the good, since the jobs that many school leavers are now taking up will not exist in the future and new skills will have to be acquired. It might well be, therefore, that much more emphasis needs to be placed on investigating the way in which children and young workers can be trained for work they know little about (and can, therefore, demonstrate little aptitude for) rather than in refining tests of different aptitudes.

The changing role of the teacher

The traditional stereotype of the teacher as one who stands in front of a class and 'tells' the children has been at odds with views of educationists for many years now. This book has attempted to show in what ways the job of the teacher no longer coincides with the stereotype. One aspect of our discussion has been the way in which social developments influence the abilities of man. We may recall once more the tremendous changes in man's abilities brought about by advances in technology. It should not be forgotten, however, that the teacher himself is part of society and that social change does not leave him unaffected. Already the accelerating tempo of scientific development is rendering much of what the teacher learns himself at school, obsolete, long before his teaching life is over. This serves to emphasize more strongly than ever the need to ensure that we do not concentrate in our teaching on specific aspects of phenomena but seek to encourage the ability to develop generalized methods of attack on problems and frameworks of understanding of general application.

The problem of educational obsolescence will undoubtedly be more acute in the future, and, of course, this means that the teacher will need to be more versatile and more adaptable than in the past. Modern developments, in what has been called the technology of education, will help the teacher to cope with the increased complexity of his job, and will also increase the possibility of our being able to implement fully some of the psychological principles which we have discussed. Skinner's point about the inefficiency of the teacher as a mechanism of reinforcement and the need to invoke some type of automatic mechanism such as he used in the laboratory, was possibly the first statement of the problem and possible solution. Since then the development of programming techniques has had the twofold effect of bringing into education the type of operational analysis that has been suggested in this chapter, together with techniques which will help to carry over the psychological principles, evolved in the laboratory study of learning, to the classroom.

As soon as a teacher introduces programmed instruction into

the classroom his function departs radically from the stereotype we mentioned. He does not become a mere machine minder as some teachers have feared, rather he becomes a more human teacher. He has more time to devote to the child who has difficulty, or the child who wishes to discuss some aspect of the subject more fully. And all the time he will know that the children are being guided through the material in a way that has already been tried, that they will be reinforced adequately, and that they will all be active. The classroom set-up changes too. The teacher does not stand down while the machine or programme takes over, he now needs to take an approach to his job in which he considers all the techniques at his disposal together. He will need to consider when and where he is to use programmed material. Will he aim to have this material separate from the rest of the teaching space so that some children can work on programmes while others join in discussion with him? What about the other aids – television, radio, films, language laboratories, models, charts, and other apparatus? How are these to be integrated into the teaching situation? Whatever his decision, the teacher should remember Gal's warning about the passive contemplation of the concrete and be sure to build into his teaching schemes the active involvement and adequate feedback which are so essential for effective learning.

The new techniques available to the teacher have already produced some changes in the organization of some schools in America. The traditional classroom with one teacher and a number of children is replaced by a more flexible grouping of children and teachers [48]. Instead of the class of thirty or over, the children are deployed in 'years' of a hundred or more. When instruction can be given effectively in large groups using a film or television the whole group works together with one teacher in charge. Small group discussions follow with twelve to fifteen children to a group. Other children might be working individually on teaching machines or using programmes without machines. The traditional idea of what a classroom and a school are, is necessarily brought into question. Self-contained standardized classrooms are, in these conditions, inappropriate; instead it is necessary to provide variety of teaching spaces. These range from the large hall for large group instruction, to individual cubicles for using programming methods, and include seminar rooms for small group work and various laboratory spaces. Schools designed in this way are mainly projects for the future, but some experimental American campuses are already in use. The idea of team teaching, however, is spreading in advance of the new building and has been tried in England. Clearly the role of the teacher in such a team is going to be very different from the stereotype which we mentioned. He will need to be more versatile and adaptable, with his role changing to fit the different demands of large group instruction and small group discussion, and he will need to be at home with the machinery of education in a way that has not been common in the past. It might well be that, in this new instructional situation, the teacher will become more aware of the problems and possibilities of effective learning. The fact that he is part of a group of teachers with a common purpose and common problems which can be discussed and tackled collectively, will help to make the work of the individual more effective. Teachers who have worked in teams in this way report that, despite the difficulties experienced in operating in buildings not designed for team teaching, they have, in fact, found the work to be more stimulating and more efiective and especially valuable to the young teacher.*

These changes in the role of the teacher are only just beginning. Some may be found to be of little value and may be dropped; others may be taken further and new ones will appear. There is little doubt, however, that developments which call into question the traditional view of what teaching is, are going to effect major changes in the classroom in the not too distant future.

Summary

This chapter argues that since man's adaptation to his environment has increased in complexity throughout history, it is reasonable to suppose that the trend will continue in our lifetime. It is also suggested that the increasing complexity of man's

* CUNNINGHAM, H.: in *Forum*, spring 1964.

environment, together with advances in our understanding of the way learning takes place, will result in children today achieving more than children in schools a generation ago. This argument is supported by the evidence of the way in which experience has been found to influence children's development. A teacher who adopts these views will see as an important part of his task the need to provide a stimulating educational environment for his children. Such an environment will be a very important factor in producing the best conditions for children's learning.

Learning will best take place when the teacher ensures that children have adequate experience of reality as a basis for the abstractions they form. The provision of aids and apparatus will help to provide the physical basis for abstraction, but the teacher needs to control the presentation of such material. The material should be organized and planned, it should be carefully controlled and not left in the classroom when no longer relevant, otherwise children may depend on it too long and it could distract other learning. When children have *derived* abstractions from the real world they should be given practice in *applying* the abstractions to reality. The process is then: concrete to abstract: abstract to concrete. The teacher should note, however, that the passive contemplation of the concrete is no guarantee that learning will take place. Children learn better when they are actively engaged in solving problems and the teacher should arrange active learning situations.

Aimless activity, however, will be inefficient. The teacher needs to programme the activity and ensure that the children are adequately reinforced to maintain the level of work and also to provide feedback.

Learning general strategies of attack on problems, such as are exemplified in Harlow's *learning sets*, Piaget's *schemas*, or Pavlov's *dynamic stereotypes*, is more efficient than learning specific bits of information. Teachers should aim to present the problem material so that children can see its structure and learn the general strategies of attack without going through long processes of trial and error like the children in Harlow's experiment. Elkonin did this by getting the children to do an operational analysis of a simple task and to look for the elements which could be transferred to other tasks.

Language is the key to concept formation and complex habits of thought. The teacher will, therefore, seek to develop children's language, especially speech, because it will develop their ability to abstract, to classify, and to symbolize, all of which are vital to human learning. He will beware, however, of the outer verbal forms which conceal a 'conceptual vacuum'.

Since negative reinforcement and punishment are linked with negative affect and negative affect inhibits learning, the teacher will avoid them as much as possible. If he does use punishment or negative reinforcement, however, he should realize that he may be able to teach children *not* to do something but he will find it very difficult to teach them to *do* something in this way. Slight anxiety in relation to the solving of a problem may help learning but such anxiety should be specific to the task and in a general atmosphere of positive affect.

Most teachers will be concerned at some time with educational guidance. Ideally guidance should be a continuous process which ensures that children get the educational treatment best suited to them at the time. Vocational guidance is the province of the secondary school and should be concerned to help children to make informed and realistic choices of careers. School records, aptitude tests, and the children's interests will help teachers and youth employment officers in their suggestions to school leavers and parents.

The role of the teacher is likely to change considerably in the near future. The good teacher will need to keep up to date in his own field, in his knowledge of educational theory, and in his grasp of the new techniques available to him through developments in educational technology. The best approach in these changing circumstances will be to consider the teacher as the controller of a system of instruction. Such a system will involve the teacher himself at key points, but will also use, as parts of the system, such things as programmed learning, television, films, and other audio-visual aids. Eventually computers are likely to be used to control some of these aids, especially the teaching machines: they will also be used for keeping pupils records and helping with guidance. All these changes are likely to bring changes in the organization of schools. A first development here is team teaching which takes the teacher out of the classroom and deploys him in a variety of ways which makes his job more varied, probably more exacting and more stimulating, and very likely more interesting. It certainly changes the conditions under which he works and drastically alters his role; but the fundamentals of his task remain. It is to be expected that future developments will help him to perform his task more effectively.

How to Calculate Standard Scores

As was suggested in the text, the most important factor to be considered when equating test scores, is the way in which the marks are dispersed or spread out. The most commonly used measure of dispersion in test procedures is called the *standard deviation.*

To find the standard deviation we have first to find out by how much each score deviates from the average or *mean* of all the scores. For example, a score of 60 on a test with a mean of 40 is a deviation of 20. So is a score of 20. This is sometimes written as −20 since it falls below the average but, for the purposes of calculating the standard deviation, a deviation of 20 is a deviation of 20 whether it is above or below the mean and we therefore ignore the sign.

Having found the amount by which each score deviates from the mean, we could ascertain the average deviation of all the scores by adding the individual deviations and dividing by the number of children who took the test. This can be seen by looking at this set of marks which has an average of 50.

	Pupil	Mark	Deviation of mark from the mean
	A	85	35 (i.e. 85−50)
	B	65	15 (i.e. 65−50)
	C	50	0 (i.e. 50−50)
	D	30	20 (i.e. 50−30)
	E	20	30 (i.e. 50−20)
Total	5	250	100

The total of the deviations is 100. The number of children is 5. Therefore the average deviation is 20 (i.e. $\frac{100}{5}$). This average deviation can be used as a measure of dispersion of scores; the greater the dispersion, the greater the average deviation.

However, while the average deviation is a legitimate measure of dispersion, the standard deviation is found more useful. To find the standard deviation we square the deviation of each score from the mean as in this set of marks.

Pupil	Mark	Deviation of mark from the mean	Deviation squared
A	85	35	1,225 (35 × 35)
B	65	15	225 (15 × 15)
C	50	0	0 (0 × 0)
D	30	20	400 (20 × 20)
E	20	30	900 (30 × 30)

Total of the squared deviations $= 2,750$

Average of the squared deviations $= 550 \left(\frac{2,750}{5}\right)$

Square root of the average of
the squared deviations $= \sqrt{550} = 23.45$
This is the *standard deviation*.

Having squared the deviation of each mark from the mean, we now add up the squared deviations: this gives us the sum of the squared deviations. We then find the average or mean of these squared deviations by dividing the sum of the squared deviations by the number of children who took the test. In our example this gives us an average of the squared deviations of 550. In order to find the standard deviation we now take the square root of the average or mean of the squared deviations. In our example we take the square root of 550 which is 23.45. The standard deviation is sometimes referred to as *the root mean square*: i.e. the square root of the average (mean) of the squared deviations.

Having found the standard deviation of a set of scores we can

396

now convert the raw marks into standard scores. A useful scale of standard scores is one using an average of 50 and a standard deviation of 15. In the example of mathematics and English scores used in the text (pp. 262) the mathematics scores had an average of 50 and a standard deviation of 15. The English scores had an average of 40 and a standard deviation of 9. To make the marks on these tests comparable we converted the English scores to the same average and standard deviation as the mathematics scores. This is the method to use when doing this kind of conversion.

1. Find the deviation of each raw mark from the average. In our two examples from the English test on p. 262, we had raw scores of 40 (pupil A) and 67 (pupil B). A was exactly average, B deviated from the mean of 40 by 27 marks $(67-40)$. A, being average, gets a standard score of 50 since he does not deviate at all from the average.

2. Multiply each deviation by the ratio between the required standard deviation and the standard deviation of the raw scores, i.e.

$$\left(\frac{15}{\text{standard deviation of raw mark}}\right)$$

In our example this is $\frac{15}{9}$.

The score of B deviates from the average by 27 marks. Multiply this by $\frac{15}{9}$ and we get $27 \times \frac{15}{9} = 45$. This is the deviation of B's score from the average on the new scale of standard scores. Since the average of the scale of standard scores is 50, the standard mark of B in English is $50+45$ which equals 95. This is now the same as the mark obtained by A in the mathematics test in our example.

The above is a simple example of the method of calculating standard scores. Usually things are more complicated because greater numbers are involved. The principle is exactly the same, however. The most difficult part of the operation is calculating the standard deviation; once this has been done standard scores can be read off from tables of standard scores. For more detailed information including techniques for dealing economically with large numbers of scores see the books suggested below:

DANIELS, J. C.: *The Teachers' Handbook of Test Construction, Marking and Records*, Crosby Lockwood, 1949.

——: *Statistical Methods in Educational Research*, University of Nottingham Institute of Education, 1953.

VERNON, P. E.: *Intelligence and Attainment Tests*, U.L.P., 1960.

——: *The Measurement of Abilities*. U.L.P., 1956.

SECONDARY SCHOOLS EXAMINATIONS COUNCIL: 'The Certificate of Secondary Education. An introduction to some techniques of examining', *Examinations Bulletin* No. 3, H.M.S.O., 1964.

——: 'The Certificate of Secondary Education. An introduction to objective-type examinations', Examinations Bulletin No. 4, H.M.S.O., 1964.

References

The references cited below are recommended for further reading and are, in the main, readily available. Articles appearing in *Scientific American* may be obtained as offprints from W. A. F. Freeman and Co. Ltd., London. A useful introduction to general psychology may be found in MUNN, N.: *Psychology, the Fundamentals of Human Adjustment*, Harrap, 1964. References are numbered in the order in which they appear in the text.

[1] BEACH, F.: 'The Individual from Conception to Conceptualisation' in WILSON, J. T. (Ed.): *Current Trends in Psychology and the Behavioural Sciences*, University of Pittsburgh Press, 1954.

This is an interesting discussion of the nature of development which refers to Spitz's investigation and work on perceptual development by M. Senden as well as other related topics.

For further information on the effects of deprivation in childhood see BOWLBY, J.: *Child Care and the Growth of Love*, Pelican, 1965. This has additional material discussing recent researches into the problem by M. D. S. Ainsworth. For a fuller account of von Senden's work see SENDEN, M.: *Space and Sight* (Trans. HEATH, P.), Methuen, 1960.

[2] WALTER, W. GREY: *The Living Brain*, Pelican, 1961.

While not an easy book for the student, it is one of the most original and authoritative sources of information about the study of the brain. It has valuable sections on homeostatic mechanisms and on learning, in addition to its exposition of brain function and the EEG.

[3] TANNER, J. M.: *Education and Physical Growth*, U.L.P., 1961.

An authoritative source for information about child growth and its educational relevance. It includes detailed accounts of normal growth processes and development curves and discusses the implications for education of the facts of physical growth and development.

[4] HARLOW, H. F.: 'Love in Infant Monkeys', in *Scientific American*, June 1959 (offprint 429).

The student will find this an absorbing study of contact comfort in young monkeys by the scientist who carried out the experiments. Illustrated and simply written, it is a most convenient piece of source material.

[5] HUNT, J. MCV.: *Intelligence and Experience*, The Ronald Press Co., N.Y., 1961.

Hunt takes up at much greater length and much more exhaustively the question of the nature of development as it is raised in this book. He discusses the changing views of the nature of intelligence with especial reference to the work of Piaget; and while the student might find the going heavy at times, he would find the subjects discussed of great importance and value in his approach to classroom practice.

[6] SANDERSON, A. E.: 'The Idea of Reading Readiness, A Re-examination', in *Educational Research*, November 1963. The quotation cited is taken from ADAMS, F., GRAY, L., and REESE, D.: *Teaching Children to Read*, The Ronald Press Co., N.Y., 1949.

This paper is one of a number dealing with the concept of *reading readiness*. It is a useful source of information relating to the changing views on the nature of 'readiness'.

[7] DANIELS, J. C. and DIACK, H.: *Progress in Reading in the Infant School*, University of Nottingham, 1960.

This monograph is the report of an investigation which compared the efficacy of teaching reading by *Look and Say* and *Phonic* methods. It has a useful introductory review of the literature on the teaching of reading and discusses the concept of reading readiness. The quotation from the Scottish Council on Education is to be found here at greater length.

[8] SIMON, B. and SIMON, J. (Eds.): *Educational Psychology in the U.S.S.R.*, Routledge and Kegan Paul, 1963.

This is a very useful collection of essays on psychology as applied to education in the U.S.S.R. It is of particular interest to students of education because of the attention it gives to the interaction between the theory of psychology and the practice of teaching.

[9] PAVLOV, I. P.: *Selected Works*, Foreign Languages Publishing House, Moscow, 1955.

This is a collection of Pavlov's lectures and seminars where most of his basic ideas are expounded. Instances of experiments are quoted which illustrate the processes involved in conditioning.

Readers are also referred to the book by CLUNY, H.: *Ivan Pavlov*, Souvenir Press, 1964. This is a biography which presents in a very readable way the main experiments and the theories which sprang from them. It is one of the most useful introductory books about Pavlov.

[10] SKINNER, B. F.: *Cumulative Record*, Methuen, 1962.

A selection of Skinner's writings which includes selections

from most of his important work. Students will also find useful articles in *Scientific American*, December 1951 (offprint 423) on 'How to Teach Animals', and *Scientific American*, November 1961 (offprint 461) on 'Teaching Machines'. These two papers will give the reader an idea of Skinner's approach to instrumental conditioning and schedules of reinforcement.

[11] KATZ, D.: *Gestalt Psychology*, Methuen, 1951.

This is a very useful source of information on the main aspects of Gestalt psychology. It has chapters which set out the main tenets of Gestalt psychology in such fields as perception, thinking, memory, and child psychology. It also develops a critique of stimulus response psychology which it refers to as the 'atomistic' or the 'older' psychology.

[12] KOHLER, W.: *The Mentality of Apes*, Pelican, 1957.

This is the classical statement of the Gestalt view of insightful learning. It gives accounts of Kohler's original experiments.

[13] SCIENTIFIC AMERICAN BOOK: *Automatic Control*, Bell, 1957.

An interesting introduction to cybernetics. Simply written and dealing with several applications of cybernetics including its relevance to psychology.

[14] HARLOW, H. F. and HARLOW, M. K.: 'Learning to Think' in *Scientific American*, August 1949 (offprint 415).

A clear and authoritative statement of the Harlows' work on learning sets with full experimental details.

[15] SAPIR, E.: *Language*, Hart-Davis, 1963.

This is a classic in the field of linguistics by a leading American linguist. It is of particular interest to the teacher because of the attention paid to the psychological aspects of linguistics.

[16] SIMON, B. (Ed.): *Psychology in the Soviet Union*, Routledge and Kegan Paul, 1957.

This is a translation of papers by leading psychologists in the U.S.S.R. Several articles are devoted to problems in educational psychology.

[17] GAGNÉ, R. M.: *The Conditions of Learning*, Holt, Rinehart and Winston, 1965.

The author suggests a hierarchical view of human learning and discusses in greater detail many of the points raised in this book.

[18] LURIA, A. R.: *The Role of Speech in the Regulation of Normal and Abnormal Behaviour*, Pergamon, 1959.

This is the most convenient source of information on Luria's work. It has details of experimental methods, experimental findings, and theoretical conclusions.

[19] PIAGET, J.: *The Origins of Intelligence in Children*, Int. Univ. Press, N.Y., 1952.

This volume is a synthesis of Piaget's present views on the development of thought and reasoning in children. Readers may find the following sources convenient for the purpose of obtaining a useful overview of Piaget's experiments with children and his views on concept formation.

LUNZER, E. A.: *Recent Studies . . . on the Work of J. Piaget*, N.F.E.R., 1960.

MAYS, W.: 'How We Form Concepts', in *Penguin Science News*, No. 35, February 1955.

PEEL, E. A.: *The Pupil's Thinking*, Oldbourne, 1960.

PIAGET, J.: 'How Children Form Mathematical Concepts', in *Scientific American*, November 1953 (offprint 420).

ISAACS, N.: *The Growth of Understanding in the Young Child*, London Educational Supply Association, 1961.

WALLACE, J. G.: *Concept Growth and the Education of the Child*, N.F.E.R., 1965.

[20] LEWIS, M. M.: *Language, Thought, and Personality in Infancy and Childhood*, Harrap, 1963.

This book outlines the growth of language and its relationship to child development. It gives an account of speech development from infancy upwards. The relation of speech to understanding is stressed throughout, the exposition is clear and the reader will find it a valuable source of information on the problems of speech and learning.

[21] VIGOTSKY, L. S.: *Thought and Language*, M.I.T. Press, N.Y., 1962.

This is a brilliantly written study of the relationship between thought and language by one of the most original thinkers in the field. Although written some thirty years ago and only recently available in translation, it discusses topics which are of great relevance to our present study. It contains detailed information of the experiments in concept formation using Vigotsky's blocks together with a consideration of Piaget's work in this field and a general discussion of all relevant aspects of concept formation including its relationship with learning.

[22] LURIA, A. R. and YUDOVICH, F. L.: *Speech and the Development of Mental Processes in the Child* (Trans. SIMON, J.), Staples Press, 1959.

This is chiefly an account of the systematic experimental observation of the identical twins referred to in the text. It gives a clear insight into the importance of unimpaired speech for adequate mental development. It also points to the fact that the teacher can intervene to improve the speech and thereby improve the intellectual life of the child.

[23] BERNSTEIN, B.: in *Educational Research*, June 1961.

This is a report of the author's investigation into the effects of social class differences on language and learning and a discussion of their significance for educators. In this article he uses the terms *public language* and *formal language* instead of the terms *restricted* and *elaborated codes*. The terms are synonymous. Other sources which may be consulted are articles by Bernstein in:

British Journal of Sociology, No. 9 (1958) and No. 11 (1960).
Education, Economy and Society, Ed. HALSEY, H. H., FLOUD, J., and ANDERSON, C. A., New York, 1961.

[24] SCHONELL, F. J.: *The Psychology of the Teaching of Reading*, Oliver and Boyd, 1945.

This is probably the most authoritative exposition of the theories and practice of the *Look and Say* method of the teaching of reading. It provides a theoretical basis for a scheme of beginning reading and argues from a Gestalt point of view.

[25] DANIELS, J. C. and DIACK, H.: Teacher's Book to *The Royal Road Readers*, Chatto and Windus.

In the first part of the book, the rationale of teaching reading is discussed and the argument for a phonic approach stated. The second part of the book shows how these are worked out systematically in the reading scheme.

[26] WILKINSON, A. (Ed.): *Spoken English*, University of Birmingham, 1965.

The reader will find this a valuable source of ideas about the nature of language and the use of language in schools. It includes a section on linguistics and the teaching of spoken English and one on spoken English in the schools.

[27] *The Use of English*, Chatto and Windus, quarterly.

A useful periodical of interest to all teachers and written mainly by teachers. A good deal of attention is paid to methods which will have the effect of helping children to build up more complex forms of linguistic expression although this may not always be the expressed aim.

[28] DIENES, Z. P.: in *Educational Research*, November 1959.

This is a useful source for Dienes's views on the formation of mathematical concepts. See also the handbook to the Dienes apparatus.

[29] LUMSDAINE, A. A. and GLASER, R. (Eds.): *Teaching Machines and Programmed Learning, A Source Book*, N.E.A. Department of Audio-Visual Instruction, Washington, 1960.

This is the best-known source book in the field of pro-grammed learning. It includes original papers by key workers in the field, a valuable bibliography and abstracts of papers not included in full. Two other useful sources of information about programmed learning are STOLUROW, L. M.: *Teaching by Machine*, OE-34010, Cooperative Research Monograph No. 6, U.S. Department of Health, Education and Welfare, 1961; and LEITH, G. O. M., PEEL, E. A., and CURR, W.: *Educational Review*, Occasional Publications, No. 1, 1964.

[30] VERNON, P. E.: *Intelligence and Attainment Tests*, U.L.P., 1960.
This book by a leading British authority in the field of mental measurement deals exhaustively with the problems of attainment and intelligence test construction. It discusses in detail the best ways of using the tests and explains how to avoid the possible pitfalls.

[31] MAYER, M.: *The Schools*, Bodley Head, 1961.
Although not directly related to educational psychology this book contains much that connects directly with some of the subjects we have discussed. Such topics as objective tests, programmed learning, team teaching, are considered in the actual context of the schools. The book is mainly concerned with education in the U.S.A., but makes some illuminating comments on British and Continental schooling. It is well written and anyone interested in education will find it absorb-ing and rewarding reading.

[32] VERNON, P. E.: *The Measurement of Abilities*, U.L.P., 1956.
This book introduces the reader to the techniques of test construction and the statistical treatment of test results. Such things as test reliability, validity, and special problems of group intelligence testing are also discussed.

[33] TANSLEY, H. E. and GULLIFORD, R.: *The Education of Slow Learning Children*, Routledge and Kegan Paul, 1960.
This is a book that would repay the attention of any teacher whether or not concerned with backward children. It discusses all aspects of the education of E.S.N. children from the problems of ascertainment to the actual teaching methods in the classroom. Many of the suggestions made are relevant to the teaching of all children.

[34] SEGAL, S. S.: in *Educational Research*, June 1961.
This paper is a very useful statement of the main features of present thinking about the treatment of backward children. It brings together most of the important current ideas in the field.

[35] WISEMAN, S.: *Education and Environment*, Manchester Univer-sity Press, 1964.

404

This is a report of research carried out in the Manchester area which investigated educational attainment and ability, the relations between social factors and attainment of children in schools in that area, and an investigation of school conditions in Salford. The reader will find some very interesting and soundly based information about the relationship between education and its social setting in this book.

[36] DANIELS, J. C.: 'The Effects of Streaming in the Primary School', in *The British Journal of Educational Psychology*, February and June 1961.

This research gives authoritative information about the effects of streaming on the intelligence and achievement of junior school children. It also discusses how teachers' attitudes towards streaming are very often based on false premises. A shorter version of the report may be found in *Forum*, summer 1963.

[37] DOUGLAS, J. W. B.: *The Home and the School*, McGibbon and Kee, 1964.

This book is part of a series reporting on a sample of 5,362 children born during March 1946. It considers the progress of the children through the primary school. Chapter 14 deals with streaming. Douglas found that streaming increased the gap between the children in the A and the B streams.

[38] CLARK, A. N. and CLARK, A. D. B. (Eds.): *Mental Deficiency, the Changing Outlook*, Methuen, 1958; new edition 1966.

This is an important collection of papers by some of the leading workers in the field of mental deficiency. Much of it is relevant to work with backward children and some of the educational methods discussed are relevant to the teaching of normal children. Readers will also find a useful discussion of intelligence and intelligence testing.

[39] MEAD, M.: *Male and Female*, Pelican, 1962.

In this book Margaret Mead unifies her extensive studies of a large number of cultures. The book is a most useful source of information about the importance of cultural factors in the development of the attitudes of the individual.

[40] SPROTT, W. J. H.: *Human Groups*, Pelican, 1958.

An interesting source of information about group dynamics. Professor Sprott outlines the way in which group attitudes affect the behaviour of individuals within the groups. He considers mainly groups other than the school but there is much of interest to the teacher and of relevance to groups within the school.

[41] EVANS, K. M.: in *Educational Research*, November 1963 and February 1964.

This is a discussion of the use of sociometry in schools which considers theoretical questions and also gives a good deal of attention to the practical application of the techniques to the classroom. There is also a useful bibliography.

[42] JACKSON, B.: *Streaming; An Educational System in Miniature*, Routledge and Kegan Paul, 1964.

The report of an investigation into streaming. It gives details of what teachers and parents think about streaming and reports an investigation into streamed and non-streamed schools. The book also gives facts which support the suggestion that A classes get the most experienced teachers and often the best accommodation.

[43] SIMON, B. (Ed.): *Non Streaming in the Junior School*, P.S.W. (Educational) Publications, 1964.

This is a collection of articles from supporters of non streaming. It gives the practical experiences of teachers who have worked in non-streamed schools in addition to discussions on the principles of non streaming.

[44] MILLER, T. W. G.: *Values in the Comprehensive School*, University of Birmingham Educational Monograph No. 5, 1961.

This is the report of a systematic study of English comprehensive schools. It gives details which suggest that the comprehensive school has a more positive influence on the attitudes of the children towards school than schools in the tripartite system.

[45] CHILD, H. A. T. (Ed.): *The Independent Progressive School*, Hutchinson, 1962.

This is a collection of articles by head-teachers of independent progressive schools. The articles describe the way in which these schools approach some of the problems considered in Chapter 14. For practical examples of the working out of these ideas and accounts of informal friendly relationships between staff and children, these articles are invaluable.

[46] PATTINSON, W.: in *Educational Research*, June 1963.

This is a short article of great interest in showing that a state school can get the same response from children as the independent progressive school when 'traditional' methods are replaced by methods based on cooperation and democratic procedures.

[47] BRACKBILL, Y.: in BAUER, R. A. (Ed.): *Some Views on Soviet Psychology*, American Psychology Association, 1962.

A collection of papers by members of the American Psychology Association following a visit to the U.S.S.R. It is of particular interest in its consideration of experiments into children's learning in the actual school situation. Other papers of interest to the teacher are those on problem solving and teaching for transfer of skills.

[48] SHAPLIN, J. T. and OLDS, H. F.: *Team Teaching*, Harper and Row, 1964. See also reference number 31.

Index

This index makes specific reference to subjects while the table of contents is the guide to their extended treatment. The index and table of contents are best used in conjunction.

speech (*contd.*):
  and problem solving, 181
  and self-regulation, 135, 169–72,
    174–5, 189–90
  and social class, 184–8
  symbolic nature of, 112, 174
  synpraxic, 183–4
Spitz, R. A., 16, 298
Sprott, W. J. H., 340, 405
Stern apparatus, 215
Stern, C., 214
stimulation, 30
  and achievement, 50
  of the brain, 20–1, 39
  deprivation of, 15–16, 23, 29, 38,
    42, 45, 309, 335
  and development, 15–17, 23–4,
    26, 40–2, 45–6, 48–50, 130,
    309, 358, 361, 392
  and the EEG, 22–3
  and intelligence, 284–5
  and learning, 362
  need for, 38
stimulus discrimination
  and adaptive behaviour, 81–2
  in classroom learning, 83–4, 104,
    363
  experiments in, 82, 84, 88
  and feedback, 81, 84
  and learning sets, 88
  in reading, 82, 84, 202–3, 307
  and reinforcement, 81–2
  in teaching concepts, 121
  teaching, to tone deaf children,
    81–2, 84
stimulus generalization, 82–4, 104
  and adaptation, 83
  in classroom learning, 83, 85, 104
  and language, 113, 119–20, 172,
    193
  and semantic generalization, 119
  and transfer of learning, 149–50
stimulus-organism-response, 63,
  68, 103
Stolurow, L. M., 404
Stott, D. H., 306
streaming
  and backwardness, 313–15, 319
  and the classroom, 347–50

effect of, 313–14, 347–9, 358
  and restricted code, 188
  and social background, 314
  and teachers' attitudes, 315,
    348–9, 352
  unstreaming, 313–14, 348–9,
    355–7, 388
structure
  in mathematics apparatus, 214–
    18
  in meaningful learning, 199,
    371–2
  in problem solving, 371–2, 392
  in programmed instruction,
    232–3
symbolization
  and concepts, 114
  and deaf children, 125
  and extension of environment,
    113, 128
  and language, 112–13, 118, 128,
    173–4, 190
  and learning, 113, 118, 178, 190
  and reading, 202, 277
  and words, 112–14, 128, 173

Tanner, J. M., 141 n., 399
Tansley, H. E., 301, 316, 325, 404
teachers
  attitudes to streaming, 315,
    348–9, 352
  and backward children, 299,
    302–3, 306, 318
  changing role of, 93–4, 389–91
  and discovery learning, 194,
    367–8, 371–5
  education of, 110
  and educational obsolescence, 389
  and guidance, 384–7, 393
  and language, 376–9
  and meaningful learning, 194–9,
    367
  and problem solving, 198, 200,
    226–7, 328–9, 370–6
  and 'progressive' methods, 357
  stereotype of, 365–6, 389–91
  and tests, 394–6
teaching
  and concept attainment, 168–9